Music
at the Turn
of Century

California Studies in 19th-Century Music
Joseph Kerman, General Editor

1. *Between Romanticism and Modernism: Four Studies in the Music of the Later Nineteenth Century,* by Carl Dahlhaus, translated by Mary Whittall
2. *Brahms and the Principle of Developing Variation,* by Walter Frisch
3. *Music and Poetry: The Nineteenth Century and After,* by Lawrence Kramer
4. *The Beethoven Sketchbooks: History, Reconstruction, Inventory,* by Douglas Johnson, Alan Tyson, and Robert Winter
5. *Nineteenth-Century Music,* by Carl Dahlhaus, translated by J. Bradford Robinson
6. *Analyzing Opera: Verdi and Wagner,* edited by Carolyn Abbate and Roger Parker
7. *Music at the Turn of Century: A* 19th-Century Music *Reader,* edited by Joseph Kerman

A *19th-Century Music* Reader

Edited by Joseph Kerman

Music
at the
Turn
of Century

UNIVERSITY OF CALIFORNIA PRESS
Berkeley • Los Angeles • Oxford

University of California Press
Berkeley and Los Angeles, California

University of California Press, Ltd.
Oxford, England

© 1990 by
The Regents of the University of California

Library of Congress Cataloging-in-Publication Data

Music at the turn of century : a 19th-century music reader / edited by
   Joseph Kerman.
      p.   cm. — (California studies in 19th century music ; 7)
    ISBN 0-520-06854-8 (alk. paper). — ISBN 0-520-06855-6 (pbk. :
alk. paper)
    1. Music — 19th century — History and criticism. 2. Music — 20th
century — History and criticism.   I. Kerman, Joseph, 1924–
II. 19th century music.   III. Series.
ML 196.M85   1990
780'.9'034 — dc20   89-28022
                                                            CIP
                                                            MN

Printed in the United States of America
1 2 3 4 5 6 7 8 9

The paper used in this publication meets the minimum requirements of
American National Standard for Information Sciences — Permanence of
Paper for Printed Library Materials, ANSI Z39.48–1984. ♾

Contents

Preface

Most of the essays in this book were solicited for the tenth anniversary of the journal *19th-Century Music*, which has sought to encourage innovative writing about music—musicological, theoretical, and/or critical writing—since its founding in 1977. We invited former contributors and some others to submit articles on the general question of the relations between nineteenth-century music and music of the early twentieth century. Responses to our invitation were published in two special issues in the spring and summer of 1987. The breadth and scope of these articles, and their collective cogency, sparked the idea of reissuing them under a single cover, as a book.

To them has been added the opening essay in the very first issue of *19th-Century Music*, in July 1977, "1-XII-99: Tonal Relations in Schoenberg's *Verklärte Nacht*" by Richard Swift. Swift's stylish pre-colon text encapsulates our theme, and does so with an appropriate sense of urgency: music of the late nineteenth century on the count-down to modernism. The substance of his study—like that of only a few others published in the journal's first decade—contributes directly and handsomely to that theme.

Music in the period prior to Europe's first World War has always held a strong interest for musicians, musicologists, and listeners, an interest that is perhaps even stronger today than in the recent past. For comprehensive brilliance, this period is unsurpassed in the history of Western music. The decades from 1894 to 1914 saw the composition—and the frequently unruly first performances—of *Verklärte Nacht*, *Pierrot lunaire*, and the early works of Alban Berg, Anton von Webern, and Béla Bartók; of the three most famous operas by Richard Strauss and the three famous ballets by Igor Stravinsky; and of practically the whole major output of Gustav Mahler, Claude Debussy, and Charles Ives. Busoni published his *Sketch of a New Esthetic of Music* in 1907, and Russolo issued his "Futurist Manifesto" in 1913. Recording technology began to make its impact during this period, as we know from a memorable chapter in Thomas Mann's *The Magic Mountain*.

It was also the period of *Madam Butterfly, The Merry Widow, Pomp and Circumstance,* and *Maple-Leaf Rag,* though nothing about these works or their like appears in the present collection. The anniversary project of inviting contributions on music at the turn of century under a broad, general charge was scarcely calculated to produce a balanced history of music at the time, even if one supposes that "history" in this sense is an achievable goal. What the project did achieve was something else: a cross-section of the best writing now being devoted to those aspects of turn-of-the-century music that particularly interest scholars today. The music of modernism, rather than the more conservative music of the time, or popular music, remains the focus of this interest.

And modernism, of course, defined itself by contrast with music of the previous century. Rejection of the values of late Romantic music was part of the new rationale. In its stance toward the past, turn-of-the-century modernism was very different from what may be called the second phase of musical modernism, the phase initiated by Boulez, Stockhausen, and others directly after World War II. It is not that composers of this second phase cut themselves off from tradition. But they selected with some care the past that they wanted: Webern, Debussy, Varèse. This luxury of choice was not available to turn-of-the-century modernists, who were involved, implicated, and often locked in a struggle with all the formidable legions of nineteenth-century music.

The focus of these studies, then, is upon modernism in relation to its immediate heritage. Given that focus, the cross-section will be seen to be reasonably comprehensive after all. Thus major modernist composers whose reflections upon the past come under consideration here include Debussy, Mahler, Schoenberg, Stravinsky, Bartók, and Ives, while older composers such as Franz Liszt and Hugo Wolf figure as precursors of modernist harmony and modernist sensibility.

There is considerable range, too, in approach. Several of the authors work to explicate the new musical languages which evolved in that era, and which are still not well understood. But if this scholarly goal may seem familiar enough, its pursuit here takes some very different and novel forms. Other authors deal with reception—directly, in the case of *Pelléas et Mélisande,* and indirectly, in the case of Bartók's copious (and copiously glossed) editions of earlier piano classics. In the academic jargon that has grown up around music, some of the essays would be described as musicological in orientation, others theoretical, others analytical. Most bring together historical, theoretical, and analytical insights to achieve a richer kind of composite scholarship than is available to traditional musical studies.

19th-Century Music has tried to encourage composite scholarship of this kind; there will be time for a few words about the journal and its role later in this preface. But first it will be appropriate to present a somewhat more detailed survey of the contents of the present volume.

For the purposes of book publication the essays have been rearranged into two groups. Under the part title "Transformations of Musical Language and Rhetoric" I have assembled studies on the evolution of—or revolutions within—traditional musical materials and modes of expression. Central here is the classic problem of dissolving tonality, associated with Schoenberg's "emancipation of dissonance" and his rethinking of structural processes, though our writers are also concerned with issues of texture, tone, and intertextuality.

Several essays in this group can be described as critical studies, or "close readings," of modernist classics. If any one work deserves to be called the musical standard-bearer of modernism, *Verklärte Nacht* of December 1899 is that work. "As he transcended program music in *Verklärte Nacht,* so Schoenberg also transformed many compositional techniques of the immediate past," writes Richard Swift, who dwells especially on that knitting together of the linear and the vertical, the local and the long-range, that he sees as a model for the hierarchical apprehension of art so characteristic of the twentieth century. *Verklärte Nacht* as a whole mirrors the psychological motion of its literary subject matter, by the *Jugendstil* poet

Richard Dehmel, by means of a duplicating, interlocking transformation of sonata form—the formal principle that in endless earlier metamorphoses had occupied the nineteenth century.

The other critical studies address works hardly less famous than *Verklärte Nacht*. In "'Quotation' and Paraphrase in Ives's Second Symphony," J. Peter Burkholder describes a typically ambivalent modernist struggle with paradigms of the past: in this case, both the American past of popular music, which Ives extolled, and the tradition of European art music, which he did not. Richard Taruskin demonstrates how the structure of an entire scene from *Petrushka* can be understood as the projection of a non-tonal practice that has been much discussed recently, derived from the octatonic scale. Descended from the "St. Petersburg common practice" of the Rimsky-Korsakov school, in Stravinsky's hands this scale can fairly be said to have founded a coherent modernist musical language.

David Lewin's essay can also be read for its striking critical insights into the work with which his discourse culminates, Debussy's Prelude *Canope* of 1912. His study extends further, however, adumbrating a more general investigation of that well-known, even notorious, practice, "Parallel Voice-Leading in Debussy." Debussy's parallel chords have sometimes been seen as a product of *fin-de-siècle* antiquarianism, but Lewin shows that their interpretation as a sort of organum—that is, as essentially sonorous "thickenings" of melodic lines—is only sometimes right. In some instances such an interpretation can take one down unsuspected paths into the niceties of medieval sonority; in others linear analysis may be more persuasive—a kind of analysis that rests on more familiar nineteenth-century models.

Issues of critical methodology, implicitly raised by Lewin, serve as the explicit impetus for Christopher Lewis in "Mirrors and Metaphors: On Schoenberg and Nineteenth-Century Tonality." Like a number of younger musical scholars today, Lewis urges that musical analysis should be conceived of as metaphor rather than model. He extends Robert Bailey's influential concept of dual tonality in Wagner—which ranks with Peter van den

Toorn's explication of octatonicism as one of the seminal musical-theoretical ideas of recent years—to music that Schoenberg wrote soon after *Verklärte Nacht*. In "Liszt's Experimental Idiom and Twentieth-Century Music," the immediate results of Allen Forte's investigation are perhaps hardly more formidable than the author's implicit methodological claims. Identifying an "experimental idiom" in Liszt's work, Forte traces dissonant chord-forms characteristic of the turn-of-the-century modernists in a long series of Liszt compositions going back to the 1850s. The underlying premise is that modern analysis—in particular, Forte's well-known pitch-class set theory—can be used to underpin broad-ranging historical studies.

Under the admittedly broad rubric "Engagements of Modernism: Personality, Politics, Perceptions," I have grouped several other essays, addressing issues of musical engagement with the nonmusical world. In an essay that is especially alert to intertextual nuance, Lawrence Kramer uses Goethe settings by Schubert and Wolf to reveal the response of one late nineteenth-century composer to the new image of personality emerging under modernism. Jann Pasler in "*Pelléas* and Power: The Reception of Debussy's Opera" examines the press notices of the opera to uncover the impact upon them of politics, both musical (academicism versus modernism) and nonmusical (the Dreyfus case). Detailed reception studies are still rare enough in musicology, at least in this country, so that Pasler's piece remains suggestive as a model.

Discussing "Wagner and Our Century," Leon Botstein finds himself revisiting the theme of Wagner as a cultural, national, and ideological force—a theme that has occupied thinkers from Nietzsche to Thomas Mann to the eminent contemporary Israeli historian Jacob Katz. (Has this discussion already been revisited often enough? It will not be laid to rest finally, I believe, until the Wagner operas themselves are.) And in "*Le Soleil des morts*: A Turn-of-the-Century Portrait Gallery," Susan Youens draws attention to a *roman à clef* of the 1890s—itself an enervated symptom of its times—that encodes significant, skeptical perceptions of major actors in the drama of modernist music during its early days in Paris.

Only one of the twelve essays in this book addresses musical performance, rather than musical texts by themselves or in extra-musical engagement. As László Somfai's contribution counts as one of the most unusual ever to have appeared in *19th-Century Music*, an editor may be forgiven for not finding a category for it. Somfai examines the details of musical notation by which Bartók sought to fix nuances of performance such as touch, phrasing, and so on. To this problem the author brings information from Bartók's recordings of his own music, the editions of eighteenth- and nineteenth-century piano classics that he prepared around 1910, and contemporaneous editions of his own works—notably those that appeared in more than one version, differing in notational detail. Like Pasler's, this essay is of significant methodological interest.

As has been said above, these studies were assembled for an anniversary; and anniversaries are times to look back.

Founded in the late 1970s, *19th-Century Music* took as its manifest charge the promotion of serious studies of nineteenth-century music. At that time such studies figured hardly at all in this country's music-academic agenda. Just how invisible nineteenth-century work was in the postwar decades, observers of today will find hard to believe; but those interested need only get hold of old volumes of *The Musical Quarterly* and the *Journal of the American Musicological Society*, and scan the tables of contents. The nineteenth was a missing century in the main musicological periodicals, in seminars at major universities, and in job advertisements. The question was put to the editors on more than one occasion: could we hope to fill three issues a year with high-level contributions on nineteenth-century topics?

Today the situation is nearly reversed. Nineteenth-century studies are now among the strongest, most fashionable holdings of American musicology. The turnaround happened so fast—our issues were filled so easily and so excellently—that we have never been able to pretend that our project played a truly functional role in the disciplinary development. It seems clear that the field was already well into the process of change, and that the most *19th-Century Music* can take credit for is being

there at the right time, as a catalyst. Being there, it was in a good position to publish a number of exceptionally strong and influential articles in the years following 1977.

We can take a little more credit for another of the journal's planks, one that was less manifest: to further a loosening-up of traditional scholarly discourse about music. This tended at that time to be positivistic and confined, even rigid. Thus while *19th-Century Music* has always been mainly historical in orientation, as its title attests, and welcomes archival, bibliographical, and biographical essays, among others, its pages are also open to practically all types of analytical, "structural" studies. Authors have been free to try out critical methodologies that would be less appreciated elsewhere. As a result, the journal has never developed a monolithic style; rather, it is marked by variety, flexibility, and experiment. These qualities are well demonstrated by the essays collected in this volume, as has already been suggested above.

To return to the neglect of the nineteenth century that characterized institutional musicology until recently: the scandal lay, of course, in what it was that came along *after* that particular century. Scholarly attention to nineteenth-century music may have been minimal; to twentieth-century music it was minuscule, and to late twentieth-century virtually nil. American musicology in the 1970s seemed to have cut itself off from current music. Work was proceeding under the tacit definition of music history as the study of a circumscribed past rather than as the study of the past running into the present. If, as some say, a major task of musicology is to show how music of the past continues to affect and impress music and reception in the present, this was not a task musicologists were addressing.

Nor, admittedly, was this the immediate task that *19th-Century Music* was founded to address. If closing the time gap between the music of the present and the music of musicology had been the journal's main impetus, it would have been called (with a nod to a distinguished contemporary) *Music: Past and Present*, or something of the sort. But while such closure was not our primary impetus, it was always at the back of the editors' minds. It still is. Operating some way behind the line of battle, we still hope that by publishing serious work on the nineteenth century, and by encouraging freer as well as broader kinds of writing about music, the journal may be accomplishing useful support work.

And in the special tenth anniversary issues, by soliciting essays at the very tip of our stated preserve, it was possible to present sustained inquiry into the music of, if not our time, at least our century (as it will be for another ten years). Perhaps the present book, growing out of those anniversary issues, can be said to make a contribution to closing musicology's notorious time gap.

While the responsibility for editing this book, in the trivial sense of reordering and introducing the articles, rests with the undersigned, launching the anniversary project and editing (as well as formatting) its outcome was the joint work of the three masthead co-editors, Walter Frisch, D. Kern Holoman, and Joseph Kerman. We should like to acknowledge here the invaluable cooperation of Robert Winter and Richard Swift, who served as co-editors in 1977–83 and 1983–84 respectively, and to editorial assistants Christina Acosta, Michael Rogan, and Janna Saslaw.

The history of the journal is somewhat complicated, but it must be at least outlined here so that we can thank the many institutions that helped make *19th-Century Music* a reality. Founded as an intercampus venture of the University of California, *19th-Century Music* was edited by a troika from the Berkeley, Davis, and Los Angeles campuses, with support (both financial and editorial) from Irvine and Santa Barbara. After the first few years the operation was run mainly out of Berkeley and Davis, and in 1984 an East Coast office was added at Columbia University in New York. A final, special word of thanks is due to the University of California Press, which after reviewing our original prospectus deliberately — even conservatively — in 1975, has ever since thrown caution to the winds and provided unstinting support and encouragement.

Joseph Kerman
for the Editors of *19th-Century Music*
Berkeley, October 1988

Transformations of Musical Language and Rhetoric

1-XII-99: Tonal Relations in Schoenberg's *Verklärte Nacht*

RICHARD SWIFT

December 1899, emotionally if not legally the end of the old century, was the month in which two compositions were completed that would point the direction for much of the dawning century's music: Claude Debussy's *Nocturnes*, almost ten years in the process of composition, and Arnold Schoenberg's *Verklärte Nacht*, composed during that autumn of 1899. Each of these compositions has been said to be indebted to Wagner, the headiest musical force of the nineteenth century: *Nocturnes* to *Parsifal*, *Verklärte Nacht* to *Tristan und Isolde*. Even as received opinions go, this falls far short of the mark; it serves here as a reminder of the muffled critical attitudes typically applied to much turn-of-the-century music. With its subtle, luminous and subversive evasions of conventional late nineteenth-century tonal and structural processes, *Nocturnes*—especially *Nuages* and *Sirènes*—would seem to be the more drastic of the two works. In *Verklärte Nacht*, however,

nineteenth-century compositional practice is confronted, embraced, and resolved: transformed by its twenty-five-year-old autodidact composer with an astonishing power and virtuosity of compositional thinking. And yet, despite its popularity in the concert hall—a fact often regretted by Schoenberg—the compositional ordering of the internal relations of *Verklärte Nacht* has remained almost uncharted territory.[1] While clinging to the bounds and

---

[1]Exceptions include Andrew Porter's youthful essay with its comments on relations among motive contours, Arnold Whittall's discussion of relations among the early chamber music of Schoenberg, and Philip Friedheim's unpublished study of Schoenberg's early music which pioneered in acknowledging the sonata structure of *Verklärte Nacht*. Andrew Porter, "Modern German Chamber Music," in *Chamber Music*, ed. Alec Robertson (Harmondsworth, 1957); Arnold Whittall, *Schoenberg Chamber Music* (London, 1972); Philip Friedheim, *Tonality and Structure in the Early Works of Schoenberg* (Ph.D. dissertation, New York University, 1963).

expectations of triadic tonality and tonal structure, it suggests, through its paradoxical combination of rigor and ambiguity, the air of other planets that would await its composer, as well as the art and craft of music, in the awakening twentieth century.

Schoenberg's obeisance to the nineteenth century's treasured notion of "program music" in *Verklärte Nacht*, and later in *Pelleas und Melisande*, is far more subtle than that of most of his predecessors or contemporaries. The symphonic poems of Liszt and his epigones are often makeshift affairs, the texts an effort to plaster over the seams of the music with literary vinegar-and-brown-paper. Often texts purporting to have some connection with the music were added later. Naturally enough, composers of such program music offered other, rather nobler, reasons for their reliance upon texts or upon literary and historical references: the "new music" of the mid-century had believed such programs were enough to guarantee its novelty, its estrangement from the "classical" past, its adherence to imagined "precepts" of Berlioz, Schumann, and the Beethoven of the *Pastoral* Symphony. For many composers, though, programmatic texts remained an easy means of assembling otherwise unrelated musical materials. Tchaikovsky, at work on *Romeo and Juliet* in 1869, received this advice from Balakirev: "Determine your plan. Do not worry about the actual musical ideas."[2] Such a cold-blooded dismissal of the musical generation of a composition would have repelled Schoenberg; for his sextet, he chose a poem with internal structural relations that could be correlated with purely musical processes. The music is not a meandering fantasy or loose improvisation illustrating an anterior verbal plan, but a determined manifestation of the tonal principles of sonata structure. If the music does suggest the action of the poem and its psychological motion, it does so because the structural processes of both the poem and the music, considered abstractly, are similar. Egon Wellesz, in his book on Schoenberg,[3] tried to make point-to-point identifications between the poem and the music in the approved nineteenth-century fashion, and Schoenberg himself, despite his fixed disavowal of such equivalences, wrote program notes as late as 1950 that attempt a similar set of connections.[4] Much earlier, in a 1912 essay in *Die Blaue Reiter*, he had stated unequivocally his opposition to program music of the common variety: "The assumption that a piece of music must summon up images of one sort or another . . . is as widespread as only the false and banal can be."[5]

As he transcended program music in *Verklärte Nacht*, so Schoenberg also transformed many compositional techniques of the immediate past. The music of the sextet does not slavishly imitate models, but it does owe much to the music of Brahms and Wagner, "to which a flavor of Liszt, Bruckner, and perhaps also Hugo Wolf was added."[6] Having confronted and having mastered those techniques—including modes of thematic construction and combination, of development and extension ("Brahms's technique of developing variation"[7])—the youthful composer achieved an intensely personal style. Gone were the times of blind partisanship for either Brahms or Wagner, for "what in 1883 seemed an impassable gulf was in 1897 no longer a problem."[8] The stylistic and technical accomplishments of those masters could now be blended without hesitation, for there was no longer any incongruity in their propinquity. Later, in "Brahms the Progressive," Schoenberg analyzed types of thematic construction to be found in Brahms's music. Many

---

[2]M. D. Calvacoressi and Gerald Abraham, *Masters of Russian Music* (New York, 1936).

[3]Egon Wellesz, *Arnold Schoenberg* (London, 1925).
[4]Arnold Schoenberg, notes for *Verklärte Nacht*, 26 August 1950, in the booklet for "The Music of Arnold Schoenberg," vol. 2, Columbia Records M2S 694. Schoenberg wrote that the music "does not illustrate any action or drama, but is restricted to portray nature and to express human feelings. It seems that, due to this attitude, my composition has gained qualities which can also satisfy if one does not know what it illustrates, or, in other words, it offers the possibility to be appreciated as 'pure' music."
[5]Arnold Schoenberg, *Style and Idea*, 2nd edn., ed. Leonard Stein (London, 1975), p. 141.
[6]Ibid., p. 80.   [7]Ibid.   [8]Ibid., p. 399.

of these—such as model and sequence, incomplete sequence, the extension and expansion of thematic contours by diminution or augmentation of temporal patterns—are similar to the essential thematic unfoldings, continuations and developments of *Verklärte Nacht.*

To cite a specific case, the melody in example 1 unfolds downward-leaping fourths that expand to fifths and sixths in a sequence (mm. 259–61) whose half measure is a diminution of m. 255. The climax of the melody (mm. 262–64) combines upward fourths and downward fifths in a rhythmic structure that includes both the previous eighth-note pattern and an irregular diminution of m. 256. The final descending scale in even eighths smooths out the linear and rhythmic angularities of the melody (ex. 1):

Example 1

Schoenberg was to dub *Grundgestalt,* or basic shape, that rationalization of the materials of music made to create relational connections at every level, to make richly congruent compositional contexts. Hierarchical reduction as a critical tool was deduced from this fundamental and universal aspect of compositional thinking; in the twentieth century, reduction becomes a primary mode of apprehending works of art (in music, from Schenker onward) and, in an extended interpretation, a mode of comprehending the relations of human nature in the world (from Husserl onward). When applied to the music of *Verklärte Nacht,* reduction reveals the inter-

relationships of one diatonic scale segment *(ut-re-mi-fa)* nested in the perfect fourth. The profound effects of this scale segment in shaping the musical structure and its textures can be traced both in relations among strands of primary and subsidiary motivic material and in large-scale tonal relations, while local tonal connections unfold a network of parallel intervallic relations.

To have begun by emphasizing the purely musical aspects of *Verklärte Nacht* is not to minimize the importance to Schoenberg of the poetry of Richard Dehmel. "At the end of the 19th century, the foremost representatives of the 'Zeitgeist' in poetry were Detlev von Liliencron, Hugo von Hofmannsthal, and Richard Dehmel."[9] Between 1897 and 1907, according to Jan Maegaard's brilliant reconstruction of the chronology of Schoenberg's music,[10] Schoenberg completed or sketched fourteen settings of Dehmel's poems, in addition to sketching two uncompleted orchestral works and composing the sextet. Three of these settings were completed shortly before or during the composition of *Verklärte Nacht: Warnung,* op. 3, no. 3; *Erwartung,* op. 2, no. 1; and *Erhebung,* op. 2, no. 3. In 1912, Schoenberg replied to a letter from Dehmel, who had expressed the pleasure given him by a recent performance of the sextet:

Your poems had a decisive influence on my development as a composer. They were what first made me try to find a new tone in the lyrical mood. Or rather, I found it even without looking, simply by reflecting in music what your poems stirred up in me. People who know my music can bear witness to the fact that my first attempts to compose settings for your poems contain more of what subsequently developed in my work than there is in many a much later composition.[11]

The estimate of the importance of Schoenberg's Dehmel settings in the development of his style

[9]Schoenberg, notes for *Verklärte Nacht,* Columbia Records, op. cit.
[10]Jan Maegaard, *Studien zur Entwicklung des dodekaphonen Satzes bei Arnold Schoenberg* (Copenhagen, 1972).
[11]Arnold Schoenberg, *Letters,* ed. Erwin Stein (London, 1964), p. 35.

contained in the last sentence quoted above has not been surpassed by later critics. Richly worked-out contrapuntal textures and a dense allusiveness of pitch and interval relations make the settings of the Dehmel poems in opera 2, 3 and 6 far superior to the settings of other texts in the same collections, admirable as these may be on their own terms.

Despite the present low ebb of his literary reputation, Dehmel's poems enjoyed considerable vogue in pre-World War I Germany and Austria. Their mildly erotic tone combined with striking post-Baudelairean and post-Nietzschean sensuousness of imagery and language to give an impression of sexual candor so typical of *Jugendstil*. The poem that serves as point of departure for Schoenberg's sextet was published with the title *Verklärte Nacht* in the first edition of Dehmel's collection *Weib und Welt* (1896), and later was incorporated into his verse novel *Zwei Menschen* (1903).[12] Although the novel postdates the composition of the sextet, it exhibits a pre-compositional planning that must have appealed to the composer. It consists of three parts, each containing thirty-six poems *(Vorgänge)* of thirty-six lines each. A twelve-line *Eingang* precedes each part; there is an eight-line *Leitlied* at the beginning, and a four-line *Ausgang* at the end of the novel. Allusions and resonances among words and themes abound among the poems in the three parts of the novel. For example, the first poem in each part has beginning and ending lines that echo back and forth, like a transformed refrain:

I.1 Zwei Menschen gehn durch kahlen, kalten Hain.
. . . .
Zwei Menschen gehn durch hohe, helle Nacht.

II.1 Zwei Menschen reiten durch maihellen Hain
. . . .
Zwei Menschen reiten in die Welt.

[12]*Verklärte Nacht* appeared on p. 61 of the 1896 edition of *Weib und Welt*; it was removed from later editions after *Zwei Menschen* was published serially in *Die Insel*, 1900–01 and in book form, 1903. I am indebted to Barbara and Roland Hoermann (who are not responsible for opinions expressed here) for discussions of Dehmel's poetry and the *fin de siècle* German literary world; also to Dorothy Swift for her usual invaluable help and advice.

III.1 Zwei Menschen gehn durch nebelnassen Hain
. . . .
Zwei Menschen stehn, als sei ein Schwur gefallen.

Similar constructional ingenuities are shared by the other poems in the novel; they are typical of Dehmel's poetry.

The *Verklärte Nacht* poem, printed in the score of the string orchestra arrangement, has irregular line groupings—six lines for the opening description of the physical scene, twelve lines for the woman's confession, four more lines of description, eleven lines for the man's avowal, and a final three lines affirming their union—and a rhyme scheme which illuminates line structure with pairs of rhymes at the beginning of each division, intricately unfolding rhymes for the woman's speech, and tightly enfolding rhymes for the man's. The "double" exposition of the poem, with direct speech of the woman and the man, must have provided an impetus for Schoenberg's novel structure—a pair of sonatas with contrasting, although closely related, motivic materials and tonal relationships. It must also have suggested the combining and blending of motives from the first sonata with those in the second. The great, if simple, shift of mode from predominantly minor in the first sonata to predominantly major in the second serves to emphasize the relative rhythmic and melodic incompleteness of the first and the relative rhythmic and melodic completeness of the second. The development of these contrasts is resolved in the tonal serenity of the coda.

Although usually described as being in five sections, *Verklärte Nacht* consists of the two intimately related sonata movements, the first of which has a truncated—if not to say impacted—recapitulation of first group materials only. The two sonata structures are preceded by an Introduction, and they are linked by a Transition in which the materials of the Introduction return in a tonal area made important in the Introduction ($\flat$vi) and are provided with a new cadence. Sonata II has a normal recapitulation. (References are to the sextet; measure numbers are the same in the string orchestra arrangement.)

Introduction (1–28) i (D minor)

Sonata I
  Exposition
    First Group, Part I (29–49) i
             Part II (50–62) ♭vi
    Bridge (63–104)
    Second Group (105–132) II
  Development
    Part I (132–168)
    Part II (169–180)
  "Recapitulation" (shortened)
    First Group (181–187) i

Transition (188–228) ♭vi

Sonata II
  Exposition
    First Group (229–244) I
    Bridge (244–48) V of iii
    Second Group (249–277) III
    Codetta (278–294) III of V—♭III of V
  Development
    Part I (294–319) ♭III—V
    Part II (320–340) III of V—V
  Recapitulation
    First Group (341–363) I
    Bridge (363–369)
    Second Group (370–390) I—(♭III–i–iv)—I
  Coda (391–end) I

Reduction of Tonal Plan:
  First Sonata   Second Sonata
  i – II – (i–♭vi) – I – III – (iv) – I

"The very essence of romance is uncertainty," Algernon remarks in *The Importance of Being Earnest*—a principle those composers commonly called Romantic were quick to discover. Algernon would have been the first to recognize the pleasures of uncertainty in the tonal ambiguity of the first movement of Schumann's *Fantasy*, or in the tensions of the open structure of the first song of *Dichterliebe*; he might have been slower to perceive the clouded whole-step progression from the beginning to the end of *Tristan*. For Schoenberg in the sextet, the shaping of rhythms, motive contours, and local tonal relationships are contingent upon uncertainty and its capacity for ambiguity. In *Verklärte Nacht*, the first of his one-movement sonata compositions—*Pelleas und Melisande*, the First Quartet, and the First Chamber Symphony are prominent among its

successors—Schoenberg was to transcend by such means the tonal principles of sonata exemplified by the neo-classicism of Brahms, Bruckner, and Strauss.

In its simplest form, the global tonal scaffolding of *Verklärte Nacht* can be reduced to: i–II–(i)–III–iv–I, or *ut–re–mi–fa*. This scale segment permeates the fundamental linear and vertical progressions of the entire sextet. It is the primary element of the Introduction, whose falling scale motive ranges over the "tonic hexachord" (the sixth to first scale degrees), initiating a contour that is at once incomplete—its many repetitions arouse anticipation for completion of the scale pattern—and static. At m. 13, completion seems near, for the motive moves to the "dominant hexachord" (third downward to fifth scale degrees); but the shift involves a conflict over the raised and lowered forms of the sixth and seventh scale degrees, a conflict that serves to extend the sense of scalar, as well as motivic, incompleteness. Rhythmic fragmentation, arising from the amassing of one-measure units, creates a temporal breathlessness that will not be dispelled fully until the broader and rhythmically more stable expanses of Sonata II are reached.

While it is in the nature of introductions to expose weakly shaped contours and immediately unresolved harmonic contexts, the motives and progressions that occur in Sonata I itself are scarcely more complete, giving rise to the uncertainty that is so prominent a part of the character of this music. The first group sentence begins with a continuation of the one-measure unit inherited from the Introduction, and the sentence motive is repeated rather than transposed. The bass line is formed from an inversion of the chief Introduction motive; its ascending diatonic scale pattern in—at first—one-measure units serves to emphasize the ambiguous nature of the sentence itself. The cadence of the first group (end of m. 57–m. 62) presents the whole step in the melody with thirds in the opposing bass; the whole step is then used as the basis for the sequence of augmented chords and chromatic motives that concludes the exposition, a sequence proceeding by whole steps in each of the voices (mm. 128–31).

The most remote tonal relations, the most complicated chromatic inflections, the lengthiest of delays in resolving non-chord tones in the sextet are rooted firmly in the plainness of diatonic reduction. Certainly the passage that begins the development of Sonata I (mm. 135–52) is the furthest removed from an encompassing triadic tonal area of any in *Verklärte Nacht*. In "How One Becomes Lonely," Schoenberg compared this passage with a similar passage in the Fourth Quartet as an instance of "more violent expression."[13] In the sextet, its expressive role is clear because its structural function as the commencement of the development—the area of a sonata in which wide-ranging tonal movement is expected—is clear. The section consists of a complex segment of music that is repeated a whole step higher. Each of the elements of the segment functions within the framework of a diatonic scale segment. First, there occurs a linear contour that creates the effect of appoggiatura-resolution by half step—a Neapolitan-derived scale-degree relation—to the members of the C♯-minor triad. When the last member (E in this spelling) is reached, the other voices have changed so that the meaning of the final resolution (mm. 135–36) becomes ambiguous. This process is followed immediately by a descending contour incorporating an augmented triad within its pattern and harmonized by minor and diminished triads. The second element consists of an expanded version of the motive of the second part of the first group, here heard in conjunction with an expanded version of the appoggiatura-resolution pattern (mm. 137–40). The final element consists of a shortened version of the motive from the beginning of the first group with a chromatic scale anticipation, its model and sequence moving by whole step in all voices (mm. 141–43). The normalizing characteristics of the diatonic scale segments, voice-leading expectations, whole-step relations, and patterns of motive expansion and reduction contrive to nest this section into the music that precedes and follows. Tonally re-

mote as this section must have seemed at its first performance, it fits smoothly into the compositional processes of the music; the dissonance treatment employed is far more rigorously and exactly controlled than in many another less tonally vagrant section of the music.

At the center of *Verklärte Nacht* (m. 188ff), there occurs the section—the Transition—that rounds off Sonata I and at the same time links the two sonatas together. Again, the whole step and diatonic scale segment provide the essential tonal scheme. The music returns to the downward scale motive from the Introduction, a return prepared for by a long, almost unaccompanied, passage. This thirteen-measure passage (mm. 188–200) conveys *in petto* the subtlety, strength, and originality of Schoenberg's manner of evolving melodic contours and contrapuntal voices, demonstrating anew the essentially diatonic nature of the musical elements, however transmuted by chromatic inflection (ex. 2):

Example 2

The downward motion of the recitative-like melodic line and its bass contains the *ur*-motive of a diatonic scale segment forming a perfect fourth (two whole steps and a half step). The passage may be considered a paradigm of those fundamental elements, a compositional reduction that reveals a capacious potential for transformation and connection. The upper and lower neighbor tones and passing tones that are introduced into the downward melodic motion focus upon its diatonic basis. The bass, too, projects the same image as it moves by whole step and by leap through the fourth. As the whole motive emerges in its usual contour (m. 201ff), it

[13]*Style and Idea*, pp. 30–33.

shocks by commencing its descent on the "wrong" scale degree: not on the sixth, as in the Introduction, but on the fourth scale degree, descending to the seventh. This is as disruptive of the sense of tonal location as are the chromatic chords within which the melody is placed, a diminished chord moving to an augmented triad. This shuddering and constantly iterated music is eventually heard in a sequence that finally reaches the tranquillity of the subdominant of ♭vi. That pitch, E♭, reaches back to the beginning of the motive in m. 201, rounding off the passage with a return to that contextually important fourth scale degree.

The whole step continues to play a major role in Sonata II, combining with the fourth and the thirds implicit in both foreground and background of the thematic material to produce the consoling—because intervallically explicit—climactic melody that concludes the development section, a melody that will be heard briefly at the onset of the coda (ex. 3):

Example 3

As the outline of major tonal areas of *Verklärte Nacht* (page 7) demonstrates, there is an astonishing absence of emphasis upon the dominant as a large-scale tonal area. This evasion of the dominant is reflected in local harmonic progressions as well, especially in Sonata I, although there are many dominant-substitute progressions, both in tonic and other chord areas, whose function is to modify their respective tonal areas indirectly, deceptively and ambiguously. Even when a dominant function is implied by a pedal—as in mm. 100–04, where the dominant of II is in the bass—the harmonic meaning of the pedal is blurred by non-dominant pitches. In this instance, the domi-

nant of the dominant appears over the dominant pedal; the pitches of that chord establish a connection with the second group material by becoming the main pitches of its first melodic contour, this time over a tonic pedal (mm. 105–07). The tension produced by these large-scale suspensions, for so they are treated contextually, is tightened by irregular temporal resolutions; often, when a resolution takes place, the note of resolution has become part of a new and uncertain harmonic context, to assume a meaning different from the one anticipated. It is through such means that restless motion and melodic incompleteness are achieved in Sonata I.

In structural positions where powerful dominant areas might be expected—such as the end of an exposition, the beginning or end of a development section—Sonata I again evades the issue. The sequence of augmented triads that ends the exposition has nothing directly to do with the dominant, although the need for resolution may suggest a typical function of the dominant. It leads to a cadence on a chord which serves as a substitute for the dominant of ♭III, and the lowest note (E) of that dominant-substitute chord becomes the initiator of the development section. This unsupported, ferociously sustained pitch refers in several directions: back to the II area of the second group, to the dominant, and to the extremely ambiguous ♭III that follows. The preparation for the recapitulation of Sonata I takes place on the dominant-substitute of the dominant. While this is scarcely an unusual procedure in itself, its significance here lies in its oblique evasion of the dominant.

In Sonata II, relations among large-scale progressions, melodic contours, local harmony, and rhythmic movement are manifestly more complete and more strongly shaped than in Sonata I, a set of circumstances that is confirmed by the more normative use of dominant area relations. The broad, succinctly presented first-group sentence, with its cloud of motives from Sonata I, cadences on iii. In the bridge, the dominant of iii is prolonged and, with a shift to the major mode, the second group begins its long, firmly structured melody. The codetta, on the dominant of III (written enharmonically as D♭), presents a new melodic contour that moves downward over the triad and whose second phrase begins with a form of the downward scale motive in diminution. Although the codetta concludes with a tonicization of ♭III—through the dominant of the dominant—the development section pivots about two powerful dominant statements. The first part of the development section cadences emphatically on the dominant (mm. 316–19), with a deceptive movement from that cadence into a new tonal area (V of III). At the end of the second part of the development (mm. 332–40), the harmony is violently wrenched from the dominant of the III area to the dominant itself in order to prepare for the recapitulation in a normal tonal manner.

The dominant, then, plays a secondary part in the unfolding of major tonal areas of the sextet. There are several other tonal areas whose importance is greater in shaping the large-scale tonal functions. The Introduction first hints at and later emphasizes strongly two chords destined to assume crucial roles in subsequent and subsidiary events in the two sonatas: ♭vi/♭VI and ♭III. The latter sometimes appears in its function as the dominant of the former; it sometimes exists as a tonal area by itself. The progression that links the two parts of the first group (mm. 41–49) moves through the dominant of ♭III, which quickly turns toward the dominant of ♭vi in mm. 46–49. Schoenberg was inordinantly proud of this progression, referring to the passage several times in his writings, notably in *Harmonielehre* where he was intent upon explaining the theoretical status of the famous ninth chord with the ninth (marked "X") in the bass (ex. 4):

Example 4

In "Criteria for the Evaluation of Music," he explained that because of this "*one* single uncatalogued dissonance," *Verklärte Nacht* was rejected for performance by a Viennese concert group.[14] But this progression has a grander function in the sextet than as a source for a particular chord-construction and usage, or even as a local linking passage, for it returns at two crucial structural points. First, it is the harmonic scaffolding for the recapitulation of the first group sentence (mm. 181–87), and is in part responsible for the ambiguity and uncertainty of that return (ex. 5):

Example 5

---

[14] Ibid., pp. 131–32.

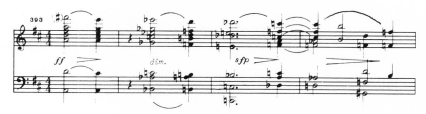

Example 6

Second, this "uncatalogued dissonance" returns in the first part of the coda as part of a succession of important motives from the composition, this time beginning on the raised third scale degree to reflect the modal shift of Sonata II (ex. 6).

The ♭vi chord, touched upon in the Introduction, emerges as the tonal area of the second part of the first group of Sonata I; it is prepared for linearly by the F♯ (=G♭) of mm. 46–49, a lowered sixth scale degree in ♭vi, which functions here as the Neapolitan of the dominant of ♭vi, a common Brucknerian relationship. The other extensive ♭vi area of Sonata I occurs in the Transition, discussed above. Its role in Sonata II is limited to minor appearances.

These third relations among tonal areas, such as i–♭vi or i–♭III or I–III, are extended to other compositional levels, particularly as intervals of transposition for sequence segments. In Sonata I, the minor third is often the basis for sequences—for example, the large-scale repetition of mm. 75–82 rising a minor third higher in mm. 83–90, or the series of sequences in the development section from m. 153 with each segment rising a minor third. The ambiguity of tonal direction that results from the linear diminished triads is especially potent in its intensification of the weak and uncertain motivic contours and harmonic progressions in Sonata I. The major third appears somewhat less prominently in such circumstances; but when it occurs, the resulting linearly and vertically stated augmented triads have a powerful effect on harmonic and melodic stability. A compelling summary of linear and vertical third relations occurs at the conclusion of the development section, Sonata I, m. 169ff, where augmented, major, minor and di-

minished triads are systematically exhibited both as melodic contours and as chords in the preparation for the dominant of the dominant.

In Sonata II, ♭III continues in its strong modifying support of the primary tonal areas. The development section begins (mm. 294ff) in the area of ♭III. In its function of the dominant of ♭vi, it is the point of arrival of the sequence arising from the end of the melody of example 3 at the beginning of m. 322, as well as the moment in which the first of the tonal abruptions occurs as the development is pulled toward the dominant. It functions in the second group of the recapitulation as part of a larger progression toward the minor subdominant (mm. 376–78), where it is heard for a final time in the sextet as a member of the global scale degree motion D–E–F–G.

The half-step relationship that has the most far-reaching consequences in *Verklärte Nacht* is that of the Neapolitan. It is encountered frequently as a modification of local linear and vertical contexts, as in the linkage between two tonal areas in mm. 46–49. In this passage, discussed above, the F♯(=G♭) assumes the function of the Neapolitan of V of ♭vi; and it later takes on the function of ♭vi of ♭vi. This resultant complex of meanings is an essential characteristic of the oblique and ambiguous tonal movement of Sonata I, encouraged by linear and vertical Neapolitan relations. By analogy, the chromatic inflection of linear elements reflects and prolongs the action of the Neapolitan relation. The Neapolitan serves as an intensification of the ii–V–iv progression in m. 34ff. Yet another instance of Neapolitan linkage, whose dramatic intensity is in part owed to those previously encountered Neapolitan relations, occurs between the Transition and Sonata II. The

Transition cadences upon the minor subdominant of ♭vi with only the B♭ remaining from the subdominant triad. The B♭, in a manner analogous to that of mm. 46–49, leads to the major tonic as the Neapolitan of the fifth scale degree, as ♭vi of I, and as a foreshadowing of the A♯ of the III region, the tonal area of the second group.

The Neapolitan also has a major function in the tonal wrenching toward the dominant that takes place near the end of the development section of Sonata II (mm. 332–36). The sequences of the preceding section halt abruptly, leaving the melody and its subsidiary contrapuntal lines stuck for some time in the same place, ♭ii, before they plunge with equal abruptness to the dominant in preparation for the recapitulation.

II has functioned, more or less conventionally, as a substitute for IV in earlier phases of the music, but from the beginning of this recapitulation, it comes to the fore as an independent entity to isolate the subdominant area in preparation for the iv–♭II–I cadence which concludes the sextet. The brief detail of the major-minor subdominant triads in the first group exposition (ex. 7):

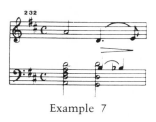

Example 7

is expanded in the recapitulation both through repetition (mm. 342, 349, 351, and 355) and through the cadence on the subdominant (mm. 358–61) that is an element in a large-scale progression: I–ii–V–IV–V (mm. 353–63). This expanded statement of subdominant function continues with equal force in the return of the second group, where, as the minor subdomi-

nant, it becomes an element in that progression toward ♭III discussed above, as well as the immediate goal of the progression of which ♭III is itself an element (mm. 375–80). The articulation of the subdominant area at this, the penultimate stage of the composition, is an affirmation of those stable and stabilizing properties of diatonic tonality. It is generally in such a position, near the end of a tonal composition, that the subdominant (or its substitute, II) is given strong functional emphasis; Schenker's analytical reduction of tonal function on the model of a complete cadence pattern—I–IV– (or II–) V–I—is rooted in the observation of this phenomenon in tonal music. Schoenberg was not blindly obeying some unwritten canon, for in *Verklärte Nacht* the structural emphasis upon the subdominant links back to the II area of Sonata I, and forward, in combination with ♭II, to the coda's concluding cadence, incorporating in its references those Neapolitan relations that function so compellingly throughout the sextet. The sustained emphasis upon the tonic from the beginning of the recapitulation of Sonata II to the end at once rights the intensely dramatic tonic imbalance of much of the preceding music, and at the same time provides a stable context in which the combined subdominant-Neapolitan cadence may make its full effect.

In this discussion of tonal functions in *Verklärte Nacht*, much has been said about the correlation between motive generation and the explicit global tonal relations of the music, particularly as an aspect of the unfolding of the diatonic intervals from the perfect fourth. The ingenuity and fluency with which linear contours represent compositional prolongations of those intervals is nowhere more clearly discernible than at the beginning of the coda (m. 391ff), where the succession of motives from earlier stages of the sextet succinctly displays that framework for motive and tonal generation (ex. 8):

Example 8

Schoenberg was justly proud of the speed and facility with which he composed the sextet, even permitting his memory to compress the actual composition time to a dramatic three weeks.[15] The sense of compression and rigor of composition conveyed by Schoenberg's exaggerated statement is matched in its intensity by the music, with its controlled contrapuntal density of motive combinations flourishing as prolongations of the basic tonal materials. Schoenberg, in the same essay, cites the passage that occurs at the beginning of the development of Sonata I (mm. 161–68), where a motive is presented in its original and inverted forms both in succession and, finally, in combination, as an instance of contrapuntal ingenuity that cost him some effort to accomplish.[16] It is precisely such a passage — and there are many others that are comparable, including the recapitulation, Sonata I (ex. 5), and the return of the second group, Sonata II—where textures display functional connections in layer upon layer of voices, that further confirms the sense of compression in the sextet. Similarly, compression is conveyed by the spatial placement of melodic lines conceived as a mingling of several voices in several registers. One such melodic contour, existing within a network of timbres and registers, occurs at the beginning of the second part of the first group, Sonata I (ex. 9).

Example 9

The upper voice, presented in octaves, is both a counterpoint to and an answering variation and amplification of the cello line. Such modes of extending and proliferating melodic contours from a single line into wider zones of instrumental space mark off other structural areas of the music—as in the second group of Sonata II—and share in non-imitative contrapuntal textures—as in the bridge of Sonata I, m. 69ff. Through such melodic configurations, Schoenberg was able to widen the forms motives may take and to deepen the connections among them with their engendering elements.

In Schoenberg's later version for string orchestra (1917, revised 1943), there are no substantive changes from the music of the original sextet. This version, with its bold and luxurious sonorities, is more familiar to the concert-goer than is the leaner, more intimate sextet version, for concerts by string sextets are rarities. There are many added or expanded indications of nuances, clarifications of tempo markings (all instructions are given in Italian instead of the German of the original), metronome markings (absent from the sextet), and occasional revisions of notation. Among the latter, there is a written-out late instance of the triplet interpretation of duple notation that occurs in the sextet (ex. 10):

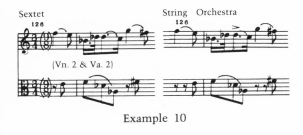

Example 10

---

[15]"Heart and Brain in Music," ibid., pp. 55–56. See Maegaard, op. cit., for details of the chronology of *Verklärte Nacht*.

[16]*Style and Idea*, pp. 55–56. The example given by Schoenberg is incorrect, presenting only those measures in which the two motive forms appear in succession (mm. 161–62), not in combination—an error future editors may wish to correct.

Among the many subtle shifts of string sonorities and masses with which Schoenberg contrived to articulate the musical structure in this new medium, the passage from m. 161— with the motive in both its original and inverted forms—is notable for its clarity and delicacy, made possible by the use of eleven solo strings and divided second violins to articulate primary and secondary contrapuntal voices. The textural clarity is aided by octave doubling and by the contrasts in sonority provided by muted solo instruments while the second violins remain unmuted.

Schoenberg often heard the plaintive remark about *Verklärte Nacht*, "If only he had continued to compose in this style," to which he replied: "I have not discontinued composing in the same style and in the same way as at the very beginning. The difference is only that I do it better now than before; it is more concentrated, more mature."[17] That vocation for composition, to which the sextet is a burning witness, radically transformed musical thinking in the new century by creating a music whose every layer and corner is permeated by concentrated relations and connections—enmeshing all, as Henry James wrote, in "the wonder of the consciousness of everything."

---

[17]Ibid., p. 30ff.

Mirrors and Metaphors: On Schoenberg and Nineteenth-Century Tonality

CHRISTOPHER LEWIS

To invoke an analogy is almost inevitably to invite criticism, for such a comparison never implies identity, but merely a selective similarity; and the potential critic is always free to draw upon a dissimilar selection.

Perhaps it is that very imprecision of meaning that has made the metaphor so essential to both poetry and poetics. From at least the time of Plato, the definition of poetry and its sister arts by the metaphor of art as the mirror of life has been so consistently recurrent as to transcend mere tautology. When that metaphor at last failed, it did so because of a change in the conception of the creative act itself—a change which caused a radical new poetic posture and language. As similar ideas began to change the language of music, the lack of a long-standing technical metaphor—or of any developed analytic apparatus—to describe the older style precluded the immediate comprehension of the

newer. Indeed, study of later nineteenth-century music is still hampered by the assumption that the principles of the earlier common practice underlie post-Wagnerian tonality, in spite of a growing body of evidence to the contrary. The later music differs from the earlier not only in its affects and its vocabulary, but in the very essence of its conception. A brief consideration of certain aspects of poetic theory and of the nature of metaphor helps clarify the relevance of certain untraditional analytical assumptions.

Plato's metaphor of the world as an imperfect reflection of an ideal archetype[1] stimulated artists as diverse as Aristotle, Cicero, da Vinci, and Johnson—to name only a few—to define their own art as a metaphoric mirror of life, and to

---

[1]Plato, *Republic* X.597, trans. Francis MacDonald Cornford (New York, 1945).

judge its quality by the accuracy of the reflection.[2] But toward the end of the eighteenth century, in place of the mimetic poet as a rationalist agent, there grew steadily a conception of the pragmatic poet who "moves into the center of the scheme and himself becomes the prime generator of the subject matter, attributes and values of a poem."[3] The single most important vehicle in English for the new, Romantic ideas is Wordsworth's "Preface to *Lyrical Ballads*," which invokes a radical new metaphor. "All good poetry," writes Wordsworth, "is the spontaneous overflow of powerful feelings."[4] Byron, Shelley, Hazlitt, and Hunt all adopt similar metaphors that imply not a static reflection of what *is*, but a process of *becoming* and an expression of the internal made external, with the artist himself as a crucial new element in the creative process.[5] Both literally and metaphorically this involves an added dimension in artistic thought that is reflected not only in criticism but also in poetic language.

The coincidence of a new metaphor in poetics with a new poetry suggests two lines of inquiry into the apparently new musical language that evolved around the middle of the nineteenth century. We will begin by considering to what extent the idea of metaphor as description may be applied to musical analysis; and we may then ask whether there does not appear, in music as in poetry, a new dimension that requires a new analytic metaphor. Our sources will necessarily be less precise than those for poetry; poets and novelists are peculiarly well-equipped to write literature about writing literature, while composers generally do not use the language of their own art to describe technical matters. In fact, it was not until Schenker's time that music theory developed a sophisticated way of expressing analysis in musical rather than in numerical or verbal notation.

We are by now well accustomed to the term "model" as a label for certain kinds of analytical statements. It is not without some hesitation that I suggest it may be profitable to think of such schemes as "metaphors": musical scholarship suffers from enough necessary catachresis to make one wary of increasing the burden. However, a "model" has distinct connotations of precision—of a one-to-one correspondence—that is lacking from almost all reductive analysis. Voice-leading graphs involve at the very earliest stages a rhythmic adjustment that amounts to a distortion of the musical surface; since the rhythm is related to "specific contrapuntal situations, it changes from level to level."[6] Indeed, the concept of prolongation itself suggests that "events or states . . . extend metaphorically through those segments of the piece which prolong them."[7]

This level of abstraction allows a more precise parallel. A metaphor is a figure with two subjects, of which the secondary one (the metaphoric subject) is to be regarded as a system of related ideas rather than a single object. The metaphor (in our case, the analysis) projects upon the primary subject (the piece) a set of associated implications that are predictable of the secondary subject. The more deeply in the background an analysis is based, the more numerous are the possible pieces (and the possible more-to-the-foreground sketches) onto which the analysis *might* be projected. Unlike a model, then, which represents something that is, an analysis as metaphor can illuminate not only what a piece does, but also what it might have done, but does not for its own internal reasons. To think of an analysis as a model can lead us to think of it as the only model, and perhaps even to substitute it for the piece itself as an artifact. While it may be gratifying to view analysis as a creative act, to do so is equivalent to confusing critical prose and literature,[8] and means that we

---

[2]Aristotle, *Poetics* I.1447a and XXIV.1460a, trans. S. H. Campbell (London, 1929); Samuel Johnson, *The Rambler*, vol. 3 in *The Yale Edition of the Complete Works* (New Haven, 1969), p. 22; and citations in M. H. Abrams, *The Mirror and the Lamp: Romantic Theory and the Critical Tradition* (New York, 1953), p. 32.
[3]M. H. Abrams, "Theories of Poetry," in *Encyclopedia of Poetry and Poetics* (Princeton, 1965), p. 643.
[4]William Wordsworth, "Preface to Lyrical Ballads," in *Wordsworth's Literary Criticism*, ed. Nowell C. Smith (London, 1905), p. 15.
[5]Abrams, *The Mirror and the Lamp*, p. 49; Alba H. Warren, Jr., *English Poetic Theory: 1825–1865* (Princeton, 1950; New York, 1966), p. 97.

[6]Heinrich Schenker, *Free Composition*, trans. and ed. Ernst Oster, (New York, 1979), I, 122.
[7]William Benjamin, "Models of Underlying Tonal Structure: How Can They Be Abstract, and How Should They Be Abstract," *Music Theory Spectrum* 4 (1982), 33–34.
[8]"Art, like nature, is the subject of a systematic study, and has to be distinguished from the study itself, which is criticism." Northrup Frye, *Fables of Identity* (New York, 1963), p. 7.

will come to believe that internal coherence and a certain elegance of expression give the analysis a degree of authority apart from its relationship to the subject work of art.

Max Black has observed that it is a violation of philosophical grammar to assign either truth or falsity to strong metaphors.[9] It is equally a violation of "critical grammar" to apply standards of scientific proof to questions of artistic theory, or to assign absolute truth or absolute falsity to analytical systems. If we can think of analyses as being metaphorically based on selective similarities among pieces, we may usefully broaden our understanding of the ways in which analyses may be correct, and may discover that two contradictory analyses, two different ways of hearing the same piece, may both be valid.[10] Of course, just as truth or falsehood can be imputed to non-metaphorical statements, so may a particular analytic statement—if sufficiently precise—be considered true or false in terms of the specific musical grammar to which it refers, and a knowledge of that grammar is a prerequisite to the creation and comprehension of a useful analysis.[11]

As a final parallel between analysis and metaphor, we find that a metaphorical statement often appears to be "perversely asserting a thing to be what it is not,"[12] and only real understanding of the complex of ideas around the secondary subject allows comprehension of the analogy. Thus the analysis of even a relatively simple passage may show rhythmic and pitch relationships that seem perversely contrary to the actual music, but that in fact arise from grammatical requirements. A case in point is shown in ex. 1. The graph shows a $\hat{2}$ that is not in the piece and is apparently implied only by a Schenkerian desire for a melodic step-descent. But the F on the first beat of m. 15, at first implying a $\frac{6}{4}$ decoration of the dominant, becomes an explicit dissonance on the second and third beats. Our knowledge of tonal grammar tells us that each of these circumstances requires the F to resolve to E♭—and our internal ears supply that resolution.[13] Therefore the analysis is an accurate representation of the abstraction underlying the music itself, however perversely it may appear to assert what is not.

The laws of common-practice grammar require that a given event have only one meaning at any given level. That meaning may arise from the literal "truth" of the music, or it may arise from our understanding of an ideal event which the actual music obscures. The "consonant passing tone" is fully conformable to the laws of the style, since it is consonant at one level and passing at another.[14] Change of function as an event is transferred from one analytic level to another, or the disappearance of an event as it is subsumed by those more structurally significant, is not only possible, but essential to the development of our view of the ultimate background of a common-practice piece. This is so because such music is "monotonal"—that is, apparent changes of key are merely prolonged chromatic elaborations of the fundamental diatonic progression that is itself prolonging the tonic triad.[15]

---

[9]Max Black, "More About Metaphor," in *Metaphor and Thought*, ed. Andrew Ortony (Cambridge, 1979), p. 41.
[10]See John Rahn's discussion of two different interpretations of a movement from Bach's Third Sonata for solo violin, in "Aspects of Musical Explanation," *Perspectives of New Music* 17 (1979), 216–17; and William Benjamin's contradictory and thus provocative views of the Sarabande from Bach's B♭ Partita, in "Models of Underlying Structure," pp. 43–45.
[11]See Steven Haflich's review of Eugene Narmour's *Beyond Schenkerism* in *The Journal of Music Theory* 23 (1979), 287–304. Haflich's discussion (pp. 296–99) of Narmour's ex. 18 makes it clear that his analysis and Narmour's cannot both be correct; one of them has gravely misunderstood the grammar of the piece. There is something of a paradox in the relationship between analysis and *a priori* knowledge of grammar, since it is apparently only through analysis that we can obtain the knowledge on which to base our analyses. Perhaps there are two stages of analysis—the "learning" and the "demonstration"—which may be likened to practice and performance. In any case, the paradox is diminished if we remember that analysis may teach us grammar, but does not create it.
[12]Black, "More About Metaphor," p. 21.

[13]See Schenker, *Free Composition* I, 51. Jonas, paraphrasing Schenker, speaks of the "ideal presence" of the implied resolution, "although in strict counterpoint the [explicit] tone of resolution remains a necessity" (Oswald Jonas, *Introduction to the Theory of Heinrich Schenker*, trans. and ed. John Rothgeb [New York, 1982], p. 98).
[14]Allen Forte, "Schenker's Conception of Musical Structure," in *Readings in Schenker Analysis and Other Approaches*, ed. Maury Yeston (New Haven, 1977), p. 15; and Schenker, *Free Composition* I, 61.
[15]See Schenker, *Free Composition* I, 8 and 112. Schoenberg uses the term in a similar, though less technically precise, way: monotonality is a principle by which "every digression from the tonic is considered to be still within the tonality," and "subordinate to the central power of a tonic" (Arnold Schoenberg, *Structural Functions of Harmony*, rev. edn. [New York, 1969], p. 19).

Example 1:
Chopin, Mazurka, op. 24, no. 4, mm. 14–16.

Let us suppose, however, that certain laws of common practice may be repealed. Can we imagine tonal music in which the principle of monotonality is abandoned; a given event may be simultaneously structural and elaborative *at the same level*; a dissonance is generated by structural harmony rather than by line; and in which conflicting foreground events may both be crucial aspects of the background?

Music exploiting these rule violations—and the many other points of detail that would necessarily follow—would differ from common-practice music just as Romantic poetry differed from its forerunners: in terms of its metaphorical dimensions. And just as Romantic critics had to postulate new metaphors of poetry, so would we have to reassess our analytic presuppositions. This is precisely the situation into which music was thrust by Wagner's *Tristan*.

The Schenkerian approach is so miraculously apt for monotonal music that it is easy to assume that it is equally apt for all music. To do so, however, is to become what Colin Turbayne calls a "victim of metaphor [who] accepts one way of sorting, bundling or allocating facts as the only way to sort, bundle or allocate them. The victim not only has a special view of the world, but regards it as the only view."[16] If we

allow ourselves another view of *Tristan*, it becomes at once evident that there are essential issues in the piece that a strictly orthodox voice-leading graph must necessarily ignore, for the piece presents instances of all the rule violations enumerated above. The "other view," the new analytic metaphor I adopt here, is the concept of the "double-tonic complex" formulated by Robert Bailey.[17]

Tristan is not the first piece to show "progressive tonality," that is, the device of beginning in one key and ending in another.[18] Schenker mentions several such works that have "deceptive beginnings," including the finale of Beethoven's Fourth Concerto and Chopin's Scherzo in D♭ Major (*not* B♭ Minor);[19] and Harald Krebs has recently discussed a number of examples from the early nineteenth century.[20] The *Tristan* prelude differs from the earlier examples in that the background progression is reflected in the musical texture right from the opening measures, which imply the two tonics both successively and simultaneously.[21] An analysis that reduces one of the implied tonics to the role of a decorative element will misrepresent the background duality.[22] That there are paired tonics is more important than that there is progression from one to the other, for Schoenberg says that the tonic "admits the rivalry of other tonics alongside it," and either may emerge as the final tonic.[23] It is this pairing of tonics established so that "either one can serve as representative of the tonic"

[16]Colin Murray Turbayne, *The Myth of Metaphor* (New Haven, 1962), p. 27.

[17]Robert Bailey, "*Das Lied von der Erde*: Tonal Language and Formal Design" (paper read before the American Musicological Society, October 1978); and *Richard Wagner: Prelude and Transfiguration from "Tristan and Isolde,"* a Norton Critical Score, ed. Robert Bailey (New York, 1985), pp. 113–46.

[18]Dika Newlin, *Bruckner, Mahler, Schoenberg*, 2nd edn. (New York, 1978), p. 129. Both the prelude and all of act I are progressive.

[19]Schenker, *Free Composition* I, 129.

[20]Harald Krebs, "Alternatives to Monotonality in Early Nineteenth-Century Music," *Journal of Music Theory* 25 (1981), 1–16.

[21]Bailey, *Tristan*, pp. 125–30.

[22]William Mitchell's brilliant voice-leading analysis (in *The Music Forum* 1 [1967], 162–203), for example, for all it reveals about the prelude, is a sketch not of Wagner's symphonic *Vorspiel* to *Tristan*, but of an occasional piece derived therefrom. The concert ending is not calculated to realize the implications of the first ninety-odd measures of the piece, but merely to allow performance of the excerpt.

[23]Arnold Schoenberg, *Theory of Harmony*, trans. Roy E. Carter (Berkeley and Los Angeles, 1978), p. 153.

that Bailey refers to as a double-tonic complex.[24] In common-practice music one can never simply boil down the foreground through successive reductions and arrive at the background; a sense of the background is needed to establish the context of the other levels. If the rule of monotonality fails, then the Schenkerian *Ursatz*, which represents the piece as the prolongation of a single tonic triad, also fails. "Background" therefore loses its precise meaning as an abstraction related to higher levels by voice-leading, and I adopt Patrick McCreless's convention that the term shall refer to those harmonic relationships that govern important structural entities.[25] Thus we understand the background of the *Tristan* prelude to be its essential tonal issue—the pairing of the tonics A and C.

For such a pairing, which generates the overall tonal structure of a piece (whether progressive or not), and prescribes certain elements of foreground harmonic language, I avoid the term "bitonal," which has conventional and useful applications to music literally in two keys for more or less extended periods. The pairing of *tonics* as a structural device is essentially different from the overlay of *keys* as a textural device, although as we shall see the latter may well be one of the techniques used to elaborate and reinforce the former.

The concept of a double tonic allows for each of our other three rule violations. The "Tristan" chord is treated by Wagner consistently as a local dissonance. At the chord's first appearance, the G♯ is an appoggiatura resolving to A, thus foreshadowing the eventual melodic resolution at mm. 16–17 and initiating a fundamentally diatonic step progression (see ex. 2b).[26] On the other hand, the G♯ is a crucial structural tone starting the arpeggiation of the "Tristan" chord of C in the upper voice (ex. 2a).[27] But even this

[24]Bailey, "*Das Lied von der Erde*."
[25]Patrick McCreless, *Wagner's "Siegfried": Its Drama, History and Music* (Ann Arbor, 1982), p. 89.
[26]Example 2a is derived from Robert Bailey, *Tristan*, pp. 127–29; Benjamin Boretz, "Meta-Variations, part IV: Analytic Fallout (I)," *Perspectives of New Music* 11 (1972), 169; and Edward T. Cone, "Sound and Syntax: An Introduction to Schoenberg's Harmony," *Perspectives of New Music* 13 (1974), 24.
[27]Bailey, *Tristan*, p. 124; see also Schoenberg, *Structural Functions*, p. 77; and Edward T. Cone, "Yet Once More, O Ye Laurels," *Perspectives of New Music* 14/15 (1976), 299–301.

a. *Tristan*, prelude, mm. 1–17.

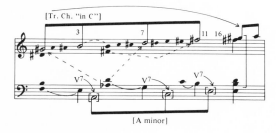

b. after Schoenberg, *Structural Functions*, p. 77.

Example 2

chord has double meaning, since it is both the "Tristan" chord of C and a foreshadowing of the V^9 of A in m. 16. A fully accurate analysis must somehow contrive to show all these implications.

Both *Also sprach Zarathustra* and *Das Lied von der Erde* close with a dissonant sonority (the first implicit and the second explicit), and in both cases the source of the dissonance is an expression of two background tonics. Such a final cadence was not possible for Wagner at the time of *Tristan*, but Bailey shows it was possible at an interior cadence to resolve to a chord containing both elements of the tonic complex (see ex. 3).[28] Of course, such a chord is "dissonant"— that is, requires resolution—only in common-practice terms; here it is precisely because the sonority derives from structural harmony that no resolution is required.

Finally, we note that the two foreground arpeggiations of mm. 1–11 are in tonal conflict (ex. 2a); the lower implies the tonic A, and the upper states the "Tristan" chord of C. It is true that locally the C implication is subordinate to that of A, just as at the end of the prelude the "Tristan" chord of A is subsumed by the domi-

[28]The cadence in question occurs on p. 193 of the Dover full score (Richard Wagner, *Tristan und Isolde*, rpt. edn. [New York, 1973]); see Bailey, *Tristan*, p. 122.

Example 3: *Tristan*, act I, sc. 5.

nant of C (see ex. 4),[29] but they are *equally* crucial members of the background complex, and neither can be deleted from any level of the analysis.

In concrete terms, then, each of our rule violations demands an added dimension in our analytic representations. Sometimes that will require sketching a given line or texture twice,

with different interpretations; sometimes it will require showing more than two ultimate structural voices. William Benjamin considers it a mistake "to embody the harmonic meaning of a passage in a two-part counterpoint of registral voices, however plausibly derived from the passage."[30] If common-practice harmony may be too full to be so embodied, then what of the examples discussed above? No two-voice reduction can do justice to Wagner's cadence, not

[29]Example 4 is derived from Bailey, *Tristan*, p. 137; and Philip Friedheim, *Tonality and Structure in the Early Works of Schoenberg* (Ph.D. diss., New York University, 1963), pp. 41–42.

[30]Benjamin, "Models of Underlying Structure," p. 40.

Example 4: *Tristan*, prelude, closing measures.

merely because the third voice may affect the voice-leading, but because there are more than two harmony-defining voices, and we must show at least three of them in our sketch or else indulge in two complementary two-voice sketches—one for each tonic in the complex.

Most of the music written in the half-century after *Tristan* may be fruitfully examined in the light of the double tonic. The remainder of this paper will be devoted to analytic observations about two of the songs from Schoenberg's op. 6, and brief remarks about op. 8, no. 5. Although written after the turn of the century (between 1903 and 1905), the songs of op. 6 derive their syntax from the post-Wagnerian tonal tradition. Schoenberg's idiosyncratic treatment of the traditional dissonances allows him to create particularly striking exploitations of paired tonics,

and the principles of construction are more readily observed than in music whose surface characteristics are more conventionally common practice.

Edward T. Cone has remarked that Schoenberg's *Traumleben* (op. 6, no. 1) "might be heard as a regretful, nostalgic farewell to the nineteenth century, [which develops a] serene uncontested E major," while the syntax of the piece is generated by cadential associations of the note C with the tonic chord of E.[31] E certainly prevails at all important cadences in the piece, including the last, but I believe that prev-

---

[31]Cone, "Sound and Syntax," p. 30–31.

Example 5: *Traumleben*, mm. 1–4.

Used by permission of Belmont Music Publishers, Los Angeles, CA 90049.

alence is not uncontested, and in many ways it is helpful to think of the syntax as deriving from background and foreground exploitation of a double-tonic complex of E and F. Christopher Wintle, in the course of an extended discussion drawing parallels between this song and the harmonic techniques described in Schoenberg's *Harmonielehre*, refers to the "extended coloring of the tonic E major by the secondary tonality of F major, with no formal close in the secondary tonality."[32] I suggest that F functions as more than a coloration, and as more than an extended neighbor; it is rather the other half of a perhaps rudimentary tonic complex. When so

viewed, a number of apparent illogicalities in the harmonic design of the song become both logical and consistent.

The only direct V–I progression in E in the song is that of mm. 1–4; the piano part, at least, is perfectly straightforward: three measures of V^7 followed by tonic (see ex. 5). The vocal line, on the other hand, is a beautiful illustration of "dissonance" arising from harmony rather than linear elaboration, for its function is clearly to announce the other member of the complex by arpeggiating the F-major triad. Even this first relatively conventional cadence therefore overlays elements of a complex tonal pairing.

The cadences of the second and third phrases (see ex. 6a) reflect an increasingly intense interaction between elements of the two tonics. Measures 8–9 must be understood as a kind of

[32]Christopher Wintle, "Schoenberg's Harmony: Theory and Practice," *Journal of the Arnold Schoenberg Institute* 4 (1980), 57.

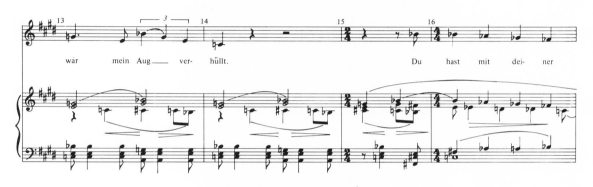

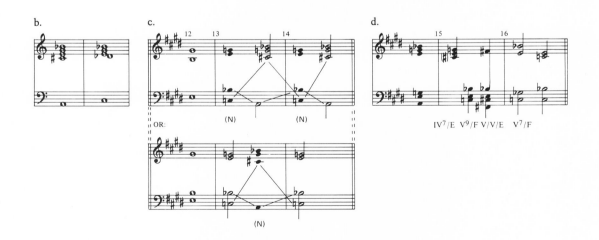

Example 6: *Traumleben*, mm. 8–16.

Used by permission of Belmont Music Publishers, Los Angeles, CA 90049.

Mirrors and Metaphors: Schoenberg and Tonality   ❧   23

plagal progression in E. The subdominant chord, however, is colored by its minor seventh, and we must ask not only why Schoenberg avoids the authentic cadence, but also why, having done so, he invokes IV$^{\natural 7}$. The answer to both questions is given by mm. 13–15, where we find that IV^9 in E and V^9 in F are so similar that their successive use allows an especially subtle shift from one tonic to the other (see ex. 6b); and singly, each has at least an ambiguous meaning.

However specious this may seem to our present harmonic understanding, we must remember that in *Harmonielehre*, published only six years after the completion of op. 6, Schoenberg adopts a strongly root-oriented view of harmony.[33] He considers that the ninth chord is a legitimate *chord*,[34] even though, like the seventh, the ninth may have first come into use as a melodic tone; and he says that altered ninth chords are particularly useful as "vagrant chords" (by which he means chords of ambiguous tonal implication that are therefore useful in modulation).[35] Indeed, precisely the technique exploited in mm. 13–15 of *Traumleben*— the substitution of roots under a common diminished-seventh sonority—is discussed at some length.[36] In the light of phrases 2 and 3 of the song, it would seem that C^7 is elaborating the presumably cadential A^7; in the context of mm. 13–16, we hear A^7 elaborating C^7. Each chord is therefore both elaborational and structural, because two tonics are being implied (see ex. 6c). In m. 15, five of the tones of the two chords are sounded together (only the A is omitted); the resolution is first to V/V in E, and then to V of F (m. 16; see ex. 6d). In m. 18, Schoenberg reverts to the plagal formula for the cadence proper (see ex. 7).[37]

Significantly, when the melodic line of phrase 1 returns in mm. 21–25, it is now harmonized with perfect felicity with the *other* tonic, F (although the melody is untransposed); but at the cadence (m. 31), V of F resolves indirectly to the "wrong" tonic (see ex. 8). Of course, such a resolution is entirely idiomatic here, for, as we noted earlier, either member of the complex can at any time (technically, at least) function as tonic, superseding the other.

The final vocal phrase and the piano postlude turn exclusively upon the pairing of E and F. Measures 25–28 effect a contrapuntal prolongation of E, and in doing so complete a melodic motion begun in phrases 1 and 2, but diverted when phrase 3 turned toward F (see ex. 8). This chromatic stepwise ascent at last reaches its goal ($\hat{1}$ of E) in m. 28; but this pitch is simultaneously the last *and* the penultimate degrees, for $\hat{1}$ of E immediately assumes its other function as $\hat{7}$ of F, and it resolves as such at the climax of the song in m. 29. The piano postlude then reinforces the symbiotic relationship between E and F by oscillating between the two in such a way as to recall for the last time the relationship between the "pre-tonic" chords in E and F which have made the whole design possible (see ex. 9).

Edward Cone has defined the "tonal normal" of a piece (or of a style) as the characteristic sonority in a piece, with which all other sonorities are implicitly compared, and which is normally used as a cadential chord—a chord which requires no further resolution.[38] He remarks that the characteristic surface sonority of *Traumleben* is B–A–F–C (the first four notes of the vocal line), and that this sonority is in conflict with the tonal normal of the piece, the E-major triad.[39] The conflict disappears, or perhaps more accurately, becomes a syntactic event, if we take as the tonal normal of the piece the double-tonic of E and F, even though the normal is nowhere explicitly sounded;[40] virtually everything in the piece, including the characteristic surface sonorities, derives logically from that normal.

Of course, just as it is often extremely dif-

---

[33]Schoenberg, *Theory of Harmony*, p. 357: "One will be inclined to consider the alterations as chromatic passing tones. But one should not, for reference to roots is always a more appropriate aid to harmonic analysis than is melodic justification."

[34]Ibid., p. 345.

[35]Ibid., p. 348.

[36]Ibid., pp. 366–67 and 380–82, especially exs. 314b and 314d.

[37]Schoenberg would undoubtedly consider the E^7 of m. 19 as an altered tonic; see *Structural Functions*, p. 99, ex. 106, m. 6.

[38]Cone, "Sound and Syntax," p. 22.

[39]Ibid., p. 31.

[40]Cone asks (ibid., p. 37) if the normal need always be stated. My own answer (and, I think, Schoenberg's as well as Cone's) is that it need not.

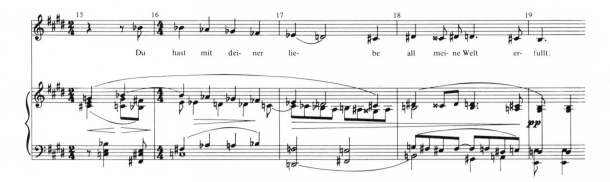

Example 7: *Traumleben*, mm. 15–19.

Used by permission of Belmont Music Publishers, Los Angeles, CA 90049.

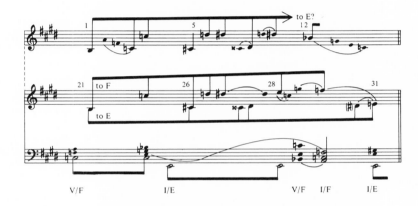

Example 8: *Traumleben*, reduction of mm. 21–31.

Example 9: *Traumleben*, mm. 31–35.

ficult to assert with authority whether a given seventeenth-century piece is tonal, modal, or somewhere between the two (if that is possible), so it is often not a matter capable of scientific proof to assert whether a given post-Romantic work is common-practice or not. The dividing line between styles, between grammars, is seldom precisely drawn. It is, however, clear from passages in both *Structural Functions* and *Harmonielehre* that Schoenberg was well aware of dual tonics in his own music and in that of his contemporaries, even though he had no developed analytic technique for dealing with them. In *Harmonielehre* he writes about fluctuating (*schwebend*) and suspended (*aufgehoben*) tonality; in *Structural Functions*, the term *schwebende Tonalität* is rendered as "suspended tonality."

In the works of Strauss, Mahler, and, even more, Debussy . . . it is already doubtful . . . whether there is a tonic in power which has control over all these centrifugal tendencies of the harmonies.[41] [This procedure] is not readily illustrated by little phrases because it most surely involves the articulation (*Gliederung*) of distinct parts of composition. Whoever wants to take a look . . . will find many examples in the music of Mahler and others.

I do not have to be ashamed of producing something of this sort myself. Two pregnant examples of fluctuating tonality from my own compositions are: *Orchesterlied*, op. 8, no. 5, "Voll jener Süsse," which wavers principally between Db and B major; and op. 6, no. 7, "Lockung," which expresses an Eb-major tonality without once in the course of the piece giving an Eb-major triad in such a way that one could regard it as pure tonic.

If the key is to fluctuate, it will have to be established somewhere. But not too firmly; it should be loose enough to yield. Therefore it is advantageous to select two keys that have some chords in common.

Further documentation is to be found in Wagner. For example, the Prelude to *Tristan*.[42]

From the outset the tonic does not appear unequivocally, it is not definitive; rather it admits the rivalry of other tonics alongside it. The tonality is kept, so to speak, suspended, and the victory can then go to [either] one of the rivals.

The harmony is nowhere disposed to allow a tonic to assert its authority. Structures are created whose laws do not seem to issue from a central source (*Zentrum*); at least this central source is not a *single* fundamental tone.[43]

Schoenberg thus speaks directly to the abandonment of monotonality, to the use of paired tonics, to the equal status and interchangeability of the two tonics; and he alludes more indirectly to the abandonment of the contrapuntal laws which are essential in linking the various higher levels in common-practice music to one another and to the central source of the *Ursatz*. It matters not at all to the present issue that many of us find Schoenberg's analysis of earlier composers' music sometimes perversely wrong. It would be even more perverse to ignore what Schoenberg tells us about Schoenberg simply because we do not always agree with what he tells us about, say, Mozart.

Schoenberg was sufficiently interested in "fluctuating tonality" to amplify his discussion of it in *Structural Functions* with what is by far the longest citation of his own music in the whole book, from *Lockung*, op. 6, no. 7.[44] The explanatory text tells us almost nothing except that the song has to do with C and Eb, and the analysis on the score is merely a double set of Roman numerals in those two keys. Of course this cannot account for many significant details of the figuration which arise from, and make coherent, the Eb/C fluctuation. Schoenberg says only that the piece is characterized by many altered chords of multiple meanings.[45] On the other hand, while a Schenkerian graph of the piece in Eb shows many interesting features, it, too, must necessarily ignore those aspects which derive from non-linear events and from the treatment of two tonics. If we can now begin to deal with those other aspects, it is only because, like Coleridge's dwarf who could see farther than the giant because he had the giant's shoulders on which to sit, we have other viewpoints and the experience of the last half-century of analytic work with which to sharpen our vision.

The monotonal view of the opening of *Lockung* interprets mm. 1–6 as a prolongation of C minor (VI of Eb), and mm. 9–15 as a prolongation of V of Eb.[46] This requires that in m. 1 Eb be

---

[41]Arnold Schoenberg, "Composition With Twelve Tones [2]" in *Style and Idea*, rev. edn., ed. Leonard B. Stein (London, 1975), p. 245.
[42]Schoenberg, *Theory of Harmony*, pp. 383–84.
[43]Ibid., p. 153.

[44]Schoenberg, *Structural Functions*, p. 112.
[45]Ibid., p. 111.
[46]See Allen Forte, "Schoenberg's Creative Evolution: The Path to Atonality," *Musical Quarterly* 64 (1978), 133–76. Note that the graph of mm. 1–16 (Forte, p. 155) shows an interruption following the sixteenth-note D in m. 16; I find it hard to reconcile this with the design of the piece. Another analysis might show an interruption following the F ($\hat{2}$ in Eb) in m. 15.

26   🔊   *Christopher Lewis*

Example 10: *Lockung*, mm. 1–4.

interpreted as an appoggiatura to D, and that the C♯/D♭ in mm. 1 and 2 be heard as a curious incomplete neighbor (see ex. 10). On the other hand, melodically the first four measures can be understood in E♭ as well as in C; an interpretation such as that of ex. 10b includes the D♭—a crucial note (not just an elaborative neighbor), since it foreshadows two important later tonal events. The only E♭ triad in the piece functions locally as V of A♭ (see mm. 50–51); thus the association of E♭ and D♭ (*not* D♮) is the most important melodic event of m. 1 (see ex. 10c). Secondly, the registral connection of D, C♯, and B (see **x** in ex. 10b) foreshadows the same line in the same register in mm. 11 and 12, where the meaning is threefold.

Lockung is structured around a primary complex of E♭ and C, with an extended diversion to B (C♭). The alterations and metric displacements of mm. 11–15 are designed to expose all three tonal references. Above the altered V of E♭ (see ex. 11a), the voice arpeggiates the dominant of C (see ex. 11b). Note that both D and D♭ are avoided—as they were in the left hand of the piano part in mm. 1 and 2—so we have here a reversal of the implications of the opening measures: the E♭ melodic line harmonized in C now becomes a C melodic line harmonized in E♭. Measures 11–12 *can* be understood purely as an altered dominant ninth of E♭, but the C♯ passing tone in the tenor register (see **y** in ex. 11c) also refers back to the motive **x** of ex. 10b and forward to mm. 31–32, where the elision of the beginning of the vocal phrase in B with the extended V[7] of E♭ produces the sonority implied by mm. 11 and 12. A single sketch, no matter how complex, cannot show these three tonal strands; yet all three are crucial to the fundamental tonal idea of the piece.

The multiple meanings of many harmonic and melodic events—one of our metaphorical extra dimensions—suggest that in this music apparent surface details become so important in foreshadowing and creating certain aspects of the tonal relationships upon which the piece is built that they become, in effect, another dimension of the background itself. The structural dissonance which provides the tonal polarization of the common-practice style[47] here operates not only between successive events, but also with alternating or even simultaneous events: the background has not only "length," but also "depth."

There remain three problematic passages that resist analysis of the linear sense, but that can be tonally understood on other terms: mm. 24–25 (and the repetition an octave lower in mm. 29–30); the extended variant of this passage in mm. 57–63; and in mm. 52–56.[48]

Schoenberg implies E♭ throughout the song by several differently altered forms of its dominant (see ex. 12a).[49] Now it is of course obvious that mm. 24–25 and their later counterparts serve simply to decorate the dominant of E♭: there is no question here of an obscuring of the tonal sense. If we understand the dominant as Schoenberg tells us *he* understands it, then the process of decoration is also clear, since it involves merely the arpeggiation of the various altered forms of the dominant (see ex. 12b). If the

---

[47]Charles Rosen, *Sonata Forms* (New York, 1980), p. 222.

[48]Forte considers these to be passages in which the tonality is momentarily suspended ("Schoenberg's Creative Evolution," p. 157).

[49]The first three chords are explained by Schoenberg in *Structural Functions*, p. 111. Note that different alterations of the same chord factor sound together in m. 21.

Mirrors and Metaphors: Schoenberg and Tonality ❧ 27

Example 13: *Lockung*, mm. 57–59.

Example 11: *Lockung*, mm. 11–15.

Example 12: Dominant variants in *Lockung*.

Db seems a worrisome note here—it is, after all, the subtonic—we need only remember how important Db has been in association with Eb right from the opening measures of the song, and to note that each time it occurs in this passage, Db is immediately followed by either the upper or the lower leading tone to Eb. Rather elegantly, in the last three measures of the piece, the final achievement of Eb is through a retrograde of the melodic cell which opened the piece by weakening Eb (see ex. 12c).

The final occurrence of the chromatic dominant flourish is preceded by three chords (mm. 57–59) that may be analyzed by Schoenberg's theories as shown in ex. 13. It will be noted that these three chords actually prolong V of Eb, and may all be analyzed as variants of that harmony (cf. ex. 12). At the same time, they make another reference to the Eb/C duality, as the second chord may also be analyzed as V of C.[50] This in turn prepares for mm. 60–62, where, over the V⁷ of Eb in the piano, the voice sustains G—not only $\hat{3}$ of Eb but also $\hat{5}$ of C.

Our last problematic passage is shown in ex. 14, and the solution to its difficulties should by

---

[50]See Schoenberg, *Theory of Harmony*, p. 252.

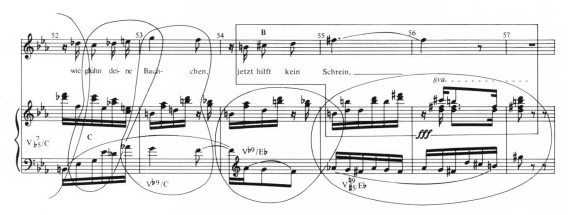

Example 14: *Lockung*, mm. 52–57.

Used by permission of Belmont Music Publishers, Los Angeles, CA 90049.

now be obvious: we have an overlay of implications of E♭, C, and B. To understand the passage in this way requires only that we think as Schoenberg has told us we must. We must abandon straight-line harmonic *progressions* and the linear connections of monotonality, and we must think very quickly![51] It is precisely this complex interweaving of the apparently conflicting implications of melody and harmony to which Schoenberg referred when he wrote that in the Chamber Symphony, op. 9, "there is established a very intimate reciprocation between melody and harmony, in that both connect remote relations of the tonality into a perfect unity."[52] He meant not the unity of a single tonic chord extended through time, but the unified realization of a more complex tonal idea—in fact, of a tonic complex.

In our two songs from op. 6, we have seen the elements of the tonic complex—perhaps merely suggested in *Traumleben*, and then clearly delineated in *Lockung*—manifested in several ways which are also the common technical resources of Wagner, Mahler, and Strauss, among others. These techniques are the following:

Exploitation of common and ambiguous harmonic functions.

Implication of the two tonics in alternation or succession.

Use of one tonic to resolve the dominant of the other.

Direct superposition of lines and textures implying one tonic upon those implying the other.

Each of these procedures, with the possible exception of the first, depends on a musical surface in which at least the remnants of diatonic monotonal practice can be discerned. But even in so pervasively chromatic and so reluctantly triadic a work as Schoenberg's op. 8, no. 5 (*Voll jener Süsse*),[53] which, in the composer's words, "wavers principally between B and D♭," invocation of diatonic imbeddings in the chromatic

---

[51]Schoenberg makes numerous references to the necessity for increased speed of harmonic processing with post-Wagnerian music; see, for example, *Theory of Harmony*, pp. 366–67.

[52]Arnold Schoenberg, "My Evolution," in *Style and Idea*, p. 84.

[53]As is so often the case with Schoenberg, the opus number is not an indication of the chronology. *Voll jener Süsse* (November 1904) falls midway between *Traumleben* (December 1903) and *Lockung* (October 1905). Dates are from Jan Maegaard, *Studien zur Entwicklung des dodekaphonen Satzes bei Arnold Schönberg*, (Copenhagen, 1972), I, 38, 40–41, 44.

Example 15: *Voll jener Süsse*, mm. 26–36.
Used by permission of Belmont Music Publishers, Los Angeles, CA 90049.

scale and of functional harmonic implications allows exploitation of the paired tonics. I give one brief example from this long, complex song, showing the close of the first stanza (see ex. 15). The chromatic passing tones of mm. 26–27 do not obscure the implication of a progression in Db (C♯), but the very strong B-major line in the highest register does. Conversely, while the outer registers announce V[7] of B in m. 28, the doubled vocal line arpeggiates a C♯ triad. As in

Lockung, the overlay of tonic implications is an intensification of the "structural" oscillation: B (m. 25), C♯ (26–27), B (28), C♯ (29–30), and B (36); I give only the strongest implications. The postlude of the song, which even more directly juxtaposes the two tonic representatives, is equally instructive, if only because it demonstrates how late in such a piece the choice of final tonic may be delayed.

An analytic representation like that of ex. 14 very much resembles the segmentation of surface sets in Fortean set analysis. Of course, in our example, the significance of a "set" is its implied function rather than its relation to an abstract prime; but like set relations, such functions are not heard in a "straight-line" processing. This leads me to suggest that a similar change in the way we think about art was being effected by Schoenberg's generation. We have only to think of the French symbolist drama; of Joyce's last two novels; of German expressionist poetry; or of Picasso's originalities in perspective and topology. If indeed there is at this time a general trend in the arts away from a linear perception toward the idea of a multi-dimensional network of implications and cross-relations in all directions, then that is both prerequisite to, and vastly more important than, any specific musical set-consciousness.

There has been enough work done with the application of sketching techniques derived from Schenker's work to pre-tonal and post-tonal music that it is unnecessary for me to point out how valuable such procedures can be. Very few analysts can today approach any remotely "tonal" work without relying heavily upon those techniques. But the universal validity of the principles of the common practice fails in much of the music of the latter half of the nineteenth century. And what appears illogical—or even atonal—to common-practice analysis often represents a set of procedures which, although perhaps not yet so rigidly defined, are on their own tonal terms fully coherent and consistent.

The best way to avoid being victimized by a metaphor is to realize when it is expendable, and then to choose a new metaphor. In particular, we must be careful not to assume that because a piece exhibits some of the surface characteristics of the common practice, and because some parts of its structure yield to the techniques of voice-leading analysis, it ultimately must express the prolongation of a single tonic triad to which all events of the piece can be made relevant. The question is not whether a given piece can be sketched—for almost any piece can be—or even whether one can learn something about the piece from the sketch, but rather whether the analysis comes to grips with the essential tonal nature of the music.

Of course, any type of analysis, like any type of metaphor, is necessarily selective in its references. No analytical method, and certainly no analysis, can fully come to grips with all the complexities of a work of art. To borrow Samuel Johnson's epigram about dictionaries, we can say that analytical systems are like watches: even the worst is better than none, and not even the best will always run true. But that knowledge is itself invaluable as a guard against complacency, for it encourages us constantly to reassess and revise our analytical premises.

"Quotation" and Paraphrase in Ives's Second Symphony

J. PETER BURKHOLDER

Charles Ives's Second Symphony, written as the nineteenth century turned into the twentieth, is crowded with "quotations." There is borrowed material or music derived from borrowed material on almost every page, some immediately recognizable, some disguised. Some of it is taken from American hymns, fiddle tunes, and popular songs, some from European art music. The extent, variety, and differing shades of recognizability of these borrowings reveal Ives's purpose: to create a symphony in the European Romantic tradition that is suffused with the character of American melody, wedding the two traditions in a single work.

The symphony was written and scored between 1900 and 1902, based in part on overtures and organ works written previously, and was not publicly performed until 1951. It has five movements, of which I and IV serve as slow in-troductions to II and V, and an unusual key structure. In the middle is a slow ternary movement in F major. The finale is a modified sonata or sonata-rondo in F, with a second theme in A♭, recapitulated in the tonic. Movement II is in sonata form, with the first theme in A♭, the second theme (m. 72) in F, and a transitional theme that mediates between the two keys, appearing first in A♭ minor/major and repeating immediately in F minor/major. In the recapitulation, both main themes are in F, while the transitional theme is at the same pitch level as before. The tonic is restored only in the coda, with the appearance in A♭ of the second theme and then of both principal themes in contrapuntal combination. The tonal polarity in both II and V is clearly between F and A♭ rather than between tonic and dominant.

Thematic links between movements contribute to a highly calculated cyclic form. Both main themes of II return in V. Moreover, IV is a shortened reprise of I, sharing the same themes and several identical passages. Both of these introductory movements begin in B minor—an unorthodox key in relation to the keys of the following movements—and move to D major; I closes in D, while IV ends on the dominant of F. The four principal keys of the symphony—B minor, D major, Ab, and F—are all related by minor thirds, and F major ultimately prevails. On one manuscript, Ives noted this intricate key structure in a prospective title: "Sym #2/ in F Maj—Ab Maj/ also in D B min."[1]

The musical borrowings in this symphony have attracted attention since its premiere. By now, most of the borrowed material has been identified, and several interpretations of the significance of the "quotations" have been offered.[2] Yet our view of the work and our understanding of its meaning are still incomplete, for three essential points have been missed.

First, what is involved here is not *quotation* but *paraphrase*, the reworking of existing music through variation, ornamentation, omission, repetition, transposition, elision, and interpolation. If little is changed, the resulting tune or

passage may strike someone familiar with the source as a direct "quotation," which it almost never is; there is always some significant alteration. On the other hand, if the transformation is more complete, the new theme or passage may sound only vaguely familiar. This means both that more is borrowed than is obvious at first hearing and also that it may be difficult to determine whether some passages are in fact paraphrased from other pieces or only coincidentally resemble them.

Second, Ives's borrowed material is not inserted into an existing framework, but forms the very basis of the music. Virtually every idea, theme, or transition in the piece is paraphrased from other music or is conceived as a counterpoint to or extension of such a paraphrase.

Third, Ives uses his sources in a thoroughly systematic way. Every one of his themes paraphrases an American vernacular tune. These are in turn varied and developed, providing material for transitions and development sections. At the same time, many transitional sections, including at least one in each movement, paraphrase transitions or episodes in the music of Bach, Brahms, or Wagner. The American sources, then, are identified with the thematic material, the European sources with non-thematic episodes and transitions. The significance of this will become clear as we examine how Ives uses each individual source.

Unaltered, the American tunes Ives uses as sources would not serve well as symphonic themes: their four-square periodicity and strong internal tonic cadences brake forward momentum just when this should be gathering steam, their frequent repetitions of rhythmic patterns and even whole phrases exhaust material before it can be developed, and they resist extension because they are complete in themselves. Ives reshapes his raw material into themes of an almost Brahmsian character, sometimes periodic, but often irregular. Through paraphrase technique, Ives (1) eliminates plainness and repetition while (2) preserving the rhythmic spark and American sound of each source tune, (3) isolates motives for development, (4) emphasizes common melodic and rhythmic patterns that link his themes together, and (5) creates themes and countermelodies that work well in counterpoint with each other, allowing him to suffuse the music with borrowed material and to

---

[1] See ms. p. #0362; quoted in John Kirkpatrick, *A Temporary Mimeographed Catalogue of the Music Manuscripts and Related Materials of Charles Edward Ives 1874–1954* (New Haven, 1960), p. 4. Ives's manuscripts are identified here by one or by two numbers: the frame number assigned to them in the master microfilms of Ives's music manuscripts in the Ives Collection, John Herrick Jackson Music Library, Yale University, and, where one exists, the negative number (preceded by a letter) by which most of them are identified in Kirkpatrick's *Catalogue*. Frame and negative numbers for each manuscript page are listed in an annotated loose-leaf version of the *Catalogue* located in the Ives Collection at Yale ("Ives Collection: Microfilm Concordance to J K Catalogue," made under the direction of James Sinclair in 1975–76 and occasionally updated).

[2] Leonard Bernstein, comments at a concert of the New York Philharmonic, printed as liner notes on a recording of the symphony by Bernstein and the Philharmonic, Columbia ML 6289/MS 6889; Kirkpatrick, *Catalogue*, pp. 3–6, with additional entries in Sinclair's "Microfilm Concordance"; Sydney Robinson Charles, "The Use of Borrowed Material in Ives's Second Symphony," *Music Review* 28 (1967), 102–11; Clayton Wilson Henderson, *Quotation as a Style Element in the Music of Charles Ives* (Ph.D. diss., Washington University, 1969), pp. 207 and 102–09; Colin Sterne, "The Quotations in Charles Ives's Second Symphony," *Music and Letters* 52 (1971), 39–45; David Eiseman, *Charles Ives and the European Symphonic Tradition: A Historical Reappraisal* (Ph.D. diss., University of Illinois at Urbana-Champaign, 1972), pp. 239–49.

achieve thematic climaxes in which themes first presented separately are played simultaneously.

I

The opening theme of the first movement appears in ex. 1. It is joined in counterpoint at m. 7 by part of the chorus of Stephen Foster's *Massa's in de Cold Ground*, at the words "Down in de cornfield / Hear dat mournful sound." (This tune is more complete at its return in mm. 43–47.) Colin Sterne has shown that Ives's theme is itself derived from this phrase from *Massa*, and Sydney Robinson Charles has demonstrated that the motive that initiates the transition to the second theme is also related to this model. Thus the entire opening passage is permeated with this phrase from Foster.[3] (Here and in later examples, passages from Ives's symphony are marked with a bracket in the left-hand margin, and passages that are related to each other are aligned vertically, showing note by note the derivation of melodies in Ives's symphony from their sources and their relationship to each other. Material enclosed in brackets is repeated in order to show its relationship to more than one parallel passage.)

The second theme paraphrases the fiddle tune *Pig Town Fling*, also known as *Warm Stuff*. As shown in ex. 2, violin I has most of mm. 1–4 of the source, and missing notes are supplied by viola and cello. The opening motive is emphasized through imitation, and the neighbor-note

motive taken from mm. 2–3 of the tune (C♯–B–C♯–A) is developed in the continuation. The two source tunes share a similar intervallic contour,[4] as shown in ex. 2. In addition, the second theme shares with the preceding transitional motive a rhythmic pattern of an eighth and two sixteenths, indicated in the examples by horizontal brackets. These links illustrate Ives's preference for themes that are melodically related and hint at his ability to turn one idea into another through progressive variation.

Both tunes return in later movements, *Massa* in III and V and *Pig Town Fling* in IV and V. Two other passages in the first movement also forecast later events. In mm. 33–36, low strings and bassoons play what will become the opening of the finale's second theme (in the horn, m. 58 of the finale), changed from common to triple time.[5] And in mm. 66–68, the horns present the opening notes of *The Red, White and Blue*, better known as *Columbia, the Gem of the Ocean*, which appears complete in the finale's coda, after being hinted at throughout that movement and heralded in the fourth movement by a reprise (at m. 16) of the passage in the first movement where *Columbia* is first heard.

Both of these forecasts in I of material from V appear in counterpoint with motives from *Pig Town Fling*. These combinations likewise anticipate events in the finale, for there a countermelody based in part on *Pig Town Fling* accompanies both the horn theme and the patriotic tune. Besides contributing to the symphony's cyclic network, the references to these tunes in I alert us to the dual role of *Pig Town Fling*, as the source for a theme in I and for a countersubject in V, and to the multiple roles of the first movement itself. This movement is at once a complete entity in its own right, an introduction to II, a longer variant of IV (which in turn serves as an introduction to V), and thus an introduction to the entire symphony.

[3]Sterne, "Quotations," p. 43; Charles, "Borrowed Material," p. 108, ex. 9c. I adapt their examples in my own. In the first sketch of this movement (ms. pp. #0353/n0303, #0354/n0319, and #0356/n0349a+0301, dated August 1900), the first theme was paraphrased not from *Massa* but from the hymn tune NETTLETON. This early sketch shares with the published version most of the second theme and the transitions that precede it; since in both versions those transitions are in part based on the first theme, there are some disguised allusions to NETTLETON that remain in the final version, notably at mm. 10–13, 16–17, and 60–61 in violin I. The sixteenth-note transitional figure in mm. 10–15 was first created as a counterpoint to part of NETTLETON, not as a paraphrase of *Massa*, but the melodic resemblance to that tune is clear; perhaps the transitional figure suggested the Foster, rather than the other way around.

What is most telling about this substitution of *Massa* for NETTLETON as the source of the first theme is how little is different. Both tunes are paraphrased, not merely quoted; both are linked motivically to the following transition; both are American tunes, reshaped to fit a European, pseudo-Baroque contrapuntal texture.

[4]Noted by Sterne, "Quotations," p. 43, although he is apparently unaware that the violin motive in m. 23 of the Ives is based on an existing fiddle tune.

[5]In the earliest sketch for this passage (#0357/n0296, replacing a segment of the first sketch), this theme appears in its original durations, syncopated against the triple-time measure lines, like the phrases from *Massa* and *Columbia, the Gem of the Ocean* in this same movement. This was canceled before the other parts were filled in and replaced with the rhythmically truncated version in the published score.

Example 1

Example 2

The examples in this article contain excerpts from Ives's Second Symphony. Copyright © 1951 by Southern Music Publishing Co. Inc. Copyright renewed by Peer International Corporation. Used by permission.

II

The first theme of the second movement paraphrases the verse of Henry Clay Work's Civil War song, *Wake Nicodemus* (ex. 3). By repeating the opening gesture and treating the cadential motive in sequence (marked with brackets in the example), Ives achieves several goals at once: he emphasizes the opening and closing motives of his source, establishing them as material for development and revealing their relationship by inversion; he relieves the unrelenting rhythm of the original, while preserving and even highlighting its characteristic pattern of dotted eighth and sixteenth leading to a quarter note; he maintains the pentatonicism and jaunty American character of his model; and he avoids the tonic cadence and introduces a colorful harmonic excursion that extends the phrase to double its length.

On repeating the phrase, Ives varies it to include the low C and rising arpeggiation in mm. 1–2 of his model—a figure that was previously omitted—and spins out the end of the phrase in a new extension based on the opening motive. In immediately varying and developing material he has just introduced, Ives shows his awareness of and allegiance to the tradition of Brahms. At the same time, Ives lays out his first theme area (mm. 1–41) in an AA'BA' format, corresponding to the AABA structure of the model's verse. Here Ives integrates into the classical European framework not only the melodic shape but also the form of an American vernacular tune.

The transitional theme at m. 42 paraphrases George A. Minor's *Bringing in the Sheaves* (ex. 4). As is almost always the case with Ives's paraphrases, the gospel song's influence continues beyond the point where the derivation is obvious. Like the second theme of the first movement, this theme is motivically anticipated: as ex. 3 shows, *Bringing in the Sheaves* shares several motives with the first theme.[6] Similarly, the latter part of this transitional theme refers back to *Wake Nicodemus* by adopting its unrelenting rhythmic pattern—a rhythmic sameness which Ives carefully avoids in his first

theme, but which he deems entirely appropriate in a transition.

The second theme presents the college song, *Where, O Where Are the Verdant Freshmen?*, slightly altered for smoothness and elegance (ex. 5). The theme's middle section (mm. 80–89) is based on the same tune, with the second half transposed down a fourth to prepare a half cadence, after which the first section is repeated. Simply by changing the repeated notes and skips of his source into a step-wise oscillation, Ives transforms its whole character, making it difficult to recognize this middle section as a paraphrase of the college tune despite the many common tones (marked with crosses in ex. 5).

This theme is prepared by a slowing to quarter-note motion and is anticipated in mm. 59–69 by the appearance of the viola obbligato that accompanies the theme, in counterpoint with motives from the first theme. In addition, the pickup to the second theme echoes the pickup of the first. The significance of this is made clear by later events.

In mm. 137–65 of the development section, under a rhythmically augmented statement of the first theme in F major, Ives gives the trombones a *cantus firmus* comprised of alternating phrases from two hymn tunes, HAMBURG and NAOMI.[7] At m. 166, the violins repeat the first phrase of this *cantus firmus* three times, answered each time by the final phrase in the horns. In the coda, the same *cantus firmus* phrase returns at m. 329, this time in counterpoint with the second theme in A♭.[8] This leads to the climactic simultaneous presentation of both themes in A♭ (mm. 342–46, anticipated at 340–41) over a variant of the *cantus firmus*. Its

---

[6]Sterne, "Quotations," p. 43, points out that *Bringing in the Sheaves* is "present in embryo in the first theme long before the direct quotation of it." He does not cite *Wake Nicodemus* as a source for the first theme.

[7]The two are interlocked, line by line: the first and third phrases of HAMBURG (which are identical) in mm. 137–45 and 153–60, and the second and final phrases of NAOMI in mm. 146–50 and 161–65. The two hymn tunes are similar in structure and character, sharing a basic rhythmic pattern of long-short-short. See Charles, "Borrowed Material," pp. 106–07.

[8]In the final version—the full score from 1900–01 (#0438/q0236) and hence the published version, but not the final sketch in short score (cf. #0404/n0339)—Ives modifies the opening of HAMBURG in cello I at mm. 329–32 to produce what seems to be a brief allusion to AMERICA, while HAMBURG continues in the other low strings and trombones; see Charles, "Borrowed Material," p. 106. This is hardly audible with everything else going on, and it suits the harmony so perfectly that it may be an accident, or perhaps a private joke with the cellists.

Example 3

Example 4

first phrase is briefly developed (trombones, mm. 358–63) and returns one last time at m. 367 in counterpoint with the opening figure of the second theme's middle section. This combination was already hinted at in the viola when the *cantus firmus* originally entered at mm. 137–38.

The first theme was thus intended from the start as a counterpoint to the second theme and to the first phrase of HAMBURG. Ives bends his source tunes through paraphrase so they combine well and adds the pickup to the second theme as a foretaste of the contrapuntal climax to come. This rich web of linear and contrapuntal relationships once again shows Ives's allegiance to the late Romantic European tradition.

III

The main theme of the third movement is based primarily on BEULAH LAND, whose distinctive rhythm, a dotted figure on the first beat, is present from the start (ex. 6). Measures 13–14 of the hymn tune appear explicitly at mm. 11–12 of the Ives, initiating a paraphrase of the last eight measures of the hymn's refrain. At the cadence, the flute briefly joins the para-

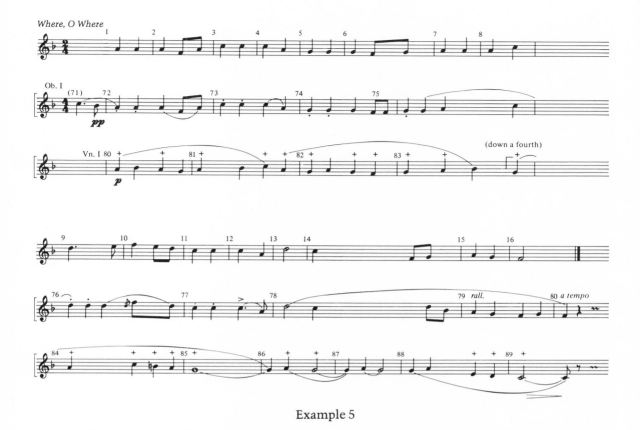

Example 5

phrase, as shown by dotted lines in the example. (At the reprise, the cadence follows the model more exactly; see mm. 116–18 in the example.) The resemblance to the model is closer in Ives's sketches, particularly the earliest ones, than in the final version, which seems to indicate that as the symphony took shape Ives sought to make the evocation more subtle.[9]

This paraphrase interlocks with another: the whole theme (mm. 7–18) is framed by mm. 5–8 of the tune—that is, the second half of its verse.

Measures 7–9 of the Ives follow the rising contour of mm. 4–6 of the model, interpolating new notes around the borrowed tones. Because the model's verse and refrain end with the same music, the cadence of Ives's theme serves at once to conclude this paraphrase of the verse and the refrain-paraphrase embedded within it. The final reprise of this theme, in mm. 116ff., is followed by a coda that presents the complete refrain (the beginning of this is shown in the example); here, mm. 5–20 of the model are heard in order, while the middle of Ives's theme is heard as an interpolation, a bit of the refrain tucked into the structure of the verse.[10]

[9]See particularly the passages corresponding to mm. 13–16 and 19–20 of the model in #0444/q3118&n2323, to mm. 13–20 in #6569/q5001&n2324, and to 17–20 in #0445/n2322. In the final version of around 1902, represented by the final short-score sketch (#0452/n0344) and full score (#0459/q0244), the cadence is even less like BEULAH LAND than it is in the published version. At some later time (probably in the 1930s or 1940s, to judge by the crabbed handwriting), Ives restored the original BEULAH LAND cadence in the margin of the short-score sketch to give something approximating the published version.

[10]This coda was apparently added in 1909 or 1910. The original ending appears on pages 12–13 of the 1902 full score (#0469–70/q0254–55), where it is crossed out; on a single leaf of a copyist's score (#7791–92, numbered as pages 13–14), which was probably part of the 1909 Tams copy, the rest of which is now missing (see reference in Kirkpatrick,

Example 6

Catalogue, p. 7); and in the surviving parts (#0474–91), apparently prepared at Tams from the 1909 copy. The new ending appears in full score on a separate double leaf (#0471–73/q0256–58) and is added in Ives's hand to one of the copyist's parts for violin I (#0480). If the original ending was part of the 1909 Tams score, it must have been detached and the new ending substituted before Ives sent the score to Walter Damrosch in 1910, who never returned it (see Frank R. Rossiter, *Charles Ives and His America* [New York, 1975], p. 152). The somewhat cryptic note on the last page of the short-score sketch (#0453/n0345) "from 112 to end about or [added at?] 1909–10, but can't find" may refer to a short-score sketch for this coda.

Embedded within this interpolation is yet another: both in the theme itself and in the complete refrain in the coda (mm. 119–30), mm. 17–18 of BEULAH LAND are replaced by a variant of mm. 13–14 of MATERNA, which have a similar rhythm, implied harmony, and melodic direction (embellished 6–5).[11] In Ives's day, MATERNA

[11]These two measures from MATERNA also resemble the opening of BEULAH LAND's refrain (mm. 9–10), transposed

was sung most often to the words "O Mother dear, Jerusalem," but it has since become inevitably identified with *America the Beautiful*. This brief reference to MATERNA is no doubt one of the passages that has brought Ives a reputation for sudden, apparently unmotivated "quotations" of familiar tunes, for it leaps out of context to startle today's listener in the United States, who, unlike Ives's intended turn-of-the-century audience, may never have heard BEULAH LAND but will instantly recognize this tune.

But the substitution serves two important musical purposes. First, it avoids the neighbor-note figure that pervades mm. 13–18 of BEULAH LAND, which has already been heard in mm. 11–12 of Ives's theme and would be anticlimactic to repeat at the peak of the phrase. That this was a concern for Ives is made clear from an early sketch for this passage that shows in place of the present measures 11–18 a variant of mm. 13–20 of BEULAH LAND, with the neighbor-note figure of measures 17–18 changed to a stepwise descent.[12] Just above this sketch on the same page is a later alternative in which these two measures of BEULAH LAND are replaced by the fragment of MATERNA, as in the final version. This not only avoids repeating the neighbor-note figure, but also provides a more satisfactory climax to the theme by touching the upper tonic octave. After the high point, there is a hint of MATERNA's final cadence in the flute (especially at the repetition in mm. 117–18). The brief passage from MATERNA is completely absorbed into the paraphrase of BEULAH LAND, as Ives exploits their melodic similarities to move seamlessly from one to the other and back.[13]

The middle section of the symphony's third movement uses three tunes, each of which is first quoted in part and then paraphrased. Clayton Henderson has shown that the hymn tune MISSIONARY CHANT, partly stated in mm. 45–46 (horns) and 47–48 (strings), is later partly paraphrased in the strings in mm. 59–67;[14] a phrase from the same hymn returns in the horn at the very end of the movement, in counterpoint with the fragment from MATERNA in the flute. The first two measures of the hymn tune NETTLETON appear in the horn in mm. 49–51 while the winds embellish it with neighbor and passing tones. Measures 46–51 are repeated, followed by an abbreviated paraphrase of the second half of this hymn in violin I, echoed in canon by the viola; since NETTLETON is in AABA form, this completes a condensed paraphrase of the model. At m. 59, there enters the phrase from *Massa's in de Cold Ground* that appeared in the first movement, now in counterpoint with the material from MISSIONARY CHANT; this is followed by a new tune paraphrased from *Massa*, presented in the flute in mm. 65–67.[15] The pattern is like that in the second movement, where each of the three themes begins

---

and reordered. That Ives heard this relationship is confirmed by a sketch in which the first MATERNA motive is replaced by the figure from m. 10 of BEULAH LAND. Compare #0448/n1299, staves 4–5, with #0445/n2322, mm. 5–13.

[12]See ms. p. #6569/q5001&2324. This alteration makes these measures resemble mm. 11–12 of the hymn tune, which do not otherwise appear in the theme; their figuration no doubt suggested the change.

[13]Other analysts have found in this theme part of the Valhalla motive from *Die Walküre* (mm. 9–10, first noted by Bernstein and echoed by Sterne, "Quotations," p. 41) and a cadential figure from Brahms's First Symphony, second movement (mm. 16–17, starting in the flute and continuing in the violins; also first noted by Bernstein, repeated by Charles, "Borrowed Material," p. 105, and Henderson, *Quotation*, p. 11), and a reference to the hymn tune *Happy Land* in the accompaniment to it (violin II, mm. 15–17;

Henderson, *Quotation*, p. 11). The similarity to Wagner's leitmotive consists of three notes in a commonplace octave leap, which disappears from the theme at its repetition 100 measures later and which has a completely different harmonic context from that of the putative source. The alleged Brahms reference, a stock arpeggio ornamenting the cadence of BEULAH LAND, is all of four notes long. The supposed segment from *Happy Land* is rhythmically distended and shares with the hymn only a six-note pitch sequence that results entirely from the underlying harmony. There is no material in the sketches to support the assertion that these resemblances were intentional.

We may be dealing here with arcane allusions or private jokes, yet it seems more likely that these are not "quotations" at all, but musical commonplaces that remind these analysts of other music because they expect to be reminded. Such a rich web of allusion as we have in the Second Symphony almost inevitably leads us to hear in it things that Ives did not intend to put in it. This hearing may even have been part of Ives's intention. For a discussion of these "questionable quotations and phantom allusions," see J. Peter Burkholder, *The Evolution of Charles Ives's Music: Aesthetics, Quotation, Technique* (Ph.D. diss., University of Chicago, 1983), pp. 316–27.

[14]*Quotation*, p. 137.

[15]This melody uses a motive introduced in the first movement at mm. 52–54, and it turns out to be intervallically related to part of the second theme of the finale, which is also paraphrased from *Massa*; see note 22 below.

Example 7

with a direct reference to its source and moves toward less explicit paraphrase, but the process is concentrated into a much shorter timespan.

IV

The finale features a still more intricate web of themes. As in the first two movements, each new theme is anticipated by previous material. Instead of one chain of ideas, however, there are three.

1. The first theme area is based on Stephen Foster's *Camptown Races*. The opening of the chorus ("Gwine to run all night") appears in the horns in the tonic F major in mm. 14–15, recurs in the dominant in low strings at m. 31, and is repeated several times in the tonic in bassoons and low strings starting at m. 35. At this point, the first trombone states the whole chorus in the tonic, its cadence altered to allow bassoons and low strings to repeat the first half of the chorus while the trombone plays the second half.[16] This makes clear in retrospect that there is also a complete statement in the dominant four measures earlier at m. 31, shared between low strings and flutes. In ex. 7, both passages are

compared with the chorus as it appeared in Foster's original 1850 print.[17]

This double chorus in dominant and tonic follows a complete paraphrase of Foster's verse in the opening theme itself (mm. 1–14), which moves from tonic to dominant and returns to F major for the cadence. This is shown in ex. 8. As is typical of Ives's paraphrases, there are elisions and overlappings, insertions and omissions: the opening C is lacking (made unnecessary, perhaps, by the prominent C at the close of the previous movement), and the paraphrase is less recognizable because several of its first few notes are missing or displaced; the segment in C major overlaps the first segment in F (mm. 3–6 of the Ives); and mm. 5, 9, and 10 of Foster's tune are elided to avoid redundancy (mm. 6–9 of the Ives).[18] In the recapitulation, mm. 6–7 of Ives's theme are dropped, eliminating some of the overlapping while condensing the paraphrase still further.

The shape of the theme is partly determined by its ultimate use as a counterpoint to *Columbia, the Gem of the Ocean* in the coda

---

[16]Interestingly, this statement in the trombone appears in the published score but not in the manuscript full score or any of the other manuscripts. Perhaps Ives later added the trombone here because he felt a need to make the allusion more explicit.

[17]Taken from Richard Jackson's *Stephen Foster Song Book: Original Sheet Music of 40 Songs by Stephen Collins Foster* (New York, 1974), pp. 14–17.
[18]Henderson, "Quotation," pp. 106 and 207, finds the first two measures of the fiddle tune *The Kerry Dance* in m. 11 of this theme, but the reference, if there is one, is quite distorted and very fleeting.

Example 8

(continued)

Example 8 (*continued*)

(m. 253).[19] Like the first theme of the second movement, this serves as both main theme and countersubject, and the parallel is made explicit obviously relate to the Foster tune. At the bottom of the same page, after several intervening attempts, mm. 1–2 of the final version appear, complete on the first try, over the first two measures of *Columbia*. It is apparently at this point, after mm. 1–4 and 11–12 were decided upon, that Ives discovered he could paraphrase *Camptown Races* in his theme, for the segments most obviously derived from the Foster—the whole-tone oscillations in mm. 6–9, 10, and 13—were added last, sometime between this and the remaining surviving sketches. Perhaps this in turn suggested following his theme with a paraphrase of Foster's chorus.

---

[19]The early sketches for the first theme all show it in counterpoint with *Columbia*. The apparently earliest surviving sketch (#0508/n3119) shows that Ives's first attempt had little or nothing to do with *Camptown Races*; only mm. 3–4 and 11–12 match the final version. Significantly, these are the segments of the theme that least

when the earlier theme briefly joins the fray at m. 253 (in the trumpets). A bit of *Columbia* in the cellos and basses in mm. 11–12 hints of the first theme's final destiny. Given the twin constraints of counterpointing one borrowed melody while paraphrasing another, it is remarkable that Ives's theme is so appealing and shapely in its own right.

There are traces of the chorus as well as the verse in this theme, as ex. 8 shows. The link between the first measure of Ives's theme and the opening of Foster's chorus is made explicit when they are played together in m. 43. Similarly, mm. 11–12 of the main theme appear in violin I as a counterpoint to the paraphrased chorus in mm. 33–34. Like the first movement theme derived from *Massa's in de Cold Ground*, these elements of the theme not only paraphrase Foster's tune but serve as counterpoints to it.

The verse's cadence in m. 14 is elided with the opening motive of the chorus in the horns. For most listeners, this is the first clear reference to *Camptown Races*, and it comes as a surprise. The first four bars of the theme return at m. 20, leading to an episode and the two full statements of the chorus already shown. Soon after this, Ives modulates suddenly, marking the transition to the second theme. Thus, the entire first theme area is an extended paraphrase of *Camptown Races*, verse and chorus, each beginning in the tonic, moving to the dominant, and returning to the tonic. What appear to be fragmentary "quotations" of the chorus are only the most conspicuous moments in this process, clues to the more subtle transformations around them. This complete rendering of the song's verse and chorus again parallels the second movement, where the AABA structure of *Wake Nicodemus* is likewise reflected in the layout of the first theme area. In both cases, Ives integrates into his classical symphonic structure not only the melodic motives but the very form of his vernacular American source.

2. In addition to the complete paraphrase of *Camptown Races*, the opening theme initiates a second line of melodic relationships. Beats 2–3 of m. 1 recall a rhythmic cell (one eighth and two sixteenths) from the first movement (bracketed in ex. 1, 2, and 8). This cell recurs throughout the theme and soon develops into a fife tune for flutes and piccolo (mm. 27–29) over

the traditional marching band roll-off in the drums.[20] During the chorus of *Camptown Races*, it appears in the countermelodies, in a segment of the first theme (violins, m. 33) and later in the verse of the fiddle tune *Turkey in the Straw*, presented off-beat in mm. 37–40 (with the rhythmic cell retrograded) and partly repeated in its normal metric placement. The motive recurs in the transition to the second theme (mm. 43–57), along with other fragments of the first theme, and eventually leads to a melody based on our old friend *Pig Town Fling* (beginning at m. 52). At the second theme (m. 58), the principal countermelody in violin I consists of elements from both *Pig Town Fling* and *Turkey in the Straw*, verse and chorus, so that sixteenth-note figuration and the rhythmic cell of an eighth followed by two sixteenths (or its retrograde) continue to be prominent. In addition, another melody based on the same rhythmic cell, the popular song *Long, Long Ago*, appears in flute and oboe in mm. 70–71, punctuating the end of the theme's middle phrase.

Except for the opening theme, the melodies linked by this rhythmic cell are all secondary ideas, counterpointing the principal themes. And since the first theme itself ultimately serves as a countermelody to *Columbia, the Gem of the Ocean*, this motive can be said to link together all the important countermelodies of the movement. This common motivic thread was of fundamental concern to Ives, as is clear from its presence in his earliest sketches. In many cases, Ives first sketched a suitable countermelody using a variant of the motive and only later found an existing tune that he could adapt for the purpose; several of the countermelodies did not coalesce into allusions to familiar tunes until later stages of composition, at the same time that the motivic connections

---

[20]This fife tune sounds like a "quotation," but is apparently only a variant of mm. 3–4 of the theme. The drum roll-off, however, *is* a quotation, one which Ives uses frequently in his music; see for instance the drums in "*Country Band*" *March* (m. 45) and *Overture and March "1776"* (m. 41), both written shortly after the Second Symphony. Both snare and bass drum give the roll-off in mm. 27–30, but the snare is missing at the reprise of this section in mm. 129–32 of the published score (Southern Music Publishing Co., 1951); this is an error, as Ives's manuscript score clearly indicates an exact repetition of the passage.

between them became more sharply focused.[21] These countersubjects, like the main themes, are all paraphrased, not directly quoted, but reshaped to fit the motivic and contrapuntal structure of the symphony while retaining enough of their individual characters to remain recognizable.

3. A third chain of melodic relationships begins with the second theme, a stately, mostly pentatonic horn melody in ABA form. The middle phrase paraphrases the same segment of *Massa's in de Cold Ground* used in movements I and III. The last four notes of this phrase (mm. 69–70) are developed after m. 78, transformed into motives that suggest *Joy to the World* (ANTIOCH) as well as *Massa* itself. This phrase and a portion of its later development are shown in ex. 9 together with these two source tunes.

In the recapitulation, the horn theme initiates a series of allusions to earlier movements. The first and second themes of II appear briefly at mm. 181–82 of V, just before the reprise of the horn theme, as if to hint of things to come. The reprise of the extension following the horn theme leads to a quotation from III (mm. 228–33 recast mm. 59–67 of III), including a prominent statement of this same phrase from *Massa*, part of MISSIONARY CHANT (in the trumpet), and the theme modeled on *Massa* that first appeared in mm. 65–67 of III.[22] This leads in turn to a still fuller reference to the opening theme of II (m. 235), in counterpoint first with itself and later with the countermelody based on *Turkey in the*

Straw. Fragments of *Columbia, the Gem of the Ocean* are mixed with elements from the first theme of V amid a general crescendo. This leads to the climax at m. 253, where the whole of *Columbia* is presented in counterpoint with the first theme of V and the countermelody to the second theme of V, with the opening bars of the first theme of II thrown in for good measure.[23] In these closing minutes, beginning at m. 228 with the quotation from the third movement, which itself quotes a theme from the first movement, the entire symphony is summed up.

V

We have seen that all of the themes and important countermelodies of this symphony are paraphrased from American tunes. But these tunes are very artfully reshaped so as to eliminate dullness and repetition while preserving their American character, isolate motives for further development, highlight common motives that link themes to each other in great thematic chains, and create melodies that work well in counterpoint. Through paraphrase, all these American tunes are transformed to fit the forms and textures of European art music, from the Bach-like polyphony of the first movement to the Dvořák-like second theme of the finale. And they are woven into a thematic web that would be coherent and compelling even if none of the tunes were recognized.

Yet we do recognize these tunes, at many levels of penetration. First, the character of each type of tune is preserved in Ives's paraphrases; no matter how drastic the changes, the themes

---

[21]The first sketch of mm. 37–42 (#2349/q0313) shows a figure that is much less obviously derived from *Turkey in the Straw* than is the final version, but shares with it the same rhythmic pattern of two sixteenths and an eighth, the retrograde form of the rhythmic cell that links all the countermelodies. (This retrograde form is present from the start, appearing right after the prime form in the transitional figure in mm. 10–21 of the first movement; see ex. 1.) The first part of the countermelody to the second theme appears in the earliest sketch of this theme (#0507/n0299) much as it does in the final version, including motives from *Pig Town Fling* and the chorus of *Turkey in the Straw*, but the middle section is completely different, lacking both *Turkey in the Straw* and *Long, Long Ago*; both these and the reference to *Turkey in the Straw* at mm. 37ff first appear in the final sketch in short score (#0514/n0362–#0515/ n0363). In all cases, the final version is both more unified motivically and more filled with allusions to existing tunes.
[22]When this theme reappears in the present context, it can be heard as a transformation of the middle section of the second theme of the fifth movement; see the discussion and musical example in Sterne, "Quotations," p. 45.

[23]"Thrown in" is literally true, for the sketches show Ives adding material to this climax as he went along. The earliest sketch (#0504/n0307), part of a two-stave continuity draft for the latter half of the movement, shows *Columbia* and the movement's first theme, accompanied only by the bass line and the horn chords. In the short-score sketch (#0526/n0374), Ives adds the second theme's countermelody (based on *Pig Town Fling* and *Turkey in the Straw*), greatly altered to fit the new harmonic context. In the full score (#0557/q0292), the first two measures of the second movement's first theme are added in the trumpet; the rest of that theme is omitted because it could not fit the harmonic context. Clearly, the addition of both this theme and the second-theme countermelody were afterthoughts. Another addition at this late stage of composition is the bugle call "Reveille," which appears in the trumpet in mm. 251–52, just before the triumphant entrance of *Columbia* and its entourage.

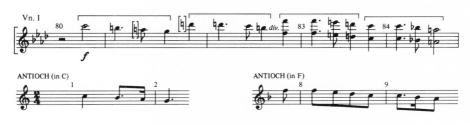

Example 9

based on hymns sound hymn-like, the Foster paraphrases sound like Foster, the melodies taken from fiddle tunes sound like fiddle tunes. Furthermore, though they vary greatly in the degree to which they resemble their models, it is striking that each paraphrased theme or countermelody includes at least one overt quotation from its source or sources. Most veer between levels of allusion from the obvious to the obscure. This variability pulls us into the music, catching our attention with the fleeting moments we can identify and inviting us to delve deeper. That the level of recognizability was a major concern for Ives is clear from his sketches, particularly those for the third and fifth movements, which show that he changed several passages to make their resemblance to their sources either more or less obvious, apparently seeking the proper balance. Although this symphony can make perfect musical sense even to a listener who recognizes not a single borrowed tune, the game of gradually recognizing

Ives's models through their transformations is part of the point of this music and part of its lasting appeal.

Why did Ives paraphrase the themes of his Second Symphony from American vernacular tunes? One clue lies in the work's adaptation from music Ives had composed for other uses between 1896 and 1898, while he was at Yale. According to Ives's annotations, the first movement is adapted in part from an organ sonata, the third from an organ prelude, and apparently all of the movements but the third from a pair of overtures titled *Down East Overture* and *Town, Gown and State*, grouped under the collective title *In These United States*.[24] The finale's

[24]According to notes Ives made on manuscripts of the symphony, quoted in Kirkpatrick, *Catalogue*, pp. 3–7. None of these earlier works survive, although sketches for some of them may be among the surviving sources for the symphony.

Which movements are derived from which overtures is

second theme is older still, having been performed in 1889 as a short piece called *The American Woods*.[25] The origin of the third movement in a piece for church explains the presence of several hymns (though not the allusion to Foster), and the descriptive titles for the overtures suggest both why Ives based his themes on vernacular tunes and why he chose the popular, college, and patriotic songs that he did. Perhaps he conceived these overtures as an American reply to Brahms's *Academic Festival Overture* (1881), a comparable exercise in treating familiar tunes with specific extramusical associations in a classical format.

Further, while Ives's other early orchestral music—a Postlude in F (1895), an Overture in G (ca. 1895), and the First Symphony (1895–98)—had shown no overtly nationalistic traits, the titles of these overtures and of the earlier *American Woods* show that in these works Ives was trying to write music that sounded American and reflected American life. Ives logically turned to the types of melody that he knew his listeners would recognize as distinctly American and would associate with particular aspects of American life: the songs of Stephen Foster, patriotic songs, traditional fiddle tunes, and gospel hymns. These are, of course, the models of American melody that return again and again in his later music.

But the Second Symphony is not exclusively American in its origins. While all of its themes are adapted from vernacular tunes, transitional sections in every movement borrow material from similar passages in European classical masterpieces. By this means, Ives emphasizes at once what the two traditions have in common and what is most distinct about them. While American vernacular music is full of potential themes, it offers few models for transitional sections, because its forms do not require them. Yet vernacular tunes do contain motives that are just as susceptible to extension and development as are those of art music, and in his transitions, as if to prove the point, Ives transforms part of a fiddle tune into a passage from Brahms and an episode from a Bach fugue into a Stephen Foster song.

The second theme of the first movement, derived from *Pig Town Fling*, includes a lower-neighbor-note figure that resembles a famous motive from the principal theme of the finale of Brahms's First Symphony, particularly as that motive appears in diminution and sequence at mm. 94–96. At the return of Ives's second theme, this resemblance is made explicit, as the fiddle-tune motive is developed (mm. 76–78) in a transition that paraphrases a passage in the Brahms (from mm. 273–78), transposed down a semitone to fit the key of B minor. Both model and paraphrase play the same role, appearing in transitions leading to the return of thematic material. Ives's transition develops so naturally out of his theme that the allusion to Brahms is not at all obvious. Indeed, Ives's first draft of these measures gives a simple rising sequence based on the fiddle-tune motive; this is crossed out and replaced with the Brahms, a substitution clearly prompted by its resemblance to Ives's first thought.[26] This same passage reappears in the fourth movement (mm. 26–28) in virtually the same context.

---

puzzling. On the short-score sketch of the present fourth movement, the introduction to the finale, Ives wrote "from Overture 'Town, Gown & State' in These United States for Brass Band 1896 played Savin Rock NH Ct." On the title page of the second sketch of the first movement, Ives wrote "Down E[ast] Overture ... 2nd part 1898." These attributions would be perfectly clear were not the first and present fourth movements adaptations of exactly the same music.

A possible solution, though not the only one, is that the title *Town, Gown and State* originally referred to an earlier form of V, for which IV is an introduction, while "Down East Overture" was the name for the "2nd part" of the Symphony, probably meaning II, to which I serves as an introduction. This is not entirely satisfactory as an explanation of either the overtures' titles or the borrowed tunes. While a full statement of the verse of *Columbia, the Gem of the Ocean* is a logical culmination for an overture entitled *Town, Gown and State*, representing patriotic sentiment, and while *Camptown Races* might well represent the town, the tune most closely associated with the academic gown is surely *Where, O Where are the Verdant Freshmen*, which is an important theme in II, not V (although it appears in passing there).

Whatever the solution to this puzzle, the titles of these overtures correspond at least to some extent to the extramusical associations of the tunes used as thematic material.

[25] See Charles Ives, "Notes on the Symphony," *Symphony No. 2* (New York, 1951), p. 1. A similar note appears in Charles Ives, *Memos*, ed. John Kirkpatrick (New York, 1972), p. 155.

[26] #0354/n0319.

Near the end of the first movement, Ives borrows an episode from Bach's Three-Part Sinfonia in F Minor: m. 93 through the next downbeat quotes m. 28, second beat, through the next downbeat of the Bach, transposed up a whole step. Ives immediately repeats this passage a minor third higher to produce a rising sequence leading to the climactic statement of a figure derived from the movement's opening theme; this corresponds to the shape and function of the borrowed Bach episode, a rising sequence that leads to a restatement of the opening material in the tonic. This passage also appears in the fourth movement, mm. 34–36, and reappears transposed and somewhat altered in the middle of the first theme area of the finale, as part of an excursion that effects the modulation from tonic to dominant (mm. 25–27 and 127–29). Like the earlier allusion to Brahms's First Symphony, these borrowings from Bach were afterthoughts, again apparently suggested by their resemblance to ideas Ives had already sketched.[27]

Measures 126–39 of the second movement present and develop a figure from the first movement of another Brahms symphony, the Third (mm. 47–48), transposed, transformed, and metrically recast. This motive leads from second-theme to first-theme material in both movements. In the Brahms, it appears only in the exposition and recapitulation, between the second theme (of which it is a transformed inversion) and the closing material, which is based on the arpeggiated figures of the first theme; in the Ives, it leads from the closing material, which is based on motives from the second theme, into a reprise of the first theme. Ives uses it as the closing tag of his exposition and recapitulation and develops it at the beginning of the development, just as Brahms treats the exposition's closing tag in his first movement.[28] These structural similarities show that Ives is using the Brahms not only as a melodic source but also as a formal model. Sydney Robinson Charles has noted a certain resemblance between the opening figures of the two movements, which may partly explain the allusion.[29]

There is yet another brief allusion to Brahms in this movement. At m. 186, in a transition leading up to the recapitulation, Ives alludes to a passage from the close of the exposition of the first movement of Brahms's First Symphony (mm. 181–88, developing a figure introduced in m. 161) and extends it considerably.[30] Once again, both model and paraphrase have the same function: leading back to the first theme. A similar passage at twice the speed appears near the end of the coda (mm. 355–66).

---

[27]In the first sketch of the first movement (#0356/n0349a +0301), the transition at this point was altogether different; the allusion to Bach first appears in the second sketch (#0360/n0317). These date from August 1900, or later: the first sketch was begun 15 August 1900 (date on its first page, #0353/n0303), and a patch for it (#0357/n0296), used in copying out the second sketch, is dated 19 August 1900; see Kirkpatrick, *Catalogue*, p. 3.

What appears to be the earliest extant full sketch for the first theme area of the finale (#2349/q0313) gives the first violin part as in m. 25 of the published version and continues this idea in sequence, but does not have the lower parts, which confirm the reference to Bach. These first appear in the short-score sketch (#0513/n0361), which is probably from 1901 or 1902. The notes that arrive on the beats in the first violin part, in both sketch and final version, alternate falling steps and rising minor thirds, as in the top line of mm. 28–29 of the Bach Sinfonia. The resemblance in the first full sketch may have suggested the borrowing here, which in turn may have prompted the borrowings from the same Bach episode in the first and fourth movements.

[28]That the motive serves as the exposition's closing tag is easier to see in the sketch, score-sketch, and full score (#0386/n0322, #0395/n0330, and #0421–22/q0221–22 respectively), all of which call for a reprise of the exposition and present first and second endings for the exposition, as does the Brahms. This reprise is suppressed in the published version of the Ives, making the end of the exposition less clear. The first ending (missing in the sketch) consists of a two-measure bridge following a slightly modified m. 127. Note that the closing tag in the Brahms is not what Ives borrows; rather, Ives borrows a figure from another spot and then treats it as the closing tag for his exposition, exactly following the pattern of Brahms's treatment of the closing tag in the model.

[29]Charles, "Borrowed Material," p. 106. The resemblance consists in the dotted figure on the 3–2–1 descent that opens Ives's melody and is paralleled by notes 3–5 of the Brahms. In mm. 149–51, Ives alters the second period of his theme (compare mm. 8–9), rhythmically augmented, so that it resembles the opening figure of the Brahms, despite the very different metric and harmonic context. The allusion is probably intentional.

[30]Kirkpatrick suspects that the principal motive for this passage may also derive from the opening four notes of the gospel song *Blessed Assurance* (*Catalogue*, p. 4); Sterne, "Quotations," p. 41, disputes it. The motive is much closer to Brahms, and the resemblance to *Blessed Assurance* is probably fortuitous.

Ives's third movement has two passages apparently based on motives from the prelude to *Tristan und Isolde*. One is the descending figure in Wagner's mm. 20–22, and the other is a quickly rising scale first played by the violins in Wagner's m. 63, immediately following the descending figure in the winds and leading directly to the return of the famous opening chord and motive at the original pitch (m. 65). Both Ives passages that are based on this material likewise lead to restatements of opening material in the tonic: the first (mm. 23–32) follows the movement's main theme and leads to a partial reprise of that theme, whereas the second (mm. 93–106) leads from the middle section to the return of the main theme. Wagner's descending figure shares the falling contour of the *Massa* theme used in the middle of the movement, a resemblance that may have suggested the borrowings. At mm. 44–45, just before the middle section, another brief reference to the *Tristan* prelude (mm. 39–40, first oboe and clarinet) marks the cadence.

A climbing figure of rising fourths and falling thirds from the finale of Brahms's First Symphony (mm. 385–88) appears in mm. 246–47 of Ives's finale, transposed down a fifth. In both cases, the figure lies over a dominant pedal and leads into the movement's triumphant coda; in the Ives, it both introduces *Columbia, the Gem of the Ocean* and reappears at its cadence (mm. 267–68). The same figure appears in more complete form at the close of the fourth movement (mm. 37–40), where it is preceded in mm. 36–37 by yet another Brahms allusion: a dramatic half-cadence from the third of the *Vier ernste Gesänge* (mm. 29–30), marked by interlocked descending augmented triads. The harmony in both Brahms's song and Ives's symphony is similar—an A-minor triad followed by an E-minor triad, leading to a half-cadence (on a B-major triad in the Brahms, a C dominant seventh in the Ives)—but Ives transposes the melodic line down a major third, reproducing the same augmented triads in a slightly more pungent harmonic context. This in turn is preceded by the sequence adapted from Bach's F-Minor Sinfonia. Thus, in the last eight measures of the fourth movement, Ives gives us three short allusions to European composers back to back.

Finally, in the reprise of the finale, the transition from the first theme to the second includes two passages (mm. 147–57 and 168–76) citing episodes from the middle of Bach's E-minor Fugue from Book I of the *Well-Tempered Clavier* (mm. 13–14, 15–17, and 22), interspersed with Bachian figuration that may or may not allude to other music. Ives carefully underlines the similarities between the sixteenth-note and arpeggiated figures in the Bach and that in his own themes. The first citation directly follows a *fortissimo* statement of the movement's opening motive, the second follows references to *Pig Town Fling*, and in both cases the sixteenth-note motion of the Bach seems to grow naturally out of the preceding material. Even more striking is the transformation in mm. 154–55 of Bach's arpeggiated figure into a reference to the chorus of *Camptown Races*. In ex. 10, Bach and Stephen Foster—the two kinds of "great music" that George Ives taught his son from an early age—meet on equal terms.[31]

VI

In almost every case, the classical allusion is woven into the texture through its resemblance to other material in the movement, making its presence far from obvious even for performers and listeners familiar with Ives's models. As is true for the paraphrased themes, the degree to which the source can be recognized varies considerably. From the sketches, it is clear that many of these allusions to European music were second thoughts, prompted by their re-

[31]See Ives's comments about his father's teaching in a letter to John Tasker Howard, printed in Ives, *Memos*, appendix 11, p. 237. Of the classical allusions noted above, Sterne, "Quotations," p. 41, lists the Brahms references in movements I and II and the longer of the two *Tristan* references in III; Charles, "Borrowed Material," pp. 105–06, notes the Bach quotation in V and the passage from Brahms's Third Symphony in II; and John Kirkpatrick noted the reference in I and IV to Bach's F-Minor Sinfonia in an annotation to his own copy of the Second Symphony score, which he kindly permitted me to consult. The references to Brahms's *Vier ernste Gesänge* and First Symphony at the end of the fourth movement (the latter repeated in the finale) apparently have not been identified before.

It is interesting and perhaps not surprising to note that every commentator has emerged with a different list of musical borrowings in the Second Symphony. Sterne, p. 42, mentions the problem of securely identifying all the references to other music and notes "the desirability of seeking safety behind [John] Kirkpatrick's convenient phrase: 'what else?'," scattered throughout Kirkpatrick's *Catalogue* at the ends of lists of borrowed material for several works.

Example 10

semblance to a passage Ives had already roughed out. Once again, this is true also of many of Ives's allusions to American music, particularly in his countermelodies; Ives clearly added references to both American and European music as he revised, until his symphony was completely saturated with borrowed material. Finally, in every case of an allusion to Classical music, the function of both source and paraphrase is similar, as episodes interposed between thematic statements, and in some cases the parallel of function is quite close.

These allusions are clearly neither accidental nor incidental, but a vital part of Ives's purpose, the integration of American melody with European form. Borrowing transition sections from well-known European compositions and weaving them through paraphrase into the fabric of his own music allows him to emphasize what is lacking in American vernacular music: symphonic development and elaborate formal schemes that require transitions, episodes, and similar material between thematic statements. By citing episodic and transitional material from classical masterworks in his own transitions and episodes, Ives acknowledges these non-thematic sections as the most distinctively European formal elements in the symphony, underlines his allegiance to European models of symphonic form, and provides an audible sign of a deeper aesthetic and structural kinship between his symphony and his European models.

The unmistakable classical borrowings are confined to these transitions. But every movement includes one or more apparent passing allusions to Classical music within the themes themselves. Two of these have been mentioned: the presence in the second theme of movements I and IV of a neighbor-note figure akin to one in the finale of Brahms's First Symphony, and the motive shared by the first theme of II and the opening theme of Brahms's Third. If these are not simply phantom allusions, they would seem intended to prepare the listener for more explicit borrowings from the same sources later on—and perhaps even to demonstrate melodic similarities between vernacular American and classical European tunes. Some analysts find hints of Wagner and Brahms in the main theme of III and of Beethoven in the coda;[32] these seem too vague and brief to be clear citations, although one cannot rule out the possibility that they may be intentional references. The allusion to one of Brahms's *Vier ernste Gesänge* near the end of IV suggests that the similar figure introduced in m. 3 as a counterpoint to the first theme (anticipated at m. 79 of the first movement) may also be paraphrased from that source.

The most interesting cases are in the finale, where I should like to suggest that two ideas

may refer simultaneously to both vernacular and classical sources. The opening figure, part of a theme paraphrased from *Camptown Races*, is also related to the pizzicato theme of the scherzo of Tchaikovsky's Fourth Symphony, also in F major, as shown in ex. 11. Similarly, the figure in violin I at m. 60 (part of the countermelody to the second theme), taken from the first phrase of the chorus of *Turkey in the Straw*, resembles a familiar motive in the first movement of Dvořák's "New World" Symphony (ex. 12). Given the many references to *Turkey in the Straw* in the surrounding measures, this motive must belong to that tune. But Ives may have intended it to sound like Dvořák as well.[33]

These may be phantom quotations, similarities that we may hear but that have no significance, like the appearance of the opening idea of Mozart's *Bastien und Bastienne* in the first theme of Beethoven's "Eroica." But there are other parallels between Ives's symphony and these by Dvořák and Tchaikovsky, suggesting that these apparent melodic allusions may have been intentional. Both Tchaikovsky's Fourth and Dvořák's "New World" are highly cyclic compositions, veritable models for the kind of piece Ives was essaying. The linear and contrapuntal combination of themes from previous movements in the finale of the "New World" is similar to that in the Ives. The principal motive of the Dvořák is a rising arpeggiated triad not unlike Ives's *Camptown Races* figure, and the final cadences of the Dvořák and Ives symphonies are very much alike.[34] Finally, the key scheme of Ives's symphony may have been in-

---

[32]On the first two, see note 13, above. Bernstein finds the "famous four opening notes" of Beethoven's Fifth Symphony in the third movement but does not indicate where he means. The closest approximation to them is in the horn at m. 130, as part of a final reference to MISSIONARY CHANT, which also is the source for the similar figures in the middle section of the movement.

[33]Bernstein includes the "New World" Symphony in his list of quotations, but none of the other writers has accepted it as genuine. (He also says that Ives quotes Bruckner, without making clear where or what he means; see the comment in Charles, "Borrowed Material," p. 103.) If we accept Ives's dating of this passage at 1889 (his date for *The American Woods*; see note 25 above), a reference to Dvořák is out of the question, for the "New World" was not composed and performed until 1893. By the time Ives completed the symphony in 1902, however, the "New World" was well known, and Ives may have adjusted this passage to emphasize the similarity.

[34]Compare the last nine measures of the Dvořák with mm. 274–78 of Ives's finale: they share a 1–3–5–6 rising bass figure in quarter notes moving through two octaves (on the tonic, rising and falling, in the Dvořák; on the subdominant, rising only, in the Ives) and an identical rhythm of closing tonic chords (twice as fast in the Ives). The 1902 full score of the Ives ends with a sustained tonic chord on the downbeat

Example 11

Example 12

spired by that of the first movement of Tchaikovsky's Fourth, in which themes presented in F minor, A♭ minor, and B major are recapitulated in D minor and F major, completing the circle of minor thirds.[35] These correspondences suggest that the hints of Dvořák and Tchaikovsky in the finale's themes may be double entendres designed both to point to broader relationships between Ives's symphony and theirs, and also to show once again—as with Ives's transformations of Bach into Foster and *Pig Town Fling* into Brahms—that the European and American traditions, however different, are closely akin.

What Ives is doing in this symphony is using models: Brahms for thematic design, Bach and Dvořák for counterpoint, Brahms, Dvořák, and Tchaikovsky for symphonic structure, and all four, plus Wagner, for texture, rhetoric, and motivic development. His themes themselves are modeled on (*not* "quoted from") American tunes. In using models and alluding to their music directly and indirectly, Ives was of course following a strong tradition in nineteenth-century European art music, as a distinguished se-

of m. 278, tied over to the next measure, and this ending resembles Dvořák's a great deal.

Measures 278–80 of the published score, including the notorious last chord, an eleven-note crunch, were substituted for the original ending at a much later date, probably in the 1940s (see Kirkpatrick's note in Ives, *Memos*, p. 155). The original ending is preferable; the final dissonance in the published version is a Bronx cheer completely out of the spirit of the rest of the work.

[35]The first movement of Tchaikovsky's Symphony No. 6 in B minor ("Pathétique") includes a similar modulation around the circle of minor thirds from B minor through D minor, F minor, and G♯ minor back to B minor (at A, mm. 30–37). Ives knew the "Pathétique" and parodied its second movement in the 1896 instrumental prototype for the song *The Side Show*. Both the Fourth and Sixth Symphonies may have served as models for this type of organization and for Ives's choice of keys.

ries of articles in this journal has shown.[36] His methods and ideals are European. The structure of the work, though novel in several respects, is still entirely determined by traditional notions of symphonic form; despite the diverse origins of his borrowed material, the symphony exhibits the thematic, intervallic, and rhythmic unity characteristic of contemporary European art music. Even paraphrase technique itself was an outgrowth of Ives's earlier work as a student with melodic transformation in variation sets and fugues, both European forms.[37] And his subject, his point, is European too: this is nationalist music, asserting the value of the music of his homeland, but it is nationalist music in an international style, like that of Dvořák and Tchaikovsky.

In my recent book on the development of Ives's ideas about music, I have argued that the year 1902 marks the end of Ives's hopes for a musical career and of his allegiance to the international idiom. Thereafter he retreated into that isolation in which he would eventually come to write the highly individual music that now seems his most characteristic.[38] After the completion of the Second Symphony in that year, Ives abandoned both the received forms of European art music and the simple nationalism of his models Dvořák and Tchaikovsky. Instead of placing national melody in an international frame, as in this work, Ives moved toward a celebration of American individuality, first of particular tunes, later of specific people, places, and events: the idealism of *Emerson* (1911–12) or of *Lincoln, the Great Commoner* (1912); the stories of *Putnam's Camp, Redding, Connecticut* (1912) or *The 'St. Gaudens' in Boston Com-*

mon (1911–12); the sound and spirit of *Decoration Day* (1912) in a small town or of a funeral hymn rising *From Hanover Square North* (1915) over the noise of New York's rush hour.

These pieces use new approaches to form to match their new subject matter. In the extended ruminations on individual hymn tunes in the outer movements of his Third Symphony (1904) and in most movements of his violin sonatas (1902–16) and First Piano Sonata (1901–09), Ives most often used a kind of cumulative form, presenting his theme, a borrowed or paraphrased tune with one or more countersubjects, in complete form only at the end of a movement, preceded by fragments and paraphrases of it. In his immense but tightly integrated collages such as *Washington's Birthday* (1909) and *The Fourth of July* (1911–13), the musical structure depends upon motivic and contrapuntal links between the many tunes Ives borrows, while the extramusical meaning relies on their character and associations.[39] Most of these pieces are unique in form, yet they too follow a few simple formal ideas—variation, verse-chorus, ABA, arch, climax-release, rondo—whose roots lie deep in the European tradition. As received forms are replaced by novel and synthetic forms, the self-conscious nationalism fades as well, replaced by a music that seeks to capture the individual musical experience of one man from Connecticut—all of it—and is therefore both American and international in its essence. Its sense of place is no longer forced but quietly understood, and its New England regionalism is offered as "a local color that will do all the world good," "a true pigment of the universal color."[40]

In this reconception of both form and content, paraphrase technique was key. In the Second Symphony, as we have already seen, para-

---

[36]James Webster, "Schubert's Sonata Form and Brahms's First Maturity," *19th-Cen Mus* 2 (1978), 18-35, and 3 (1979), 52-71; Charles Rosen, "Influence: Plagiarism and Inspiration," *19th-Cen Mus* 4 (1980), 87-100; Carolyn Abbate, "*Tristan* in the Composition of *Pelléas*," *19th-Cen Mus* 5 (1981), 117-41; Nicholas Temperley, "Schubert and Beethoven's Eight-Six Chord," *19th-Cen Mus* 5 (1981), 142-54; Oliver Neighbour, "Brahms and Schumann: Two Opus Nines and Beyond," *19th-Cen Mus* 7 (1984), 266-70. For an extended argument emphasizing European influences on Ives's First and Second Symphonies, see Eiseman, *Charles Ives and the European Symphonic Tradition.*
[37]See Burkholder, *Evolution of Charles Ives's Music*, pp. 373–84.
[38]See J. Peter Burkholder, *Charles Ives: The Ideas Behind the Music* (New Haven, 1985), pp. 80–82*ff.*

[39]There are European precedents and parallels to these new forms in the music of composers such as Smetana, Mahler, Sibelius, and Stravinsky. It is as yet unclear what models Ives may have had for these procedures, if any, and indeed the history of collage technique and cumulative forms among European composers remains to be written.

For a fuller discussion of cumulative setting, collage, and other uses of existing music in Ives's music, see J. Peter Burkholder, "'Quotation' and Emulation: Charles Ives's Uses of His Models," *Musical Quarterly* 71 (1985), 1–26, and Burkholder, *The Evolution of Charles Ives's Music*, pp. 385–460.
[40]Charles Ives, *Essays Before a Sonata and Other Writings*, ed. Howard Boatwright (New York, 1964), p. 81.

---

phrase technique had allowed Ives to achieve several apparently contradictory objectives at once: to pay homage to the European tradition of art music at the same time that he saluted the American vernacular tradition; to integrate the two traditions while emphasizing what is most distinctive about each; to write unmistakably nationalist music within an international idiom; and to create an extraordinarily original symphony based on borrowed, unoriginal tunes. But the same skill in reworking existing material that permitted him to remake *Wake Nicodemus* into a theme of Brahmsian shape and potential also made it possible in his mature music to create pieces with strong extramusical associations whose structure, like that of the Second Symphony, nonetheless depends squarely upon musical relationships. These mature works are still Romantic in ethos; Ives was still committed to the formal and expressive aesthetic of European art music he had learned from Horatio Parker at Yale. Yet they move beyond Ives's nineteenth-century models as decisively as contemporary works by Schoenberg and Stravinsky. In these later compositions, the tension between European and American traditions that is so palpable in the Second Symphony is no longer felt. Ives has absorbed all of his influences and has found his true subject: the idealism that he attributed to Emerson and Beethoven, Lincoln and gospel singers, Bach and Stephen Foster alike.

Parallel Voice-Leading in Debussy

DAVID LEWIN

There is a traditional view that parallel voice-leading was for Debussy a method of elaborating monophonic ideas, the extra voices being added for acoustic coloration or for poetic effect of some sort, archaic, primitivistic, "Oriental," or whatever else the tone painting might suggest. In this view, the piano part for mm. 1–9 of Debussy's Violin Sonata is an essentially monophonic conception. The music, with its continuation through the opening phrase (mm. 1–14), is shown in ex. 1.

Exposed to the traditional view when I was young, I tried to hear the essential pitch structure for the piano part over the first nine measures in some melody projected by one of the voices within the parallel triads, either in the melody D–G–D–G–B♭ that appears on top of the triads, or in the melody G–C–G–C–E♭ that appears in the bass. But I found this attitude uncomfortable when I listened to the music, or

when I played it. The succession of G-minor, C-major, and E♭-minor triads seemed arbitrary if not perverse. Beyond that, I could not fathom a continuous musical impulse connecting mm. 1–9 to mm. 10–14 in the piano. True, the G-minor and C-major triads did return in mm. 12–14; still, their return seemed no less arbitrary or perverse for being harmonically consistent with mm. 1–4. The traditional dominant harmony of mm. 10–11 confused me all the more in this context. I found the major rather than the minor ninth in that harmony especially perplexing, since the point of the preceding E♭-minor triad had seemed to be precisely to deny the harmonic power of E♮.

So matters stood until the spring of 1958, when I was given twenty-four hours to produce an analytic essay on the movement as part of an

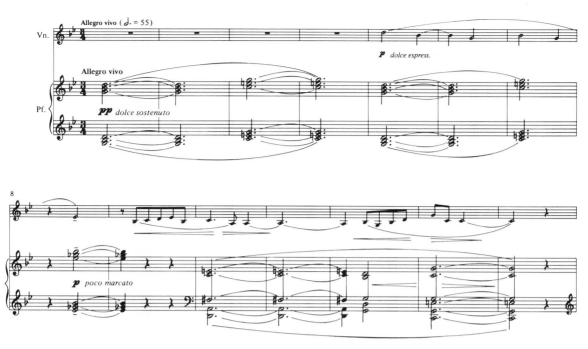

Example 1

examination. In those days I analyzed motivically when I had to analyze quickly, and so I began my task by exploring the motivic organization of the movement, especially the violin part. As I did so, I was overwhelmingly struck by the violin's octave leaps at mm. 61–63, which stood out of the motivic and compositional fabric. Example 2 gives the score from m. 56, the first big climax, through m. 65.

The music just before m. 56 seems to be modulating away from G with increasing momentum; in that context the climax and cadence over the insistent G bass, as shown in ex. 2, are all the more striking. Are the violin's octaves during mm. 61–63 primarily a sonorous coupling with the piano bass, supporting the cadence? That seems like an intolerable indignity for a solo instrument that has just soared to the rhapsodic heights of mm. 56–59. No, that cannot be a valid hearing, I thought, there must be a definite motivic/thematic meaning for the violin's octaves. But where could such a motivic idea be coming from? All at once I heard the opening of the piece in a completely new light. The violin's octaves in mm. 61–63 come precisely from mm. 1–4 and following, where one can hear melodic octave G relations in the piano. To hear those relations, one must "orchestrate" the opening not as in ex. 3a, but as in ex. 3b.

This feels much more comfortable to play. In addition, it makes good modal sense of the E♮ in m. 3; the E♮ of the rising G mode eventually finds its way to F♯, specifically to the F♯ of m. 8 that is spelled as G♭ in the E♭-minor triad. And once one hears *that*, one can hear a clear and forceful structural voice-leading governing mm. 1–14 as a whole in the piano part (see ex. 4).

The example shows how the E♮ of m. 3 fits into a voice that begins on D in m. 1, rises through the E to F♯ at m. 8, and then returns back down, through the pungent but no longer perplexing E of m. 10, to D in m. 12; this voice then moves on to C at m. 13, where it converges cadentially with the lower voice on the top staff of ex. 4. That lower voice alternates between B♭ and C, coming to a provisional rest on C at m. 13. The voice on the middle staff of the example is the "octave-leap voice": it leaps up the octave G, inflects the Gs with their leading tones, leap-

Example 2

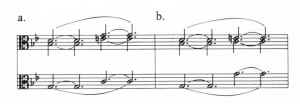

Example 3

Example 4

ing down the F♯ octave, then restates the lower G (m. 12), and finally leaps up the G octave yet again, this time holding the low G coupled on to reinforce the cadence at m. 13. This voice is the motivic/thematic source of the octave leaps in the violin during mm. 61–63. On the bottom staff of ex. 4, the voice whose stems point up echoes the D–E gesture of mm. 1–4 in a lower register. The stems pointing down on the same staff notate a fundamental bass that supports the cadence by a root-progression in fifths. (The progression might have satisfied D'Alembert, if not Rameau.) The fundamental bass has upper fifths added on, projecting real "parallel voice-leading."

One and only one pitch class of the piano part is conspicuously absent from the sketch of ex. 4; that is the E♭ of m. 8. So far as the voice-leading of the example is concerned, E♭—not G♭–F♯—is the "weird note" of the piano's harmony in m. 8. The E♭ in the *violin* at m. 8 is "correct" for *that* instrument. The piano can hear E♭ as the property of the violin here because of the rhythm: the E♭ comes at the right time for the violin, but at the wrong time for the piano, given their respective rhythmic patterns so far. Measure 8 thus initiates a rich structure of dramatic inter-relationships, a structure involving at once violin *vs.* piano, E♭ *vs.* E♭, and regular *vs.* syncopated rhythmic patterns of various sorts, especially in hemiola relationships. Each of these components can be followed through the movement, indeed through the three movements of the piece; so can the special way in which instrumentation, chromatic work, and rhythmic technique all interrelate.

Pleased with my analysis of the Violin Sonata, I made a mental note of the methodological benefits to be accrued in not taking parallel voice-leading for granted. I was further pleased, then, by Allen Forte's analytic commentary on *La Cathédrale engloutie* which appeared shortly afterward.[1] Forte's analysis, like mine, investigated thoroughly *each* voice-leading strand from a thematic idea that traditional theory urged us to hear as monophony-with-parallel-organum, or monophony-with-coloristic-couplings. All this made me more reflective about performing and analyzing passages from Debussy's music in which traditional approaches to parallel voice-leading were making me uncomfortable. (The traditional performing advice I had received went with the analytical theory: balance and regulate the voices equally, or else bring out one of them uniformly as a tenor or cantus firmus throughout.) A phrase that had always bothered me when I played it in this way was mm. 9–14 of *Le Vent dans la plaine*, shown in ex. 5.

The traditional view urged me to fix either the upper or the lower voice of the left hand in mm. 9–12 as a Hauptstimme for the entire melodic contour involved. In this case, the choice seemed straightforward enough: the upper voice of the organum drops out at the bar line of m. 13, where the lower voice attains a cadential B♭ as its melodic goal. "Therefore" the lowest voice in mm. 9–12 is the Hauptstimme, and the

fifth above that voice is organal coupling. This hearing fits well with the strong root sense about the low E♭ of m. 9. (Debussy could hardly have written the left-hand sonority, in a tone-poem about a natural phenomenon, without hearing at least subliminally the opening sounds of Wagner's *Ring*.) And it is not far fetched to hear Debussy's E♭ as a tonic: E♭ seems to resolve B♭ harmonically; the rhythmic relaxation after the bar line of m. 9 seems to resolve the rhythmic bustle of mm. 1–8; and the wide-open spacing of m. 9 seems to resolve the taut registral compression of mm. 1–8, measures that lie completely within the ambitus of a B♭ octave except for a neighboring C♭.

I can respect this hearing of the passage, but I cannot myself hear it. I know I cannot, because I cannot hear a left-hand Hauptstimme for mm. 9–12 that consistently follows the lowest notes, starting on E♭ at m. 9 and ending on B♭ at m. 13. When I first picked out a Hauptstimme by ear, I found myself singing and playing not E♭–A♭–G♭–E♭–G♭–A♭–B♭, but rather B♭–E♭–D♭–B♭–G♭–A♭–B♭ in the left hand. My structural melody begins on B♭, at m. 9, and then follows the short–short–long rhythmic motive so as to arrive on B♭ at each subsequent downbeat: E♭–D♭–B♭ of my Hauptstimme leads into m. 11, and G♭–A♭–B♭ leads into m. 13. Hearing this principal line, I am attributing less structural priority than does the other reading to E♭ as a harmonic root, and more priority to B♭ as a melodic incipit and final. The E♭–D♭–B♭ of my Hauptstimme approches B♭ from above through tones of a black-note pentatonic scale; the subsequent G♭–A♭–B♭ of my line approaches B♭ from below through the remaining pitch-classes of that pentatonic scale.

B♭ as both-lower-and-upper-bound for pentatonic melodic activity is strongly projected by the music of the first eight measures, where its ceaseless ostinato figure delimits the registral ambitus of B♭³–B♭⁴. Within that ambitus, the first eight measures present a pentatonic melody (mm. 3–4) that ends on the descent E♭–D♭–B♭ (m. 4); the descent is varied and echoed over mm. 5 and 6. Example 6a shows the melody and the first echo, extracting this material from the surrounding ostinato figure. The stems in m. 5 are from the Durand edition.

At the end of ex. 6a I have put a vertical B♭ octave in parentheses. This is the octave that

[1]Allen Forte, "Schenker's Conception of Musical Structure," *Journal of Music Theory* 3 (April 1959), 1–30. Rpt. in *Readings in Schenker Analysis*, ed. Maury Yeston (New Haven, 1984), pp. 3–37; see pp. 32–33.

Example 5

Example 6

delimits the ambitus of mm. 1–8, bounding both the ostinato (not shown) and the pentatonic activity of the melody. The tune of ex. 6a rises only as high as Gb⁴; the segment Gb⁴–Ab⁴–Bb⁴ of the pentatonic scale is as yet inactive.

Example 6b aligns beneath ex. 6a the Hauptstimme I hear over mm. 9–13. I have changed the registers of the pitch classes within my Hauptstimme so that the pitches of ex. 6b all lie within the tonic ambitus of ex. 6a. My alignment suggests that the segment Bb–Eb–Db–Bb of the Hauptstimme over mm. 9–11 develops the cadential Bb of the melody in m. 4, followed by the echoing descent-figure of m. 5. The alignment also suggests that the segment Gb–Ab–Bb of the Hauptstimme over mm. 12–13 is structurally cadential, precisely because it activates the as yet inactive segment of the pentatonic

scale, leading it unidirectionally up to Bb as a goal. My Hauptstimme, one might say, thereby completes the pentatonic diminution of the Bb octave which was begun by the melody of mm. 3–4.

In this hearing, the downbeat of m. 9 is not a structural downbeat for mm. 1–14 as a whole; m. 9 does not resolve tension and then lead back to another state of tension at mm. 13–14. Rather, m. 9 is a point of large-scale contrast, of rhythmic and registral dilation. It complicates a situation which began normally at m. 1 and will close normally by the end of m. 14. Bb as melodic incipit and final governs the large-scale structure throughout; at m. 9 the Eb of the bass provides acoustical support for the melodic tonic Bb, which enjoys no upper fifth within the black-note pentatonic scale. The pitch classes sounded at the bar line of m. 9, that is E♭, B♭, D♭, and G♭, are all present within the pentatonic theme of mm. 3–4; indeed the thematic tune comprises exactly the same four pitch classes. Thus the downbeat sonority of m. 9 can be heard as a "harmonic inversion" of a sonority that was "arpeggiated in fundamental position" by the theme of mm. 3–4, given the context of the piece. Hearing m. 9 as a harmonic inversion helps us hear it "dilating" and "expanding" mm. 1–8 through registral space, stretching that space away from the norm of opening, a registral norm to which the music snaps back over mm. 13–14.[2]

The G♭–A♭–B♭ that leads the bass line to the cadential B♭ of m. 13, a melodic gesture asserted as Hauptstimme by both readings for mm. 9–12, expands to govern larger-scale structural melodic activity over the rest of the piece. The harmonic-metric reduction of ex. 7 clarifies the point.[3]

The cadential melodic gesture G♭–A♭–B♭, aiming at a B♭ downbeat, is easily heard governing the coda, m. 54 to the end. Over the span we encounter the melodic gesture filled in chromatically to become G♭–G–A♭–A–B♭, as displayed on ex. 7, and on the score itself. Example 7 as annotated helps us hear the same chromatic cadential gesture governing a yet larger span of the piece, that is, the span between the crashing G♭-major chord of m. 28 and the downbeat B♭ for the reprise of the theme at m. 44. The G♭-major attack at m. 28 recalls in its "dilated" spacing the "E♭-minor" attack of m. 9; the association of registers and densities is strong despite differences in other respects, like dynamics. Embedded in the chromatic voice-leading which ex. 7 asserts for mm. 34–44, there is also a gesture A♭–G–G♭. This figure retrogrades the G♭–G–A♭ of mm. 28–34, giving rise to a palindrome G♭–G–A♭–G–G♭ over mm. 28–34. The palindrome binds the G♭ chord of m. 28 together with the tone G♭ in the reprise of the main theme following m. 44.

Elements of the chromatic gesture G♭–G–A♭–A–B♭ direct structural voice-leading elsewhere as well. The ostinato of mm. 1–8 and 13–14 changes at m. 15, B♭ being replaced by B♭♭ or A♮. B♭–A is a retrograde segment of our chromatic gesture. The outer voices of ex. 7 over mm. 22–27 project the voice-leading elements A–B♭ and G–A♭; both elements belong to the chromatic span under discussion.

Now there is no contention about the cadential primacy of G♭–A♭–B♭ under any reading for any Hauptstimme in the left hand during mm. 9–13, so the reader may be wondering why I am going into the higher-level structure of ex. 7 here, whatever its intrinsic interest. What does it have to do, that is, with my announced topic, parallel voice-leading? To be sure, parallel organum is manifest in ex. 7 over mm. 54–57 and 28–34, but we need no special discussion to help

---

[2] I had always imagined mm. 1–8 as the swirling wind, and mm. 9–12 as the wide-open empty plain whose registral space the wind was "in," until one day a student said that he had always imagined the textural images corresponding in just the opposite way: for him, the hypnotic ostinato of mm. 1–8 and 13–14 represented the unchanging uniformity of the plain extending on without limit in time, while the slow cascades of mm. 9–12 represented an intermittent chill wind seeping down from the tundra. For him the wind was "in" the plain temporally rather than registrally. A deconstructive pursuit of these metaphors, elaborating what is "in" what, and how, could probably reveal interesting things about the piece. It could engage things we have already discussed about musical contrasts involving mm. 1–8, 9–12, and 13–14. It could also engage some larger-scale structures we shall examine presently.

The metaphor for music being "in" something deserves more general theoretical investigation. Here it underlies the sense of one hearing: that m. 9 sets the piece "in" some sort of harmonic E♭-minor tonality. The same metaphor is involved when the alternate hearing I have proposed sets the piece "in" a melodic mode bounded by B♭, both registrally and temporally.

Schenker's theory of the Ursatz, with all its ramifications in the middleground and the foreground, can be regarded as a mammoth exegesis of just what sort of creature we think a tonal composition is "in," in just what sort of sense, when we say that the composition is "in" a certain key. The creature depicted by Schenker's Ursatz is characterized by a certain species of *coordination* between harmonic tonality and melodic finality.

[3] A quarter-note of the reduction represents a measure of the music. Two-measure groups and (from m. 19 through m. 33) three-measure groups of the piece are articulated by dotted or solid bar lines in ex. 7; the solid bar lines articulate metric pulses that function at some rhythmic level still higher than that. Further metric interpretation is not attempted in the

example: it would not affect the points I intend to make. Neither would certain alternative readings that could be proposed at the metric levels of ex. 7 itself. The example is explicitly designed to be playable; its musical syntax can be checked by performance, at a reasonable tempo for the reduction-quarter. The reduction can also, of course, be read in comparison with the score, at the tempo of the composition. The note heads in the reduction for mm. 34–43 will be discussed later.

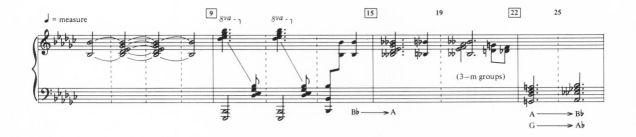

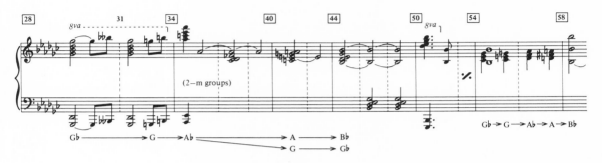

Example 7

us hear that. We do, however, need the special discussion to hear and entertain seriously the voice leading I have indicated on ex. 7 for mm. 34–44. That voice-leading, which follows "the law of the nearest way" chromatically, must be inferred from our desire in this context to hear a linear connection leading the A♭ of m. 34 to the B♭ of m. 44 through an intervening A♮. The voice-leading asserted by ex. 7 for mm. 34–44, is also supported by our willingness to entertain a linear connection between the A♭ of m. 34 and the G♭ of m. 44, through an intervening G♮. Without such support from the large-scale context, we would hardly follow the law of the nearest way over these measures; we would rather follow the sequential pattern of the thematic entries, which would give us the reduction of ex. 8.

This example asserts in the structure of the passage five-part parallel organum at the major third, fifth, major sixth, and octave below, on the motive A♭–F♭–B♭, the "Love's Peace" motive from *Tristan und Isolde*. Perhaps there is something to all this, but it is a far cry from the structure asserted by ex. 7, one which we should certainly not want the parallelisms of ex. 8 to conceal from our ears.

Our investigations so far may suggest that I am saying, "Always mistrust apparent parallel voice-leading in Debussy's music," but that is far from my message. Indeed we have encountered in the two pieces discussed so far several instances of parallel voice-leading that I have taken at face value. My message is rather, "Do not make *any* a priori assumptions about parallel voice-leading in Debussy's music. Take each instance as a highly individual phenomenon in its own musical context." To develop the message further, let us now look at some aspects of *Canope*. Example 9 gives the score for mm. 1–12.

Canopus was an ancient Egyptian city near Alexandria, the site of a temple to Serapis, who

Example 8

Example 9

ruled over the land of the dead and was the god of medicine (so far as he is represented as distinct from Osiris). The word *canope* in French also denotes the Canopic jar, a special sort of burial urn that came from the city. One finds such jars in museums today, often with jackals' heads atop their lids. The jackal, I imagine, represents Anubis guarding the remains. Canopus is also an exceptionally bright star in the sky.[4]

(New York, 1969), entries for "Canopic" and "Canopus," p. 197; *Bulfinch's Mythology* (New York, n. d.), see p. 234 on Serapis and Anubis; and *Larousse de poche* (Paris, 1912). This edn. of the *Larousse*, presumably representing common usage among the educated classes at the time Debussy composed the piece, gives only one meaning for *canope*, calling it a "vase of ancient Egypt." The definition does not mention the funeral function of the urn, but one presumes that Debussy, to the extent he had the urn in mind, used the word *canope* as a metonym for the city, the temple, the associated rites, the dead civilization itself, and funereal ideas of a more general nature. One also presumes that Debussy was familiar with the star Canopus by name; I cannot guess to what extent he might have known anything more about it.

[4]I have collated this background from three sources: *The American Heritage Dictionary of the English Language*

Debussy's piece is saturated with the atmosphere these associations suggest. Things preserved from a remote and bygone past impinge upon a modern sensibility; we are fascinated by these things in spite of—and because of—the cognitive dissonances arising from our relations to them. So, for instance, I am compelled by the persistent and immanent brightness of the star-right-now, while also aware that what I am seeing "right now" happened before Chaucer was born.[5] I am similarly beset by fantasies about the person buried in the beautiful Egyptian urn, the potter who cast that compelling art-work, and so on. I imagine the activities of these people, experiencing their life "as they experienced it" (*wie es eigentlich war*)—yet all the while very much aware that the "life" in my fantasy ceased to exist thousands of years ago.

Debussy's music, in just this vein, contemplates the "long dead" sound of its opening organum through the ears of a cosmopolitan European musician from the early twentieth century. His ears can experience cognitive dislocations, like those of mm. 4–5, for example, in a cultural present within which such dislocations can make musical sense. And what *is* the musical sense of the excursion over that last three beats of m. 4, together with the return to D minor at the bar line of m. 5? *Inter alia*, those events substitute for the events of ex. 10.

Example 10

I shall call ex. 10 "the Dorian cadence" for the theme; what I mean by "the Dorian version" of the theme is a hypothetical variant that proceeds according to the score through the first beat of m. 4, and then continues with the Do-

rian cadence. The plausibility of the Dorian models will emerge in subsequent discussion. For now, the reader should simply hear that the Dorian version of the theme makes good sense by ear; the reader should hear that the melody of this version is plausible by itself as well. Readers who want to perform explicit modal, melodic, or set-theoretic analysis on the Dorian melody will discover easily enough many things about its cadence that work well with its antecedent/consequent balance, its essentially palindromic large contour, its balancing of trichordal, tetrachordal, and pentachordal (pentatonic) segments up through the first quarter of m. 4, its local centers of inversional symmetry up to that point, the balance of transpositional fifth-relations among its segments, and so forth. We shall explore a few of these things later.

Then what generates the musical impulse for a cognitive dissonance whereby, according to my reading, Debussy hears the cadence of the actual music instead of the Dorian cadence? To explore the matter, let us return to the opening of the piece. The first four events of the organum expose the complete family of "white notes." The first of those events projects a D-minor harmony. The melody, after exposing an incipit D, dips to the A below and then surrounds the incipit D by its two white-note neighbors, C and E. The fifth event restates the melodic incipit D and the opening D-minor harmony.

We begin to form two presumptions. First we begin to presume D tonicity of some sort; second, we begin to presume a white-note mode as a tonic collection of pitch classes for the piece. The two impressions together lead us to start expecting some kind of D-Dorian modal organization for the composition. Our expectation is fortified by the continuation of the organal melody over its fifth through eighth notes, to the end of the first phrasing slur. After restating the incipit D, the melody rises and cadences on the C–A above; we can easily associate the complete profile of this melody under its first slur with "Dorian" modal behavior.

Only the B♭ in the harmony of the sixth event gives us pause. There is no strictly *organal* reason why our presumably diatonic B♮ should not appear within that harmony. True, a G-major harmony for the sixth event would sound awkward in other ways, if the rest of the phrase were

[5]I write in 1985; the star Canopus is 650 light-years distant; Chaucer was probably born around 1340.

left unchanged. But Debussy was not, after all, obliged to write a G in the organal melody just here. Nor was he obliged, once he had put a G in the melody here, to follow it directly with a C.[6] The sixth and seventh events of the piece thus lead us to modify our original D-Dorian presumptions in two ways. First, we begin to suspect that B♭, rather than B♮, may be a diatonic form of B for the piece. Second, we associate the soft B with the melodic gesture G—C, the melodic gesture of the sixth and seventh organal events.

The soft-B modifications of our D-Dorian presumptions are subtly reinforced by the parallel voice-leading. For while there is no strictly organal reason for B♭ to appear in the sixth harmony, rather than B♮, there is very good organal reason for B♮ to appear in the fourth harmony, rather than B♭. Thus the B♮ in the harmony of the fourth event is consistent with an assumption of soft-B modality, given the organal premises, but the B♭ in the harmony of the sixth event cannot be heard as consistent with hard-B modality in the same way.

Events nine through twelve in the organum are grouped in the right hand under another phrasing slur. The organal melody continues to project priority for the note D, while the organal harmony continues to project soft-B modality. Beneath the organum a new voice enters, independent of the parallel voice-leading; it is the first hint we have heard of a functional "bass voice" in the piece. Significantly, the new voice isolates and projects the characteristic dyad G—C that we have come to associate with soft-B modality. Up through the first beat of m. 4 both the organal melody and the new pseudo-bass remain entirely within the pentatonic set (C, D, E, G, A). Neither the melody nor the pseudo-bass has yet committed itself on the issue of hard-B vs. soft-B modality, though for other (compositional) reasons we have come to associate the melody, and its presumption of D-priority, with hard-B modality, while we have come to associate the pseudo-bass, and its characteristic dyad G—C, with soft-B modality.

Our analysis has now brought us back to the second beat of m. 4, where the Dorian cadence of ex. 10 would accomplish certain things, and the actual cadence of the music accomplishes certain other things. The Dorian cadence would close very strongly on D, completing a number of symmetries within the sixteen-note Dorian melody. The Dorian cadence would also emphatically celebrate the return of hard-B modality, and its local victory over the soft-B modifications of mm. 2–3; those would be reassessed as temporary mutations within a gesture that begins and ends in the hard modality. The triumph of hard-B modality would be particularly audible in the melodic approach to the final D from a penultimate B♮ in the melody, as displayed by ex. 10. That B♮ is particularly flagged in the homophonic texture by its sounding a *third* above its bass; so far every preceding tone in the Dorian melody has been supported by a bass that lies an octave below. To hear the penultimate B♮ in the melody of ex. 10 as a third above a bass G is highly apt: in the theme, the rival B♭ has so far always appeared as the third over a bass G; conversely, the organal bass G has so far always carried the minor, not the major, third above it. Thus the emphasis on B♮ as the major third of a bass G, in the Dorian cadence, is especially well-suited to telling us that hard-modality has triumphed.

Another telling feature of the penultimate melodic B♮ in the Dorian cadence is precisely that it *is* melodic, i.e., that it appears within a principal melodic line that has so far restricted itself to notes within the pentatonic set (C, D, E, G, A), eschewing both the hard B and the soft B. The hard B in the melody of ex. 10, which extends the pentatonic set to the hard hexachord (G, A, B, C, D, E), makes a decisive impression in this context, telling us that we are in hard-B modality of some kind. Nothing in the pseudo-bass and bass of the Dorian version contradicts that impression; in fact, the G—C pseudo-bass of m. 3 combines with the subsequent E—A—G—D in the bass of ex. 10 to project the referential pentatonic set $P = (C, D, E, G, A)$ in another of its manifestations.

The hard hexachord can be analyzed as the union of the pentatonic set P with the set $P' = (G, A, B, D, E)$. P' is the transposition of P by a characteristic interval i. Depending on our point of view, we can describe i as a fifth (= five

[6]For example, he could have written the first four events as they stand and then continued his melody: D⁵—G⁵—A⁵—C⁶—(D⁶-or-A⁵), and so forth. There would have been no awkwardness about the white-note organum in this situation, or in a number of other situations one might imagine.

steps along some mode we infer from the music); or the harmonic ratio 3:2 (as heard within the organal symphony); or that interval which transposes the natural hexachord into the hard hexachord; or that interval which can generate P if we continue to extend the pseudo bass of m. 3 backward and upward from its C; or in a number of other ways. Extending the pseudo-bass backward and upward is not such a purely fanciful idea as it might seem on first consideration: in moving up beyond the C^4 and G^4 of m. 3 in this way, we would take in the incipit D^5 of m. 1 and the cadential A^5 at the end of the slur in m. 3, finishing our generation of P with the high E^6 of m. 11 that follows directly after the first return since m. 3 to A^5 and its high register, at the end of m. 10.

Since the first eight notes of the melody ascend under a slur and the second eight notes of the melody descend under two slurs in a reasonably balancing way, it makes sense to analyze the Dorian melody as projecting the pentatonic set P over its first eight notes, and the transformed pentatonic set P′ over its second eight notes. Transposition-by-i and transposition-by-the-complement-of-i relate not just P and P′ but also pairs of smaller sets within the Dorian melody as well. This feature is not surprising in a highly motivic pentatonic tune. Later on, we shall see how transposition-by-i engages larger aspects of the music.

Now let us try to reconstruct a thematic chain of transformations, from the Dorian version to the actual music.

First transformation: the penultimate B♮s of the Dorian cadence become B♭s; the G-major triad of that cadence becomes a G-minor triad. Rationale: the piece is *not* going to exhibit hard-B modality in the way projected by the Dorian version, but some kind of soft-B modality. The G harmony has a B♭, as it has always had so far (in mm. 2–3).

Second transformation: the B♮ within the E triad that begins the Dorian cadence also becomes a B♭. Rationale: it was the E triad of m. 2, with B♮ as its fifth, that gave us our presumption of hard-B modality in the first place. That presumption, which would have been confirmed by the Dorian cadence, is not only to be kept somewhat in abeyance here; it is to be utterly denied. So B♮ is not to appear at all in the cadence segment, even as the organal fifth of E. We have now reached a stage of transformation, from ex. 10, whose note heads are set down in ex. 11.

Third transformation: the E♮ within the first harmony of ex. 11 becomes E♭. Rationale: the organal

Example 11

premises, still in effect here, forbid a diminished fifth in the harmony. No longer does the diatonic E generate a B♮ (possibly diatonic, possibly raised); now B♭, seizing structural priority, generates an E♭ which is definitely chromatic.

Fourth transformation: the E♭ in the first chord of transformed ex. 11 remains within the second harmony of the example, and the A♮ becomes a flat in that second harmony. Rationale: the organal premises tell us to avoid the relations (E♭)–(E♮) and (E♭)–(A♮), in moving from the first harmony to the second harmony of the cadence passage. They also tell us to avoid an (A♮)–(E♭) relation within the second harmony. In this connection we might note that the B♭s of mm. 2–3 do not create cross relations that involve the immediate succession of B♭ and B♮ (in any organal voice), or the statement of any diminished interval within the organal melody itself. We have now reached a stage of transformation whose note heads appear in ex. 12.

Example 12

Fifth transformation: the D of ex. 12 becomes D♭, to continue the melody (E♭)–(A♭)–(B♭) according to the melodic motive of the Dorian cadence. The rest of ex. 12 adjusts itself to produce the entire Dorian cadence a chromatic half-step below the level of ex. 10, as shown in ex. 13.

Example 13

Rationale: the cadential Db in the melody has just been discussed above. Transformations 1 through 4 have produced Bb for B♮, Eb for E♮, and Ab for A♮, all in very rapid succession. The impetus carries one along to Db and Gb, and thence to ex. 13. The five black notes make up a thematic pentatonic set P″ = (Gb, Ab, Bb, Db, Eb). The melody and bass of ex. 13 project P″, just as the melody and bass of the original Dorian cadence (ex. 10) project P′ = (G, A, B, D, E). P″ is of course a *ficta* version of P′.

I use the word *ficta* here with some deliberation, because the process that generates ex. 13 from the progressive impetus of Bb, then Eb, then Ab, suggests very strongly a view of *musica ficta* recently propounded by Margaret Bent. She writes:

> B fa and B mi are both equally available in the *recta* system, and . . . neither of them has priority over, or is merely a modification of, the other. . . . *Musica recta* is not an arsenal of fixed pitches but denotes a set of relationships . . . more like a flotilla at anchor than a Procrustean bed or a pre-tuned keyboard. The "operation of *musica ficta*" . . . could mean that the absolute frequency of the As, Bs, Cs that follow may not be the same as they were before, although the local interval relationships of small segments will remain intact. The . . . substitution of a tone for a semitone or vice-versa . . . anywhere in the system [that is, D–Eb going into the beginning of ex. 12] may change the actual pitches following that point [from the form of ex 10. to the form of ex. 13] without changing the relationships except at that point.[7]

The reader who plays over the actual music through the first beat of m. 4 and then continues with the cadence of ex. 13 will find that the *Gedankenthema* sounds quite plausible—perhaps surprisingly so. The overall effect may be compared to that of Bent's examples, in particular her version of Obrecht's Kyrie *Libenter gloriabor*.[8] According to Bent's view, we should not think of the *ficta* in ex. 13 as giving us "new notes" at all; it is only that the flotilla has dipped a bit during the ebb of a maritime tide.

Sixth transformation: the minor thirds of the first two chords in ex. 13 become major, reverting from Gb and Cb to G♮ and C♮ respectively, where they were in ex. 12. Rationale: in so doing, the tones echo and prolong (in register) the thematic dyad G–C that we just heard in the pseudo-bass of m. 3. That dyad is thematically bound up with the power of soft B, and the dyad is preserved while the power of Bb is being developed and amplified by the *ficta* that affects other notes. The organal premises allow either major or minor thirds for the two chords at issue. We are thus brought to the actual pitches of the music, except for one more crucial transformation.

Seventh transformation: the Db-minor harmony

of ex. 13 reverts to the D-minor harmony of ex. 10, producing the actual music. Rationale: as the theme ends, the tide floods back in on the flotilla. Debussy notices his phonograph running down as it is playing its record of Egyptian organum, and winds it back up.[9] No wonder the phonograph runs down ("*Cédez—*"), what with all those flats burgeoning out every which way, while the texture thickens and deepens. Less poetically: this will not be a composition of the Bent species; the cadence event in the treble clef of m. 5 is to match the incipit event of m. 1 in absolute accoustical location as well as in the solfège function of its melodic tone (as *sol* of some appropriate hard hexachord, with whatever *ficta* applied).

The sixth and seventh transformations isolate and articulate the notes Bb, Eb, Ab, Db, and Gb, the notes of the pentatonic set P″. Those five black notes are separated from their comrades-in-*ficta*, the Cb and the Fb of ex. 13: we are not permitted to hear either of the two white *ficta* tones. Nor is the *ficta* idea allowed to proceed to its logical cadence, as in ex. 13. We do hear the notes of P″, but then we are instructed by the D-minor cadence *not* to hear those notes as simple *ficta*. We become less disposed to hear the black notes as *ficta* equivalents for their white-note counterparts; correspondingly, we become more disposed to hear the black notes as functionally *new* entities in the white-note world of the piece.

The opening organum has generated an abundance of musical ideas and cognitive worlds over the first four measures. Let us follow some of these ideas and worlds along over the next eight measures, seeing how they continue to develop and interact. As new notes, the tones of P″ complete the total chromatic just when the music is threatening to come to a dead halt, at the moment directly preceding the D-minor ca-

---

[7]Margaret Bent, "Diatonic Ficta," *Early Music History* 4 (1984), 1–48; see p. 10.
[8]Ibid., pp. 34–40.

[9]Edison's new invention was a featured attraction at the Exposition Universelle of 1889 in Paris. There, at the same time, "dancers and national orchestras from Africa, Arabia, the Orient, Scandinavia, and Russia introduced their primitive and exotic musics. The dancing of the Javanese Bedayas to the music of their national *gamelang* incited comparisons with the flower-maidens of *Parsifal*! . . . In the summer of this year the whole musical universe passed through Paris" (Edward Lockspeiser, *Debussy* [New York, paperback edn. 1972], 40–41]. I am indebted to James Levy for having pointed out to me the importance of the coincidence, that the phonograph, a well-nigh indispensable adjunct for cognitive studies in ethnomusicology, was introduced to the European intellectual world on precisely the same occasion. See also Richard Mueller, "Javanese Influence on Debussy's *Fantaisie* and Beyond," this journal 10 (1986), 157–86 [eds.].

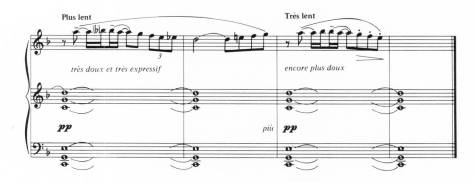

(. . . Canope)

Example 14

dence harmony of m. 5. We now hear that total chromaticism, and even aggregate-completion, are to belong within this piece.

In mm. 5–6 the first phrase of the organal melody is echoed, but now the slur extends only through seven notes, from the incipit D through the low A and on up to the high C of the tune. Then D, A, and C are bound together by the harmony of m. 7. The concomitant F♯ turns modal D–A–C harmony into potential tonal dominant of G minor/major, and both the G functions appear in the harmonies of mm. 11 and 12. The change there from G-minor to G-major harmony, with the change from B♭ to B♮ therein, is of course a pregnant thematic and compositional event.

The C♯ of m. 7, and the C♯ an octave above in m. 9, recall the D♭ cadence tones of ex. 13, the *ficta* Dorian cadence tones that "ought to have been" at the bar line of m. 5 all along, according to the *ficta* theme. The exotic, archaic-sounding entrance of the "Egyptian instrument" on the C♯ of m. 7 is thus a *cognitive* dissonance against the acoustical D♮s of m. 5 and m. 7, not just an accoustical dissonance. According to the archaic hearing of ex. 13, C♯ ought to represent *tonic function* here.

The chromaticism of the tune that begins on the C♯ has all sorts of connections with matters we have been discussing, e.g., the D–E♭ in the melody of m. 4, where E♭ "replaces" E♮, and so on. There is not space here to cover all such details of the chromaticism. A more global aspect of the tune is the way it picks up and develops the discourse of total chromaticism and aggregate-completion. The chromaticism of pitches

in register actually begins with C⁴(♮), the highest pitch of the organal melody from m. 6, and the highest pitch of the D⁷ harmony that fills the first beat of m. 7. Then there ensues C♯⁴ at the entrance of the Egyptian instrument, followed in close order by D⁴, E♭⁴, and E⁴ in that imaginary instrument; F⁴ also appears as a neighbor to E⁴. The chromatic span of pitches continues to extend upward through register 4 during m. 10, where the instrument varies its tune so as to provide F♯, G, and A♭ (in retrograde order), followed by A⁴. Thence the chromatic line continues in register, proceeding to B♭ (A♯?!) in m. 11 and B♮ in m. 12. The pregnant thematic semitone B♭–B thus *completes an aggregate*, the linear aggregate that began with C♮ of m. 7 (or m. 6). This is indeed a fancy modern dress for our friends the soft B (m. 11) and the hard B (m. 12). The chromatic line does not continue chromatically in register to C⁵ (or to any C in any register at all) past m. 12.

The big event of mm. 11–12 discharges the tonal implication of the "dominant seventh" harmony over mm. 7–10. The spacing of D⁵–A⁵–E⁶ in the right hand of m. 11 suggests that the middle C and treble-clef G of m. 3 have been extended on upward by *i*-intervals, as suggested earlier. E⁶ is a new high point for the piece. One can associate the B♮(s) of m. 12 with the bass-and-root G under the D–A–E of m. 11; the resulting harmony, G–D–A–E plus B, projects the P′ pentatonic set.

The tune of mm. 11–12 recurs at pitch during the last four measures of the piece; there it is supported by the sustained chord C²–G²–E³–C⁴–G⁴–D⁵ (see ex. 14).

The chord recalls in its spacing the sonority of m. 12, and indeed the final chord, together with the incipit A^5 of the melodic motive over it (the motive from m. 11), projects the P pentatonic set. Thus the P' set of mm. 11–12, with its G bass-and-root, is transformed by the inverse of our interval i into the P set of the final cadential gesture, where P appears with a C bass-and-root.

This is a manifestation of the characteristic dyad G–C on a grand scale, amplified from the pseudo-bass of m. 3 to a large structural bass motion that continues to resonate over the last four measures of the piece in the low G^2 and C^2, low tones that give us the fifth and bass-*cum*-root of the ultimate tonic harmony. Just as the characteristic G–C dyad of m. 3 was associated with soft-B modality, so the big C-major event of the final four measures is associated with the same modality; there are no B♮s in the four measures, and the B♭ of the tune from m. 11 sounds over the low G–C, at first *très doux et très expressif*, and then again *encore plus doux*. (Has the structural softness of the B liquidated itself into an affect? Note that the high B♭ is now *tenuto*, not *staccato*.) Only the chromatic E♭ remains in the music four measures before the end, from the motive of m. 11, now *plus lent*, to remind us of the *ficta* from m. 4. And then two measures further on, *très lent*, the motive runs

down and stops on E, the last attack of the piece, without ever quite reaching E♭, or the D that might lie beyond. We have to imagine E♭ and the melodic final D during the measure of written-out resonance that follows, ending the piece. The *ficta* E♭ and the priority of D as a melodic final have receded into a vague and fragrant memory of things past.

I must halt the analysis here, lest this essay turn into a study of *Canope* rather than a study of parallel voice-leading.[10] Our analytic work on the Violin Sonata and on *Le Vent dans la plaine* showed us that we would miss a lot by always taking such voice-leading at face value. Our work on *Canope* shows that we would also miss a lot by *never* taking parallel voice-leading at face value. The moral, once again, is not that parallel voice-leading "is" this or that in Debussy's music, but rather that it is not *anything* as an abstract "technique." In each passage where it occurs, it manifests some particular, often uniquely idiosyncratic, approach to the compositional and poetic situation at hand.

---

[10]One cannot appreciate fully even the world of organum in *Canope* without much more analysis. The reprise of the opening, with its radically different cadence, is naturally central to any such study.

Chez Pétrouchka: Harmony and Tonality chez Stravinsky

RICHARD TARUSKIN

In an appreciative comment on Pieter van den Toorn's recent study of Stravinsky,[1] Stephen Walsh remarks that thanks to the work of van den Toorn, Arthur Berger, and some others, we are now beginning to approach the stage of possessing a "background theory" for describing and understanding Stravinsky's harmonic mechanisms, "such as we take for granted when we discuss tonal music."[2] Around Stravinsky's music, in other words, there is at last a growing literature that begins to fulfill Berger's prediction-*cum*-demand for a "new branch of theory" that is equipped "to deal with the nature of twentieth-century music that is centric (i.e. organized in terms of tone center) but not tonally functional,"[3] in a way that transcends the purely statistical, inductive, or *ad hoc* (read: hit-or-miss) methods that have served in the past. Elsewhere I have argued that proper attention to the historical dimension is necessary if we are ever to be able to measure Stravinsky's achievement against a relevant context of common practice—something I conceive as an essential component of any "background theory"—and have made some attempt to provide such a context by describing the historical

---

[1] *The Music of Igor Stravinsky* (New Haven, 1983).
[2] "Review-Survey: Some Recent Stravinsky Literature," *Music Analysis* 3 (1984), 205.

[3] Arthur Berger, "Problems of Pitch Organization in Stravinsky," in *Perspectives on Schoenberg and Stravinsky*, ed. Benjamin Boretz and Edward T. Cone (Princeton, 1968), pp. 123, 154.

evolution of certain aspects of Stravinsky's harmonic and tonal idiom.[4] Now it is time to attempt a couple of further steps, both as the logical extension of the progress made thus far, and in answer to some legitimate objections that have been raised to van den Toorn's work.

The background theory in question locates the source of many of Stravinsky's most characteristic harmonic and tonal practices in a predisposition toward symmetrical partitions of the octave, most often involving the use of the "octatonic" scale (so christened, I believe, by Berger, and now the generally accepted term for a referential pitch collection that may be represented as a ladder of alternating tones and semitones). But it has been observed that up to now no critic has managed to analyze any complete Stravinsky composition along these lines, in such a way as to account for the long-range direction and coherence we now routinely demand to be shown in analyses of tonal or serial pieces. Too often the analysis merely establishes local referability to the octatonic collection, along, perhaps, with a description of various partitioning devices. Joseph Straus, in a prominent review of van den Toorn's work, has laid particular stress in this methodological shortcoming:

Selecting a short passage (usually under twenty measures in length), he extracts its pitch content as an unordered, unregistered, unrhythmicized collection of notes, then identifies the collection as representative of one of the three octatonic collections, one of the diatonic collections, or some amalgamation of the two. Finally, in a multi-level display, he shows the partitioning of these collections.[5]

As far as it goes, this is an accurate description of van den Toorn's method.

But of course to show partitioning is to establish something beyond mere referability. The way in which certain partitions crop up time and again suggests the existence of routines, which in turn suggest a common practice, which can in turn be shown to have historical

precedent. Van den Toorn quite explicitly identifies three such octatonic routines: (0 3 6 9) symmetry, meaning a matrix or axis of triadic roots (potential tonal centers) a minor third apart; the partitioning of the collection into (0 2 3 5) minor tetrachords, again available at each of the (0 3 6 9) nodes, but with strong preference shown for the (0 6) tritone relationship that exhausts the collection; finally, with particular reference to Stravinsky's neoclassic period, the partitioning of the collection into (0 3 7 / 0 4 7) major-minor triadic interactions.[6] Further Stravinskian routines specified by van den Toorn include the interaction of the (0 2 3 5) partition with the "D scale" (Dorian) and that of the (0 3 7 / 0 4 7) partition with the "C-scale" (major) diatonic modes; this provides an excellent lens for viewing Stravinsky's stylistic progress from the "Russian" to the neoclassic phases of his career. And finally, van den Toorn makes some compelling generalizations about the differing properties of the (1, 2) ordering of the scale ("Model A") and the (2, 1) ordering ("Model B"). These are already considerable achievements.

Still, the fact that his analyses are as a rule confined to short passages has given rise to skepticism as to the explicative power of these analytical models, and the continued hope that a key to Stravinsky's tonal (or centric) system may yet lie in "a wildly Schenkerian-derived kind of theory of pc [pitch-class] set 'prolongation' in various pitch-structural and rhythmic-structural 'levels'."[7] Another shortcoming often adduced is the fact that beyond a rather pragmatically flexible notion of ad hoc "octatonic/diatonic interactions," no one has come up with a satisfactory means of taking "chromaticism" into account. That is, there lacks a firm means of accounting for pitches not present in a given

[4]See my "Chernomor to Kashchei: Harmonic Sorcery; or, Stravinsky's 'Angle'," Journal of the American Musicological Society 38 (1985), 72–142.

[5]Review of van den Toorn, The Music of Igor Stravinsky, in Journal of Music Theory 28 (1984), 129.

[6]The numbers within the parentheses are those of the degrees of the chromatic scale, with an arbitrary starting point at zero. The method, first used in the analysis of serial music, has the advantage of enabling the "ideal" conceptualizing of intervals without their embodiment in actual pitch classes, to say nothing of register.

[7]John Rahn, Basic Atonal Theory (New York, 1980), p. 79. This book appeared before van den Toorn's (though later than the Perspectives of New Music article in which van den Toorn originally set forth his viewpoint: "Some Characteristics of Stravinsky's Diatonic Music," Perspectives 14 [1975], 104–38; and 15 [1977], 58–96).

octatonic collection within a context that is generally referable to the collection. As Straus has put it, van den Toorn "never tries to distinguish between structural and embellishing pitches or to account for a sense of directed motion from point to point."[8] *Never* is rather a strong word,[9] but this is indeed an aspect of the Berger–van den Toorn approach that could use some shoring up. Straus has implied[10] that a van den Toorn analysis of Stravinsky accounts for little more than would an analysis of the "Jupiter" Symphony that merely demonstrated its referability to the "C scale." The objection is overstated, but its grain of truth is this: just as we get our sense of Mozart's C major not only from his use of the "C scale on C" but also from the way the "black keys" are related hierarchically to the tones of the scale, so, if we are to be able to conceive of the octatonic collection as a tonality, we must be able to account for the use of the "other" four tones in relation to it.

This neither Berger nor van den Toorn has tried very rigorously to do. On the contrary, by their, it seems, too easy recourse to "diatonic-octatonic interaction" they have given the impression that the octatonic collection in Stravinsky is in point of fact structurally subordinate to the diatonic. Defending himself against Straus's strictures, van den Toorn has even admitted that "there are no works by Stravinsky which are wholly octatonic in conception."[11] If by this he means that there is no work by Stravinsky every note of which is refer-able to a single octatonic collection, then his statement is true. But by that token one would be hard put to come up with a composition by Mozart that is "wholly diatonic in conception," since even the simplest minuet or sonatina movement will contain tones foreign to the C scale that defines its key. If, on the other hand, the concept of octatonicism is broadened sufficiently to encompass what we normally have in mind when we speak of a diatonic key, then I believe there are Stravinsky works that are essentially, if not "wholly" octatonic in conception.

To be sure, an octatonic tonality will never be precisely analogous to a diatonic key, since the structure of the collection precludes the exclusive a priori hierarchical dominance of a single pitch class.[12] Nonetheless, there are Stravinsky compositions in which an octatonic *complexe sonore* (to borrow, after Berger, a useful term from the *Poétique musicale*[13]) is maintained as a stable point of reference governing the whole span of a composition, whatever the vagaries or digressions along the way.

The second tableau of *Petrushka* (*Chez Pétrouchka*) is such a composition, and I propose to attempt an analysis of the entire piece based on what has been learned up to now of the common practice out of which Stravinsky emerged, plus what has been established thus far in terms of "background theory" to Stravinsky's "harmonic mechanisms," amplifying or augmenting the latter as necessary to accomplish the job.

---

[8]Review of van den Toorn, p. 132.

[9]Indeed, van den Toorn's lengthier analyses of pieces such as *Le Sacre du printemps*, *Les Noces*, *L'Histoire du soldat*, the Symphony in Three Movements, and *Agon* cannot be said to ignore directed motion through structural pitch hierarchies. He does show frequently how one Stravinskian "block" leads to another, how priority is established by preserved connecting links and registrally fixed pitches. See, for example, his discussion of E♭, and later, E♭ and C, as structural tones governing the progress of *Le Sacre* from the beginning of the *Augures printanières* through the end of the *Jeu de rapt*—a lengthy span indeed (*The Music of Igor Stravinsky*, pp. 102*ff.*). Van den Toorn's ex. 27, which by the way extends through twenty pages[!], takes in great chunks of the first tableau of Stravinsky's ballet and interrelates them impressively (see, for summary, the charts in his ex. 29 on p. 123).

[10]Joseph Straus, "Stravinsky's Tonal Axis," *Journal of Music Theory* 26 (1982), 264.

[11]"Letter to the Editor," *Journal of Music Theory* 28 (1984), 321–22.

[12]This is something to which Straus evidently cannot reconcile himself. He complains that van den Toorn "never establishes workable criteria for asserting the priority of a single pitch class in a given passage of music" (p. 133). But the failing, if such it be, is not the analyst's; it is the failing of the collection (not to say the composer). To think that a single pitch class must always be assertable in this way within any "centric" situation is an arbitrarily restrictive condition that equates out of preconception what Berger was careful to distinguish in the passage quoted near the beginning of this essay, and renders the whole quest for a Stravinskian "background theory" futile. (It seems to be an identifiable "Yale" position; see the remarks by Forte quoted and discussed below.) Van den Toorn, like any unprejudiced observer, recognizes that pitch-class priority in an octatonic situation—or, to be precise, in Stravinsky's (0 3 6 9) symmetrically partitioned octatonic situations, where by definition there are four potential tone centers—can only be asserted contextually. See *The Music of Igor Stravinsky*, pp. 178–79, or his "Letter to the Editor," pp. 323–25.

[13]*Perspectives on Schoenberg and Stravinsky*, p. 137.

Both Berger and van den Toorn have made pertinent and valuable observations about *Chez Pétrouchka*. To Berger we owe the first analysis of the illustrious "*Petrushka* chord" that "subsumed [it] under a single collection with a single referential order, i.e. the octatonic scale, [so that] the dubious concept of 'polytonality' need no longer be invoked."[14] But beyond such purely operational observations Berger was not prepared to go: "it is not the intention . . . to make exalted claims for this scale, but rather, to observe its behavior in such concrete manifestations as the '*Petrushka* chord'."[15] In particular, Berger held back from positing the scale as an a priori concept for Stravinsky, granting it no more than an inferential, and therefore provisional, analytical status. Van den Toorn went some distance toward demonstrating Stravinsky's "*in-the-act* awareness" of the collection and its "referential implications" when he noted that when the "*Petrushka* chord" reappears along with Petrushka himself at the end of the third tableau of the ballet ([77]), it "features the (0 6) tritone-related (0 4 7) triadic subcomplexes not at C and F♯ but at the remaining two (0 3 6 9) symmetrically defined partitioning elements of Collection III, E♭ and A," which exhausts the collection of reference and suggests that it did in fact possess for Stravinsky an a priori conceptual status (see ex. 1).[16] Van den Toorn also took the first steps toward demonstrating that the concept had been imparted to Stravinsky by Rimsky-Korsakov.[17] His main historical point was that Stravinsky was the first to combine (0 3 6 9) symmetrical triadic derivations from the octatonic collection vertically, as simultaneities (his redoubtable "polytonalisms," of which the "*Petrushka* chord" is the most famous). "The distance separating [Rimsky] from *Petrushka* suddenly becomes enormous," he comments.[18]

But in fact the difference remains one of degree (of harmonic boldness and voice-leading freedom) rather than kind. By understanding the origins of Stravinsky's triadic-symmetrical octatonicism in Rimsky-Korsakov's work and teaching, one can distinguish his "*Petrushka* chord" from the ones in Ravel's *Jeux d'eau* (1901), for example, or in Strauss's *Elektra* (1908), which have very different historical backgrounds and different functional explanations, but which an analyst unarmed with historical perspective might be tempted to adduce as precedents for Stravinsky's usage.

There is, in fact, at least one forerunner to the *Petrushka* chord within the particular sphere of theory and practice that gave rise to Stravinsky's. It is found in Maximilian Steinberg's *Symphonic Prelude* in memory of Rimsky-Korsakov (1908), which was a companion piece to Stravinsky's own *Chant funèbre* in memory of his teacher, the one important Stravinsky composition that is lost to posterity. What is especially remarkable about Steinberg's passage, which combines major triads on B and F, and consequently refers to what van den Toorn calls "Collection II," is that it is one of three passages in his *Prelude* that quote from his father-in-law's own sketches for a work he had in progress at the time of his death: an oratorio ("Heaven and Earth") after Byron (see ex. 2). Rimsky's explicit reference in these sketches to the "interstices" provides the octatonic "background theory" for the Stravinsky usage demonstrated in ex. 1.[19]

Thus it would appear that by the time he died, Rimsky-Korsakov had traveled a longer journey down the octatonic path than he is normally credited with, and hence that the congruence between his octatonic "routines" and those of his most eminent pupil extends at least

---

[14]Ibid., pp. 134–35.

[15]Ibid., p. 138.

[16]*The Music of Igor Stravinsky*, p. 463, n. 5. Van den Toorn numbers the three possible transpositions of the octatonic scale with Roman numerals, and we will follow him here, even though I wish he had called this collection (which contains the C-major triad as a constituent of its *complexe sonore*) no. I.

[17]See his discussion of Rimsky's *Sadko* and Stravinsky's *Scherzo fantastique* as background to *Petrushka* and beyond, pp. 35–39.

[18]Ibid., p. 37.

[19]The Rimsky sketch has been published in a supplemental volume to his complete works: N. A. Rimsky-Korsakov, *Polnoe sobranie sochinenii: Literaturnye proizvendeniia i perepiska* IV (dop.): *Notnye zapisnye knizhki* (Moscow: Muzyka, 1970), p. 277. Steinberg's prelude was published in the author's reduction for piano by Edition Belaieff (Leipzig, 1910). The citations from Heaven and Earth sketches are set forth with asterisks.

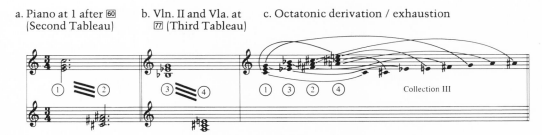

a. Piano at 1 after 60 (Second Tableau) b. Vln. II and Vla. at 77 (Third Tableau) c. Octatonic derivation / exhaustion

Collection III

Example 1

a. Rimsky-Korsakov, Sketch for *Heaven and Earth* (1908).

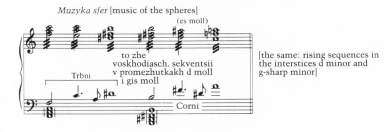

Muzyka sfer [music of the spheres]

(es moll)

Trbni

to zhe
voskhodiasch. sekventsii
v promezhutkakh d moll
i gis moll

[the same: rising sequences in
the interstices d minor and
g-sharp minor]

Corni

b. Maximilan Steinberg, Symphonic Prelude, mm. 99–103.

Trb. *marcato*

Hn.

ppp   *ppp*   *ppp*

Example 2

as far as the second tableau in *Petrushka*. It is my contention here that *Chez Pétrouchka* (conceived originally, as everyone knows, as an independent *Konzertstück* for piano and orchestra in the late summer of 1910), is based on a *complexe sonore* consisting of an (0 3 6 9) symmetrical partitioning of "Collection III," according to what was a fully elaborated St. Petersburg common practice, established by Rimsky, handed down to *all* his pupils, and

fully described in my earlier historical study.[20] Example 3 reproduces a chart given in that essay, which originally accompanied an analysis of the opening of the second scene (the Underwater Kingdom) in Rimsky's opera *Sadko* of 1897 (also touched on by van den Toorn[21]).

---

[20]See n. 4 above.

[21]*The Music of Igor Stravinsky*, pp. 36–37, including ex. 15a.

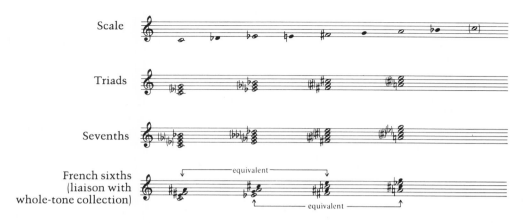

Example 3: the Collection III *complexe sonore.*

Another Rimskian technique traced in the earlier article, one that also has a bearing on Stravinsky's usages in *Chez Pétrouchka*, consists in the alternating or even simultaneous use of the (1, 2) and (2, 1) orderings of the octatonic scale arranged around the same set of (0 3 6 9) symmetrical nodes. Following Rimsky's explicit and demonstrable usage, these are labeled "harmony scale" (the 1, 2 ordering) and "melody scale" (the 2, 1 ordering: see ex. 4). Rimsky's habit was to derive the harmony of a given passage from the (1, 2) ordering and the melody from the (2, 1) ordering, as in ex. 5, also from *Sadko*. In this way the entire chromatic could be employed within an explicit octatonic framework. This passage was actually discussed by Rimsky-Korsakov with his disciple Vasilii Yastrebtsev, in such a way that we may be sure our analysis of it follows his conscious practice.[22]

Before proceeding, let us consider the special status of the French sixth chord within Rimsky's harmonic practice, for this is something previous writers have not mentioned. Just as any one of the triads or (particularly) dominant-seventh chords referable to the octatonic *complexe sonore* can provide a pivot for modulation to a diatonic scale, so the French sixth (0 4 6 10), like the tritone (0 6) itself, can act as a bridge between the octatonic collection and the whole-tone scale (0 2 4 6 8 10), another "mode of limited transpositions" (to use Messiaen's suggestive term) based on a symmetrical division of the octave (0 4 8). This scale, too, figures prominently in the Russian "fantastic chromaticism" that forms the immediate background to Stravinsky's harmonic idiom in *Petrushka*.[23] Chord formations based on the whole-tone collection interact spectacularly with octatonic formations in the second act of Rimsky's *Le Coq d'or*, to mention a famous example. Moreover, it is a commonplace of Scriabin's harmonic practice to partition the French sixth chord into two "incomplete" dominant sevenths a tritone apart, often within an explicitly octatonic frame of reference.[24] If these partitioning chords are completed by the addition of their fifths, the *Petrushka* chord is the result.

The theoretical models thus far expounded

---

[22]See "Chernomor to Kashchei," pp. 79*ff.*

[23]For a tracing of its historical evolution in nineteenth-century music, and a demonstration of its original functional congruence with the octatonic collection, see "Chernomor to Kashchei," pp. 79–99.

[24]See Varvara Dernova, "Garmoniia Skriabina," in *A. N. Skriabin: Sbornik statei,* ed. S. Pavchinsky (Moscow, 1973), pp. 352–57. For many insightful comments on Scriabin's use of the French sixth as generator of whole-tone and octatonic collections and as mediator between them, see Jay Reise, "Late Skriabin: Some Principles Behind the Style," *19th-Cen Mus* 6 (1983), 220-31. Reise also has useful things to say about the handling of "chromaticism" within whole-tone and octatonic contexts.

Example 4

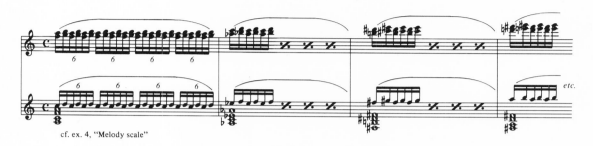

cf. ex. 4, "Melody scale"

Example 5: *Sadko*, act I, sc. 2, 78.

were derived in the first instance from an analysis of the Underwater Act in *Sadko,* chosen for this purpose because Rimsky had discussed it theoretically to some limited extent with Yastrebtsev. There is every reason to assume that Stravinsky knew that music intimately; it was performed by Diaghilev's company, as a matter of fact, during the same Paris season that saw the premiere of *Petrushka.* But if an immediate and historically demonstrable forebear to *Chez Pétrouchka* is required, it can easily be found in another of the very many Rimsky-Korsakov compositions that embody these procedural norms: the symphonic suite *Shéhérazade,* op. 35, the hoariest Rimskian chestnut of them all.

Now why should this work of 1888 have been a more direct stimulus on the imagination that produced *Petrushka* than the opera *Sadko* of 1897, not to mention any of the later fantastic operas, from *Kashchei the Deathless* to *Le Coq d'or,* that were actually composed or revised during the period of Stravinsky's tutelage? The reason is that *Shéhérazade,* choreographed by Fokine to a scenario by Benois, and with epoch-making sets and costumes by Bakst, had been, along with the *Firebird,* the other *succès fou* of the Diaghilev *saison russe* of 1910. The two works frequently shared the boards, and in any case, Stravinsky still had vivid memories of the

ballet as late as 1958, when he described it to Robert Craft—at least with respect to Bakst's contribution—as a masterpiece.[25] He heard Rimsky's score any number of times, then, in June and July of 1910, and he began work on the *Konzertstück* that would become *Chez Pétrouchka* in late August or September. There can be little doubt that it was *Shéhérazade* that got Stravinsky thinking again in terms of strict (0 3 6 9) octatonic symmetry, something of which there is actually rather little in *The Firebird.* (That ballet is based to a very large extent on a special "ladder of thirds" technique Stravinsky had derived from octatonic practices, but which transcended them.) The example of *Shéhérazade* reminded Stravinsky that there was, to paraphrase Schoenberg, "still a great deal to be said in C major"—or, to be precise, in Collection III with a strong initial orientation on C, and with a good deal of diatonic and whole-tone contamination.

Shéhérazade contains a number of striking passages in which the (0 6) octave-bisecting tritone relationship is strongly asserted. The very

[25]Igor Stravinsky and Robert Craft, *Conversations with Igor Stravinsky* (Berkeley and Los Angeles, 1980), p. 97.

opening is a case in point. The successive down-beats of Sultan Shahriar's four-bar motive sound a descending whole-tone scale through the fourth degree, that is, the midpoint (see ex. 6). In the middle of the first movement of the suite, the first three notes of the theme are broken off from the rest and treated in a typically Rimskian sequential progression that covers the same distance, but in an octatonic (Collection III) progression. In ex. 7, all tones foreign to Collection III are circled. They will be seen to be conventional appoggiaturas, an important precedent to recall in connection with *Chez Pétrouchka*.

In the middle of the second movement, the Shahriar motive in its full four-measure form is linked with a passage that seems to stand midway between the famous bell-ringing progression in *Boris Godunov*, with its oscillating tritone-related dominant-seventh chords, and the cries of Petrushka. In ex. 8, the (0 6) limits of the Shahriar theme are filtered out, as Berger might say, and held as a pedal while the trumpet and trombone play their antiphonal fanfares. The latter are derived from the third measure of the

theme. Their starting notes, heard pretty ineluctably as roots of dominant sevenths *à la* Mussorgsky, are pitched a tritone apart, as per the implied harmony of the third and fourth measures of the theme (cf. ex. 6b). These fanfares, by the way, show Rimsky-Korsakov thinking, as early as 1888, in terms of an embryonic octatonically referable "polytonality," for the fanfare figures outline minor triads, the thirds of which contradict the pedal tritone (F♭ in the trombone against the F; B♭ in the trumpet against the B). The clashing pitches, no less than the invariant ones, are full-fledged members of the Collection III *complexe sonore*. Rimsky's particular harmonic filtering of that complex—the "common tritone" pedal plus the emphasized fourths in the brass fanfares—yield that contents of the *Petrushka* chord. It is plausible, moreover, that Rimsky's fanfare figures provided a model for the opening phrases of *Chez Pétrouchka*: Rimsky's opening fourth is inverted to a fifth, and there is the same use of triplet upbeats containing passing tones foreign to the octatonic collection in force, but which are prepared and resolved in a fully conven-

a. Shahriar's motive

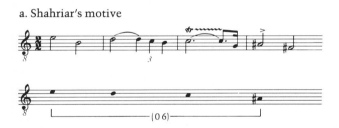

b. A typical harmonization (9 before ⒠)

cf. *Petrushka* chord and ex. 13, below.

Example 6

a. *Shéhérazade*, 7 after [B]

b. Harmonic reduction

Fr6 °7 Dom 7   6   Fr6   °7 $\frac{6}{5}$ $\frac{6}{4}$ Fr6   °7 $\frac{4}{3}$

"terminating
convenience"

b: V ———————— I

c. Neighbor relationships condensed

Example 7

tional, hence comprehensible, way (see ex. 8c).[26]

---

[26]Reise says something similar about Scriabin; see his analysis of *Étrangeté*, op. 63, no. 2 ("Late Skriabin," pp. 224–26).

Rimsky's passage (ex. 8a) continues. The "common tritone" is resolved in one of the two ways possible: "inward," to C (the "outward" resolution would have been to F♯). The F♯ is quickly provided through a sequencing of the

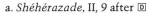
a. *Shéhérazade*, II, 9 after ▢D

b. Reduction and analysis

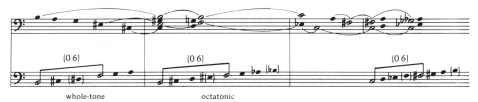

c. Rimsky's theme compared with Stravinsky's

Example 8

triplet figure from the brass fanfares, and the new tritone, C–F♯, replaces the old as a pedal for a sequential repetition of the whole passage described in the last paragraph. This time the antiphonal-fanfares idea is developed through fragmentation and an accelerated harmonic rhythm (shades, again, of those *Boris* bells), until it is time for the inevitable contrapuntal combination of the Shahriar theme and the fanfare theme. Rimsky achieves this through a common-tone progression in which the fanfare passage, centered on A, is repeated endlessly,

a. *Shéhérazade*, II, 6 before F

b. Reduction and analysis

Example 9

with the A progressively redefined as root, third, seventh, and fifth. This passage ought to be quoted (ex. 9) since in it Rimsky hammers away at the phrase that seems to have been echoing in Stravinsky's ear (and no wonder) as he began his *Konzertstück* in 1910. And the passage it leads to at the end of ex. 9 also reverberates in *Petrushka:* the three clarinet cadenzas over static harmonies provided the model for the big cadenza bar (one before ⑤⑨) in *Chez Pé-trouchka*, where the same clarinet, immediately aped by the piano, holds forth in virtuosic cascades over a sustained harmony in the cellos.[27] Rimsky's cadenza passage, moreover, following ⑤, is exclusively and exhaustively octatonic, referable to Collection III. The harmonies of the second and third bars, in fact, sum up the exact contents of the *Petrushka* chord. As a progression they adumbrate what might be called (with apologies to Siegmund Levarie) the "tonal flow" of *Chez Pétrouchka*, which begins with a passage centered on C and ends with a cadence on F♯.[28]

III

This observation is the first step toward an understanding of Petrushkian tonality. The (0 6) C/F♯ tritone polarity exists not only in the vertical conjunction that has become so famous, but is extended in the temporal dimension to govern the overall tonal coherence of the music. And—shades of *Shéhérazade!*—the (0 6) polarity exists in an important tonal sense as a subset both of the octatonic and of the whole-tone collections, between which it represents the point of intersection. As an expression of the midpoint of the whole-tone collection it provides a frame for the modulatory plan of the movement, which, though rather rigorously octatonic in its referential ordering through ⑤②, is nonetheless centered through m. 42 on C, as will be demonstrated below. The Adagietto at ⑤② is centered on D and carries a signature of two sharps, while the music from ⑤④ to ⑤⑧ has E at its center. (From ⑤④ to ⑤⑥ the key signature of E minor is actually employed.) As noted above, the final cadence is on F♯. Thus the sequence of tonal centers forms an ascending octave-bisecting whole-tone progression C–D–E–F♯, which mirrors the descending progression so suggestively embodied in the Shahriar leitmotif from *Shéhérazade* (ex. 10).

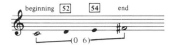

Example 10: *Chez Pétrouchka*, overall tonal flow.

The C of the opening section is not a conventionally established tonic, certainly, but a *primus inter pares*, the favored member of the four-fold array of potential centers implicit in the Collection III *complexe sonore*. Berger accounted for its dominance by citing the "liaison" of the opening phrase with the end of the first tableau, a clear and almost conventional authentic cadence in C major. Thus the G is heard as the "supporting fifth" of the C.[29] Even without reference to the first tableau (which, of course, did not exist when the beginning of the 1910 *Konzertstück* was composed), it is possible to justify the ear's assignment of unmistakable priority to C by virtue of the quasi-cadential approach to it at m. 6, for which purpose the downbeat B♮, not endemic to Collection III, functions as an imported leading tone (as it would, say, in C minor). Though its resolution to C is indirect, since its position in a chromatic stepwise descent is alone what justifies its intrusion within an octatonic context, it surely reinforces the contributions of the other half-step resolutions (F♯–G, D♯–E) to what is in weak but nonetheless sufficient effect a tonicization of the C-major triad—despite presentation of the latter inversion, both in m. 6 and one measure later.[30] In m. 7, the tonicized role of C is reinforced by the way the E♭ harmony (a potential rival as

[27]It might be argued that a model nearer Stravinsky lay in the first movement of Ravel's *Rapsodie espagnole*; but Rimsky was Ravel's model, too, and, as pointed out above, no piece was closer to Stravinsky than *Shéhérazade* right before he embarked on his *Konzertstück*.

[28]See Siegmund Levarie, "Tonal Relations in Verdi's *Un Ballo in maschera*," *19th-Cen Mus* 2 (1978), 143-47.

[29]*Perspectives on Schoenberg and Stravinsky*, p. 135.

[30]Berger's point (*Perspectives on Schoenberg and Stravinsky*, p. 136) about the holding in reserve of the octatonically referable A♯ and its suppression in m. 6 in favor of a repetition of the cadential B, seems to have been founded on a misprint. Both in Stravinsky's four-hand arrangement of the ballet and in the *Trois Mouvements de "Pétrouchka,"* the B♮ in m. 6 is followed by a B♭, which maintains the regularity of the chromatic descent. As the *lectio difficilior*, it probably represents Stravinsky's original conception of the passage, even if he did not correct the B♮ to B♭ in the 1947 version of the score.

This may have been an oversight, since Stravinsky did not make any changes in the fist violin part in mm. 5–6—the only part that contains the note in question—and may not, therefore, have proofread the exemplar from which he was working. On the other hand, he may have retained the B♮ deliberately: the revised version of the passage contains other changes of actual notes, including at least one as conspicuous as the one in question. (The chord of arrival in m. 6 is C minor in 1947 instead of C major). Whatever the case, when Stravinsky made his piano solo transcription in 1921 he kept the B♭—which he had to copy out by hand; this makes it clear that as of then (and consequently, in 1910) he considered B♭ the correct reading.

Example 11: *Chez Pétrouchka*, mm. 1–8.

an octatonic center) is applied to it as an acciaccatura, restating on a more structural plane the local resolution of D♯–E in m. 6. The whole passage is given in ex. 11, with tones foreign to Collection III circled, as in the *Shéhérazade* excerpt above. (See also the *Sadko* excerpt analyzed in "Chernomor to Kashchei," ex. 22.) As in Rimsky's compositions, all the foreign pitches are applied to Collection III pitches by means of the most ordinary techniques for handling "nonharmonic" tones: either as passing tones, or, in the case of the chord preceding the French sixth in m. 4, as neighbors, complete (D–E♭) or incomplete (G♯–A, B–C♯).

When the *Petrushka* chord is first sounded by the clarinet arpeggios in m. 9 (|49|), the C-major component retains its dominance because it is on top, and also (as Berger noted) because it is in the same stable form it had assumed at the beginning—to which we associate it on rehearing—while the F♯ arpeggio, previously unheard as a discrete harmony, is voiced in its § position, making it more difficult to identify aurally than its companion.

As Berger also pointed out, the "principal defining agency of the total configuration" produced by the pair of clarinet arpeggios is the dyad A♯/C,[31] both because it is the high point, and because it is prolonged in notes lasting as much as two measures and more (mm. 10–11, 13–15). Stravinsky capitalizes on this dyad's property of belonging both to the octatonic and the whole-tone collections that share C/F♯ as their defining (0 6) midpoint, by introducing a figure in the bassoon that completes the whole-tone tetrachord from C to F♯. The foreign tone thus introduced, G♯, is a borrowing such as Rimsky-Korsakov himself might have made from the octatonic "melody scale": literally a "nonharmonic" tone. It is immediately contradicted by the first clarinet's "harmonic" G♮ in m. 12, and then (m. 16) resolved indirectly—that is, through a diminished-seventh arpeggio consisting of all the potential centers of Collection III—to A, the one Collection III nodal point that has not been heard

up to now, however briefly, as a chord root. It is sounded in m. 16 only as a sixty-fourth note, but it is a functional root nonetheless, for it immediately picks up a third and a seventh, C♯/G, the latter pitch introduced by the bassoon's G♯, now given to the muted trumpet, as appoggiatura: the melody scale gives way to the harmony scale.[32] The C♯/G tritone now transiently assumes the status of focal point. It is a far weaker one than C/F♯ had been, since its constituent pitches are not available as triadic roots within the Collection III *complexe sonore*. Its main function is to provide a pair of thirds—or, in Rimskian terms, a "common tritone"—for the roots E♭ (D♯)–A, which fill in the interstices between the C and F♯ of Collection III. This happens in mm. 21 and 22. The cascades in the piano part are a kind of composed-out *Petrushka* chord, reminiscent of the complex arpeggio figuration in Stravinsky's *Fireworks*, op. 4, and, indeed, constructed according to methods Stravinsky had worked out in composing that piece. There, a complex whole-tone-derived chord (one that appears prominently in *Le Coq d'or*) had been slyly resolved as a sort of inverted augmented-sixth chord to a more stable dominant-seventh harmony as shown in ex. 12.

The same kind of multiple voicings and resolutions operate in the *Petrushka* cascade. Both the precedent set in *Fireworks*, and the fact that half of the cascade is repeated independently (by the clarinet) in m. 22, suggest that the ten-note cascade is to be heard as two groups of five. The first of these exhibits a very clear neighbor progression to the dominant seventh on D♯/E♭ (ex. 13a); the second is a more abstruse progression that relies, for its interpretation, on the precedent set in mm. 3–4 (ex. 13b). The basic harmony is a fifthless dominant seventh on A, which together with the D♯ harmony yields the content of the *Petrushka* chord.

The extraordinary passage adumbrated in m. 19,

---

[31]*Perspectives on Schoenberg and Stravinsky*, p. 136.

[32]The use of a perfect fifth as dissonant appoggiatura to a stable diminished fifth has ample precedent in Rimsky-Korsakov. See "Chernomor to Kashchei," pp. 114–15.

Example 12: *Fireworks*, 1 after ⑪.

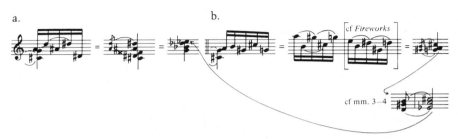

Example 13: *Chez Pétrouchka*, m. 22.

and developed fully beginning in m. 23, shows that despite the octatonic interpretation of its genesis, there may be some validity after all in regarding the *Petrushka* chord as a polytonality. In m. 19 the C♯/G tritone generates another burst of arpeggios, in which the piano joins (or rather, opposes) the clarinets. The latter confine themselves to the C-major and F♯-major triads as before (the G and C♯ of the generating tritone assuming the identity of chordal fifths). The piano right hand, however, builds a triad from the root G to clash against the F♯ arpeggio in the left hand. This G-major arpeggio, which borrows two tones from outside Collection III, could be looked upon as an appoggiatura to the F♯ arpeggio, following the many neighbor-note precedents already established in *Chez Pétrouchka*.[33] Another way of looking at the chord would be simply to regard it as the dominant of the first clarinet's C-major arpeggio. This has the "dramaturgical" advantage of casting the opposition of piano and orchestra, which we know to have been at the core of the programmatic idea that motivated the *Konzertstück*, into higher relief. It further enhances our sense that C enjoys priority within Collection III, for it alone is licensed to import auxiliary harmonies from outside the octatonic field.

At any rate, the application to C of its conventional diatonic dominant—foreshadowed, one recalls, by the accented B♮ in m. 6—shows that

Stravinsky regarded the two triadic subsets of the *Petrushka* chord as potentially independent functional agents. This interpretation is corroborated by many passages later on in the piece (to be noted on their occurrence); it is therefore the one I favor. During the passage at m. 19—and the one following (mm. 23–26) in which the piano and first clarinet exchange harmonies, the latter taking over the G-major arpeggio, while the piano reverts to C—it seems proper to speak of "music in two keys," as Stravinsky continued to do throughout his life,[34] so long as it is borne in mind that the keys in question were chosen not at random but from among the circumscribed and historically sanctioned wares of the octatonic *complexe sonore*.

The ensuing passage for the piano—the first of several cadenzas in which, according to the original conception of the *Konzertstück*, the soloist was envisioned as a mad genius in a *frac*, rolling "*objets hétéroclites*" up and down the keyboard[35]—combines both G and C chords in the right hand against the F♯ arpeggio in the left, which by now has taken on the character of a non-harmonic pedal. The white-key / black-key opposition, which plays a role of ever-in-

[33]That is van den Toorn's way of looking on it. See *The Music of Igor Stravinsky*, p. 64, and the discussion of polytonality in this essay, below.

[34]See *Expositions and Developments* (Berkeley and Los Angeles, 1981), p. 136.

[35]Florent Fels, "Un Entretien avec Igor Stravinsky à propos de l'enregistrement au phonographe du *Pétrouchka*," *Nouvelles littéraires*, 8 December 1928; rpt. in *Stravinsky: Études et témoignages*, ed. François Lesure (Paris, 1982), p. 248.

a. m. 29, 2nd beat

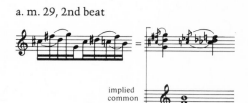

implied
common
tritone:

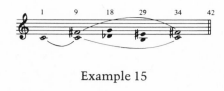

Example 15

b. mm. 31–32

Example 14

creasing prominence in the piano's rhetoric, is nothing if not "heteroclite." By the third measure, however, the figuration has been modified so as to conform to the *Fireworks*-like "cascade" figure heard shortly before (compare m. 29 with m. 21). Two more white notes—C and F—are added to the pitch repertoire of the piano's white hand; but more important, the new pitch configuration demands a reinterpretation of the relationship between F♯ and G. The former, up to now a stable element, is heard at this point as an appoggiatura to the latter, until now a mere epiphenomenon. A modulation, in other words, has been effected which implies a new governing tritone: B/F (see ex. 14a). Sure enough, these very tones are filtered out by Stravinsky and conspicuously prolonged in mm. 31 nd 32 (ex. 14b).

This momentary departure prepares the climactic return of the original uncontaminated Collection III complex at ⑤1, the *Malédictions de Pétrouchka*. Once again C is asserted as the key of priority, if for no other reason than because the curse itself, blared out by four muted trumpets in unison, *fortississimo*, is confined for the first five bars to the notes of the C-major triad, and thereafter the notes of the F♯ subset are used exclusively in an ornamental capacity. This concludes the first major section of *Chez Pétrouchka*, if by section we mean a closed tonal span. The essential tonal motion it encloses consists of a double-neighbor relation to the "governing (or common) tritone," which could be represented graphically as in ex. 15. The tonality-defining progression F/B–F♯/C, which in the present context acts like a dominant proceeding to the tonic, was encountered, one recalls, in precisely this form in *Shéhérazade* (cf. exs. 8 and 9 above).

Whether or not one accepts all the details of this analysis, the essential point seems clear enough: namely, that the octatonic collection (here, Collection III) satisfies at least some of the criteria of "key," in that it affords not only a referential vocabulary of pitch classes but also a set of stable structural functions, and that departures from it and returns to it—on various levels from that of local "chromaticism" to that of "modulation"—are possible without compromising its referential integrity. Stravinsky's methods of effecting departure and return, though necessarily *ad hoc* to some degree given the novelty of the material, are based, as one might only expect from a pupil of the super-fastidious Rimsky-Korsakov, on traditional principles of voice leading in tonal music, principles prominently exemplified in Rimsky's own works, like *Shéhérazade* and *Sadko*. They are both consistent and salient to the ear.

IV

On to the second section, which begins with the surprising resolution of the *Petrushka*-chord, two measures before ⑤2, to a strongly voiced D-major triad. This is actually the first complete and uncontaminated triad, in block form and in root position, to be sounded thus far in the course of *Chez Pétrouchka*, so it seems to presage, not another octatonic *complexe sonore*, but, purely and simply, the key of D.

And such seems to be the case—with one telling exception. The "D major" of the Adagietto at ⑤2 is consistently contaminated by a G♯ in place of the normal fourth degree. This pitch, persistently sounded against the tonic triad, maintains the level of tritone saturation we have by now come to regard as normal for this piece. It would make little sense, though, to try to explain it away by invoking the "Lydian mode." Nor does this particular "raised fourth" behave in the standard way for such altered degrees. With one apparent exception to be dealt with later, it is never applied to the fifth degree, but consistently falls back onto the third, both within the main tune and in the piano cascade that interrupts it in m. 48 (ex. 16). Indeed, the note A (the fifth degree) is the one pitch that has been suppressed from the cascade. In short, what we have here is a composing-out of the bassoon's G♯–F♯ *lamentoso* motive from mm. 11–15, providing a thematic and an affective link between the sections.

The apparent exception to this generalization as to the behavior of the G♯ comes in m. 49, when it is used to initiate a piano cascade like the ones already heard in mm. 21 and 29 (ex. 17). The meaning of this cascade, though, has little to do with the behavior of the previous G♯s. Instead, it reidentifies the last G♯ as a center in a *Petrushka*-chord-like deadlock with D, and only enhances the structural importance of the "borrowed" tritone. Moreover, the implied fulcrum of the progression, the "common tritone" that links the D and the G♯ components of the cascade, is the original "tonic" tritone, C–F♯. This is very much like what Rimsky-Korsakov had had in mind when he wrote of his care to govern the tonal relations within his "fantastic" music so that no matter how chromatic and *recherché* the local context, all is ruled by "the *invisible presence* of the tonic at all times," lest the music degenerate into "artistic thoughtlessness and caprice."[36] It is evident that Stravinsky inherited this concern.

The piano cascade is immediately echoed in m. 49 by the original perpetrators of the G♯ (the English horn standing in for the bassoon, since the passage in question, in this pre-*Sacre* composition, must have seemed to Stravinsky to lie too high for that instrument). They repeat the second quintolet a step higher, so that it actually ends on G♯, providing a pivot back to the opening tune (⟨53⟩, Andantino). Here the flute joins in and contradicts the G♯ (m. 53) with a G♮—the piano meanwhile abandoning all Gs in its figuration, sharp or natural—in preparation for the modulation to E minor at ⟨54⟩. Both the preparation of this new key and its initial presentation are saturated with double neighbors. These diatonic neighbors reflect, on the surface level, the chromatic structural progression we uncovered in examining the first section of *Chez Pétrouchka*.

The new tonality is, if not entirely conventional, at least entirely diatonic as far as ⟨55⟩, when some very characteristic Russian chromaticism is applied to it. This again involves the use of ornamental double neighbors (see the piano part, mm. 65–67, where chromatic double neighbors decorate the descending Phrygian line from B to E), and also a variety of passing chromaticism one finds very often in the work of

[36]Letter to E. M. Petrovsky, 11 January 1903; *Sovetskaia muzyka* [XVI], no. 12 (1952), 69.

Example 16

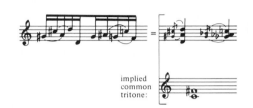

implied common tritone:

Example 17: m. 49.

Glinka and the Five, especially when they were writing in an "oriental" vein. Borodin's *Arabian Melody* (1881) has a turn of phrase so like the end of the *Petrushka* passage as almost to suggest itself a model (ex. 18).

The frenzied passage beginning at ⟨56⟩ is harmonically a rather ambiguous one. It starts with a C-major triad, and students of the score may be encouraged to think of that chord as tonic, since the F♯ is removed at this point from the key signature. But the F♯, now specifically signed on each occurrence, persists; the melody continues to center quite obsessively around E (in fact, it is a variant of the tune quoted in ex. 18a); and there are no chord progressions in the vicinity that assert any of the primary functions of C major. The upper-voice E, then, is best construed as a continuing tone center, even though it is not used as a local harmonic root. The pitches that are so used most frequently, on the other hand, are the very ones that had figured in the Borodinesque bass line that accompanied the repeated Es of the melody in ex. 18a. They have been promoted from a purely linear, ornamental status to that of a series of *ersatz* roots, but their functional status with respect to the static tonic E is unchanged. A reduction of the passage such as the one in ex. 19, similar in appearance to the actual surface of the music in ex. 18a, will make this clear.

a. *Chez Pétrouchka*, mm. 69–70.

b. Borodin, *Arabskaia melodiia*, mm. 33–40.

O take pity on me, you see that I perish on your account.

Example 18

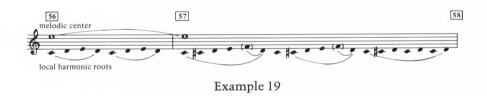

Example 19

At 58 the F♯ is finally cancelled and the harmony begins to pile up diatonic thirds in a fashion that in the context of the complete ballet recalls the end of the *Danse russe* from the first tableau (though the actual order of composition was the reverse). The largest of these pile-ups actually incorporates the whole white-key collection, in final summary before octatonicism reasserts itself through a D/F pivot, and with a vengeance (ex. 20). The cadenza bars are based on octatonic Collection I, the collection that is missing precisely the C–E♭–F♯–A "tonic matrix" of the opening section. It is partitioned, Scriabinesquely, into two diminished-seventh chords.[37] There can be

Example 20

no doubt that Stravinsky knew exactly what he was doing here, and that the harmony sustained by the trumpets and then the solo cellos consists precisely of the collection of those pitches that are foreign to the collection on which the piece commenced, and to which it will return. A position has been assumed at a maximum distance from the tonic matrix, and it has been assumed deliberately.

[37]See George Perle, "Scriabin's Self-Analyses," *Music Analysis* 3 (1984), 102–03.

Just as in the case of the two triads that add up to the *Petrushka* chord, the two diminished sevenths here are obsessively and grotesquely made to clash as a polychord. The *ad libitum* cadenza cascades in clarinet and piano treat the diminished-seventh complex Bb–G–E–C# as a vast appoggiatura to the sustained harmony. The lowest pitch in the cascades is the Bb, part of the sustained harmony (i.e., a "chord tone"), to which the clarinet descends from its high Bb in a rush, and which it then sustains for whole beats at a time, leaving no doubt that it is the "structural" pitch. Repeatedly the clarinet takes flight into the appoggiatura region, only to be dragged back to the Bb. The last ascent breaks free of the cellos' gravitational field, however, and the clarinet concludes with the very striking sigh figures, on E and C#, which Stravinsky marks *lamentoso assai.* This is the one really "atonal" sounding moment in the composition, since the octatonic collection has been partitioned here into mutually exclusive elements, neither of which can function as a tonic sonority in common practice.

The piano immediately tries to duplicate the clarinet's feat, and makes it as far as the high C#, which it pounds seven times in a vain effort to break through to the E. Failing to accomplish this, it comes plummeting down to the Bb where it had started. The B is taken up by the English horn in seeming mockery of the piano's efforts. The Bb is then maintained by the English horn as a kind of pedal-pivot against the piano's activity, through which a return to the tonic matrix (Collection III) will eventually be vouchsafed. Here we can try to make a long story short. As soon as the English horn has entered, the piano repeats and extends the cascade discussed above, illustrated in ex. 14. The extension consists of an extra quintolet inserted between the two original members of the cascade, which recapitulates the harmonic content of the Adagietto at ⑤. The effect of the middle quintolet is to add D and A to the B–F tritone that underlies the cascades to create a complex of tones that will eventually resolve to the tonic matrix (ex. 21).

The biggest "heteroclite" white-key / black-key roulade now begins, this time rather consistently accompanied by other instruments that ferret out its structural pitches. The harp in the measure before ⑥ does the best job of this, picking out all the Bs and Fs, the right hand of the piano filling out the white-key component with the aforementioned Ds and As to form a half-diminished chord which cries out for resolution to the C of Collection III. When resolution comes, though, it is clouded by suspension. The three notes from the white-key component of the roulade that make up the D-minor triad (filtered out and obsessively arpeggiated no fewer than nine times in succession in mm. 94–98) are filtered out again from the half-diminished chord in the last descending cascade and applied as an appoggiatura to the C-major component of the *Petrushka*-chord at ⑥.

The trumpets, blaring their fanfare of Petrushka's despair just as they did in the first section (⑤), now reinforce the appoggiatura progression with arpeggios on both the D-minor and C-major triads.[38] At ⑥ the complete half-diminished chord is applied to the C-major triad in the pianist's right hand, doubled by the cornets and trumpets, *fortissimo*. The F# triad, confined to the piano left hand and the string tremolo that mixes the two triads, can hardly be called the equal partner of the C triad any longer.[39] When the last progression (half-diminished seventh to C major) is repeated by the horns in the next measure (m. 108), the F# component of the *Petrushka* chord is dropped altogether, replaced in the accompanying bassoon by a G, which completes a dominant ninth whose resolution to C (albeit in $\frac{6}{4}$ position) suggests that the F# triad has been vanquished by the C, or that the diatonic collection has vanquished the octatonic. Or—to put it in terms of the 1910 *Konzertstück* as Stravinsky described its scenario years later—that the orchestra has vanquished the obstreperous "heteroclite" at the keyboard. The whole passage is summarized in ex. 22.[40]

The triumph, however, is fleeting. Like the eventual ghost of Petrushka himself, the *Petrushka* chord suddenly "comes to" in the same pair of clarinets that gave it birth (mm. 108–111)— up an octave in fact, alive and kicking. The F#, seizing its chance, dragoons its old associate G#—recall the original *Petrushka*-chord passage at ㊾—into providing it with a preparation. The G# arrives with the rest of "its" triad

[38]The device is repeated (transposed down a minor third, at which transposition the octatonic collection is invariant) at the reappearance of the Petrushka music at the end of the third tableau (㊆): B minor applied as appoggiatura to the A-major triad that is paired with a triad on Eb to complete the *Petrushka* harmony.

[39]On the other hand, Forte in *Contemporary Tone Structures* (New York, 1955) states flat out that "the tones [of the *Petrushka* chord] are not of equal structural value; F# is by far the more important" (p. 136). If I understand Forte's analysis aright, it is based on the assumption that "harmonic functions in *Petrushka* are entirely secondary to the linear movement" (p. 129). The linear movement that establishes F# for Forte as primary within the *Petrushka* complex is one that carries over from the first tableau (see p. 136 and the analytical chart on p. 187). But *Chez Pétrouchka* was composed before the first tableau and without premonition of it. Therefore, Forte's explicative construct is based on an ontological fallacy, at least as regards the analysis of *Chez Pétrouchka* on its own terms.

[40]The horn–bassoon music in the measure after ⑥ is so like the *garmoshka* (concertina) effects in the first and fourth tableaux of the as yet undreamed-of *Petrushka*, that one has to wonder whether it was a later interpolation. The relevant documents, in particular the 1910 sketchbook for the *Konzertstück*, are at present in private hands and inaccessible to scholarly investigation. See Vera Stravinsky and Robert Craft, *Stravinsky in Pictures and Documents* (New York, 1978), p. 612, n. 136.

mm. 89–90

Example 21

Example 22

in tow, the formerly triumphant C now transformed into a subservient, enharmonic B♯. F♯ gains the upper hand to end the piece with a cadence—or if not a cadence, at least what van den Toorn would call a suitable "terminating convenience"—that effectively tonicizes the note seemingly left for dead a few measures earlier.

V

I have cast the description of the final pages of *Chez Pétrouchka* in these blatantly anthropomorphic and academically disreputable terms, because I believe something of the sort was very much on Stravinsky's mind when he wrote his *Konzertstück*. His harmony is animistic; the *Petrushka* chord is conceived, nay motivated, by a sense of struggle, an antagonism of order and chaos reflecting the roles of pianist *vs.* orchestra. Once again I wish to emphasize that there is practical and poetic—if not "theoretical"—validity in the "polytonal" idea. We are meant to hear C and F♯ in terms of an active, not static, polarity—as competing centers, not merely as docile components of a single, static, octatonically referable "hyper-harmony," to borrow another apt term from Rimsky-Korsakov's vocabulary.[41] The recognition of the octatonic source of the *Petrushka* complex was a breakthrough in Stravinsky analysis, and is absolutely essential both to an understanding of

the techniques by means of which *Chez Pétrouchka* was composed, and to a proper assessment of Stravinsky's stylistic patrimony; still, to go on from there to assert that in consequence, "questions regarding the 'bitonality' or 'polytonality' of certain passages in [Stravinsky] can no longer be taken seriously,"[42] is to commit a genetic fallacy. The end of *Chez Pétrouchka* shows that the *Petrushka* chord is more than an embodiment of a tonal stalemate among centers "of equal and thus independent weight."[43] The centers are potentially equal and independent, to be sure, but in the actual composing of the individual piece, the weighting may be unequal indeed. Stravinsky, as heir to traditions of both octatonic and diatonic common practice, felt free to give the component subsets of the *Petrushka* chord independent diatonic support when it suited his purpose, as it did most spectacularly at the very end of the tableau.

Van den Toorn calls notions of bitonality or polytonality "real horrors of the musical imagination" that have "widely (and mercifully) been dismissed as too fantastic or illogical to be of assistance."[44] He relies on a comment of Allen Forte's, that polytonality is "a logical contradiction—for a tonality, by definition, requires the ascendancy of a single tone."[45] But this is mere legislative fiat; and in any case, Forte's definition of tonality here is an operational one, not a "logical" one. To deny the possibility of existence to a phenomenon simply by framing axioms so as to exclude it a priori will no more prevent a composer (Ives, for example, besides Stravinsky) from employing that phenomenon

[41]Letter to Semyon Kruglikov, 11 April 1902; Andrei Rimsky-Korsakov, *N. A. Rimskii-Korsakov: Zhizn' i tvorchestvo*, vol. V (Moscow, 1946), p. 67.

[42]Van den Toorn, *The Music of Igor Stravinsky*, p. 63.
[43]Berger, *Perspectives on Schoenberg and Stravinsky*, p. 137.
[44]Van den Toorn, p. 64.
[45]*Contemporary Tone Structures*, p. 137.

than man's theories of aerodynamics will prevent the bumblebee from flying. Forte's later comment, that "it's better to discard the old terminology of polychords and polyharmonies," since "you end up with something that's neither tonal nor atonal" even more strongly suggests an unwarranted apriority in the formulation of his categories.[46]

Van den Toorn objects further that "bitonality" logically implies the "simultaneous (tonally functional) unfolding of two keys," while the *Petrushka* chord is merely the superimposition of two chords without any implied tonal function.[47] He rejects the contention advanced here, that almost immediately after the initial presentation of the *Petrushka* chord ([49]) the C-major component is provided with a functional dominant. "In place of initiating a tonally functional definition of the 'key of C-major'," he writes, "the (G B D) triad merely prompts surface tendency-tone behavior on the part of F♯, A♯, and C♯ of the (F♯ A♯ C♯) component in relation to G, B, and D; that is to say, the F♯ tending to the G, the A♯ to the B, and the C♯ to the D."[48] Leaving aside the question as to whether van den Toorn's invocation of a triple leading-tone relationship does not in fact strengthen the functional status of the G-major chord, I will leave it to the reader to decide whether his analysis accurately describes the voice-leading situation between [49] and [51]. The only spot where, it could be argued, the F♯ resolves to G, the A♯ to B and the C♯ to the D, is in the cascade at [50], by which time the G–B–D configuration has been obviously associated with the C–E–G in the opposition of piano and clarinet. The ear has been thoroughly prejudiced to hear the cascade in terms of separate contents of the two hands: a cadential function in the right hand against a constant pedal harmony, or "irritant," in the left. Indeed, the initiation of "a tonally functional definition of the 'key of C-major' " is a self-evident feature of the musical surface, as I hear it, and its careful preparation, beginning at eleven after [49], is evidence of the composer's intention. This particular tonicization of C

within the *Petrushka* complex, moreover, is only one of a number of such functional applications, culminating in the ii–I and vii⁷–I progressions to C in [60] and [61].

Or will it be objected that ii–I is not a viable cadential function? If so, then we have deprived ourselves of any way of understanding the final cadence in the piece: F♯ major prepared by G♯ major. We would be in the position of those Rimsky-Korsakov epigones who railed at the incorrectness of Stravinsky's parallel triads. Conversely, if we were to argue that the G♯–F♯ progression is not a tonal cadence because Stravinsky's music, by definition, is "centric . . . but not tonally functional," then we would be in the equally untenable position of denying Stravinsky's connection to a background of common practice, despite his academic schooling at the hands of Rimsky-Korsakov and the latter's pupils. The "background theory," the very breakthrough Walsh and others have justly celebrated, would be sacrificed for the sake of a foolish consistency.

We would also be at a loss to understand perhaps the greatest stroke of genius in *Petrushka*—the inspired concluding pages of the fourth tableau, in which Petrushka's ghost rears up to jeer at the charlatan. More than once Stravinsky confessed his pride in having authored this music,[49] which takes the interpenetration of the octatonic and diatonic collections to a new level, unprecedented both within the ballet and within the traditions that fed it. The whole twenty-eight-measure passage, from the Lento after [130] to the end, consists of a magnificent composing-out of the ii–I progression we are calling cadential, now very explicitly associated with the *garmoshka* harmonies of the crowd scenes.

At first the D-minor chord is a mere appendage to the C-major triad that emerges from a *Petrushka* chord, as in the second tableau at [60]. At [131], the C–D oscillation takes on a new dimension. The C chord is given simultaneous upper and lower triadic neighbors, a direct reminiscence of the opening of the fourth tableau (and the end of second, too: the ii and the vii add up to the half-diminished vii⁷ at [61]). Surprisingly, the

---

[46]See the question-and-answer transcript following Forte, "Ives and Atonality," in *An Ives Celebration*, ed. H. Wiley Hitchcock and Vivian Perlis (Urbana, 1974), pp. 185–86.
[47]*The Music of Igor Stravinsky*, p. 64.
[48]Ibid.

[49]*Expositions and Developments*, p. 137; *Memories and Commentaries* (Berkeley and Los Angeles, 1981), p. 67: "it is obvious to any perceptive musician that the best pages in *Petroushka* are the last."

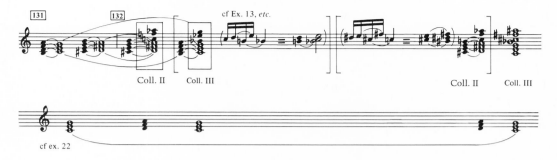

Example 23

whole complex is then jacked up a whole step, as if to tonicize the D. (This had been the tonality at the opening of the tableau, and thus the allusion may have a recapitulatory aspect.) After the two major triads on D and C have gone through another oscillation, each accompanied by its own set of double neighbors, the D complex is sustained. And all at once Petrushka's ghost appears—in a piercing trumpet arpeggio on the notes of the F-minor triad. Now F minor is part of the same octatonic *complexe sonore* as D major, and this puts the final stamp of certainty (if one is still needed) on Stravinsky's consciousness of the octatonic complex as a referential set. For only by conceptualizing the collection in its typically Rimskian partition would the minor-third relationship have occurred to Stravinsky as a viable substitute for the tritone of the original *Petrushka*-chord complex.

The ascending F-minor trumpet arpeggio is answered by a descending arpeggio on the notes of the E♭-major triad, the accompanying *garmoshka* harmony simultaneously slipping down to the original C major / D minor. As summarized in ex. 23, the whole "apparition" is a muted, varied and harmonically enriched reprise of the "despair" music at 60 in the second tableau, where the trumpets and cornets had blared their woe in D-minor (ascending) and C-major (descending) arpeggios, while the accompanying harmony D minor had been applied as an appoggiatura to the C major of the *Petrushka* chord, the constant F♯ triad acting as the harmonic glue. In the reprise, we now have an oscillation of two different octatonic complexes—Collection II, which contains the D- and F-minor triads, and which had furnished the harmony for the *ad libitum* cadenzas in *Chez Pétrouchka*, acting as cadential supertonic to Collection III, the old tonic matrix of *Chez Pétrouchka*. And both collections are made to accommodate diatonic double appoggiaturas (the *garmoshka* effect) such as was represented by the D-minor triad alone in the second tableau: E minor / C♯ diminished to D in the Collection II complex, and D minor / diminished to C in Collection III.

In the orchestral score, the arpeggios (played on transposing instruments) are spelled conventionally within the keys of the transposition. In the contemporaneous piano four-hands reduction, however, Stravinsky's spelling of the arpeggios at 132 amounts to an analysis. They are spelled F–G♯–C and D♯–G–B♭ respectively, in fastidious reflection of their place within their respective octatonic scales. The spelling tips us off that these are embellishing harmonies, to be heard as subordinate to the chords that are provided with diatonic, quasi-cadential neighbors—i.e., D and C, with C enjoying priority by analogy with the second tableau at 60, as the center of the complex to which the descending arpeggio is applied.

And then, just as in *Chez Pétrouchka*, the hegemony of C is challenged at the last minute by its octatonic antipode F♯. This is very adroitly signalled in the four-hands arrangement by means of the peremptory respelling of the C as B♯ the moment the original *Petrushka* chord is heard for the last time (six measures before the end). After one last attempt at resurgence, again accompanied by its attendant supertonic in the horns, the C is finally dislodged by the F♯ in the final, famously enigmatic (Diaghilev: "But you finish with a question?"[50]) pizzicati. The approach to F♯ by a direct tritone leap down from C, moreover, mirrors the pizzicato descent *from* F♯ by which C has been confirmed as tonic at the very beginning of the "apparition" coda (three before 131).

In the end, the best one can do, in answer to the question "What is the key of *Petrushka*?", is to say "Collection III." It is more than a collection, though: if key means anything at all, then in this ballet it is a key; for it governs a hierarchy of pitches—contextually established, to be sure, but eminently consistent and regular.

[50]Igor Stravinsky and Robert Craft, *Retrospectives and Conclusions* (New York, 1969), p. 265.

Chez Pétrouchka, Summary

Within *Chez Pétrouchka*, at least, Collection III is a much more stable referent than the transient diatonic collections that supplant it in the middle sections, and in this Stravinsky has neatly reversed the perspective encountered in *Shéhérazade*, where the diatonic keys were stable and the octatonic passages fugitive (chiefly "modulatory"). In *Petrushka*, Collection III is a point of harmonic reference from which departures and to which returns are effected by a variety of clearly articulated techniques. These departures and returns, which are of measurable distance, organize very lengthy spans indeed. No, not every pitch in *Petrushka* is referable to Collection III. But then, there are plenty of black keys in the "Jupiter" Symphony.

Liszt's Experimental Idiom and Twentieth-Century Music

ALLEN FORTE

The question of historical precedents for the remarkable new music that suddenly—or so it seemed to contemporaries—appeared on the scene in 1908–09 has always fascinated musicians. The question has necessarily been reformulated, however, as a result of changes in theoretical and analytical approaches over the last fifty years or so. While older studies, such as

Ernst Kurth's *Romantische Harmonik*, suggested in somewhat less-than-precise terms the existence of certain evolutionary processes in late nineteenth-century music, recent work has provided more specific analytical information in an effort to establish a firm technical basis for a better understanding of the emergence of the music of the twentieth-century avant garde.[1]

In this emergent phase (one hesitates even to suggest that it was any kind of orderly evolu-

I am indebted to the American Council of Learned Societies and to the Nationale Forschungs- und Gedenkstätten der Klassischen Literatur in Weimar, Goethe- und Schiller-Archiv, for the opportunity in October 1984 to study Liszt's manuscripts, sketches, and letters. For bibliographical assistance my thanks to Judith Silber. Liszt's sketches published by kind permission of the Goethe- und Schiller-Archiv, Weimar.

Musical examples for this article were prepared by David Budmen.

[1] Ernst Kurth, *Romantische Harmonik und ihre Krise in Wagners "Tristan"* (Berlin, 1923). See especially pp. 183–228. Two more recent studies are relevant: James M. Baker, *Alexander Scriabin: The Transition from Tonality to Atonality* (Ph.D. diss., Yale University, 1977), and Allen Forte, "Schoenberg's Creative Evolution: The Path to Atonality," *Musical Quarterly* 64 (1978), 133–76.

tionary progression) the music of Liszt appears to have played an important precursory role. Indeed, there is a rather extensive specialized literature concerned with what is regarded as his main contribution to this transition, the late music (after 1880), and with certain of its striking surface features, such as the "augmented triad" and various exotic scales.

In view of these writings—many of which will be cited in the course of this article—it may seem presumptuous to address, once again, the topic of Liszt's music as precursor of early twentieth-century music. Still, careful study based upon more effective analytical techniques may produce a deeper and more comprehensive view of the music of Liszt that is most closely related to that of the early twentieth century, the music composed in what I shall call his experimental idiom.

Under the term "experimental" I mean to include not only the radical late works, but also segments of earlier works, extending back into the pre-Weimar period, before 1848. This view is based upon the assumption that there are two general categories of music represented in Liszt's œuvre: the traditional music of triadic tonality and the experimental music, which represents innovational departures from the norms of tonal syntax. In the latter there is an increasingly stronger movement toward a different sphere of sonic organization, one that came into full view some twenty-three years after Liszt's death in the new music of Bartók, Schoenberg, Webern, Scriabin, and Stravinsky.

It is not my intention to assert that there is a direct connection between Liszt's non-traditional music and the music of the avant-garde composers of the early twentieth century, but rather to show that when he created music that was remarkably similar in specific general structural aspects to the innovative music that followed the *Jahrhundertwende*, he anticipated a significant historical development. This disclaimer requires qualification, however, since, with the exception of the late works (most of which were unpublished and unperformed when the twentieth-century avant garde appeared on the scene), Liszt's music forms part of the repertory of concert music of the later nineteenth century and was known to Schoenberg, Bartók, and others. Yet, in the absence of explicit testimonials from those composers, the extent to which its unusual features exerted influence upon them remains moot.[2]

Music in the experimental idiom exhibits specific surface characteristics. For example, it is often recitative-like, occurring in the introductions to such longer works as the last tone-poem, *Hamlet*. Very often it is threnodic in quality, even when the title does not explicitly indicate an elegiac program, as it does in *Am Grabe Richard Wagners*. Finally, there is the definite impression that a specific tonal focus is in abeyance, or has at least become very attenuated—a feature that has been observed by other writers. Often the absence of a key signature underscores this characteristic, even though a conventional key signature may appear later in the music when the more traditional idiom enters.

This brief description of some of the general surface characteristics of the experimental idiom is intended only as the most casual kind of introduction to this extraordinary music. Far more penetrating analysis is required to reveal its inner workings.

That statement leads naturally to a brief overview of published analytical work relevant to the present study. Within this extensive literature, the writings that relate most directly to the present one are those by James M. Baker, Robert P. Morgan, R. Larry Todd, and Paul Wilson.[3] It is no accident that these are all American authors whose work reflects, to a

[2]Both Schoenberg and Bartók published laudatory essays on Liszt in the centennial year 1911, some time after both had broken with traditional modes of composition. Of these, the Schoenberg essay is the more suggestive. He writes, for example: "A man like this is no longer an artist, but something greater: a prophet" ("Ein solcher Mensch ist nicht mehr ein Künstler, sondern bald etwas Grösseres: ein Prophet"). Arnold Schoenberg, "Franz Liszts Werk und Wesen," *Allgemeine Musik-Zeitung* 38 (1911), 1009–13, English trans. in *Style and Idea*, ed. Leonard Stein (New York, 1975), 442–47; Béla Bartók, "Liszt zenéje és a mai közönség," *Népművelés* (Budapest), 1911, pub. in English as "Liszt's Music and Our Contemporary Public," *New Hungarian Quarterly* 2 (1961), 5–8. In this encomium, Bartók deplores the public's failure to perceive Liszt's true worth and writes of Liszt's "almost fanatical striving for what is new and rare" (p. 6).
[3]Baker, *Scriabin*; Robert P. Morgan, "Dissonant Prolongations: Theoretical and Compositional Precedents," *Journal of Music Theory* 20 (1976), 49–91; R. Larry Todd, "Liszt, Fantasy and Fugue for Organ on 'Ad nos, ad salutarem undam'," *19th-Cen Mus* 4 (1981), 250-61; Paul Wilson, "Concepts of Prolongation and Bartók's Opus 20," *Music Theory Spectrum* 6 (1984), 78-89.

greater or lesser degree, the influence of Heinrich Schenker.[4] Additional references to their work as well as to the work of other scholars will appear at appropriate points below.

In general, much of the literature that touches upon aspects of the experimental idiom (primarily the late piano music, as noted above) is disappointing. Perhaps the most obvious of the defects is the virtual absence of studies of complete compositions.[5] Moreover, although many authors assert that the music has atonal characteristics, they do not pursue the technical implications of such an assertion.[6] In the worst cases, the studies are desultory, impressionistic, and based upon models that are demonstrably inappropriate in that they do not produce substantive analytical results.[7] Prime examples of the latter are the recent Hungarian writings based upon the "scalar" approach,[8] a

literature also often burdened with political and ethnic platitudes.[9]

Of greater significance, however, is the general disregard of the concept of structural levels and its expression in large-scale linear motions as they relate to details of structure—a disregard that goes along with a seeming preoccupation with the identification of certain easily recognized entities, notably, the "augmented triad," the "diminished seventh chord," the whole-tone scale, and the "Hungarian" scale. Once these components have been identified, no further conclusions ensue. Exceptions to this criticism, in addition to the publications by Morgan and Todd cited in footnote 3, will be mentioned as we proceed.

The analytical technique employed in the present study derives from, but is not identical to, the linear methods of Heinrich Schenker. It also incorporates pitch-class set analysis, which offers a range of interpretive tools that seem to be effective in illuminating the innovative music that is the main topic of this essay.[10] Since pitch-class set names are now used more and more in the literature, it seems that no explanation is required here. However, I refer those readers who wish an introduction to this nomenclature to my study, *The Structure of Atonal Music*, pp. 11–13 (see fn. 10). Although no attempt has been made in this article to be absolutely rigorous in the application of pitch-class set names, so that informal designations such as "diminished triad" and "augmented triad" may be used in place of 3-10 and 3-12, respectively, the reader should bear in mind that those traditional rubrics may imply certain tonal functions, whereas pitch-class set names are neutral. In addition, the reader will see that there are many harmonic formations in the composer's experimental music that lack any such familiar traditional names. In such cases,

[4]However, examples of Liszt's music, experimental or otherwise, are virtually absent from Schenker's own writings. Exceptions are his discussions of two passages from the Piano Sonata (vis-à-vis modal attributes) and one from the ninth of the Transcendental Etudes. See Heinrich Schenker, *Neue Musikalische Theorien und Phantasien*, Band I: *Harmonielehre* (Stuttgart and Berlin, 1906), pp. 94, 139, 403. An excellent study of Liszt's tonal music, using Schenkerian methods, may be found in David Damschroder, *The Structural Foundations of "The Music of the Future"* (Ph.D. diss., Yale University, 1981).

[5]Morgan and Todd, the only authors cited in fn. 3 who deal directly with Liszt, are exempt from this criticism.

[6]The earliest contribution to this tradition would appear to be Werner Danckert, "Liszt als Vorläufer des musikalischen Impressionismus," *Die Musik* 21 (1928–29), 341–44. Then, around 1950, English and French writers gave the late music of Liszt some attention: William Yeomans, "The Late Piano Works of Liszt," *Monthly Musical Record* 79 (1949), 31–37; René Leibowitz, *L'Évolution de la musique de Bach à Schoenberg* (Paris, 1951), ch. 7: "Les Prophéties de Franz Liszt"; Humphrey Searle, "Liszt's Final Period (1860–1886)," *Proceedings of the Royal Music Association* 78 (1951–52), 67–81.

[7]Among recent publications is an article by Bengt Johnsson, "Modernities in Liszt's Works," *Svensk Tidskrift för Musik-Forskning* 46 (1964), 83–117, which, although it forgoes in-depth analytical techniques and the results those might afford, offers interesting comments on many pieces.

[8]See Lajos Bardos, "Ferenc Liszt, the Innovator," *Studia Musicologica* 17 (1975), 3–38; and "Die volksmusikalischen Tonleitern bei Liszt," in *Franz Liszt: Beiträge von ungarischen Autoren*, ed. Klara Hamburger (Budapest, 1978); Zoltan Gárdonyi, "Neue Tonleiter- Sequenztypen in Liszts Frühwerken," *Studia musicologica* 11 (1969), 169–99. Of the fourteen scales codified by Bardos in "Die volks-musikalischen Tonleitern bei Liszt," five are reducible to set class 7-32, one of the basic harmonies in Stravinsky's *Rite of Spring*.

[9]For example, on p. 67 of Bence Szabolcsi, *The Twilight of Ferenc Liszt* (Budapest, 1959), we find: "Thus the old Liszt's art becomes a phantastic synthesis of Hungarian and Russian, French and German, Italian and Gregorian elements, a synthesis which is, however, pervaded by an utterly new, revolutionary, sharp [sic] East-European atmosphere."

[10] Heinrich Schenker, *Free Composition*, trans. and ed. Ernst Oster (New York, 1979). Allen Forte, *The Structure of Atonal Music* (New Haven and London, 1973).

the use of pitch-class set names is not only a convenience, but perhaps also a necessity.[11]

The following study contains three main sections. In the first, examples of Liszt's experimental idiom will be discussed through excerpts from his early music. In the second and larger section, his late visionary music provides excerpts for analytical discussion. The third section consists of an analysis of an entire composition, well known as an example of Liszt's most advanced writing, the piano piece *Nuages gris*.[12] It is hoped that these interdependent sections will carry out the two-fold goal of the article: to examine in some detail the structure of the composer's experimental music and to point out correspondences that it bears to music of the early twentieth-century avant garde.

Before we proceed to matters analytical in connection with the musical examples, a word about the latter is in order. Because space limitations do not allow for the presentation of complete scores, most of the musical illustrations consist of analytical sketches in quasi-Schenkerian notation annotated with pitch-class set names and other symbols. The main part of the article is based upon these sketches.

THE EXPERIMENTAL IDIOM IN THE EARLY WORKS

Vallée d'Obermann (1855). As an early instance of the experimental idiom, let us consider the second version of the piano composition *Vallée d'Obermann*, which appeared in the first volume of *Années de pèlerinage*, though its composition (or—in the case of most of the numbers—recomposition) goes back half a dozen years. The first version, which was composed in 1835–36 and is the longest work in the *Album d'un voyageur*, differs radically from the recomposed version, as can be seen in ex. 1. Indeed, the two versions share only certain basic motives at the foreground level, notably the melodic motive that spans a minor third. In ex. 1a, which follows a porten-

tous introduction of twenty-one bars, the motive occurs in the tenor, initiating the long thematic scalar figure based upon the minor-seventh chord in the right-hand accompaniment. After the resolution upon the tonic triad in m. 2 a consequent phrase of two bars leads to the mediant harmony, G major, a completely traditional progression.

In ex. 1b, the first four bars of the recomposed version, the bass has vanished (to return in m. 34) and a chromatic passing tone, A♯, is introduced to delay the entry of the tonic triad. However, the most striking difference between the two versions is seen in the consequent phrase, which ended on the mediant harmony in the original version and which now modulates to G minor, with a suspended seventh delaying the tonic note in the upper voice. This modulatory process continues over the next four-measure group, producing the large-scale motions shown in ex. 2. (The bass from m. 34 is included there, enclosed in brackets.)

Overlaid on the unusual tonal organization of this opening music (ex. 2) is an analysis that shows by means of beams connecting stemmed noteheads the basic pitch-class set structures that are formed in the middleground. The upper voice forms the trichord 3-10 (the "diminished triad"), as does the bass, while the tenor melody in each four-measure group sets forth a form of the trichord 3-12 (the "augmented triad"). With reference to Liszt's experimental music, the analytical selection of these harmonies requires little justification, as will be substantiated below.[13]

Trichords 3-10 and 3-12 also occur in the contrapuntal detail of ex. 2. Specifically, 3-12 is formed in m. 9 by the pitches (from the bass up) A–C♯–E♯; 3-10 follows, in m. 10, as G♯–B–E♯. When F♯ in m. 9 is added to the 3-12 trichord, tetrachord 4-19 results. Similarly, when E is added to 3-10 in m. 10, tetrachord 4-18 ensues. In both cases these pitch-class sets come into existence as a result of decorative motion in the foreground: the 5–6 suspension in m. 9 brings 4-19 into play, while the appoggiatura E in m. 10 forms 4-18 with 3-10. Both of these tetrachordal sonorities play a fundamental role in Liszt's experimental idiom, as does the five-note sonority 5-31, which comprises the total content of m. 10 in ex. 2.[14]

Of all the foreground sonorities in the opening music of this composition, perhaps the most characteristic is 4-26, the tetrachord in the right-hand part of m. 1, duplicated a minor third higher in m. 5. In traditional nomenclature this is a minor-seventh chord. Here, in the absence of a clear-cut harmonic function, consideration of its intervallic organization

[11]See, however, Serge Gut, *Franz Liszt: Éléments du langage musical* (Paris, 1975), in which the author presents a method of harmonic analysis that features multiply altered chords and polyharmony with accompanying Roman numerals and figured bass symbols. However attractive this alternative might be to those oriented exclusively to vertical slices of music, it should be recognized that analysis carried out on this basis alone may preclude serious consideration of other structural spans and levels.

[12]As an indication of the attention that this short work has recently received we note that it is now included in a standard textbook: Donald Jay Grout, *A History of Western Music*, 3rd edn. with Claude V. Palisca (New York, 1980), p. 583.

[13]See Todd, "Liszt, Fantasy and Fugue," in which the author points out long-range relations involving the diminished triad.

[14]Set 5-31 has long attracted the attention of students of nineteenth-century music. For example, Kurth (*Romantische Harmonik*, p. 412) cites an instance from Strauss's *Salome*, describing it as a "combination of fundamental chord with the diminished-seventh chord in C minor."

Example 1: *Vallée d'Obermann*

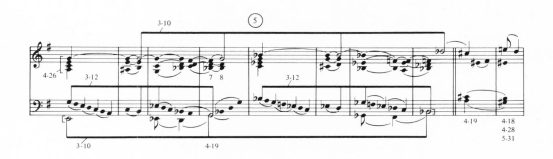

Example 2: *Vallée d'Obermann*, second version

seems more to the point, and therefore we observe that pitch-class set 4-26 is one of the thirteen symmetrical tetrachords—in this case symmetric about the major third C—E or the major second G—A. Although the composer's harmonic palette is by no means restricted to such symmetrical sonorities, he did use them frequently in the experimental music. In the present instance, the minor and major third constituents of 4-26 relate directly to the trichords 3-10 (minor thirds) and 3-12 (major thirds) and thus offer a cogent initial example of the relation between detail and motions of larger span that is so typical of Liszt's experimental works, as well as a demonstration of the unification of harmony that is so characteristic of his experimental idiom.

Set 4-26 is also prominent in other works of Liszt, such as *Les Préludes* (1848); it is endemic to *fin-de-siècle* art music. For example, it is the opening sonority in Schoenberg's *Gurrelieder*, and, in addition, the prelude to part II of that work is remarkably Lisztian from the harmonic standpoint, featuring tetrachords 4-20 and 4-24, the latter a whole-tone tetrachord which incorporates 3-12. Pitch-class set 4-26 also occurs throughout Berg's *Wozzeck*, where it serves as one of the primary musical symbols of Marie; see act I, sc. 3, where it is heard precisely at the end of Marie's long aria (the lullaby). While interesting examples of such correspondences are legion, correspondences of larger scale are even more intriguing, and characteristic instances of those will be pointed out as we proceed.

To sum up, the analysis presented in ex. 2 shows prolongations at two structural levels. Over the span of the eight-measure phrase, the bass projects 3-10, while within this grouping the inner voice projects a form of 3-12 over each four-measure constituent, creating a remarkable and completely innovative structure and providing, for the purposes of this article, an early example of the way in which the composer combined these two radically different sonorities over long spans of music in the experimental idiom.[15]

***Hamlet* (1858).** The tonal orientation of the introduction to the tone-poem *Hamlet* (ex. 3) is clearly governed by the B-minor tonic triad upon which the work is based, as indicated by the key signature. Although the introduction strongly hints at that centric sonority, mainly by way of the bass motion F♯—B, its main interest lies in the projection of structures theoretically outside the traditional tonal sphere.[16]

The large-scale upper voice motion comprises pitch-class set 3-12, the pitches E♭—G—B shown as the stemmed and beamed open noteheads in ex. 3. Attached to the opening E♭ is again 3-12, graphed as stemmed and beamed closed noteheads. With respect to pitch class this form of 3-12 is identical to the one of larger scale in the upper voice, exemplifying the correspondence of musical spans found in many compositions of the early twentieth century. The *Bagatelles*, Bartók's op. 6, offer many examples of more complex, but related, correspondences, involving more than one set class—for example no. 8 of that work. It is not difficult to imagine these Lisztian structures as prototypes, in the metaphorical sense, of course, of such avant-garde musical phenomena.

At m. 5 the surface configurations suggest for a moment that the passage is to be merely a transposed replica of the music that begins in m. 1. This, however, is not the case, for instead of 3-12, 3-10 now unfolds, a demonstration of the striking ways in which the composer often juxtaposes these two sonorities (cf. ex. 2). Here and elsewhere in the work the two sonorities are, of course, musical emblems associated with the program.

Closer study of ex. 3 reveals that the lower-level trichords 3-12 and 3-10 do not occur in isolation. Set 3-12 has an "upper neighbor note," C, attached to its last component, while 3-10 has a "lower neighbor note," D♯, attached to its last component. These half-step motives are labelled *a* and *a'* on ex. 3. As indicated, they combine with 3-12 and 3-10 to form 4-19 and 4-18, respectively. This is but one instance of a general aspect of Liszt's harmonic language in the experimental idiom: tetrachords 4-18 and 4-19 are fundamental components of much of that music.[17] This feature seems to have escaped the attention of students of Liszt's music in the experimental idiom. Other important aspects, such as the large-scale linear-harmonic projections that seem to be universal

[15]Several authors have recognized the important role the augmented triad assumed in music of the later nineteenth century. Among these are Robert P. Morgan ("Dissonant Prolongations") and Gregory Proctor, *Technical Bases of Nineteenth-Century Chromatic Tonality: A Study in Chromaticism* (Ph.D. diss., Princeton University, 1978).

[16]In "Franz Liszt und die Vorgeschichte der Neuen Musik," *Neue Zeitschrift für Musik* 122 (1961), 387–91, Carl Dahlhaus touches upon foreground harmonic relations in the introduction to *Hamlet* and states: "An attempt to refer

every harmonic event to B minor would be a distortion." See also his *Between Romanticism and Modernism: Four Studies in Music of the Later Nineteenth Century*, tr. Mary Whittall (Berkeley and Los Angeles, 1980), pp. 46–47.

[17]Instances of 4-19 are to be found everywhere in the nontonal music of the early twentieth century. Indeed, if there is a single harmony that is emblematic of that music it is 4-19. A few occurrences in familiar works are: the "*Wir arme Leut*'" motive in Berg's *Wozzeck* (see Janet Schmalfeldt, *Berg's* Wozzeck: *Harmonic Language and Dramatic Design* [New Haven and London, 1983], p. 87); Bartók, Fourteen Bagatelles, op. 6 (see James E. Woodward, "Understanding Bartók's Bagatelle, Op. 6/9," *Indiana Theory Review* 4 [1981], 11–32); Stravinsky, *The Rite of Spring* (see Allen Forte, *The Harmonic Organization of* The Rite of Spring [New Haven and London, 1978], p. 104); and Scriabin, Sonata No. 7 ("White Mass"), upper voice of mm. 1–3. Set 4-18 is almost as prominent in this repertory. It is, for example, a major component of Stravinsky's *Petrouchka*, and it occurs at the very beginning and throughout Schoenberg's *Pierrot Lunaire*, a work in which 3-10 (4-18) and 3-12 (4-19) are primary harmonic symbols.

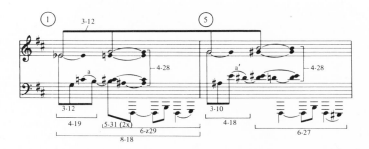

Example 3: *Hamlet*

in this music, have also gone virtually unrecognized.[18]

The passage from *Hamlet* (ex. 3) suggests even more strongly than did ex. 1 that as early as the Weimar period, and probably even before, Liszt was composing with tetrachords that are essentially non-tonal in nature, independent sonic objects that are not treated according to the syntactic rules of tonic-dominant tonality. With the advent of atonal and other non-tonal music around 1908, the tetrachord became the basic harmonic building block of new music, replacing the triad in that role. Liszt had already made that replacement in the music of his experimental idiom shortly after the middle of the nineteenth century, at the latest.[19]

Among the other twentieth-century harmonies in the excerpt shown in ex. 3 is the pentad 5-31, mentioned earlier (see fn. 13). This occurs in two ways: first, as the "diminished seventh chord," 4-28, plus bass F♯; second, as that same chord plus bass B. Thus, the change of bass from F♯ to B alters the pitch content but does not change the harmony (set class). This remarkable passage, which is not at all atypical of the experimental idiom, could serve as a model for many in Schoenberg's atonal or in Stravinsky's early non-tonal works.[20]

The two hexachords in ex. 3, labelled 6-z29 and 6-27, reflect a still larger sphere of harmonic activity, the octatonic.[21] Extended discussion of this aspect of the composer's experimental idiom as well as consideration of the octad 8-18 here, as an instance of complementation, is reserved for a subsequent part of this article.

***Blume und Duft* (1860).** The song *Blume und Duft*, a striking instance of the experimental music of Liszt, has attracted attention recently and deserves additional study.[22] Example 4 shows some of the organizational features of the song.

Readers conversant with the lore of pitch-class sets will recognize immediately that all of the sets in the three parts of the example (a, b, and c) are subsumed by the octatonic collection, pitch-class set 8-28. However, as remarked above, more extended discussion of this set with respect to Liszt's music will be postponed until later, since the reader can understand the essentials of the illustration here without being subjected to theoretical digressions.

Example 4a is an analysis of the introductory music, mm. 1–4. This reading avoids the obvious "dominant seventh" label that might be attached to the four verticals, a label that has no analytical consequences whatsoever since the sonorities so designated play no functional role within a tonality, explicit or implied. (For a strikingly similar instance of

[18]However, Morgan ("Dissonant Prolongations") and Todd ("Liszt, Fantasy and Fugue") have recognized large-scale motions, as have the following authors, to whom we will refer again later: Howard Cinnamon, "Tonal Structure and Voice-Leading in Liszt's 'Blume und Duft' " *In Theory Only* 6 (1982), 12–24, and Edwin Hantz, "Motivic and Structural Unity in Liszt's 'Blume und Duft'," *In Theory Only* 6 (1982), 3–11.

[19]See Istvan Szelényi, "Der unbekannte Liszt," *Studia musicologica* 5 (1963), 311–31, for speculations on the role that Liszt's study of Greek theory and scales (especially tetrachords, p. 314) may have played in his composing. In Lina Ramann, *Lisztiana; Erinnerungen an Franz Liszt (1873–1886)* (Mainz, 1983), pp. 317–18, is an amusing account of Liszt's outrage upon learning that the "Herren von der Theorie" had asserted that the "Hungarian" scale was not of Indian origin, hence, presumably, not of sufficiently respectable antiquity.

[20]See Forte, *Structure*, ex. 43, and *Harmonic Organization*, ex. 54 for examples in Schoenberg and Stravinsky, respectively.

[21]See Pieter C. van den Toorn, *The Music of Igor Stravinsky* (New Haven and London, 1983), pp. 48–60, for an extended theoretical exposition of the octatonic collection with reference to the music of Stravinsky.

[22]The two articles on this song cited in fn. 18 present analyses and analytical graphs. Of the two, Cinnamon's is the more conservative, complete with Roman numerals. Hantz deals with "harmonic ambiguity" and emphasizes the role of "symmetrical harmonic structures," asserting that "the home chord, . . . the Urklang, is an augmented triad" (p. 11). Neither author recognizes the octatonic component, and both seem to regard the song as a kind of aberration within Liszt's œuvre. But the experimental idiom is clearly displayed not only by *Blume und Duft*, but also by other Liszt Lieder, such as *Ein Fichtenbaum* (c. 1855), in which 4-19 is prominent, and, even earlier, by *Es Rauschen die Winde* (c. 1845), where both 4-19 and 4-18 occur in the foreground.

the non-functional use of a "dominant seventh" chord [4-27] in a non-tonal passage, see Forte, *Harmonic Organization*, ex. 60; there 4-27 is a subset of 8-28, the octatonic collection.) Indeed, these verticals group in pairs, as indicated, to form the hexachordal succession 6-27/6-27 in which the second form of 6-27 is a transposition of the first up three semitones. In each case, 6-27 includes a form of 4-18, presented as a pair of sonorities in the upper voices. Perhaps most interesting, however, is the outer-voice configuration shown in example 4b: not only does the tetrachord 4-3 unfold in the horizontal dimension (the upper form a minor third higher than the lower if they are compared in unordered form), but also each pair of components in the vertical dimension sums to that set class (4-3). And again, those two forms of 4-3 are transpositionally related by a minor third, since the second dyad in the lower part repeats the first dyad in the upper part.

The extent to which the composer was aware of all these relations is perhaps moot. However, this passage, and the entire song, prefigure the modern music of his very last period, a period in which the evidence of conscious manipulation of such structural properties seems incontrovertible. Liszt was certainly aware of the unusual nature of his experimental music; consider the amusingly defiant gloss that appears in his handwriting at the end of the manuscript of the experimental work, *Ossa arida* (1879), with a final shift into Latin for added emphasis:

Professors and apostles of the conservatories most strongly disapprove of the dissonance of the continuous thirds-construction of the first twenty bars, which is not yet customary. Nevertheless, so has he written. Liszt (Villa d'Este, 18–21 October 79).

(Professoren und Jünger der Conservatorien haben die noch nicht gebräuchlichen [sic] Dissonanz des fortgesetzen [sic] terzenweisen Aufbau der 20 ersten Takte gründlichst zu missbilligen: nichts destoweniger scripsit.)

Example 4c extracts still another octatonic con-

figuration from *Blume und Duft,* the climactic passage of the song in mm. 18–20, where the voice expresses pitch-class set 4-3 (D♯–E–F♯–G) followed by C♯. Unlike the passage in ex. 4a, the music in ex. 4c consists of the complete octatonic collection, 8-28. It might well serve as a model for a passage in a work by Stravinsky around the time of *Firebird*.

Blume und Duft shares a notational characteristic with much of the other experimental music, one that was mentioned earlier: it lacks a key signature until the last four measures, where the composer adds a signature of four flats. Although the absence of a key signature alone does not support a non-tonal reading, just as the presence of a key signature does not rule out such an interpretation, it does provide an interesting and provocative clue to the composer's experimental musical thought.

Mignons Lied (Kennst du das Land?).

Mignons Lied was composed in 1842 and revised and arranged for orchestra in 1860. In the course of revising, Liszt wrote an introduction which, like the beginning of *Vallée d'Obermann*, offers the student of his music a lucid instance of his experimental thought. Example 5 shows 4-18 (by now a tetrachord familiar to the reader) in the context of a standard tonal configuration, the dominant seventh chord in the key of F♯ major. As indicated, the two successive forms of 4-18 a major sixth apart sum to the hexachord 6-27. In this setting the origin of 4-18 can be traced to the thematic sonority, the chord that sets the word *du*. This sonority, 5-22, has a special subset structure: of its five tetrachords two are of class 4-18 and two are of class 4-19—both highly characteristic of the experimental idiom, as noted earlier. (The remaining tetrachord of 5-22 is 4-8, also a staple component of Liszt's harmonic palette.) As can be seen on example 5, the upper tetrachord of 5-22 is a form of 4-18, a form identical to the second tetrachord in the introduction. Moreover, the lower tetrachord in 5-22 is also a form of 4-18, inversionally equivalent to the upper tetrachord transposed by a major third. The two forms share trichord 3-10, the diminished triad, B–D–E♯.

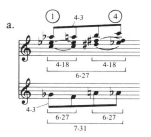

Example 4: *Blume und Duft*

Example 5: *Mignon*, orchestral arrangement

Thus, the first two phrases of the introduction comprise a linearization of the vertical tetrachordal subsets of the thematic sonority—a remarkable prefiguration of a process that can be observed in much of the non-tonal music of the early twentieth century.[23] In 5-22, 4-19 occurs twice as a non-contiguous formation, a secondary component in this case. It is interesting to recall that 4-18 contains 3-10 and 4-19 contains 3-12, representing the diminished triad and augmented triad spheres of harmonic activity, respectively. The combination of 4-18 and 4-19 in pentad 5-22 is a very special circumstance on other grounds too, since among all the pentads only 5-22 and 5-26 contain both 3-10 and 3-12.

***Faust* Symphony (1854–57).** Many surveys of Liszt's music, as well as specialized articles that touch on the experimental music, cite the beginning of the Faust Symphony for its daring use of the augmented triad.[24] Yet not one of these analyses incorporates the opening A♭ in violas and cellos, which is marked *ff* and is to be played with downbow (ex. 6). Set 4-19 results when this initial A♭ is followed by 3-12, G–B–E♭, after which the remaining three forms of 3-12 complete the total chromatic (with one repetition). Because of a special chromatic relation between 3-12 and 4-19, each of the augmented triads expands to a form of 4-19, so that the subject, after the initial form of 4-19, consists of the series of interlocking forms of that tetrachord—seven in all, as shown in ex. 6. The

subject also exhibits harmonies larger than the tetrachord. As shown at the bottom of ex. 6, the eighth rests partition the subject into sets 7-21 and 6-20; both collections are common in early twentieth-century music, especially in the works of Bartók and Schoenberg.[25] Thus, although 3-12 is the most obvious surface feature of the subject, the initial A♭ generates a structure of considerably greater intricacy, the fundamental component of which is the tetrachord so basic to the composer's experimental idiom, 4-19.

LATE MUSIC IN THE EXPERIMENTAL IDIOM[26]

Before we move to the main part of this article, devoted to exs. 7–10, some informal theoretical information about relations among sets should be set forth. Among these, the most important for the present study is the inclusion relation.[27] We have already seen an illustration of this:

[23]See, for example, George Perle's analysis of Webern's Five Pieces for String Quartet, op. 5, no. 4, in *Serial Composition and Atonality*, 2nd edn. (Berkeley and Los Angeles, 1968), p. 16.

[24]See László Somfai, "Die Metamorphose der 'Faust-Symphonie' von Liszt," *Studia musicologica* 5 (1961), 283–93. In this article, which includes a study of the compositional sketches, Somfai asserts that the theme of the introduction is "the first known dodecaphonic melody in music history" (p. 286), a view elaborated by Fred Ritzel in "Materialdenken bei Liszt: eine Untersuchung des 'Zwölftonthemas' der Faust-Symphonie," *Die Musikforschung* 20 (1967), 289–94.

[25]For an example from Bartók, see Paul F. Wilson, "Atonality and Structure," p. 164. Set 6-20 is everywhere in Schoenberg's atonal music, and in the advanced twelve-tone music it is equally prominent. For example, it is the main hexachord in his *Ode to Napoleon*, op. 41 (1942), where he exploits its special combinatorial properties.

[26]The publication status of the late music is provided by Szabolcsi in *Twilight*. p. 68ff., and by Humphrey Searle in *The New Grove*. Of the late works cited in the present article, only one, Psalm 129, was published during the composer's lifetime (Leipzig: C. F. Kahnt, n. d. ; repr. in *Franz Liszt, Six Psalms [1864–81]*, Gregg International Publishers, Ltd., England, 1972). The late piano works were published in vol. IX of the collected works in 1927, with the exception of *Trauer-Vorspiel* and *La lugubre Gondola* (1887 and 1886, respectively). *Via crucis* appeared in the collected works in 1936. Therefore, as indicated earlier, it is unlikely that the few works in the experimental idiom available to composers in the early twentieth century could have exerted any direct influence on compositional practice.

[27]See Forte, *Structure*, pp. 24–28, for a more detailed explanation.

Example 6: *Eine Faust-Symphonie*, movt. I

3-12 is included in 4-19 and 4-19 includes 3-12. In equivalent language, 3-12 is a subset of set 4-19 and 4-19 is a superset of set 3-12.

Certain of the specific inclusion relations among the Lisztian harmonies require brief comments, since they represent unusual circumstances among pitch-class set inclusion relations in general, reflecting the composer's special sense of selectivity. First, 3-10 and 3-12 occupy quite different domains with respect to four-note and five-note sets. None of the total array of twenty-nine possible tetrachords contains both 3-10 and 3-12 (else the composer would certainly have found it), and only two of the thirty-eight possible pentads contain both of the trichords: 5-22 and 5-26, as noted above. Of these pentads, only 5-22 contains both 4-18 and 4-19. Therefore when this pentad occurs in an experimental passage (as in ex. 5), it has—in two senses—a special resonance. Among composers in the early twentieth century who were aware of this unusual pitch-class set kinship, Alban Berg comes to mind. In his *Wozzeck*, 5-22 is always a composite symbol of Marie, whose primary tetrachordal emblem is 4-18, and the protagonist, who is associated with 4-19, the set that underlies the *"Wir arme Leut'"* motive, which is the basic musical symbol of the entire opera (see fn. 17).

To complete this preliminary theoretical information, we observe that 3-12 has only two tetrachordal supersets, 4-19 and 4-24, the latter a "whole-tone" tetrachord. No other trichord has such restricted relations with respect to its tetrachords. For example, 3-11, the "major/minor triad" can be enclosed in tetrachords of nine different set classes. This means that the addition of any note to 3-12 will produce either 4-19 or 4-24, a simple but rather remarkable fact that has

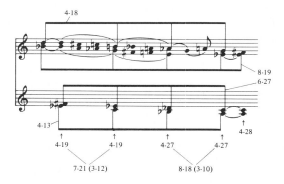

Example 7: *Via crucis*, Station 8

to do with the way in which 3-12 partitions the basic store of twelve pitch classes. Specifically, if a note a whole-step away from any note of 3-12 is added to 3-12, set 4-24 results; if a note a half-step away from any note of 3-12 is added to that trichord, set 4-19 is formed.

For the convenience of the reader, table 1 provides an index in ordinary music notation of the twenty-six pitch-class sets represented in the musical examples that accompany this article. In each case the noteheads stand for the prime form of the set.[28]

Via crucis, **Station 8.** The opening of Station 8 of *Via crucis* (ex. 7) is entirely in the experimental idiom, without any referential tonality. Most striking, and most important for an understanding of Liszt's musical thought, is the chromatic motion in the upper parts. This prolongs a form of 4-18, identified by

---

[28]See Forte, *Structure*, pp. 3–5, for a definition of prime form, a basic referential pitch-class form for each set class.

Table 1: Pitch-Class Sets in the Musical Examples

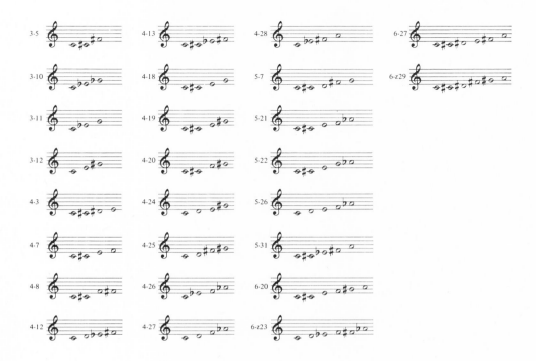

beams. After the initial component of 4-18, D, the arrival on each of the succeeding three components (B, A♭, and G) is signalled by the simultaneity formed with the lower parts. While the upper parts progress in vertical major thirds, the lower parts progress in vertical minor thirds. Contrary to what one might expect in such an apparently "schematic" composition, the horizontal motion in the lower parts is not uniform; each of the two voices projects a form of tetrachord 4-13 (F♯–E♭–D♭–C and E♭–C–B♭–A). As a result, the four-note verticals created when upper and lower parts coincide are not of the same type. The first two are forms of 4-19, while the last two are forms of 4-27. As shown at the bottom of the lower stave in ex. 7, the two 4-19 tetrachords sum to 7-21, which represents the augmented-triad harmonic domain, while the two 4-27 tetrachords sum to 8-18, representing the diminished-triad harmonic domain.[29]

In this remarkable way, the composer has juxtaposed the two fundamental harmonic areas that we encounter throughout the experimental music, not merely in the foreground as 3-12 and 3-10, but also in the horizontally prolonged tetrachord 4-18 and in the large-scale harmonies indicated on the graph, 7-21 (representing 3-12) and 8-18 (representing 3-10). In addition, tetrachord 4-18 and octad 8-18 are complement-related sets. This important relation, complementation, is amply illustrated in subsequent examples.

With respect to general shape and organization, the beginning of Station 8 of *Via crucis* (ex. 7) is strikingly similar to the eighth of Bartók's *Fourteen Bagatelles*, op. 6 (1907), one of the earliest non-tonal works of the twentieth century, and one associated chronologically with the first atonal works of the Viennese school, composed by Anton Webern. Although more complex and less "schematic," the Bartók work also features direct chromatic progressions that prolong slower-moving projections of sets. Even at the surface level, in its presentations of 4-19, it resembles the Liszt work.

The direct chromatic motion in example 7 represents a special instance of a general process, the traditional process of diminution, an understanding of which is essential to the correct analytical reading of Liszt's music in the experimental idiom. As in more

---

[29]Throughout this religious work, the two sets 3-12 and 3-10 appear to be emblematic—the first of the Holy Trinity, the second of the act of crucifixion. The direct chromatic motions (as in ex. 7) are symbolic of Mary and also depict the traversal of the stations of the cross.

Example 8: Sketch-Draft for *Via crucis*

conventional music, diminutions belong to the foreground and cannot be completely understood without reference to structures at the middleground level. These middleground structures offer no significant obstacle to the student of the composer's experimental idiom, for they conform to only a few types, based upon the linear projection of a limited number of special sets, several of which we have already encountered during the foregoing exposition. These projections are made audible in a number of ways, of which metric-rhythmic placement is perhaps the most apparent.

That Liszt was fully aware of the traditional practice of diminution—one would hardly expect otherwise—is apparent not only from his finished composition, but also from some of his sketches and drafts. A particularly compelling demonstration is afforded by ex. 8, a diplomatic transcription of a portion of a sketch-draft of music related to *Via crucis*.[30]

What we have in ex. 8 is a four-part texture consisting of bass and upper voices. The essential bass line, notated on the middle staff, is a linear projection of 4-18: B–F–G♯–E. On the lower staff the composer has written a diminution of this line, involving an upper neighbor note and two passing notes within each two-measure pattern. The second passing note in each case is accented, displacing the main note of 4-18 from its position of metrical priority. Notice that the composer strikes out the first two whole notes on the middle stave, clearly indicating that had he carried the sketch through to completion to form a part of the final version of *Via crucis*, the diminutions on the lower stave would have replaced the long notes on the middle stave. In that case the end notes of each pattern would have expressed the underlying essential bass progression of 4-18, which is the simplified pattern that would have emerged had the bass been analyzed following the procedures used in this article. That the bass whole notes were to have been replaced by the faster diminutions on the lowest stave is further indicated by the crossing out of the whole notes in the first two measures and the confusion of durations in m. 2 of the diminutions. The composer reminds himself to correct these features in the rapidly notated incipit of the piece by the annotation above the top stave, *"2 Takte neu umschreiben."*

Virtually all of *Via crucis* is in the experimental idiom. Some of the movements lack key signatures and clear tonal orientation, while others have key signatures and referential tonalities, frequently occluded. For example, Station 10 bears a key signature of four flats (suggesting F minor), yet the linear configurations projected in bass and soprano are not dependent upon the tonal frame for the coherence of their structural roles. This is provided, in a way similar to that shown in ex. 7, by controlling pitch-class set structures to which stepwise diminutions are attached. For example, over the first seven measures of the piece these sets are 4-19 and 4-18 in the upper voices, while 4-20, a symmetrical set for which the composer had a predilection in the experimental music, governs the bass, unadorned.

Trauer-Vorspiel (1885). This work, from the next-to-last year of Liszt's life, encapsulates the 3-10/3-12 di-

---

[30]In the Liszt Archive in Weimar this material occupies folder Ms b, 6c–d, labelled by the former curator, Raabe, as "Entwurf und 3 Skizzenblätter—ungedruckt." Although the music in these sketch-drafts does not correspond to the music of the final version of *Via crucis*, there are a few similarities. For instance, the pitches of 4-18 in the sketch (ex. 8), B–F–G♯–E, are identical to those in the bass solo at the end of Station I in the final version (*"In-no-cens, ego sum . . ."*). From the Roman numeral designations it seems likely that these drafts represent Liszt's initial musical ideas for the work.

The drafts provide other significant information. Since the earliest date on these documents—in Liszt's hand—is 1876 (the place, Villa d'Este), the year 1878 often given for the beginning of Via crucis is incorrect. Liszt had begun composing his largest work in the experimental idiom two years earlier.

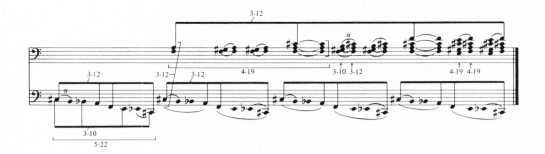

Example 9: *Trauer-Vorspiel*

chotomy at the surface level and presents a greatly distilled—indeed, almost a schematic—image of the complex compositional vision evident in some of the earlier music. In this respect it serves as a key illustration in this article.

Pitch-class set 3-12, in the upper-voice form that dominates *Trauer-Vorspiel* (C♯–A–F–C♯), is marked by up stems and by a beam at the beginning of ex. 9, while down stems and a beam show the interlocking form of 3-10 (C♯–B♭–E–C♯). Here the combination of 3-12 and 3-10 produces the special pentad 5-22 mentioned earlier in connection with ex. 5 as one of only two pitch-class sets that contain both trichords.

Trauer-Vorspiel, in common with many other of the very last compositions, does not exhibit tonality, as a vestigial feature or otherwise; its musical structure is entirely dependent upon pitch-class sets and their interrelations, as expressed over the temporal span of the work.

Unstern (after 1880). Like *Trauer-Vorspiel*, the long introduction to the late piano work, *Unstern*, is based primarily upon sets, such as 4-19, familiar from previous examples.[31] However, the opening passage is remarkable and novel even in Liszt's innovative works because it exhibits a highly structured pitch-class set hierarchy. At the highest level this consists of 7-7, an atonal set that is very distinctive among the thirty-eight heptads. With respect to interval content

it is the only heptad to contain five minor seconds and five perfect fifths. Moreover, it is one of only six heptads to contain three tritones. Among its many early twentieth-century manifestations we might note that set 7-7 and its five-note complement, 5-7, are the predominant sonorities in the first of Webern's *Orchestra Pieces* (1913, published posthumously in 1971), and those collections also occur frequently in that composer's other orchestral music, such as op. 6, no. 5 (1909) and op. 10, no. 1 from 1913.

With respect to subset organization, the most characteristic trichord of 7-7 is 3-5, a common formation in early twentieth-century music that we have not seen in the excerpts until now. Set 7-7 contains nine forms of 3-5, more than any other heptad. It is this trichord that dominates the foreground of the music up to m. 21, with three interlocking forms of that sonority comprising the opening subject (ex. 10). Perhaps most extraordinary, however, is the fact that these forms of 3-5 combine to produce two transpositionally equivalent forms of 5-7, the complement of the large harmonic set 7-7.[32] Moreover, when 5-7 is transposed up five semitones, as here, a trichord of type 3-5 will always be preserved between the two transpositionally related forms, affording a strong and specific pitch-class set bond between the two occurrences of 5-7. Transposition alone does not guarantee that the common trichord will occupy contiguous positions in each set. Here, however, 5-7 is ordered in such a way that the last trichord in the second form of 5-7 is pitch-class equivalent to the first trichord in the first form: E–F–B—incidentally, a pitch motto often found in the late works. It is significant that this form of 3-5 returns (four times) at the

---

[31]See Dieter Rexroth, "Zum Spätwerk Franz Liszts: Material und Form in dem Klavierstück 'Unstern'," in *Internationaler Musikwissenschaftlicher Kongress*, ed. Carl Dahlhaus *et al.* (Kassel, 1971), 544–46. This is an abstract of a paper that apparently contains a number of worthwhile analytical perceptions. The same cannot be said for John Ogdon, "Solo Piano Music (1861–86)," in *Franz Liszt: The Man and His Music*, ed. Alan Walker (London, 1970), pp. 140–65.

[32]See Forte, *Structure*, 73–82, for the significance of the complement relation in non-tonal music. In this connection, I note that the special harmony 5-22 often found in the experimental music, for reasons detailed above, is the complement of 7-22, one form of which is the "Hungarian" scale.

Liszt's Experimental Idiom

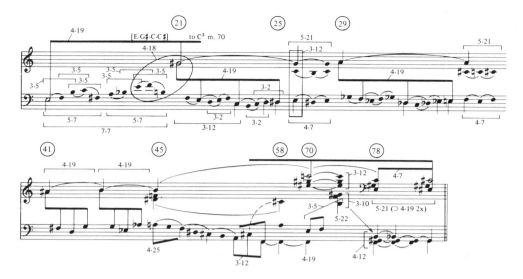

Example 10: *Unstern*

climax in m. 70, as noted on the graph (ex. 10). This opening passage, in its austerity and its economy of means with respect to the musical processes it represents, is strongly reminiscent of the music of Anton Webern, which we have already had occasion to mention in connection with this excerpt from Liszt's experimental music.[33]

The final 3-5 in this opening passage then merges with G♯ in the upper voice (m. 21) to create 4-18, the only strong manifestation of that "diminished triad" set in this music—although 3-10 itself returns, together with 3-12, in the climactic music that begins in m. 70.

At the middleground level, the upper voice G♯ in m. 21 links to E in the opening measure, as indicated by the stemmed open noteheads and beam in ex. 10.[34] From this point on, the upper-voice motion is completely regular, consisting of ascending semitones, each of them prolonged, which fill in the diminished fourth from G♯ to C, the penultimate goal of the passage and the climactic pitch in the highest register in m. 70. As in previous examples, the prolongations of the ascending chromatic line are "organic," in the specific sense that they are linear projections of

4-19, the set that is gradually being unfolded in the middleground.

In addition to 4-19, set 4-7 also serves a prolongational function at two points: after m. 25 and before m. 41. In both cases the set is created by lower neighbor notes to elements of 3-12, a motivic reflection of the semitone motives in the first section. Parallel intervals of this kind are always significant in Liszt's experimental music, just as are the seemingly mechanical directly chromatic motions. For instance, the "parallel fifths" in the late work, *Csardas macabre*, express the symmetrical set 4-8. Similar usage is common in early atonal music, for example in Schoenberg's song *Am Strande* (1909).

At m. 45 the symmetrical whole-tone tetrachord 4-25 suddenly appears as a vertical, supporting the next-to-last passing note, B, within the large-scale diminished fourth, G♯ (m. 21) to C (m. 70). Here the function of this set, which does not fit neatly into Liszt's experimental harmonic vocabulary, is analogous to a half-cadence. Precisely because 4-25 does not relate closely to any of the other sets in the work, it performs this caesural role effectively and interrupts the continuity established by the previous regular succession of forms of 4-19.

Immediately after the melodic climax on c³ in m. 70 set 5-22 is created in the vertical dimension. It will be recalled that this is one of only two pentads that contain both 3-10 and 3-12. Here the two trichordal components are lucidly presented: 3-12 is tied over from the climax, then 3-10 is adjoined, completing 5-22. In addition, a horizontal form of 3-5, pitch-identical to the first trichord in the piece (the Lisztian motto E−F−B), completes the roster of trichordal constituents.

---

[33]Of many similar passages, the opening of Webern's op. 7 is representative. Paul Wilson ("Atonality and Structure," p. 186) shows a striking passage in Bartók's op. 18, no. 3, based upon sets 5-7 and 3-5.

[34]Sandor Kovacs, "Form Prinzipien und Ungarische Stileigentümlichkeiten in den Spätwerken von Liszt," in *Liszt-Studien* 2, ed. Serge Gut (Munich−Salzburg, 1981), pp. 114−22, emphasizes the role played by the "Zentraltöne" E and F in *Unstern*.

From m. 78 to the double bar (ex. 10), three basic events of significance transpire. First, the arrival on C♯ completes the large-scale 4-19 in the upper voice. Second, 4-7 refers back to the occurrences of that set in support of the chromatic line that ascends from m. 21. And third, the 3-10 and 3-12 domains merge, with the right-hand part expressing 5-21 (3-12), while the left-hand part reiterates 3-10 from the preceding climactic music, within the context of 4-12.

Via crucis, Station 5. The most extended manifestations of the 3-10 genus in the composer's experimental idiom are those that engage the octatonic collection (see fn. 21), a pitch-class set with which Liszt was probably the first to compose in a thorough-going way. The technical reason for the association of 3-10 with the octatonic collection, 8-28, has to do with complementation and inclusion. As is explained in my study, *The Structure of Atonal Music*, of the seven trichordal classes represented as subsets of 8-28, each an equal number of times, only 3-10 is in the symmetric set-complex relation Kh with 8-28.[35] This close relation between 8-28, the complement of 4-28, the "diminished seventh chord," can be grasped intuitively, without recourse to arcane theoretical explanation, when it is realized that any note added to a form of 8-28 will always produce a nine-note set of class 9-10, the complement of 3-10.

Although octatonic structures have appeared in previous examples (e.g., ex. 4), they will be discussed in greater detail here. In this connection it is important to recall that octatonic elements may be both "ordered" and "unordered." That is, while we expect to find octatonic structures set out as scalar formations or portions of scalar formations, we will also regard as octatonic other configurations that may not represent a fixed linear ordering. For example, if two vertical trichords that have no referential linear ordering combine to form one of the six octatonic hexachords, we will take that hexachord to be just as octatonic as one of its scalar brethren.

Station 5 of *Via crucis* (ex. 11) offers a compelling instance of Liszt's sophisticated octatonic usage. The octatonic component becomes evident with very little analytical coaxing: from the beginning of the piece to the double bar the upper voice projects a linear form of 7-31, which, it will be recalled from the discussion of ex. 4, is the only seven-note class within 8-28, the total octatonic collection. Example 11b displays the diminished seventh (4-28) constituents of this line as they ascend from the initial B to the climactic D. The octatonic basis of the music is also apparent in the large harmonic groupings marked by brackets below the lower stave in ex. 11b. These comprise, in order, 7-31, 8-28, and finally 5-31, which is the prolonged upper-voice motion, as indicated by the beamed stems. Here 5-31 prolongs D, or, more precisely, the sixth from D down to F. In m. 10 a

descending structure also prolongs the main upper-voice note B♭, but in this instance the set is 4-26, a special tetrachord that appears often in the experimental idiom (see ex. 2). In this work the set has a special significance, for it is the melodic configuration at the opening, where it occurs in a pentatonic context and is identical to the one here with respect to pitch class. It is one of the principal sonic symbols of *Via crucis*.[36]

While the upper voice is organized in terms of 4-28, the bass is set out in terms of another tetrachordal subset of 8-28, 4-12. The two beamed forms of this set are transpositionally related by major sixth (minor third). As in the upper-voice prolongations in m. 10 and at the end of the section, the octatonic sets incorporate non-octatonic elements as passing and neighbor notes, shown as filled-in noteheads slurred to the main stemmed and beamed elements and marked *P* in several instances.

At the double bar, m. 25, with the introduction of a key signature of four flats, a more traditional idiom replaces the octatonic music. Nevertheless, the octatonic characteristics persist, in the 4-28 and 5-31 formations as well as in the bass's 6-z23, one of the six hexachordal classes of the octatonic collection, which here spans the interval C–A♭ within the A♭-major tonality.[37] And, as might be expected, with the new music come strong references to the 3-12 domain, a trichord totally unrepresented in the preceding introductory section, which featured 3-10 and its kindred. Thus, the first chromatic motion in the upper voice, from E♭ to E, brings in 4-19, and set 4-24 then occurs as a result of the passing motions in bass and soprano. For both tetrachords the core, 3-12, is C–E–A♭, and this finally appears in pristine form at the end of the excerpt.

Example 11 provides an appropriate occasion for a general comment on Liszt's music, one that is relevant to further research. Study of the experimental

---

[35]See Forte, *Structure*, pp. 96–100.

[36]The pentatonic aspect of some of Liszt's music is well known. His use of pentatonic sets, prefiguring their function as pitch-class sets independent of tonality, occurs as early as "Sposalizio" (*Années de Pèlerinage* II, 1838, in which 4-23, the archetypical pentatonic tetrachord, is the motto set stated at the very outset (cf. Leon Plantinga, *Romantic Music* [New York, 1984], pp. 186–88). The same set plays a basic role in an early hybrid tonal/atonal work by Schoenberg, the *Entrückung* movement of the Second String Quartet.

[37]The octatonic collection is not always fully present in this music—just as it is not always completely spelled out in Stravinsky's octatonic music—but may be represented by one of its subsets, by 6-z23 in this instance. Similarly, although "*Sunt lacrymae rerum*" (*Années de Pèlerinage* III, 1872) bears the subtitle "*en mode hongroise*," a reference to the "Hungarian" scale, 7-22, the scale does not appear in its entirety at the beginning of the music, but is represented by one of its subsets, 6-z44, in an ordering that presents the characteristic interval-patterns associated with the complete scale.

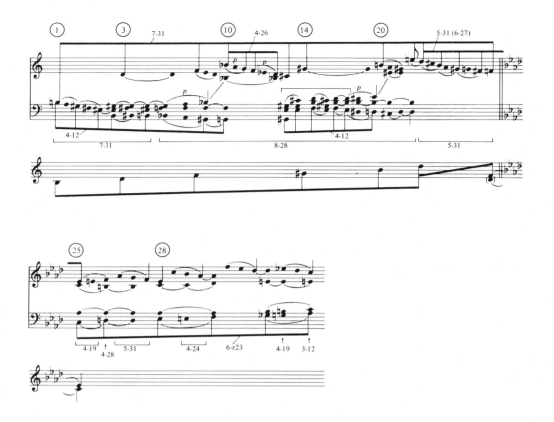

Example 11: *Via crucis*, Station 5

music with effective analytical method may illuminate certain facets of the more traditional diatonic music, as here, where we find structures supposedly endemic to the experimental idiom appearing in the traditional language. This, of course, is the converse of the situation pointed out earlier in this article, where the experimental sonorities were shown to have originated in the traditional forms.

Before proceeding to the final section of this article, which contains an analysis of a complete and quite well-known composition, I would like to say something about a work that is not well known, but which deserves attention for several reasons.

Psalm 129 (1881). Even in its external, notational appearance this choral composition resembles a distillation of the music of Webern, especially the twelve-tone music, and in its severity it even suggests a kinship with a very late religious work by Schoenberg, his incomplete *Moderner Psalm*, op. 50c (1950). At a deeper structural level, the work presages many of the procedures that are characteristic of the non-

tonal music of the early twentieth century, as we shall see.

The composition begins, uncompromisingly in the vernacular of the early twentieth century, with the symmetrical tetrachord 4-8, which we have seen before in ex. 11.[38] In the first section (delimited by double barlines in ex. 12) 4-8 is presented in two different ways: first, as a succession of two ascending major sevenths, and second, as a vertical sonority that emphasizes its perfect fifths, an arrangement effected by an exchange of voices, as indicated by crossed arrows on ex. 12. When the chorus enters in m. 10 the set assumes still another shape, one that emphasizes the major third as well as the minor second. What could be more characteristic of the foreground of much early twentieth-century music than

---

[38]The use of this essentially atonal set is itself astonishing. In what is perhaps the most "classical" of all the early twentieth-century atonal works, Berg's *Wozzeck*, this set underlies the subject of the *Ländler*, act II, sc. 4, m. 412*ff*.

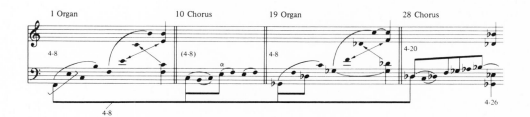

1 Organ   10 Chorus   19 Organ   28 Chorus

4-8   (4-8)   4-8   4-20

α

4-8   4-26

Example 12: Psalm 129

this rearrangement of musical materials to show new facets that suggest other possibilities for structural development?

In the next section of the composition 4-8 occurs in one-for-one transposition up a minor second with respect to its statement in the first section of the work. As a result of this transformation the pitches F and C remain fixed between the two forms. The longer-range result of the transposition, however, engages the middleground. As shown by the beamed stems over the first four sections (mm. 1–28), the lowest voice projects still another form of 4-8, one that is identical, with respect to pitch-class, to the form in the third section (mm. 19–28). Again, as is typical of the experimental music of Liszt, there are strong unifying factors, factors that involve more than one aspect of the music. In this case we have the succession of transpositionally related 4-8 tetrachords that comprise each section and over the span of the first three sections we perceive a linear projection of the same set class, a remarkable way of coordinating musical spans and one that is usually attributed to the pioneers of early twentieth-century music.

With the entry of the chorus in m. 28, the harmonic components change, now summing to the diatonic hexachord 6-32. When tetrachord 4-20 enters, its association with 4-8 is unmistakable due to the ascending major thirds Db–F and Gb–Bb, the interval it shares with 4-8 in its appearance in the second section. The arrival on 4-26 at the end of the section would seem illogical in pitch-class set terms, were it not for the fact that this tetrachord shares two perfect fifths with both 4-8 and 4-20, the only interval-type they have in common. In this way 4-20 carries forward the primary intervallic characteristic that is projected in the middleground bass form of 4-8. Although we have seen 4-8, 4-20, and 4-26 in other examples (see table 1), their appearance here together suggests that a basic structural feature of this music is determined by shared interval content. In this respect, again, the experimental idiom, as represented in this extraordinary work, prefigures in a highly significant way the music of the early twentieth century.

A COMPLETE WORK IN THE
EXPERIMENTAL IDIOM

Nuages gris (1881). Except perhaps for *Unstern* (ex. 10), the best known of the composer's final works in the experimental idiom is the piano piece known as *Nuages gris*. (Liszt's primary title was *Trübe Wolken*.) Probably this is due to the attention accorded it in Szabolcsi's book on the composer's late years and its subsequent inclusion in the 1972 edition of a widely used history of music textbook.[39]

As indicated by double bars and upper-case letters on ex. 13, the work comprises four sections. Section A is organized around the major third D–Bb in the upper voice, with Bb in the bass, decorated by its lower neighbor note to form an ostinato figure. The upper-voice major third, D–Bb, proves to be the initial interval of 4-19, the tetrachord that is projected over the entire span of the work, as indicated by stemmed open noteheads on the analytical sketch.

Because the verticals in the upper voice, after the initial embellishment of the G-minor triad, consist of a regular succession of 3-12 trichords while the bass ostinato remains constant, multiple forms of 4-19, together with two forms of 4-24, are produced. Note, however, that the first two tetrachords in the piece are marked 4-18, a set class that reappears in section C (m. 25ff.) together with its complement, 8-18.

In the B section (m. 21), which is a short interlude,

[39]Szabolcsi, *Twilight*; Grout, *History* (see fn. 12). Jim Samson includes a discussion of *Nuages gris* in his *Music in Transition* (New York, 1977). He remarks (p. 17): "the most distinctive features of Liszt's late style are present in this short work—the avoidance of a conventional cadential structure, the importance of semitonal movement, the use of the augmented triad as the central harmonic unit and of parallelism as a principal means of progression." Bernard C. Lemoine offers a curious, Schenker-like analysis of the work in "Tonal Organization in Selected Late Piano Works of Franz Liszt," in *Liszt-Studien*, ed. Serge Gut (Munich, 1981). Among other peculiarities, the final chord is misspelled.

Example 13: *Nuages gris*

the bass ostinato figure A–B♭ (marked δ) combines with the initial upper-voice dyad, C♯–D (marked α), to form set 4-7. (Set 4-7 is not new in the music; it is a subset of 5-21 in the upper parts of m. 9.) This interlude is effectively a condensation of the main melodic components of the A section. Thus, 4-7 has motivic as well as harmonic significance with respect to the preceding section; not only does it incorporate motives δ and α, but it also includes B♭ and D, beamed in ex. 13, a repetition of the interval spanned by the upper voice of the A section. tion.

Section C (m. 25*ff.*) introduces new elements in the upper voice, namely, prolonged melodic forms of trichords 3-10 and 3-11, beamed on the graph. Here 3-11 as the minor triad is the referential tonic sonority, which, in the context of this piece—despite the key signature of two flats—may even be regarded as subsidiary to 3-12, so predominant is the role that set plays, particularly in the large-scale upper voice. The conflict between 3-11 and 3-12 is emphasized in the upper voice from m. 29 to m. 33, where the head-note D of the 3-11 (G-minor) configuration stretches across to incorporate B♭ and, finally, F♯, forming 3-12 at the middleground level.

The final section of *Nuages gris* is designated D, with A' given in parentheses because up to the final chord the lower parts are identical to the entire opening section. Above this progression the upper voice traverses the ascending octave from F♯ to F♯ chro-

matically. The ultimate destination of this motion, however, is high G (g^2), which completes the large-scale 4-19 in the upper voice: D–B♭–B♭–D–F♯–G.

Since the final chord has been the subject of some speculation in the published writings about this work, the sketch includes a partial analysis of its structure. In its entirety the chord is a representative of set class 5-26, which shares with 5-22 the special property that it contains both 3-10 and 3-12, as explained earlier. Here the lower tetrachord of 5-26 is 4-24, taken directly from the left-hand part, as indicated by the brackets and arrow on ex. 13. The upper tetrachord of 5-26 here is 4-19, representing the primary tetrachord of the piece.

With the final ascent to G in the upper voice over the sustained 4-24, the entire sonority reduces to 4-24 and is pitch-class identical to the next-to-last vertical in the A section. Thus, the work closes with a reference to the opening music and on one of the two tetrachordal supersets of 3-12, which constitutes a "resolution" into that attenuated harmonic domain and an appropriate and logical setting for the final note of the large-scale linear motion of the upper voice, a projection of the other tetrachordal superset of 3-12, 4-19.[40]

---

[40]See Lawrence Kramer, "The Mirror of Tonality: Transitional Features of Nineteenth-Century Harmony," *19th-Cen Mus* 4 (1981), 191-208 for a different view of the unusual

The penultimate vertical, 5-26, contains 3-10 in the same form in which that trichord occurred in m. 9: F♯–E♭–A. This provides a somewhat concealed reference to the 3-10/4-18 domain, which is prominent in the C section (mm. 25–32), where 4-18 is reiterated in the left-hand part and mirrored by its complement, 8-18, which is formed by all the pitches in the section.

Below the lower stave of section D in ex. 13 is a further analysis of the upper voice which shows that if we take as middleground components the notes that begin and end the five-note chromatic figure (a procedure entirely consistent with previous readings of chromatic prolongations), two interlocking forms of 4-19 are brought to the analytical surface, both incorporating 3-12 as B–E♭–G, the core sonority in the penultimate chord, 5-26. These observations comprise a demonstration that even on the "subliminal" level certain basic musical phenomena highly characteristic of the Lisztian experimental idiom penetrate the structure.

To sum up, *Nuages gris*, for all its brevity, represents a high point in the experimental idiom with respect to expressive compositional procedure. Set organization is manifested in the most artistic and coherent ways throughout the musical fabric, and the long-range melodic structure as it relates to the harmonic content of the individual sections could hardly be projected more clearly.

CONCLUSION

From the theoretical standpoint, what makes the experimental music of Liszt so special and so interesting is not its unusual surface features—which are, of course, extraordinary—but the fact that it represents a systematic expansion of traditional voice-leading and harmonic models, an expansion that incorporates, as basic harmonies, sonorities (pitch-class sets) that are not part of the central syntax of tonal music, but that derive, in the most extreme instances, from a process of accretion to the augmented triad and the diminished triad, to form the 3-12 and 3-10 domains mentioned so often in the course of this article.

Example 14: *Harmonies poétiques et religieuses*

It is also remarkable that these sonorities appear in Liszt's music at more than one level long before their more obvious occurrences in the later music. When did these unusual features first surface in the composer's creative output? Harold Thompson states categorically: "The octatonic scale . . . enters Liszt's works first in the *Sonetto* (c. 1846)."[41] The octatonic collection, however, is clearly represented at the beginning of the first piece in the first version of *Harmonies poétiques et religieuses* (1834) by 5D31, and elsewhere by the octatonic heptad 7-31 and the octatonic hexad 6-z49.

This entire work is especially interesting with respect to the question of the origin and development of certain experimental features, for upon completing the second version in 1843, the composer declared the first version invalid, perhaps because of certain refinements he had introduced into the second. For example, the untitled first piece in the first version became the basis for the movement entitled *Pensées des morts* in the second; there the composer altered the upper-voice melody as shown in ex. 14a, changing F♯ to F, so that the augmented triad became the central melodic symbol. A similar discrepancy between the two versions crops up later on (ex. 14b), where the revision introduces overlapping contiguous forms of 4-19 and 4-24 that rotate about their common satellite, 3-12,

---

ending of this work (pp. 205–06). Of the penultimate vertical, Kramer writes: "Reading the problematic chord as an unresolved atonal formation, Liszt resolves its F♯s to G, just as if he were moving from leading-tone to tonic, but he keeps the E♭ and the A in place. The result . . . is that celebrated whole-tone chord which closes the piece. . . ." Kramer appears to regard the close as highly unusual and enigmatic, which, indeed, it is in the context of this piece. However, in the general harmonic language of Liszt's experimental idiom it is but one of many instances of progressions that engage the 3-12/4-19/4-24 structure.

[41]Harold A. Thompson, *The Evolution of Whole-Tone Sound in Liszt's Original Piano Works* (Ph.D. diss., Louisiana State University, 1974).

and brings those harmonies into the immediate foreground.[42]

A second question of interest to students of late nineteenth-century music in general and Liszt's music in particular is: how pervasive are what have been termed the experimental features in his music? Among the works that invite further study along these lines are the tone poems—such as, notably, *Prometheus* (1850).[43] Also the six psalm settings, which span a period of eighteen of the later years (1864–81), contain symmetrical and other special non-tonal har-

monies that are highly suggestive in this respect.

The two topics broached above are just two among many that invite further study, as contributions to a larger and more precise picture of the development of Liszt's musical thought, not only as it pertains to the experimental idiom, as we have termed it, but also to the entire range of his diversified output. We are still far from a comprehensive picture of his position in nineteenth-century music and his relation to the twentieth century.

---

[42]Here and elsewhere the whole-tone aspect of Liszt's music has been overly emphasized. In general, sets such as 4-19, 5-21, and 5-22, which are highly characteristic of the experimental idiom, relate directly to 3-12 by inclusion, whereas they are not subsets of 6-35, the whole-tone hexachord.

[43]*Prometheus* was viewed as a radical work at the time. See C[arl] F[riedrich] Weitzmann, *Die Neue Harmonie im Streit mit der Alten* (Leipzig, 1861), in which *Prometheus* serves as an exemplar of the new harmony. Other studies relevant

to this area of research are: Norbert Nagler, "Die verspätete Zukunftsmusik," in *Musik-Konzepte 12: Franz Liszt*, ed. Heinz-Klaus Metzger and Rainer Riehn (Munich, 1980), pp. 25–36, and Dieter Torkewitz, *Harmonisches Denken im Frühwerk Franz Liszts* (Munich–Salzburg, 1978). And finally, Diether de la Motte, *Harmonielehre* (Kassel, 1976), a work that deals with some unusual features of Liszt's music such as occurrences of the augmented triad in the early music (see pp. 237–48).

Engagements of Modernism:
Personality, Politics, Perceptions

Decadence and Desire:
The *Wilhelm Meister* Songs
of Wolf and Schubert

LAWRENCE KRAMER

The lyrics from Goethe's novel *Wilhelm Meisters Lehrjahre* haunted more than one generation of German composers. What Friedrich Schlegel called their "music and romantic enchantment" prompted important settings from Beethoven, Schubert, Schumann, and Wolf, among others.[1] Hugo Wolf's *Wilhelm Meister* songs are among his finest, but they are exceptional among his fifty-odd Goethe Lieder in one respect. Wolf ordinarily avoided setting texts by Goethe that had already been set by Schubert. The only other exceptions of consequence are *Prometheus*, *Ganymed*, and *Gren-*

zen der Menschheit: the trilogy of songs about mortal limits that closes Wolf's Goethe collection, as the trilogy of harper songs from *Wilhelm Meister* opens it.

The standard explanation for this state of affairs, established by Ernest Newman in the biography he published in 1907, three years after the composer's death, is that Wolf would not set a text if he felt that Schubert had set it effectively. Writing as a partisan, Newman takes up the cudgels to justify this practice. His Schubert, naively scribbling pieces in Viennese coffeehouses, failed to understand the psychopathology of Goethe's harper and Mignon, perhaps because he did not trouble to read Goethe's novel, or perhaps because of his inferior "general culture." He set the *Wilhelm Meister* lyrics "in a more or less mechanical

---

[1]Friedrich Schlegel, "On Goethe's Meister," trans. Peter Firchow, rpt. in *German Aesthetic and Literary Criticism: The Romantic Ironists and Goethe*, ed. Kathleen Wheeler (Cambridge, 1984), pp. 59–73; see p. 73.

way, vaguely sensing their underlying emotions but never realizing them in terms of music as profound as themselves. . . . [F]or him they were just pretty poems."[2] Where Wolf unerringly penetrates "into the very depth of Goethe's mood," poor Schubert fails "to get very far beneath the surface of it."[3]

The best of Wolf's later commentators—Frank Walker, Philip Radcliffe, Eric Sams, Mosco Carner—have not fallen into Newman's trap of crassly undervaluing Schubert in order to praise Wolf, but neither have they escaped Newman's frame of reference. The idea lingers that Wolf understood Goethe better than Schubert did, that his settings have a psychological penetration and intensity that Schubert's lack, that Wolf is sophisticated where Schubert is naive.[4] What is most problematical about this point of view is not that it misconceives Schubert, whose songs routinely triumph over the misconception from their place at the center of the repertoire. The real trouble with the critical tradition established by Newman is that it positively inhibits a productive understanding of the relationship between Schubert's and Wolf's settings of the same texts.

That relationship is my subject. My discussion will turn on three claims, all of which run counter to the standard account. First, no composer is responsible to the poet's sense of a text, much less to a commentator's sense of that sense. The composer appropriates the text and makes a song with it. The results need not be "true" to the poet—and rarely are; they need only be convincing on their own terms.[5] Second, Wolf's *Wilhelm Meister* songs are not sim-ply attempts to best or dethrone Schubert's versions: they are attempts to revise or recompose what Schubert wrote. The two composers' songs are bound together dynamically, on both literary and musical planes of opposition. Wolf's songs could supplant Schubert's only at the cost of their own expressive value. Finally, Wolf's rewriting of Schubert's settings depends less on his "understanding"—that is, his interpretation—of particular texts than on his adherence to a culturally ascendent model of human personality that differs from Schubert's. Wolf's expressive differences from Schubert can no more be extricated from late nineteenth-century representations of the self than his purely musical differences can be extricated from the influence of Wagner.

The impetus for hearing a dynamic relationship between Wolf's and Schubert's shared Goethe settings comes from certain developments in literary criticism. In recent years, critics have increasingly concerned themselves with the ways in which literary texts repeat, revise, or reinterpret earlier texts, a situation covered broadly by the term "intertextuality." In the troubled and pluralistic world of contemporary criticism, there are almost as many theories of intertextual processes as there are critics. Texts may be studied through their implication in a variety of literary and cultural codes; through their repeated exposure of their own literariness and rhetoricity; or as vehicles of an Oedipal power-struggle between poets and their precursors.[6] For present purposes, I will simply assume without a *parti pris* that the expressive design of one work of art may include, and even found itself upon, a critical understanding of another. Following Paul de Man, I am persuaded that critical interpretation depends on the same rhetorical and expressive practices that are basic to works of art, so that creative activity and

[2]Ernest Newman, *Hugo Wolf* (London, 1907; rpt. New York, 1966), p. 196.
[3]Ibid., p. 192.
[4]Frank Walker, *Hugo Wolf: A Biography* (London, 1951); Philip Radcliffe, "Germany and Austria: The Modern Period," in *A History of Song*, ed. Denis Stevens (New York, 1960); Eric Sams, *The Songs of Hugo Wolf* (London, 1961); Mosco Carner, *Hugo Wolf: Songs* (London, 1982). Jack M. Stein's *Poem and Music in the German Lied from Gluck to Hugo Wolf* (Cambridge, Mass., 1971) should be mentioned here also, but only as a kind of nadir of the Newman tradition. Stein goes Newman one better and condescends to *both* Schubert and Wolf as interpreters of Goethe—thus making it impossible for him to interpret their settings.
[5]For detailed discussions of this issue, see Edward T. Cone, *The Composer's Voice* (Berkeley and Los Angeles, 1974); Steven Paul Scher, "Comparing Poetry and Music:

Beethoven's Goethe-Lieder," *Sensus Communis: Festschrift for Henry Remak*, ed. Janos Riesz et al. (Tübingen, 1986), 155–65; and chapter 5 of my *Music and Poetry: The Nineteenth Century and After* (Berkeley and Los Angeles, 1984).
[6]These literary approaches may be exemplified, respectively, by Roland Barthes, *S/Z*, trans. Richard Miller (New York, 1974); Paul de Man, *Allegories of Reading: Figural Language in Rousseau, Nietzsche, Rilke, and Proust* (New Haven, 1979); and Harold Bloom, *The Anxiety of Influence* (New York, 1973).

critical understanding are inescapably entailed in each other.[7]

A SHORT HISTORY

Wolf's critical understanding of the Goethe songs that he found problematical in Schubert seems to pivot on Schubert's dramatization of the Romantic ego—the vital core of subjectivity that dominates both literature and philosophy in the first decades of the nineteenth century. According to the literary historian M. H. Abrams:

> In its central tradition Christian thought had posited three primary elements: God, nature, and the soul. . . . The tendency in innovative Romantic thought . . . is greatly to diminish, and at the extreme to eliminate, the role of God, leaving as the prime agencies man and the world, mind and nature, the ego and the non-ego, the self and the not-self, or (in the favorite antithesis of post-Kantian philosophers) subject and object.[8]

Two consequences of conceiving the subject in these terms concern us at present. The first is a celebration of inwardness in all its forms: memory, self-reflection, imagination, and desire, among others. Recalling his first conscious discovery of these things, Wordsworth writes:

> Of genius, power,
> Creation and divinity itself,
> I have been speaking, for my theme has been
> What passed within me. Not of outward things
> Done visibly for other minds—words, signs,
> Symbols or actions—but of my own heart
> Have I been speaking, and my youthful mind.[9]

And Novalis, echoing Schiller, claims: "The highest task of education—is to master one's own transcendental self—and at the same time to be the Self of one's Self."[10]

Inwardness, however, also embraces the inwardness of pain. For the Romantic subject, intense mental suffering is as primary as the exhilarations of sentience, and it is equally capable of being idealized. Romantic writers frequently seek in guilt, grief, or despondency the evidence of what Wordsworth called "intellectual strength": an internalized heroism that engenders

> Sorrow that is not sorrow but delight,
> And miserable love that is not pain
> To hear of, for the glory that redounds
> Therefrom to human-kind and what we are.
> —*The Prelude* (1805), XII, 245–48.

No matter how anguished it becomes, the Romantic ego retains a core of unity, resiliency, and latent power that limits its alienation and blocks its collapse.[11] The figure of Prometheus personified this "patient energy"—what Nietzsche called "the glory of passivity"—for Byron, Shelley, and Goethe. Its other archetypes include wanderers like Coleridge's ancient mariner; heroic artists who "learn in suffering what they teach in song";[12] and marginal figures who suddenly intrude on the eye: beggars, solitaries, obsessives, the silent, the emaciated.

The hurdy-gurdy man of Schubert's *Winterreise* is a marginal figure of this sort: an extreme one, through whom the patient energy of self travels to the border of annihilation. *Winterreise* enacts an ordeal that tests its wanderer-protagonist's ability to endure the endless symbolic repetition of his thwarted desire. In the final song, the almost insentient figure of the hurdy-gurdy man, with his empty cup and mechanical music, beckons toward a subjective void:

> Wunderlicher Alter, soll ich mit dir gehn?
> Willst zu meinen Liedern deine Leier drehn?
>
> (Strange old man, shall I go with you?
> Will your hurdy-gurdy turn to my songs?)

[7]See chapter 1 of de Man's *Allegories of Reading* and chapters 2 and 3 of his *Blindness and Insight: Essays in the Rhetoric of Contemporary Criticism* (New York, 1971).

[8]M. H. Abrams, *Natural Supernaturalism: Tradition and Revolution in Romantic Literature* (New York, 1971), p. 91.

[9]*The Prelude* (1805), III, 171–77. Cited from *The Prelude: 1799, 1805, 1850*, ed. Jonathan Wordsworth, M. H. Abrams, and Steven Gill (New York, 1979).

[10]From *Miscellaneous Writings*, trans. Joyce Crick, in *German Aesthetic and Literary Criticism*, p. 88. For the reference to Schiller (and Schiller's reference to Fichte!) see p. 239, n. 4.

[11]But not its death—the exemplary case of Goethe's Werther, Byron's Manfred, and many others, who die in order to affirm themselves.

[12]"Patient energy" is from Byron's *Prometheus*; Nietzsche's phrase is from his discussion of Goethe's *Prometheus* in *The Birth of Tragedy*, trans. Walter Kaufmann in Nietzsche, *The Birth of Tragedy and The Case of Wagner* (New York, 1967), pp. 69–70. "They learn in suffering what they teach in song" is from Shelley's *Julian and Maddalo* (l. 546).

As he sings these closing lines, the wanderer half-consciously opposes the question that they ask and finds a saving scruple of resistance to the lure of his nerveless double. For only here does he abandon the two-measure scraps of jingling melody that have so far matched his song to the mindless turning of the hurdy-gurdy.

As the nineteenth century wears on, however, the Romantic ego wears out. Werther becomes Emma Bovary; Faust turns into Ibsen's Master Builder. Increasingly, the inner resonances of both desire and suffering merge with intimations of solipsism, morbidity, and self-destructiveness. Looking back on the century from the mid-1880s, Nietzsche remarks on "that typical transformation of which G. Flaubert offers the clearest example among the French and Richard Wagner among the Germans, in which the romantic faith in love and the future is transformed into the desire for the nothing, 1830 into 1850."[13] The reflexive awareness, or irony, celebrated by German Romantics like Jean-Paul, Tieck, and Friedrich Schlegel, metamorphoses into a perverse and paralyzing self-consciousness. Thus Baudelaire, in *L'Héautontimorouménos* ("The Self-Tormentor"):

Ne suis-je pas un faux accord
Dans la divine symphonie,
Grâce à la vorace Ironie
Qui me secoue et qui me mord? . . .

Je suis la plaie et le couteau!
Je suis le soufflet et la joue!
Je suis les membres et la roue
Et la victime et le bourreau!

(Am I not a false accord in the divine symphony, thanks to the voracious Irony that shakes me and that gnaws at me? . . . I am the wound and dagger both! I am the slap, I am the cheek, I am the body and the rack and the victim and the torturer.)

Pain becomes a vocation; desire fastens increasingly on images of decline, the "passing sweetness / Of autumn splendor or a setting sun."[14]

[13]From *The Will to Power*, trans. Walter Kaufmann and R. J. Hollingdale, ed. Walter Kaufmann (New York, 1968), p. 66.
[14]Text of *L'Héautontimorouménos* from the complete bilingual edn. of *Les Fleurs du mal: Flowers of Evil*, ed. Jackson and Marthiel Matthews (New York, 1955). "Passing sweetness": my translation from lines 27–28 of Baudelaire's *Chant d'automne*; text from the Matthews's edn.

When this devaluation of the ego is coupled with a certain masochistic pleasure, a heightened sensuousness, and a love for artifice, we can begin to speak of decadence: the ethos of Swinburne and Mallarmé, of Klimt and Beardsley, of unfocused eroticism and the archetypes of fatal desire, Salome and the Medusa. In turning now to a comparative account of some representative *Wilhelm Meister* settings by Schubert and Wolf—the harper trilogies and Mignon's *Nur wer die Sehnsucht kennt*—I will suggest that Wolf's critique of Schubert founds itself on the replacement of a Romantic by a decadent model of the self. Wolf's "Schubert" songs, typically for their composer, carry forward a process that begins in music with Wagner and culminates in the self-flagellations of Schoenberg's *Book of the Hanging Gardens* and Berg's *Lulu*.

THE HARPER TRILOGIES

Goethe's harper, the father by incest of Wilhelm Meister's ward, Mignon, is consumed by a remorse that he barely manages to sublimate in his songs, three of which apply covertly to his own sufferings. Goethe gave these songs an independent life by extracting them from the novel and rearranging them to form a lyric trilogy. Free of their narrative context, the poems break the grip of the harper's obsessions and enact an archetypal Romantic progression from self-alienation to self-mastery. *Wer sich der Einsamkeit ergibt* dwells on despair and a longing for death; *An die Türen will ich schleichen* seeks life again through the role of the Romantic wanderer and attains a degree of self-conscious detachment from the pathos that the wanderer evokes in others; *Wer nie sein Brot mit Tränen ass* voices a bitter but dignified accusation of the heavenly powers for their injustice to humanity.

Both Schubert and Wolf set the three poems as a group. Schubert ties them together by setting all three in the same key, A minor. Wolf is more tenuous—or attenuated: his first song closes inconclusively with bare parallel fifths (Eb–Bb/D–A) in the bass—a texture resumed by his third song, which closes with a decisive cadence a full step lower (C–G/F–C). In the first version of *Gesänge des Harfners*, Schubert followed Goethe's lyric order, but then reversed the second and third songs for the final version, published as op. 12. The change freed him to reconceive Goethe's scenario of self-mastery as a movement toward resignation or stoical acceptance. He reads the *Meister* lyrics much as Friedrich Schlegel does, "as if their sorrow would tear our hearts in two, but this sorrow has the form, the tone, of some lamenting dignity."[15] Wolf, despite his apparent feeling that his settings refer to the half-mad harper of the novel, keeps strictly to the lyric order, but recasts it as a descent into an all-consuming rage of almost infantile ferocity. The disparity between Schubert and Wolf expresses itself most broadly through their tempos. Both composers write the whole harper sequence as slow music, but Schubert's pace quickens a little as the songs succeed each other, while Wolf's remains leaden from first to last.

Goethe's *Wer sich der Einsamkeit ergibt* begins in detachment and ends in despair:

> Wer sich der Einsamkeit ergibt,
> Ach! der ist bald allein;
> Ein jeder lebt, ein jeder liebt,
> Und lässt ihn seiner Pein.
>
> Ja! lasst mich meiner Qual!
> Und kann ich nur einmal
> Recht einsam sein,
> Dann bin ich nicht allein.
>
> Es schleicht ein Liebender lauschend sacht,
> Ob seine Freundin allein?
> So überschleicht bei Tag und Nacht
> Mich Einsamen die Pein,
>
> Mich Einsamen die Qual.
> Ach, werd' ich erst einmal
> Einsam im Grabe sein,
> Da lässt sie mich allein![16]

(He who devotes himself to solitude, ah! he is soon alone; everyone lives, everyone loves, and leaves him to his pain. Yes! leave me to my torment! And if I can once be truly solitary, [even] then I will not be alone. A lover steals up and listening seeks if his mistress is alone; so steals over me, night and day in my solitude, pain, in my solitude, torment. Ah! when one day I am solitary in the grave, then it will leave me alone!)

The first stanza portrays the solitary man as a

[15]*German Aesthetic and Literary Criticism*, p. 73.
[16]Goethe's texts are taken from *Gedenkausgabe der Werke*, ed. Ernst Beutler (Zurich, 1949), I, 345.

pathetic figure alienated from the life and love that others enjoy. The succeeding stanzas, however, suggest that this alienation is precisely what the solitary desires—a desire the harper acknowledges as his own with the line, "Ja! lasst mich meiner Qual!" It is a desire condemned to frustration. Alone though he may be in a literal sense, the harper finds that his personified torment visits him in secret just as a lover visits his mistress. The presence of others cannot be refused: it reconstitutes itself in the deepest reaches of the self. The simile of the lover suggests that the harper feels the inevitable internalization of others as a sexual violation, an unwanted penetration of the ego, compelled by the alliance between life and love. The harper thus longs for the grave as that fine and private place where true solitude can be at last accomplished.

Goethe's harper, then, is less in flight from his suffering than from the sexualized presence of other selves. By contrast, the harper of Schubert's song wants only to be "left alone" by his unintermitted suffering. A solitary life only heightens his vexed self-awareness, so he turns for mitigation to the solitude of death, in which even sentience leaves one alone. The expressiveness of the song comes chiefly from the quasi-allegorical use it makes of its full cadences, which occur only on the words *Pein*, *Qual*, and *allein*, and which thus create a subtext that outlines the harper's essential conflict as Schubert recreates it.

The first half of the song seems to dramatize a reluctance on the harper's part to admit the reality of his suffering. The opening section divides into a pair of eight-measure periods, with regularly occurring full cadences at mm. 4, 8, and 12. The pain (*Pein*) of the pathetic solitary of the first stanza is referred to over the last of these. The torment (*Qual*) of the harper himself, however, disrupts the periodic rhythm. After the piano has glumly echoed the *Pein* cadence, in m. 14, the harper's half perverse, half defiant demand to be left alone with his torment takes the form of an abrupt move onto VI (F major) in mm. 15–16. Schubert's harper thus limits, even as he admits, his identification with the generalized figure of the solitary. *Seiner Pein* and *meiner Qual* become antonyms rather than synonyms: the one linked with closure, acceptance, the other with continuation, resistance.

In the measures that follow, the harmony becomes digressive. It first skirts the "painful" sonority of the tonic, then passes through it en route to a stronger cadence on VI (m. 25), which accompanies the first half of the simile of the lover. Only as he goes on to apply the simile to himself does Schubert's harper assume the burden of his own torment with a full cadence on the tonic at "mich einsamen die Qual" (m. 31). Heard *subito piano* (then *pianissimo*) after a rending *subito forte* on *Pein*, this cadence answers the submediant cadence at "Ja! lasst mich meiner Qual" (mm. 15–16) which had evaded the emotional truth and initiated the harmonic digression.

The remainder of the song finds a melancholy peace in the aftermath of this catharsis. Marked "mit leiserer Stimme," it dreams of an easeful death by drawing out the process of closure. In this section, lines of text are repeated for the first time, as if the harper were trying to invoke, to call forth, the mortal solitude that the lines envision. In the process, the cadential allegory of the song is brought to fulfillment. The section consists of two eight-measure periods followed by a brief piano postlude. Each period moves in four measures to a half cadence on the dominant at "im Grabe sein" (V at m. 35, V^6 at m. 43), and in four measures more to a perfect authentic cadence on the tonic closing the phrase "da lässt sie mich allein" (mm. 39, 47).

The relation between the terms singled out by the cadences could not be drawn more directly or simply: death is the dissonance that resolves in solitary rest.

Early in this passage (m. 36), "Da lässt sie mich allein" is set to a startling dissonant outburst that disturbs the gathering calm, and, before it subsides onto the dominant, gives an edge of desperation to the harper's wishful prophecy. But the music quickly hushes itself, and as it ebbs away the finality of the closing cadences merges increasingly with the longed-for finality of the grave. In the end, Schubert's harper sings himself to sleep.

Wolf's setting of *Wer sich die Einsamkeit ergibt* alludes to Schubert's in both detail and design without ever sounding like the earlier song. Like Schubert, Wolf begins with an arpeggiated piano prelude to evoke the sound of the harp and rounds back to the harmony of the prelude near the close; he culls his main accompaniment motif from a snatch of descending melody that Schubert dwells on briefly, then abandons (ex. 1); he even follows Schubert in giving Goethe's resentful "dann bin ich nicht allein" a wistful cast by ending the phrase on a somewhat incongruous cadence to a major key. There is also a parallel in the harmonic drama of the two songs. Like Schubert, Wolf sets "Ja! lasst mich meiner Qual" to an "alienated" harmony (G minor, the nominal tonic, as V of C mi-

a. Schubert, mm. 11–14 (piano only)

b. Wolf, mm. 1–2

Example 1

nor),[17] then finds an answering harmony at "mich Einsamen die Qual" (V⁷/V in G minor), which thereupon marks a moment of self-recognition. The effect of these allusions is to incorporate a critical awareness of Schubert into Wolf's expressive design. They establish Wolf's differences from Schubert as explicit acts of revision, and even, as it turns out, of admonishment. The setting of "mich Einsamen die Qual" forms the turning point in this process. Wolf has the voice close this phrase with a sickening descent of a tritone, the most wrenching vocal discontinuity in the song. In so doing, he contradicts the cathartic effect of the cadence with which Schubert sets the same words, and intimates the grim conclusion that the harper's pain can never be mastered.

Wolf's large expressive purpose in *Wer sich die Einsamkeit ergibt* is to revoke the peace of mind that Schubert's harper achieves through the contemplation of his death. Wolf's harper may look forward to oblivion, but he is nonetheless condemned to go on living. His longing for the grave can do nothing to still his unrest: in the final analysis, it *is* that unrest.

Like Schubert, Wolf makes a quasi-allegorical use of full cadences on the tonic to dramatize the harper's quest for assuagement, but his cadential pattern forms a studied antithesis to Schubert's. Of the four full cadences on G minor in Wolf's song, the first two are only fictitiously tonic; their G minor functions as the dominant minor of C minor, which acts throughout as a

polar or shadow tonic. As ex. 2 shows, this splitting of the song into competing tonics is the process that calls forth the entry of the voice. The G-minor Neapolitan sixth of m. 1 becomes a German sixth of C minor through the addition of a G♭, so that the cadence at m. 6 hovers somewhere between V⁷–i in G minor and V⁷/V–v in C minor. This splitting, which is reenacted in mm. 11–14,[18] represents Wolf's version of decadent irony: the quasi-masochistic anguish of a personality that has divided itself into the roles of victim and torturer.

The third G-minor cadence emerges as the harper's thoughts first turn toward the grave. Evolving from a much-prolonged dominant (mm. 18–29, with digressions), the cadence seeks to recover Schubert's association of the peace of death with the release of harmonic tension, but it quickly leads to a reprise of the clash between G minor and C minor (ex. 3). Only with the setting of the last line of text, "Da lässt sie mich allein," is there an uncontested tonic cadence on G minor. As the voice "dies away"— Wolf marks it *ersterbend*, a wishful expansion on Schubert's "leiserer Stimme"—something like peace, repose, release, seems to have been won. Indeed, it is only at this point that the vocal and harmonic cadences coincide, as if the voice finally had made the harmonic repose its own; earlier, the vocal line has either anticipated or followed cadential harmonies.

And then Wolf subverts the whole labor of assuagement with a single stroke. The brief piano postlude seems intent upon echoing the dying fall of the consummating cadence, as Schubert's postlude does. The last two measures, however, intrude the hollow sounds of their parallel fifths and close unexpectedly on the dominant. The music breaks off in the unsatisfied anticipation of a death that lies forever in the future.

The rest of the harper's songs, both Schubert's and Wolf's, steadily work out the emotional logic of the first. Schubert's *Wer nie sein Brot mit Tränen ass* is an unusually protracted song, especially given the brevity of the text, which is matched by Schubert's two earlier settings of it. Schubert requires these antiheavenly lengths in order to play out the drama of the text

---

[17]Wolf's harmony in this passage requires some comment. Mm. 13–14 seem to articulate a full cadence to G minor, but the passage is governed by the German sixth of C minor, which occupies mm. 11³–12, and persists, respaced, through 13¹. (In this context, the D⁷ at 13³⁻⁴ becomes a version of the supertonic chord from which the augmented sixth theoretically derives.) Wolf thus evokes the normal expectation for a G-major chord as V, probably preceded by i⁶₄ of C minor. By moving to V/V and cadencing on G minor, however, he gives the G minor sonority a credible but illusory tonic feeling. If the chord is played in the major, its dominant quality becomes obvious. Another way to understand this passage is to say simply that a tonic G minor appears where a dominant G major is expected. G minor, however, receives no immediate confirmation as a tonic, and turns to a clear G-major dominant in m. 15, followed by a C-minor cadence in m. 16. I prefer to think of the G minor in m. 14 as a purely fictitious tonic, but on either account the G-minor chord comes out sounding defamiliarized, not quite right, and that is what counts in the expressive design of the song.

[18]See fn. 17.

Example 2

Example 3

as an internal rather than an external conflict. Goethe's harper accuses the "heavenly powers" of crassly making guilt the basis of human life:

> Ihr führt ins Leben uns hinein,
> Ihr lasst den Armen schuldig werden,
> Dann überlasst ihr ihn der Pein:
> Denn alle Schuld rächt sich auf Erden.

(You lead us into this life, you let the wretched one grow guilty, then you abandon him to pain: for all guilt calls forth its retribution upon earth.)

Schubert is less concerned with the moral force of this accusation than with the psychology of defying a higher power. The gods of Schubert's harper have their power only in the harper's reverence for them; in Freudian terms, they personify the punitive excesses of his own superego.[19] The song, we might say, unfolds not in textual time but in psychological time.

Schubert's design for *Wer nie sein Brot mit Tränen ass* consists of four variations on a single dramatic gesture, followed by a long coda. The gesture is a crescendo of protest at divine injustice which is abruptly curtailed by a terse decrescendo or a *subito piano*. The first three curtailments also coincide with an abrupt cadential turn from minor to major harmony—a Picardy third. This feature has been much criticized as blandly inappropriate to the text.[20] Assuming that Schubert knew what he was doing, however, it makes expressive sense to take the Picardy thirds as gestures of self-restraint. The major cadences block the anger of the crescendos, perhaps with awe, perhaps with a mechanical but psychologically useful expression of piety. The fourth and most powerful crescendo brings with it the harper's climatic outcry, "alle Schuld," set to a wrenchingly discontinuous harmony that just happens to be in the tonic (ex. 4: A♭ major, approached abruptly from B♭ minor, left unrationalized, and given dominant support in mm. 49–50, is reinterpreted enharmonically as G♯, the leading tone to the tonic, on the downbeat of m. 51). This crescendo curtails itself all the way to triple *piano* without the Picardy third, as if the harper's resurgent outrage had again brought catharsis, as it did in *Wer sich der Einsamkeit ergibt*. Schubert's harper can now gravely accuse the gods of injustice without raising his voice, at peace with himself if not with them. The coda, which restores the Picardy third but omits the crescendo, bears out this impression, but the brief piano postlude reveals the effort of self-denial or of repression that underlies this final calm. The song closes with violently dissonant appoggia-

turas that resolve only with the greatest reluctance onto the major triad (ex. 5).

Schubert achieves a less problematical calm in *An die Türen will ich schleichen*, a simple, dignified, wholly untortured song. Marked *Mässig, in gehender Bewegung*, the music envelops its melancholy in an aura of resignation by means of steady quarter-note motion in the accompaniment and a sustained *piano* dynamic that only rarely admits dramatic accents, and those modest ones. In modified strophic form, with a simple melody of markedly narrow compass, the song is a candid evocation of the *Volkston*. The harper of Goethe's lyric sequence reenters the social world as a kind of holy fool who makes others feel fortunate wherever he wanders, and who wanders everywhere. Schubert's harper makes a far fuller reconciliation: he returns as the archaic, anonymous voice of communal experience itself.

To an unfriendly critic, the resignation won by Schubert's harper might seem no more than a rationalization of passivity, his stoicism a thinly veiled moral failure. That view is implicitly Wolf's, whose harper's protest against the gods in *Wer nie sein Brot mit Tränen ass* rises to an operatic triple *forte* over ponderous two-hand chords that compete for audibility even with the baritone's loud upper register. The outcome for Wolf's harper, however, is neither catharsis nor defiant grandeur but paralysis. The burden of his song is not the Promethean power of moral outrage but its Job-like futility.

Wolf approaches *Wer nie sein Brot mit Tränen ass* by way of a bleak, almost featureless setting of *An die Türen will ich schleichen*, which reduces that detachment from pathos characteristic of Goethe's and Schubert's harpers to a frozen insensibility. The first half of *Wer nie sein Brot mit Tränen ass* allows the harper's feelings to reawaken; the second half releases them into uninhibited rage. At Goethe's accusatory, "Ihr himmlischen Mächte," Wolf alludes to the Picardy third with which Schubert sets the same phrase, though Wolf's unexpected major chords are dominants. The prospect of Schubertian restraint, however, is rejected as soon as it arises. Wolf's crescendo of protest begins over a series of rumbling arpeggios and reaches a first climax as the arpeggios give way to chordal attacks, as if the harper were too distraught to command his instrument. (It may not

---

[19]As one who always tries to yield to Freudian temptations, I should point out the classically Oedipal character of cruelly paternal gods who usher one into life and leave one to incur a primal guilt. My sense is that Schubert's song makes more of this latent textual element than Goethe does.

[20]Newman (p. 196) speaks of the "complete obscuring of Goethe's meaning"; Walker (p. 241) suggests that Schubert misunderstood the text and wrote as if "the singer were finding reconciliation to his fate in the knowledge it has brought him of the heavenly powers."

Example 4

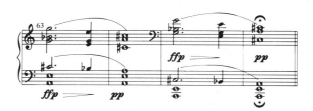

Example 5

Example 6

be fanciful to hear in this a distant echo of Schubert's *Gretchen am Spinnrade*, with its famous suspension of the spinning figure at Gretchen's climactic outburst.) Harshly declaimed, the outcry consummates itself as Schubert's does, with an unexpected, indeed a wrenching, return to the tonic (ex. 6). Unlike Schubert's, however, this tonic finds no cadential confirmation until the last measure of the song. Harmonically enervated, it undercuts the expression of rage that it accompanies.

Then, while the harmony hovers somewhere

in a limbo between iv and V⁷, the piano postlude quickly sinks from *ff* to *p* and enters onto a plane of complete immobility. The melodic cadence of the main accompaniment figure begins to stammer; it fails to complete itself three times in the space of two measures. The sudden decrescendo is a recreation of Schubert's gesture of restraint, but in Wolf it becomes a consummate musical image for paralysis, exhaustion, utter dejection. Even the closing cadence, harmonically decisive though it may be, has an alienated sound to it, thanks to the parallel fifths that link it to the bleak close of *Wer sich die Einsamkeit ergibt*.

NUR WER DIE SEHNSUCHT KENNT

Goethe's Mignon is bound to Wilhelm Meister by half filial, half erotic feelings that she is incapable of understanding but is continually expressing. In one of the novel's most startling episodes, she acts out the racking ambivalence and need for repression that Wilhelm elicits from her:

He raised her up, and she fell upon his breast; he pressed towards him, and kissed her. . . . All at once [she] gave a cry, which was accompanied by spasmodic movements of the body. She started up, and immediately fell down before him, as if broken in every joint. . . . All at once she again became quite stiff, like one enduring the sharpest corporeal agony; and soon with a new vehemence all her frame became alive; and she threw herself about his neck, like a bent spring that is closing. . . . Her rigid limbs were again become relaxed; her inmost soul was pouring itself forth; in the wild confusion of the moment, Wilhelm was afraid she would dissolve in his arms.[21]

The barely suppressible violence of Mignon's desires also forms the essential subject of her song, *Nur wer die Sehnsucht kennt*, which she sings in the novel as a duet with the harper:

Nur wer die Sehnsucht kennt,
Weiss, was ich leide!
Allein und abgetrennt
Von aller Freude,
Seh ich ans Firmament
Nach jener Seite.

Ach! der mich liebt und kennt
Ist in der Weite.
Es schwindelt mir, es brennt
Mein Eingeweide.
Nur wer die Sehnsucht kennt,
Weiss, was ich leide!

(Only the one who knows longing knows what I suffer. Alone and cut off from all joy, I gaze at the sky yonder. Ah! he who loves and knows me is far away. It makes me dizzy, it burns my bowels. Only the one who knows longing knows what I suffer.)

The poem pivots on the sudden extravagance of Mignon's rhetoric at "es schwindelt mir, es brennt / Mein Eingeweide." The abrupt rise in intensity corresponds to an abrupt shift of focus from outer to inner reality, from distance and absence to vertigo and a burning in the bowels. Mignon's longing threatens to become insupportable when it "swindles" her thoughts away from the person she longs for and turns them on herself.[22] For both Schubert and Wolf, the main expressive issue in setting *Nur wer die Sehnsucht kennt* is how to realize the rhetorical discontinuity of "Es schwindelt mir, es brennt / Mein Eingeweide" in musical terms. Schubert tried four times in 1815–16 to find a solution, evidently without feeling that he had succeeded; the canonical version of the song, published as op. 62, no. 4 (D. 877), was not composed until 1826.

For most of its course, Schubert's *Nur wer die Sehnsucht kennt* is *sotto voce* music of utter simplicity. The seven measures devoted to a double statement of "Es schwindelt mir, es brennt / Mein Eingeweide," however, are incommensurate with the rest. The voice shifts from melody to declamation and abandons its steady *pianissimo* for a dramatic swell; the gently rocking accompaniment suddenly turns agitated, and the limpid harmony travels ambiguously through a series of diminished-seventh chords before subsiding onto the dominant.[23] Without actually changing tempo, meter, or underlying harmony, Schubert forms a gripping musical image of self-alienation.

---

[21] Goethe, *Wilhelm Meister's Apprenticeship*, trans. Thomas Carlyle (New York, 1962), p. 144.

[22] "Es schwindelt mir": it makes me dizzy. "Schwindeln": to swindle, defraud.

[23] The progression marks its singularity by starting with a low B♭ —the only echo in the body of the song of the powerful B♭ in the piano introduction, m. 3.

The psychological drama of the song turns on the ability of Schubert's Mignon to make peace with her suffering. As she declaims her climactic phrase for the first time, she yields to a crescendo, only to curtail it as it rises above *forte* at "Eingeweide." Then she repeats her phrase decrescendo with scarcely a pause for breath. In context, this gesture could suggest either self-mastery or exhaustion, an uncertainty that Schubert plays out in harmonic terms (ex. 7). Mignon's second "Eingeweide" comes to rest as the music casts off its mystification and arrives on the dominant. The voice falls on G♯, the third of the dominant chord, in a melodic cadence that is, and is meant to be, remarkably unsatisfying. The unsettled feeling persists for two measures as a terse piano interlude extends the dominant harmony, ending with a fermata on the dominant-seventh chord. In the resolution that follows, the voice both revives the cantabile line of the refrain, "Nur wer die Sehnsucht kennt, / Weiss, was ich leide," and restores simplicity and stability to the harmony. The refrain begins as the voice rises a half-step from the G♯ of "Eingeweide" onto the root of the tonic chord—which is to say, as the voice resolves the G♯ upwards as the leading tone. In dramatic terms, this deferred release of harmonic tension enacts a moment of self-integration. Mignon's pain may not be assuaged—it sounds again through a brief swell on the last "Sehnsucht kennt"—but it can no longer threaten to annihilate her.

Fortunately, Schubert's Mignon was not dealing with Hugo Wolf. The revisionary effort of Wolf's *Nur wer die Sehnsucht kennt* is to abrogate the moment of recovery at the center of Schubert's song. Like Schubert's, Wolf's Mignon declaims her climactic phrase to a crescendo in harmonically unstable surroundings. Wolf's crescendo, however, is completed, not curtailed, and his harmony—a chain of augmented triads that continues almost uninterrupted for eleven measures—is not merely uncertain but genuinely indeterminate. The quiet simplicity that dominates Schubert's song posits a world of common feeling in which Mignon's pain, however fierce and however inward, is anchored. Here the anchor is missing. Everything is edged toward an extreme, even in register; the piano does not descend more than a half octave below middle C until the closing measures. Tempo, too, is unstable; it changes continuously until the return of the refrain.

Following Schubert, Wolf silences the voice after "Eingeweide," but with a telling difference. Wolf's piano interlude lasts for a full twelve measures in constantly retarding tempo. The passage is marked "allmählich ruhiger werden," but as with the curtailed crescendo in Schubert's setting the effect is ambiguous. The gradually but unevenly ebbing music might suggest a slow recovery of composure in the aftermath of a catharsis, or it might suggest mere enervation, a sinking away into a deathly stupor, as if Wolf's Mignon had been actually consumed, deprived of a voice, by the force of her own longing. The gloomier interpretation owns the margin of preference, not only because the interlude is so drawn out, but because the harmony does not clarify itself as the interlude proceeds. When the chain of augmented triads

Example 7

Example 8

is broken, the harmony slowly progresses onto a remote dominant-seventh chord that turns out to herald the return of the voice. But the voice does not resolve the dominant seventh: far from it.[24]

What the voice does do is to immobilize the music on the home dominant, where the close comes a few measures later on a protracted half cadence. The dominant: the very sonority that Schubert's Mignon resolves in order to appropriate her desire as a bearable torment.

This dominant ending is not obvious from a casual look at the score, though its debilitating effect is plain enough to the ear. Wolf's song is written with a key signature of G minor, but the one thing it lacks is a G-minor cadence. As ex. 8 shows, the song begins in a tonal fog with an unanchored $A\flat^6$ chord, then cadences into $E\flat$ minor from $B\flat^7$. This cadential progression remains the primary point of tonal orientation amid much coloristic sonority until the chain of augmented triads that begins with "Es schwindelt mir" effaces all tonal bearings. When the music eventually closes on D major, the supporting details make it clear that Wolf intends the song as a whole to be heard as a large-scale progression from the submediant to the dominant of G minor. As ex. 9 shows, the closing refrain and the piano postlude rationalize what has been heard earlier. The mysterious $A\flat^6$ chord is reinterpreted as a Neapolitan sixth; the $E\flat$ minor that pervades the first half of the piece is reprised as $E\flat$ major, the unaltered sixth degree of G minor; and the D-major chords of the postlude appear as extensions of the D^7 that emerges as the voice brings the refrain to a close.

The effect of this dominant ending is far more frustrating than the abrupt dominant close of *Wer sich die Einsamkeit ergibt*. Supported by its expressive detail—an almost nonexistent melodic cadence in the voice; the long-deferred descent of the piano part into the bass registers—this music bespeaks the disintegration of personality that follows upon a desire that is at once idealized and thwarted. Yet the disintegration is not without a certain seductiveness. The attenuated harmony, long drawn out, evokes a sensuous weariness that is far from the tone of Goethe, but very much that of the Symbolist and Pre-Raphaelite poets who flourished after mid century:

Stand still, fond fettered wretch! while Memory's art
  Parades the past before thy face, and lures
  Thy spirit to her passionate portraitures:
Till the tempestuous tide-gates flung apart
Flood with wild will the hollows of thy heart,
  And thy heart rends thee, and thy body endures.
     —Dante Gabriel Rossetti, *Parted Love*.[25]

POSTLUDE IN LIEU OF A CONCLUSION

In his *Interpretation of Dreams*, Freud discusses a dream that alludes to Hugo Wolf. The dreamer is identified only as a woman of Freud's acquaintance, but I assume that she was a daughter of Freud's early collaborator, Josef Breuer, some of whose children were Wolf's devoted pupils in the early 1880s. In the dream, a

---

[24]A similar discontinuity accompanies an earlier return of the opening at m. 26, the non-resolving dominant seventh being first introduced at m. 21, then prolonged.

[25]Text from *The Pre-Raphaelites and Their Circle*, ed. Cecil B. Lang (Chicago, 1975), p. 103.

Example 9

man with the features of Hans Richter paces back and forth in a violent sweat on the caged-in top of a tower. He is trying to conduct a Wagner opera that has lasted all night. Freud is able to identify the man as Wolf, and he gives a fascinating account of the dream as an expression of the dreamer's predicament.[26] It is also, however, an expression of Wolf's predicament, an astute insight from a pupil who has once loved her teacher. What we have here is a rare opportunity to turn a psychoanalytic dream analysis into music criticism.

The man of the dream is a consummate image for Wolf's harper or Mignon or the persona of dozens of his songs, or, indeed, for Wolf himself. Distraught, harried, a failure on the tower of potency who cannot get the opera done before dawn, a man unable to be himself, to wear his own features, yet someone still trapped by his own identity—the cage that encloses the Wolf: the portrait is recognizable at once. It is a portrait, however, that fits a generation, several generations, and not a man. Wolf recomposed Schubert as he did, not because Wolf's poetic insight was superior—it was not: it was just more articulate—but because he was a man of the late century who had to make music from the top of that tower.

[26]Sigmund Freud, *The Interpretation of Dreams*, trans. James Strachey (New York, 1965), pp. 377–79.

Pelléas and Power: The Reception of Debussy's Opera

JANN PASLER

The premiere of Debussy's opera *Pelléas et Mélisande* at the Paris Opéra-Comique in 1902 provoked a reaction comparable in historical importance to those produced by Hugo's *Hernani* in 1830, Wagner's *Lohengrin* in 1887 and 1891, and Stravinsky's *Le Sacre du printemps* in 1913. At the open dress rehearsal on 28 April, much of the public at large responded with surprise, laughter, and hostility. Ill-disposed to the work by a parodying pamphlet circulated before the performance, they entered the theater resistent to the simplicity of the story, laughed heartily at Mary Garden's English accent when she sang "Je ne suis pas heureuse," shouted "petit guignol" ("little clown") at Yniold, and left indignant because the opera was so different from those to which they were accustomed. Others in the audience, largely Debussysts, clapped excessively—even during the orchestral preludes—and argued vehemently during intermissions with anyone who refused to regard the work as a total triumph. For the premiere on 30 April, Debussy agreed to some prudent cuts, but both sides con-

This essay is based, in part, on a paper presented to the Eleventh Annual Conference, "Social Theory, Politics, and the Arts," at Adelphi University on 27 October 1985. All citations from the reviews of *Pelléas* derive from the articles listed in table 2, and all translations from the French are by the author unless stated otherwise.

Allegorical postcards of Parisian newspapers from the Belle Epoque, reproduced in René de Livois, *Histoire de la presse française*, vol. II (Lausanne, 1965), betw. pp. 360–61. Caricatures of the audience from Albert Millaud, *Physiologies parisiennes* (Paris, 1887).

tinued to respond to the opera with an equal lack of dignity and discrimination.

Even though these conflicts did not result in any riots or arrests—as there had been for *Lohengrin* a decade earlier—nor any interruption of the production, the work clearly inspired intense controversy. Every major newspaper and journal carried a review of *Pelléas* (sometimes more than one), whether the critics were seduced by the opera's charm or felt their values threatened by its scorn of traditions. Moreover, the heated discussions continued well past the first two weeks of performances; they extended over ten years, through the hundredth performance of the opera on 28 January 1913. Despite (or because of) the controversy, the work made more money than such established repertoire items as *Carmen* and *Manon* and for most of its performances, significantly more than the monthly average of all operas (see table 1).

The reasons *Pelléas* triggered such a response have not been examined. Many of those who subsequently wrote about the first performances of the opera, such as Vuillermoz, Laloy, Koechlin, Peter, and Inghelbrecht,[1] were among the original group who worked arduously to have it accepted, both through their faithful attendance at every performance and with their pens. Because they felt that the music critics of the time were "almost unanimous in their condemnation" of the work,[2] any discussion by such Debussysts is tinged with the propaganda they first used to defend the work. Two more objective reviews of the *Pelléas* criticism—by Léon Vallas in his classic monograph on Debussy, and, more recently, by Christian Goubault in his study of music criticism in the French press, 1870–1914—reveal that there were proponents as well as adversaries of the opera among the established critics.[3] These studies, however, do not analyze which critics had the most influence with the public, nor what motivated the various critics to take the positions they did. They also fail to take account of some of the most interesting reviews in nonmusical journals.

By examining and categorizing some four dozen reviews *Pelléas* received during its first season together with selected memoirs and novels of the period, this article will show that the controversy associated with Debussy's opera extended far beyond that caused by the first performances, and that it was fueled more by the clash of values held by the various groups in the opera's first audiences than by the intrinsic nature of the work itself. The rich ladies who enjoyed the air of aristocracy surrounding the opera house, the professional musicians who cherished the traditions of the beloved genre, and the Wagnerian fanatics who sought quasi-religious experiences through music—each of these groups had preconceived notions of what would or could please them and came to the opera with positions fixed in advance. Debussy's friends and supporters, who had been waiting "with curiosity and sympathy" for nine years since the composer began the work and had heard excerpts in salon performances, knew the work would be important[4] and came prepared to defend it, as their red-vested predecessors had defended *Hernani*. Up in the top gallery, the *amateurs de toute condition*—young musicians, composers, poets, and students who had never had the least contact with Debussy, but who had grown to love his orchestral music—listened for what new avenues the work might suggest for the future of French music and music theater. "Licensed" critics came representing every musical persuasion as well as much of the theatrical and literary worlds, which were intrigued by the idea of setting Maeterlinck's play to music.

In effect, the *scandale* of *Pelléas*—the shock, indignation, and outrage caused by the opera—resulted from all these writers using the work to argue for a number of opposing, even contradictory, views on the use, purpose, and nature of opera, music theater, and music in general throughout the first ten years of the century.

---

[1]Émile Vuillermoz, *Claude Debussy* (Geneva, 1957); Louis Laloy, *La Musique retrouvée* (Paris, 1974); Charles Koechlin, *Debussy*, (Paris, 1927); René Peter, *Claude Debussy* (Paris, 1944); Germaine and D. E. Inghelbrecht, *Claude Debussy* (Paris, 1953).
[2]Laloy, p. 106. In his 20 May review, Pierre Lalo also argues that the work had few supporters.
[3]Léon Vallas, *Claude Debussy: His Life and Works*, trans. Marie and Grace O'Brien (New York, 1973); Christian Goubault, *La Critique musicale dans la presse française de 1870 à 1914* (Geneva, 1984).
[4]Henri de Regnier, "Page sur Debussy," in *Vues* (Paris, 1926), p. 87.

Table 1: Receipts for Opera Performances in 1902.

DATE		OTHER OPERAS		PELLÉAS	
		Opéra			
February	17,865 [a]	Siegfried	18,424 [b]		
		Faust	16,276		
March	14,803	Lohengrin	15,825		
		Faust	18,927		
May	16,997	Lohengrin	21,284		
		Faust	20,010		
June	15,677	Valkyrie	18,985		
		Faust	13,445		
September	18,401	Lohengrin	17,815		
		Faust	20,005		
		Samson et Dalila	18,796		
October	17,883	Tannhäuser	19,637		
		Faust	17,781		
		Don Juan	17,192		
November	15,806	Valkyrie	18,168		
		Lohengrin	19,451		
		Faust	17,781		
		Opéra-Comique			
February	6,004	Manon	5,801		
		Carmen	5,916		
		Louise	5,513		
		Grisélidis	6,933		
April				premiere 30	1,131 [c]
May	6,930	Manon	6,332	2	3,938
		Carmen	6,014	3	5,981
		Louise	6,602	8	7,364
		Mignon	8,455	10	6,819
		La Troupe Jolicœur		15	6,517
		premiere	774		
				20	6,221
				25	6,138
				28	5,807
June	5,632	Manon	6,965	1	3,815
		Carmen	5,671	6	7,395
		Louise	3,600	11	5,322
		Mignon	3,761	20	7,798
		Lakmé	7,583	26	6,699
October	6,726	Manon	8,813	30	7,007
		Carmen	9,796		
		Louise	6,138		
		Mignon	6,100		
November	6,254	Manon	7,264	6	6,759
		Carmen	5,909	14	6,331
		Louise	5,698	21	4,939
		Mignon	6,991	29	7,646

SOURCE: From *Le Monde musical*, April through December 1902.
[a] Average receipts for all performances, in francs.
[b] Average receipts per performance.
[c] Date; receipts.

Unlike today, artistic *scandales* occurred relatively often in Paris at the turn of the century. For one thing, theater, and particularly music, served as arenas in which the society could work out its political and social differences. In his 1902 essay, "The Metropolis and Mental Life," the eminent sociologist Georg Simmel analyzes this polemical spirit and suggests that a "latent antipathy" and "practical antagonism" were a necessary part of life in growing urban centers.[5] By effecting distances and aversions, such devaluating responses protect a person from becoming indifferent or indiscriminate in a world of unending sensual stimuli. Any new art work automatically received some hostility. Building support and understanding for a work—i.e., creating a public—was a process that took time and strategy. Audiences were members of a variety of social, political, and cultural groups which could be threatened or appealed to in a number of ways.

Table 2 lists the reviews of *Pelléas* from May to July 1902. About half were drawn from Claude Abravanel's bibliography on Debussy;[6] the other half were turned up by a lengthy search through the numerous journals of the time. I have devised the categories in this table in order to identify the order in which the reviews appeared, the publics to whom they were addressed, and the biases that the critics brought to the opera. In its construction, then, the table aims to suggest in capsule form a number of forces that may have informed the critics' judgements and influenced the way they shaped public opinion.

The political orientation of the newspapers and the social class of their readers readily present two sets of potential forces that the critics must have taken into account. From the table, it is clear that in general the newspapers' re-

jection of or receptivity to *Pelléas* aligns directly with their politics. Monarchist papers—*Le Gaulois* and the *Gazette de France*—attacked the opera viciously, while republican ones—*Le Petit Parisien*, *Le Temps*, the *Journal des Débats*, *La République*, *La Petite République*, and the *Revue de Paris*—supported it. There were exceptions, however, depending in part on the degree of the paper's appeal to its readers' social class. The most important critical journal, the *Revue des deux mondes*, took a stance which would satisfy the *haute bourgeoisie* rather than other republicans among its readership; consequently, in both tone and argument, its review sounds remarkably like those published in the quasi-official papers of the aristocracy, *Le Gaulois* and the *Gazette de France*. These attacks were dangerous to the work because they addressed the very public whose subscriptions and taxes supported the Opéra. By contrast, one monarchist paper, *Le Soleil*, reviewed the opera favorably, perhaps because it had slightly different readers than the other two. Like *La Liberté* and *Le Matin*, which praised *Pelléas*, *Le Soleil* was read by businessmen rather than the nobility, many of whom lived in the provinces.

There also appears to be a correlation between the various papers' stand in the Dreyfus affair (which began in 1894 and reached its peak in 1898–99) and their disposition toward *Pelléas*. Anti-Dreyfus papers (*Le Petit Journal*, *L'Éclair*, and *Le Gaulois*) took a negative view of the opera (except for D'Indy who, in *L'Occident*, surprisingly reversed his earlier opposition to the opera), while the pro-Dreyfus *Le Soleil*, *Revue de Paris*, and *Revue blanche*, were perhaps more inclined to urge their readers to give Debussy's opera a chance. The papers' views on nationalism, however, seem not to have carried much weight, for the nationalists split over the opera, depending on whether the paper or its critic was socialist (*La Presse* and Bauër came out for *Pelléas*) or anti-socialist (*L'Echo de Paris*'s review was somewhat negative) and to the extent some nationalists were also anti-Dreyfus (*Le Petit Journal* and *L'Éclair*).

The type of interest held by the readers suggests a third force to which the critics responded. To the degree that the paper addressed bourgeois socialites (*L'Echo de Paris*, *Gil Blas*, and the *Magasin pittoresque*), its critics were reluctant to give much praise; but when writing

[5]*The Sociology of Georg Simmel*, trans. and ed. Kurt H. Wolff (New York, 1950), p. 409–17. I am indebted to Chandra Mukerji for directing me to this article and to Pierre Bourdieu, Bennett Berger, Gaye Tuchman, Yaffa Schlesinger, and Tia DeNora for valuable discussions with them concerning the sociology of the arts. I also wish to thank Ann Feldman, Joseph Kerman, and William Weber for their helpful comments.

[6]Claude Abravanel, *Claude Debussy: A Bibliography* (Detroit, 1974), p. 111.

Table 2: Critical Reviews of *Pelléas et Mélisande,* May–July 1902.

Paper[a]	Emphasis (Readers)	Critic	Critic's Status, Tastes	Date, Evaluation[b]
Large Circulation Daily Newspapers				
*Le Matin (200,000) ↑	news, rep. all political views, not clerical (politicians)	André Corneau	critic at the *Revue blanche*	1 May⁺
Le Petit Parisien (1,000,000) ↑	republican (mass market esp. in provinces)	Montcornet		1 May⁺
Le Petit Journal (900,000) ↓	nationalist, anti-Dreyfus (mass market esp. in provinces)	Léon Kerst	"intellect moyen"	1 May⁻
Le Journal (600,000) ↑	literary, pro-Dreyfus (writers, intellectuals, mass market)	*Catulle Mendès	writer, librettist, Wagnerian	1 May°
Other Daily Newspapers				
*L'Echo de Paris (80,000) ↑	nationalist, catholic, fearing socialism (bourgeois socialites)	*Henry Gauthier-Villars (Willy)	novelist, Wagnerian	1 May°
L'Eclair (60,000) ↓	political, nationalist, anti-Dreyfus	Samuel Rousseau	composer	1 May⁻
Le Soleil (35,000)	defends big business, pro-Dreyfus (moderate monarchists)	O'Divy		1 May⁺
*Le Figaro (20,000) ↑	attempts to be a-political [low sales, but respected reviews] (bourgeois, republicans)	Eugène d'Harcourt	composer	1 May⁻
Le Figaro (20,000) ↑	*see above*	*Un monsieur d'orchestre*	concert-goer	1 May°
*Le Gaulois (25,000)	monarchist, bonapartist, anti-Dreyfus (aristocracy, some *haute bourgeoisie*)	Louis de Fourcaud	Wagnerian, art historian, professor	1 May⁻
Gil Blas	short stories, gossip (socialites)	Gaston Serpette	composer	1 May⁻
La Liberté (50,000) ↑	financial business (bourgeois)	Gaston Carraud	composer, pro-Schola Cantorum	2 May⁺
La République (3,500) ↓	(educated republicans)	Litte (*alias* André Suarès)	writer, prefers Beethoven, Wagner	2 May°
La Petite République (100,000) ↓	open to all types of socialism (less-educated republicans)	Camille de Saint-Croix	literary critic	⁺
La Presse (50,000) ↑	socialist, nationalist, Boulangist	Gustave Bret	conductor	⁺
Gazette de France (5,000)	monarchist [one of oldest] (upper class, esp. in provinces)	Henri de Curzon	musicologist, archivist	3 May⁻
Le Figaro (20,000) ↑	*see above*	Henry Bauër	socialist, politically *engagé*	5 May⁺
Gazette des Beaux-Arts supplement	(art lovers)	*Paul Dukas	composer	10 May⁺

(continued)

Table 2 (*continued*)

Paper[a]	Emphasis (Readers)	Critic	Critic's Status, Tastes	Date, Evaluation[b]
Journal des Débats (15,000) ↑	[old, established] (moderate republicans, academic elite)	Adolphe Jullien	pro-Wagner and Germans, musicologist, pro-Maeterlinck	11 May⁺
Le Figaro (20,000) ↑	*see above*	Robert Flers	Interview of Debussy on his critics	16 May
Le Temps (35,000) ↑	politically moderate [most respected] (republican bourgeoisie)	*Pierre Lalo	anti-Wagner, critic, son of the composer E. Lalo	20 May⁺

Journals

Paper[a]	Emphasis (Readers)	Critic	Critic's Status, Tastes	Date, Evaluation[b]
*Le Ménestrel	conservative, anti-Wagner (musical public)	Arthur Pougin	editor, arch-conservative musicologist	4 May⁻
La Revue Musicale	music history, analysis (musicologists)	Louis Schneider	music gossip columnist like Willy, musicologist	May⁺
Revue d'Art dramatique et musical	(writers, theater-goers)	Robert Brussel	drama critic	May⁺
La Revue dorée	(young writers)	Emile Vuillermoz	young critic, Debussyste	May⁺
Revue bleue (30,000)	(politicians, writers)	Paul Flat	theater critic, Wagnerian	10 May°
Revue des deux mondes (32,000)	ideas, Catholic (*haute bourgeoisie*, conservative republicans)	*Camille Bellaigue	Catholic, *haut bourgeois*, music critic, prize-winning pianist	15 May⁻
Revue de Paris (20,000)	ideas, pro-Dreyfus (*haute bourgoisie*, conservative republicans)	André Hallays	ex-editor of the *Journal des Débats*, music critic	15 May⁺
La Revue (15,000)	ideas (writers)	Paul Souday	literary critic	15 May°
Le Courrier musical	(progressive musical public)	Victor Debay	writer, opera reviewer	15 May⁺
Le Guide musical [Brussels]	anti-Wagner (musical public)	Hugues Imbert	journal editor, critic, prefers chamber music (born 1842)	15 May?⁻
Le Monde musical	making of instruments (musical public)	Auguste Mangeot	journal publisher	15 May°
L'Art moderne [Brussels]	(writers, artists)	M. D. Calvocoressi	young critic	15 May°
Magasin pittoresque, supplement	(bourgeois)	Emile Fouquet		15 May⁻
L'Art moderne [Brussels]	*see above*	Octave Maus	journal editor	25 May⁺
Mercure de France (10,000)	ideas, some symbolist (independent writers)	Jean Marnold	young critic, Debussyste	June⁺
Le Courrier musical	*see above*	Paul Locard	orchestra concert reviewer	1 June⁺

Table 2 (*continued*)

Paper[a]	Emphasis (Readers)	Critic	Critic's Status, Tastes	Date, Evaluation[b]
Revue d'Art dramatique et musical	*see above*	*Paul Dukas	composer	June: rpt. of above
L'Occident	anti-Dreyfus [founded 1902] (artists)	*Vincent D'Indy	composer, professor	June[+]
Le Théâtre	(theater-goers)	Adolphe Jullien	musicologist, *see above*	June[+]
Le Théâtre	*see above*	Louis Lastret	theater critic	June[+]
La Renaissance latine	interest in provincial culture	Florencio Odero	prefers Charpentier	June[o]
L'Ermitage	symbolist (writers)	Henri Ghéon	poet, critic	July[+]
Revue universelle	ideas (writers, intellectuals)	Camille Mauclair	poet, novelist, aesthetician	July[+]
Le Grande France	(libertarian politicians)	Amédée Rouques	poet	July[+]
La Grande Revue	ideas (writers)	Alfred Bruneau	composer, pro-Dreyfus	July[+]
Revue blanche	ideas, pro-Dreyfus (writers)	Julien Benda	philosopher, writer	July[+]

SOURCE: Information on political orientation of the French press and its readership from Claude Bellander, et al., *Histoire Generale de la presse française*, vol. III (Paris, 1972); René de Livois, *Histoire de la presse française*, vol. II (Lausanne, 1965); Theodore Zeldin, *France 1848–1945*, 2 vols. (Oxford, 1977); and Christian Goubault, *La Critique musicale dans la presse française de 1870 à 1914* (Geneva, 1984). Information on the critics, their status, and their tastes gleaned from their own writings and from Vallas and Goubault.

NOTE: The more important journals and critics are marked with an asterisk.

[a]Approximate circulation; rising or falling in 1902.

[b]Positive, negative, mixed.

for writers and art-lovers (*Le Journal*, the *Gazette des Beaux-Arts*, *L'Art moderne*, the *Mercure de France*, *L'Ermitage*, etc.), the reviews were mixed at worse and full of acclamation for the most part. The musical public received perhaps the most diverse response from its critics, depending, predictably, on whether it was perceived as interested in progressive new trends or conservative traditions.

A fourth consideration underlying the critics' evaluation of the opera derives from their own principal occupation and its perspectives. Most of those who wrote criticism, poetry, and/or novels as their main form of employment (the greatest percentage of the critics on this list) found it easy to appreciate the opera whether they understood it or not, and none panned it outright. But the composer-critics swung both ways. It may be suspected that the three who attacked the opera—D'Harcourt, Serpette, and Rousseau—may have felt that the lit-

tle attention their music had received was called into jeopardy by the new opera, whereas those who defended *Pelléas*—Dukas, Bruneau, and even D'Indy, all well-known composers—felt secure enough to admire something that actually challenged their own compositional approaches. The greatest resistance to the opera came from professional musicologists and historically-minded music critics, most of whom remained committed to an earlier form of opera. Four of the six critics falling into this category were deeply disturbed by *Pelléas* and wrote scathing reviews.

The particular way these political, social, and cultural forces were brought into play during the first two weeks of the opera's life explains why Debussy's supporters had reason for concern about its survival, let alone its success. For the first week, 30 April–5 May, the criticism was largely divided. Each of the four large-circulation daily newspapers printed reviews. The

tery" and the "indecisiveness of its emotions, thoughts, and language"—and even though Debussy "never used his wonderful talents with more skill," he regretted the composer's "systematic exaggeration of monotony" in the vocal parts and his "stubborn determination to 'musicalize' even the least musical phrases." Surely some of Debussy's writer friends knew that Mendès might have harbored a lingering resentment over Debussy's refusal to finish their mutual project *Rodrigue et Chimène* when he began *Pelléas;* nonetheless René Peter considered Mendès "the most qualified [*designé*] of them all to penetrate this surprising work."[7] When the critic addressed the very issues most dear to

---

[7]Peter, p. 191.

most powerful paper in town was *Le Matin;* its critic, André Corneau, who had known Debussy from the *Revue blanche,* wrote favorably, but had little influence, having worked at the paper for only a year. The two papers addressed to the working classes, *Le Petit Parisien* and *Le Petit Journal,* disagreed. Montcornet, writing for the former, found that the music served its atmospheric function in the theater well, while Léon Kerst, writing for the latter, simply told people not to go hear *Pelléas,* since they would not understand it.

Catulle Mendès, a much more respected writer at the fourth major paper, *Le Journal,* insisted that the collaboration had not been a fruitful one. Mendès left the theater, he said, wanting to see the music and the play performed separately. This attack posed a real threat to the work, for even though Mendès liked the play, he found that, in the opera, the text loses its most valuable qualities—its "mys-

Debussy's symbolist supporters, such as the relationship between the music and the text, and concluded that the musico-poetic analogies were entirely superficial and that "we have been deceived" in placing our hopes in Debussy, his review had the potential of scaring away Debussy's base of support.

On the next level, the twelve critics from the other daily newspapers who reviewed the work also disagreed with one another. Five who admired the work (O'Divy, Carraud, Saint-Croix, Bret, Bauër) did not pretend to understand it, but praised its novelty; some of them said that if people went without any expectations, it would delight them. Suarès was also mystified, but while he applauded Debussy's skill and originality, he also registered a few reservations concerning the excessive importance given to the text. As noted earlier, these relatively favorable

reviews came in papers read by businessmen, republicans, and socialists. Four critics who condemned the work (D'Harcourt, Fourcaud, Serpette, Curzon) attacked the composer and his alleged contempt for conventions more than the opera itself. They directed their words primarily to socialites and the high society. Among those who rejected the opera, only Rousseau appears to have examined the music in detail.

But probably the most important critic of the daily press, Willy (Henry Gauthier-Villars), refused to cast his vote definitively either for or against the opera. This was another serious impediment to the opera's success. Not only were Willy's *Lettres de l'ouvreuse* very popular with all kinds of concert-goers and salon people, but, like Mendès, he knew the composer, he had heard excerpts of the work as it was being composed, and he was well aware of how his comments would be read by the public. Remarks tinged with disapproval interrupt his otherwise sympathetic review. For example, although he scolded readers who had laughed during the opera (wondering if many of them, like Golaud, had also been cuckolded by their wives!), he made light of the story himself with a humorous plot summary. And while he called Debussy a poet and succinctly identified the opera's innovative declamation, unusual orchestration, and harmonies built of fourths, fifths, and ninth chords, he also expressed some reservation as to their aesthetic effect. Debussy's unresolved dissonances evoked his strongest objection: "My God, yes! How harsh they are! What can I say? I am without a doubt becoming a *pompier* [academic]; it's my turn, I confess that these scraping noises annoy me a little." From such a writer, these criticisms were taken to heart. (Perhaps Willy was the "impenitent Wagnerian" that Laloy dubbed him, after all.[8])

These equivocal, highly favorable, and downright dismissive early reviews fueled the controversy surrounding the work. Some of the criticism that came out the next week began to examine the resistance to the work and defend it against specific criticisms. Paul Dukas, who wrote perhaps the most important of these, said that the opera was just too different for anyone to think it could be understood right away. Given his position at one of the oldest papers in Paris, the *Journal des Débats*, and his long-time devotion to Wagner, Adolphe Jullien surprised his readers by placing Debussy's originality on a par with Wagner's and by suggesting that if the listener allowed himself, he would find the impression often agreeable, and even sometimes a bit profound.

Before this defense of *Pelléas* could win many sympathizers, however, the journal critics, who had not yet voiced their opinions, initiated a new series of attacks and counterattacks in the 15 May and 1 June issues of the important monthly and semimonthly journals. In the *Revue des deux mondes* and *Revue de Paris*, the most respected periodicals of Parisian high society, and in *Le Temps*, their daily equivalent, the success or failure of Debussy's opera became an issue involving some of the society's most pressing questions.

AESTHETIC ISSUES

What kept *Pelléas et Mélisande* such a controversial topic of discussion throughout the spring and summer of 1902? From the musical perspective, the debate revolved around Debussy's approach to form, development, orchestration, and the "holy trinity"—that is, the three musical elements: harmony, melody, and rhythm. For some, the work lacked any nuance, any real "melody, motive, phrase, accent, form, and contour" (Kerst, Corneau, Pougin, Serpette, D'Harcourt, Curzon, Bellaigue); yet others heard in it an "infinity of nuances" and not a moment without all of the elements of music, only in new forms and guises (Dukas, Locard, Debay, Mauclair). Many objected to a total absence of development in the work, though Marnold claimed that Debussy used all the resources of leitmotifs, including the developmental, but in his own unusual way. As far as harmonies were concerned, those like Willy and Imbert, who found them ugly, harsh, and irritating, or like Rousseau, for whom they were too numerous, argued with Hallays, who heard not a grating sound in the opera, and Locard, who claimed that the work's "tonal uncertainty was more apparent than real." For Mauclair, Debussy was "the most original harmonist of the times."

In addition to examining the opera's music, discussions sometimes extended to Debussy's other compositions and to his musical background. Depending on how they viewed his orchestral music, the critics of music journals

---

[8]Laloy, p. 129. In his memoirs, *Souvenirs littéraires . . . et autres* (Paris, 1925), Willy mentions that he got nasty letters during the war "for having confessed to remaining an 'unchanged' partisan of Wagnerian music" (p. 94). Even though he had moved in the same circles as Debussy, in these same memoirs he writes, "And Debussy himself could not cure me completely of what he considered a mortal sickness. Certainly, an invincible charm emanates from the tenderness with which Pelléas showers Mélisande with her long hair; I felt it, but it does not make one forget one's old loves . . . the memory of Siegfried's horn" (p. 95).

By the turn of the century, neither for Willy, Mendès, or the other Wagnerians could it be said that they "were committed to furthering the cause of forward-looking trends in French culture," as Gerald D. Turbow mistakenly concludes in his essay, "Art and Politics: Wagnerism in France" in *Wagnerism in European Culture and Politics*, ed. David C. Large and William Weber (Ithaca, 1984), p. 166, even though this may have been true in the mid-nineteenth century.

sought either to attract more concert-goers by comparing *Pelléas* favorably with this other music (Debay, Schneider), or to put them off by making this same comparison (Imbert). To bolster his argument, Pougin went so far as to undermine Debussy's credibility with the conservative musical public of *Le Ménestrel* by noting how few works the composer had written and how, at forty years old, it was really too late to try to establish a reputation. (Perhaps in response to this manipulation of public opinion, Locard wrote in his 1 June review, "Let fearful souls be reassured, [Debussy] is an excellent musician: his musical training is solid, he cherishes Renaissance music, defends Bach, and works on his scores for many years.")

But whether the work's opponents found the music of *Pelléas* threatening or just monotonous, their criticisms were certainly not graced with much originality. After reading the first three weeks of criticisms heaved at Debussy's opera, Pierre Lalo writes on 20 May:

Listen to the adversaries of *Pelléas*: you would think you were reading an article by Scudo or Oscar Comettant on *Tannhäuser*.[9] And what about this? 'He abolishes melody; it's the vocal or instrumental discourse that preoccupies him, not the song.' Is this Debussy? No, Bizet. It's the critic of *Le Figaro* judging *Carmen* this way. And who, other than Debussy, can one reproach for his 'obscure harmonies' and the 'murky depths' of his inspiration? Why Mozart, in 1805.

Yet even with this defense of Debussy's musical choices, the debate continued.

Beyond the music, broader aesthetic issues and particularly the problem of music theater also created controversy. Most critics devoted the first one-third to one-half of their review to discussing the play. Symbolist writers applauded the work for its use of a drama based on sentiment and sensation, rather than on metaphysics or romance. Henri Ghéon called the opera "a dramatic event" and, in the July issue of the symbolist journal *L'Ermitage*, he devoted the fifth of his series on a renaissance in contemporary theater to an analysis of the work.

But those devoted to Wagner or Massenet complained bitterly. Paul Souday pointed out in *La Revue* that literary decadence was dead and buried, having been killed by boredom, and that in consequence Debussy's symbolist opera—also *mortellement ennuyeux*—was behind the times rather than ahead of them.

Perhaps the greatest divergence of opinion came in discussing the relationship between Maeterlinck's play and Debussy's music. Hallays defended the few cuts Debussy made in the original text, in an attempt to reassure and attract Maeterlinck fans, and considered the text responsible for inspiring many qualities of the music. Ghéon, Mauclair, Mangeot, Imbert, and Bruneau, however, regretted Debussy's choice of libretto and would have wished for more cuts in the original play. The play was "too obscure, naive, and complicated," said Mauclair, "too fragile and internal"; it is better read than staged. In general, the critics agreed that Debussy's music faithfully translated the poet's thought, but there was also considerable dissension about whether the text dominates or should dominate the music. The composer Dukas saw a perfect union between its music and words, whereas, ironically, it was such writers as Suarès and Mauclair who thought Debussy had gone too far in following the text.

One could say a great deal more about the musical and aesthetic issues at stake in this opera. Vallas and other Debussy biographers have already explained various ways the music was heard and understood. But the manner in which the opera was perceived as music theater calls for more than a study of the reception of *Pelléas*, and indeed a discussion of the relationship of the opera to other symbolist theater at the time. In this paper, these matters will be taken up only as they play roles in the larger social-political context.

SOCIAL, MORAL, AND POLITICAL ISSUES

Behind the words used by the critics, particularly those writing for *ancien régime* or high society publications, lurk a number of social, moral, and political presuppositions. In the following, I shall examine four such issues raised by *Pelléas et Mélisande*: first, the use and purpose of opera, including the function of opera-going; second, the ability of text, music, and a

---

[9]In his *Le Goût musical en France* (Geneva, 1905), p. 327, Lionel de la Laurencie quotes these critics as blaming *Tannhäuser* for having a "formless melody, colorless and deafening, that condemns you to deadly boredom."

composer's lifestyle to affect the morality of the audience; third, the notion of opera as a place for confronting political differences and a political tool for lauding French music over German music; and fourth, the idea of artistic innovation as a model of either individual freedom or anarchy.

Social Issues. For many, the Opéra was of course first and foremost a meeting place, a place to see and be seen, as it had been for many years. For a certain social class, indeed—the wealthy opera subscribers—such an "institution of luxury, that luxury upholds, and that is made only for it"[10] served as an important if nostalgic reminder of the days when the aristocracy flourished. By donning the right clothes and attending the opera, anyone, especially the *nouveaux riches*, could give the impression that they belonged to the upper classes. Octave Mirbeau, a writer who frequented the same circles as Debussy, wrote in 1885 that

The Opéra is an elegant meeting place for a certain social class that can pay 34,000 francs per year for the right to show up in tuxedos and strapless gowns three times a week, from ten to midnight, in one of the boxes. It is sort of a grand banal salon, divided into an infinity of small individual salons. . . . Consequently what one asks from it is not art but elegance, and luxury, and all the conveniences for holding fashionable receptions.[11]

From this standpoint *Pelléas* was no different from any other opera. Three of the more enlightened wealthy ladies known to have attended its premiere were the Princesse de Polignac, the daughter of Isaac Singer who returned from Venice especially for the opening, Mme de Saint-Marceaux, and the Comtesse Greffulhe, Robert de Montesquiou's cousin and a great arts patroness who had supported the only performance of Maeterlinck's *Pelléas et Mélisande* in 1893. Such listeners occupied the main floor and the principal boxes. Attending *Pelléas* on 10 May, the writer Jules Renard perceived this public as "consisting of rich ladies who go only there or to the Opéra," and he arrived at the same conclusion as Mirbeau: "It's a kind of

huge café where strapless gowns and diamonds and the deaf (who want to give the impression that they can hear) hold their *rendez-vous*."[12]

At the turn of the century, the opera began to attract another type of elite, the snobs. In his *Chez les snobs* (1896), the novelist Pierre Veber derided snobs as those "who follow the latest fashion," "who want to understand everything or at least seem to," "*bourgeois-gentilhommes de l'esthétique*," "who only esteem the rare and the precious."[13] Their attraction to a personality or an artist depended not on personal taste or critical sense, but on the prestige surrounding his work. For them, performances were meeting places where they hoped to be seen associated with the avant-garde.[14]

The notorious writer Jean Lorrain called the particular snobs who attended Debussy's opera *Pelléastres*, and he described them with considerable malice in a novel with that name. According to him and the critic Florencio Odero, many had been devotees of the Théâtre de l'Œuvre where Maeterlinck's play was given its premiere. Most were quite young and dressed very elegantly. These aesthetes—dandies who "loved their mothers," "composed Greek verses," and "were good musicians" together with their mistresses—"beautiful," "useless," "concerned about intellectuality," and "scornful of the masses"—mixed with the socialites in the best seats in the house.[15] Vuillermoz notes that Lorrain painted these musical snobs with his own vices, and that their fervor exasperated Debussy.[16] Fernand Gregh says in his memoirs,

---

[10]Octave Mirbeau, *Des Artistes*, 2nd series (Paris, 1924), p. 253.

[11]Mirbeau, pp. 259–60.

[12]Jules Renard, *Journal 1887–1910* (Paris, 1965), pp. 751, 760. Renard found *Pelléas* to be "un sombre ennui" ("a dismal bore") (p. 751).

[13]Pierre Veber, *Chez les snobs* (Paris, 1896), pp. 9, 41. In her autobiography, *Earthly Paradise* (New York, 1966; trans. from various French sources), Colette names Veber as one of several ghost writers for her husband Willy.

[14]Emilien Carassus, *Le Snobisme et les lettres françaises de Paul Bourget à Marcel Proust 1884–1914* (Paris, 1966), pp. 38, 170.

[15]Jean Lorrain, *Pelléastres* (Paris, 1910; excerpts first published in *Le Journal*, 22 January 1904), pp. 24, 26, 28; Willy, *Maîtresses d'esthètes* (Paris, 1897), pp. 50–54.

[16]Vuillermoz, *Debussy*, p. 100. After reading the first installment of Lorrain's essay in *Le Journal*, Pierre Louÿs wrote Debussy that he could sue, but it would be preferable simply to ignore the writer (*Correspondence de Claude Debussy et Pierre Louÿs*, ed. Henri Borgeaud [Paris, 1945], pp. 176–77).

however, that he and his literary friends were proud to be *Pelleástres*.[17]

In reality, *Pelléas* did attract many writers, some of whom were snobs and others who were serious intellectuals, for ever since he had begun working on the opera in 1893, Debussy had built substantial support and interest in his opera among writers by frequently playing excerpts of it in various salons and literary circles—especially those of Pierre Louÿs, Mme de Saint-Marceaux, and the *Revue blanche*. When *Pelléas* finally opened, Debussy put pressure on these friends to come. "It is necessary for our friendship that you be there," he wrote to Pierre Louÿs, and he urged Louÿs to bring along Lebey and Valéry. Louÿs agreed to bring five friends so that the group would "fill the ground floor box with applause."[18] Such writers as Paul Valéry, Henri de Regnier, André Lebey, Octave Mirbeau, Curnonsky, Jean-Paul Toulet, and Léon Blum were among this group.[19]

For both groups—the social and the intellectual elite, including their feigned members—the self-definition they sought in going to the opera depended on a certain kind of art. Only that which upheld tradition could reinforce the class identification the social snobs sought. Only the new and unknown, however, could fulfill the desires of the *chercheurs de l'inédit* ("seekers of the novel"), who rapidly became the "zealots of new aesthetic enterprises."[20] And to the extent that some zealots (like the Wagnerians) became convinced of one aesthetic direction, they became intolerant of any other one. The critics were clearly aware of these underlying motivations in their readers and appealed to them directly in their reviews. To discourage their readers from attending, many of those who addressed the high society (such as Fourcaud and Bellaigue) placed emphasis on Debussy's rejection of traditions, while to lure

their readers to the opera, those who wrote for libertarians and intellectuals (such as Bauër, Brussel, Corneau, Dukas, and Mauclair) stressed the composer's profound originality.

The kind of opera they defended also depended on what opera-goers considered the purpose of opera to be. Mirbeau writes that opera subscribers were satisfied and charmed with whatever was sung for them, that is, as long as they could see the latest fashions and admire beautiful women.[21] In the Goncourts' journal, one gets this perspective from both the male and female points of view. Returning from a gala at the Opéra in 1893, Edmond de Goncourt shares his desire to see beautiful women there, but regrets that it was not sated:

A deception. Really this hall is not favorable for the exhibition of a woman's beauty. Those old lights at the back of the boxes kill everything, wipe everything out, especially the soft glow of the light-colored outfits and strapless gowns.[22]

He also reports that the Comtesse Greffulhe, "who was quite charming in white," was upset that evening that the large number of military uniforms attracted too much attention away from the women. Writing of her own experience at the opera in an essay she asks Goncourt to help her publish, the countess describes how the "great anonymous caress" of all the eyes that admire her there totally transforms her each night. "What a blood transfusion this communication with the eyes of the crowd gives me. How to live without it. . . ."[23]

Of course, many opera-goers had more precise demands of the art form. One group sought entertainment through the music—romance, "melodic emotions," as Debussy called them, and charm for the ear. With their beautiful melodies, Mozart, and more recently Massenet, pleased them the most, Wagner the least. Some critics who stressed the sensual qualities of Debussy's music thought that *Pelléas* should satisfy these listeners. Carraud ranked the composer with Mozart; Vincent D'Indy found the

[17]Fernand Gregh, *L'Age d'or: Souvenirs d'enfance et de jeunesse* (Paris, 1947), p. 313.
[18]*Correspondance de Debussy et Louÿs*, ed. Borgeaud, p. 170.
[19]The building of this audience was discussed in a paper presented to the joint meeting of the Northern California and Pacific Southwest chapters of the American Musicological Society at the University of California, Santa Barbara, 27 April 1985.
[20]André Hallays, "De la mode en art et en littérature,"*Revue de Paris*, 1 May 1896, pp. 205–24.

[21]Mirbeau, p. 258.
[22]Édmond et Jules de Goncourt, *Journal: Mémoires de la vie littéraire, 1891–1896*, vol. 4, ed. Robert Ricatte (Paris, 1956), p. 473.
[23]Ibid., p. 611.

The Snob

music comparable with Rossini's, though he also primly judged it inferior for seeking the "damnable pleasures" of sensualism.[24] The majority of those, however, who advocated this kind of opera—conservative musicians and many who favored the *ancien régime*—were quick to denounce *Pelléas* when it did not fulfill their fixed expectations. Corneau addressed them immediately in his review on 1 May:

You will look in vain in the 283 pages of this score for a piece to detach, a melody to extract. Well-loved *romance* flourishes nowhere. Characters do not declaim, and avoid singing. . . . It is uniquely the orchestra that has the task of expressing everything, or better, of making one feel everything.

In *Le Ménestrel*—a journal which, according to Goubault, was read by those who liked only Ambroise Thomas and Massenet and which was owned by the music publisher Heugel, a firm anti-Wagnerian—the reactionary critic Arthur Pougin told his readers that *Pelléas* would leave them cold with boredom and, at most, would give them only "mediocre pleasure."

A second group argued that entertaining, often anecdotal music like Massenet's only existed for the purposes of the theater for which it was written, and that, like the stage itself, the seductions of this kind of music were momentary and incapable of penetrating the depths of one's soul.[25] This faction of the public came to the opera for a quasi-religious experience. In what some called "this century without faith," music became the new religion and the opera house, the temple of high art. The eminent Wagnerian Louis de Fourcaud explains, "What we aspire to is a really deep, human art, not continual effects of titillation which are fundamentally morbid."[26] After calling *Pelléas* "nihilist art," unable "to rouse any deep emotion in our hearts," he continues, "one cannot serve ideals without ideas, one cannot quench the thirst of

[24]Émile Vuillermoz, *Gabriel Fauré*, trans. Kenneth Schapin (Philadelphia, 1969), pp. 34–35.

[25]Robert Burnand, *Paris 1900* (Paris, 1951) p. 181.
[26]Vallas, pp. 126–27.

souls with questionable pharmaceutical beverages."

In spite of this criticism, many *Pelléas* enthusiasts sought the same experience from listening to Debussy's opera as the Wagnerians sought from Wagner's. Lorrain, a staunch anti-Wagnerian, makes fun of how the snobs turned Debussy into the head of another religion. According to him, at each performance of *Pelléas* the Salle Favart took on the atmosphere of a sanctuary:

One only went there with solemn expressions on one's face. . . . After the preludes were listened to in a religious silence, in the corridors there were the initiates' greetings, the finger on their lips, the strange handshakes hastily exchanged in the dim light of the boxes, the faces of the crucified, and the eyes lost in another world.[27]

Lorrain goes on to point out that while the Wagnerians came from all social classes and thus occupied seats throughout the theater, the *Pelléastres* were more elegant and sat principally in seats on the main floor and in the lower boxes.

A third group of opera-goers looked to Debussy's opera as a means of escaping their daily routines and of being transported into an enchanted world—the young. For them, the opera was a stimulus for dreaming. More than orchestral music which, for the symbolist poets, offered a similar experience—opening them to inner experiences they had heretofore never known and inspiring in them a sense of communion, a oneness in feeling—*Pelléas* captivated many young writers. As the twenty-five-year-old Jacques Rivière put it in 1911:

Pelléas was for us a certain forest and a certain region and a terrace overlooking a certain sea. There we escaped, knowing the secret door, and the world no longer meant anything to us.[28]

The young musicians Vuillermoz and Koechlin

also considered the opera "an enchanted garden";[29] but, as their contemporary, the critic Marnold, clarified, they did not feel that the opera transported them "into an unreal sphere, into an external invented world, but rather into [their] own most profound depths." By attracting the young as well as the middle class, the opera expanded its appeal beyond the elite to new audiences during this period.

Moral Issues. Underlying these social issues, there are also a number of moral questions, raised particularly by the critics who wrote for the *haute bourgeoisie*, those who still believed in the *ancien régime*, and the conservative musicians. These critics included Bellaigue, Fourcaud, Imbert, Curzon, D'Harcourt, and Pougin.

At the dress rehearsal, the story and text itself presented problems, even though the story was a classic; many compared it to the love affair of Paolo Malatesta and Francesca da Rimini in Dante. The play *Francesca da Rimini* had been done just recently at the Sarah Bernhardt Theater.[30] Nonetheless, some were unwilling to drop the scurrilous title, *Péderaste et Médisante* ("Pederast and Slanderer"), that had been coined at the dress rehearsal,[31] and others were so upset by the Yniold scene that the Undersecretary of State for Fine Arts forced Debussy to cut four measures before the opera opened, so as to expunge any reference to Pelléas's and Mélisande's proximity to the bed. Given the period, this cut must have seemed pretty silly, yet the producer Albert Carré himself blamed the poor initial reception of the work on the text and he too advised modifying several scenes.[32]

More important were the critics' attacks on Debussy himself and on his way of life. He was classed with the "decadents," a name once invented by journalists to describe adherents of a

---

[27]Lorrain, *Pelléastres*, p. 25. In his second, pre-season review of the opera in the *Revue dorée* (August 1902), Vuillermoz directly contradicts Lorrain's description of audience response to *Pelléas*: "Debussy's music does not encourage foolish swooning, empty looks of ecstasy, and plaintive mutterings as easily as Wagner's. . . . The musical thought is too simple, too pure."

[28]Jacques Rivière, *Études* (Paris, 1944), p. 127.

[29]Vuillermoz, *Debussy*, p. 105; Koechlin, p. 86.

[30]This story clearly was quite popular that year, for in the 15 April 1902 issue of the *Revue des deux mondes*, Téodor de Wyzewa reviews two other plays on the same subject: Stephen Phillip's *Paolo and Francesca*, which was playing in London at the time, and Gabriel d'Annunzio's *Francesca da Rimini*, which was playing in Milan.

[31]Pierre Lalo, *De Rameau à Ravel: Portraits et souvenirs* (Paris, 1947), p. 368.

[32]Henri Busser, *De Pelléas aux Indes galantes* (Paris, 1955), p. 114.

The Decadent

In his review of *Pelléas* in one of the oldest newspapers in Paris, the *Gazette de France*, the archivist and musicologist Henri de Curzon cites Imbert's recent description of Debussy as "enigmatic and sensual, indolent and living his life as if in a kind of dream, attracted only by poets and prose writers of the avant-garde whose troubled and trembling works he uses for his musical creations." Curzon implies a connection between the apparent formlessness of Debussy's music and a life filled with smoke, if not drugs, when he compares it with the formlessness of contemporary painting and blames that on painters who "see through a fog, a smoke, and who ignore precise lines and colors." Bruneau, too, links Debussy's music with the decadent movement and finds the play's "fatality," "disinterested approach to life," and other decadent notions as "suiting [Debussy's] temperament in the most exact way." Perhaps, as Lalo points out in a later review, this "suspicion of defects" in the composer's character developed from the displeasure that "people of taste" experienced at having to sit beside "certain degenerate aesthetes" during performances of *Pelléas!*[34] Not everyone, however, felt this way.[35]

The ultimate attack on *Pelléas* was that the music, if listened to, would ruin one's character. Although he avoids almost all discussion of the music, Curzon reaches this conclusion first by noting that the characters in *Pelléas*, like Debussy, also "act as if in a vague stupor" and then by suggesting a connection between the listener's experience and that of the characters on stage. "As if moved by some external and supernatural forces, they live, and we live with them, in the unconscious and the mysterious depths," he remarks, bemoaning the repulsive "nihilism and negation of all faith, of all guide" which informs their actions. For Curzon, as well as D'Harcourt, Fourcaud, and Bellaigue, *Pelléas* was essentially *maladive* or unhealthy music, music "without life." Bellaigue claims that "after listening to it, one feels sick" and not unlike

literary movement—precursor to the symbolists'—that flourished in the mid-1880s and is best represented by J. K. Huysmans's *A Rebours* ("Against the Grain"). Known for their invented words and concentration on ornamental detail at the expense of the shape of a whole work, the group was criticized for its extravagant writing style as well as for its life-style—dressing in the latest fashions, always lost in the clouds (or seemingly drugged), and smelling of perfumes. The press loved to caricature them. In his *Physiologies parisiennes*, Albert Millaud gives an amusing portrait of the decadent:

Son of the modernist, grandson of the idealist, nephew of the impassible, great-nephew of the Parnassian, . . . the decadent is a young man, very pale, skinny, and respected in certain literary *brasseries.* . . . He doesn't have any ideas; he doesn't want any. He likes words better. . . . When a word does not come to him, he invents it. It's up to the reader to understand and to put ideas under his words. The reader refuses to do so generally. From that comes the decadent's scorn for the reader.[33]

[33]Albert Millaud, *Physiologies parisiennes* (Paris, 1887), pp. 201–03.

[34]Cited in Vuillermoz, *Debussy*, p. 104. According to Vuillermoz, Debussy took offense at this statement because he thought it implied that *Pelléas* was "music for riffraff."
[35]In his review of *Pelléas*, addressed to the theatrical world, Robert Brussel leapt to Debussy's defense. To him, Debussy appeared to live a "modest life"—that of an "upright artist"— "far from newspapers and salons."

Pelléas himself, who sighs, "Nothing is left for me, if I continue in this way."

The powerful music critic Camille Bellaigue went the furthest in condemning the work on moral grounds. Writing for the *Revue des deux mondes*, perhaps the most important journal of the *haute bourgeoisie* and one which was known for having a moral authority, Bellaigue was himself from a family of the *haute bourgeoisie* and wielded considerable influence, having won a first prize in piano at the Conservatoire in 1878. In reviewing *Pelléas*, he builds credibility with the reader by referring to an episode from his youth when he knew Debussy as a fellow student in the piano class of Marmontel. The story is quite a nasty one: he says that the class laughed at Debussy while he played piano because he breathed heavily on every strong beat, but that now he clearly has been cured of this bad habit— all the beats in this music are weak ones. Then, after attacking the work on every possible musical ground and accusing Debussy of presiding over the "decomposition of our art," he addresses his readers, "distinguished, even superior men," and concludes:

We are dissolved by this music because it is in itself a form of dissolution. Existing as it does with the minimum of vitality, it tends to impair and destroy our existence. The germs it contains are not those of life and progress, but of decadence and death.[36]

In a November 1901 article in the same journal, Bellaigue reveals what he would prefer to have in its place—"melodic opera," especially that of Mozart, for his operas "express or realize an ideal of life itself." He gives the characteristics of this ideal as simplicity, even familarity, then peace, joy, and love, without violence or excess.[37] Sure enough, a light-hearted comic opera first performed only weeks after *Pelléas*, Arthur Coquard's *La Troupe Jolicœur*, met with Bellaigue's approval, even though he admitted it could have been "a little more profound and original."[38]

One of *Pelléas*'s staunchest supporters, Louis Laloy, also raises the issue of morals. In his memoirs, he recalls a conversation he had with Jean Lorrain concerning the opera. Lorrain's first words were "I don't like the subject," to which Laloy responded, "Protestant!" According to Laloy, Lorrain's biting parody of *Pelléas* supporters in his novel *Pelléastres* was due to a protestant education that prevented him from understanding the moral import of the story:

I don't want to imply that a protestant is incapable of appreciating *Pelléas*. But all moral codes that treat human nature harshly and that, considering it evil by nature or since original sin, correct it only to constrict it to the commandments and to make it do penance, will necessarily be leery about an artwork so completely emancipated from any constraint and repentance. [He continues, reminding the reader that catholics, by contrary,] do not believe in predestination and, through the help of grace, can always hope for forgiveness for any sin.[39]

Laloy goes on to explain that the moral message he finds in *Pelléas* is not that men and women should abandon themselves to their instincts, but rather try to preserve the state of innocence into which they were born. For him, "*Pelléas* teaches pardon."[40]

Political Issues. In addition to these social and moral issues, many critics upheld or opposed the work for political reasons, some almost entirely so. Since the Opéra was considered by some to be an extension of the state—a meeting place for government officials and a salon for entertaining visiting dignitaries[41]—this intermingling of music and politics was to be expected.

The most obvious and clear-cut of the political issues touching opera at the turn of the century was the question of nationalism—French

---

[36] "Pelléas et Mélisande," *Revue des deux mondes*, 15 May 1902, p. 455; trans. in Vallas, p. 128.

[37] Camille Bellaigue, "Les Époques de la musique: l'opéra mélodique, Mozart," *Revue des deux mondes*, 15 November 1901, p. 904.

[38] In reviewing the opera for the *Revue des deux mondes*, 1 June 1902, pp. 920–21, Bellaigue praises *La Troupe Joli-*

---

cœur's lack of excess together with the sincerity and delicacy of its expression, finds many "excellent things" in it, and considers it "worthy of esteem and sympathy." Bruneau, by contrast (in the same article as his review of *Pelléas*), found the Coquard comedy flawed by "inconsistent and insufficiently drawn characters, predictable *péripéties*, and easy sentimentality." The public seems to have concurred with the latter, for the work was performed only once.

[39] Laloy, p. 110.

[40] Ibid., pp. 112–13.

[41] Mirbeau, pp. 259–61. In his *Paris 1900* (Paris, 1931), Paul Morand also calls the Opéra "a combination of government office, brothel, and political club" (p. 223).

The Man Who Listens to Wagner

rian manifestos and parodies in the press.[42] The caricatures in such books as *Physiologies parisiennes* depicts "the man who listens to Wagner" as not only serious but also stark. Albert Millaud calls him generally "preoccupied and unhappy. One knows he is prey to a continual overexcitement. . . . He both delights and suffers at the same time—a blessing normally given to morphinism."[43]

But these efforts to do away with Wagner had little long-lasting effect in face of the Wagnerians' campaigns. Catulle Mendès, for example, lectured on *Lohengrin* in all the provincial cities where the opera was performed—together with Raoul Pugno, Debussy even accompanied a lecture he gave at the Opéra in 1893 by playing excerpts from *Das Rheingold* (see the list below), and Louis de Fourcaud busily translated as many of the operas as possible into French.[44] The number of concert performances of Wagner's music in Paris grew steadily throughout the 1880s and 1890s, climaxing in the period 1897 to 1900. A decrease in their number in 1900 and 1901 only reflects the fact that entire Wagnerian operas began to be produced regularly in the opera houses. The following table gives the frequency that Wagnerian operas were performed at the Opéra in Paris from the last years of the century through 1902 (compare table 1):[45]

Table 3

Lohengrin	1891–1902	201 times
Die Meistersinger	1897–1902	65 times
Tannhäuser	1861; 1895–1902	116 times
Die Walküre	1893–96; 1898–1902	132 times
Das Rheingold	1893 (two pianos)	1 time
Siegfried	1901–02	20 times

Even Edmond de Goncourt, who rarely concerned himself about music, objected to the Opéra playing Wagner four times a week in 1895.

music *vs.* German music (i.e., Wagner). Nationalism was a wild card that cut across other basic issues and caused unexpected realignments. The conflict began in the 1880s as the French concert halls, and eventually the opera houses, opened their doors to the German master, despite the fact that the Germans had recently taken Alsace and the French public increasingly resented the support of foreign music in their state-supported theaters. Violent riots protesting the performances of *Lohengrin* in Paris at the Eden Theater on 3 May 1887 and in front of the Opéra throughout the month of September 1891 were followed by numerous anti-Wagne-

[42]See especially the exposition catalogue, *Wagner et la France*, ed. Martine Kahane and Nicole Wild (Paris, 1983).
[43]Millaud, *Physiologies parisiennes*, pp. 267–68.
[44]*Wagner et la France*, p. 165. The intellectual journal *L'Ermitage*, however, harshly criticized Fourcaud's translations of Wagner's libretti in its May 1902 issue (p. 190).
[45]The information in this table has been culled from *Wagner et la France*, pp. 158–73.

"And there are sixty-five operas that await performances and will perhaps never be put on!" he points out in his journal.[46] On 31 December 1901, the heated confrontation between those advocating Wagner's music and those crying for more French music became lively again at the dress rehearsal for the first production of *Siegfried* and remained an undercurrent in critical writing throughout the spring of 1902, in preparation for the French premiere of *Götterdämmerung* on 17 May 1902.

To exacerbate the political situation, Wagnerism at the turn of the century became linked with the Dreyfus Affair and with anti-Semitism. Although Debussy claimed neutrality in the Affair, Debussy's supporters and friends were mostly pro-Dreyfus, which did not help the conflict with the Wagnerians; only Pierre Louÿs was passionately anti-Dreyfusard, according to René Peter.[47] Lorrain recognized many in the audience for *Pelléas* from productions at the Théâtre L'Œuvre which, according to its director Lugné-Poë, was a favored *rendez-vous* for the Dreyfusards.[48] The *Revue blanche*, for which Debussy and many of his friends wrote articles, including Regnier, Mirbeau, and Valéry, was another important center for Dreyfusard activity and in 1898 published an article protesting Dreyfus's imprisonment.[49]

Critics who embraced *Pelléas* as an alternative to Wagner did not hide their motivation. Henri Bauër, a politically committed writer who was forced to leave the newspaper *L'Echo de Paris* for supporting the First International, backed Debussy in *Le Figaro*, a newspaper whose principal critic, D'Harcourt, had panned the work only four days earlier. Even though at the time of *Lohengrin*, Bauër had defended Wagner from the "absurd chauvinism" of his compatriots, in 1902 he objected to Wagnerians gaining control of the Opéra and impinging on other composers' freedom to have their works performed. "Finally someone who will liberate French music from Wagnerian oppression!" he exclaimed. In a letter of 8 May 1902, Debussy thanked him for his strong words of support.[50]

Pierre Lalo, the respected son of the composer Édouard Lalo and the critic for the most important paper in town, *Le Temps*, also saw *Pelléas* as strong encouragement for young composers "to emancipate themselves from the tyranny of the Wagnerian formula and to conceive and create with more freedom." Lalo goes so far as to say, "There is nothing or almost nothing of Wagner in *Pelléas*," and backs up this statement with a long list of elements that the work does not share with Wagner's music.[51] Lalo's blatantly polemical essay reflects, in part, his personal feelings of gratitude for Debussy and Carré—Debussy had expressed so much enthusiasm for Édouard Lalo's ballet *Namouna*, which flopped in 1882, that he was almost thrown out of the Conservatoire; and in 1902 Carré put on a totally new production of his father's opera *Le Roi d'Ys* that Lalo and his mother found enchanting[52]—but it also stems from the strongly nationalist feeling which pervaded his life. Throughout his memoirs, Lalo boasts of his French heritage, the fact that five generations of Lalos were military officers and that the family still possessed a commission appointing one of them captain, signed in 1709 by Louis XIV. The only music he praises, such as that of Fauré and Charpentier, is music that is "entirely our own." With *Pelléas*, Lalo felt Debussy "was serving in his own way the cause of France in the world."[53] The French composers Dukas and Koechlin also voiced nationalist cries at the time, complaining that little French music was being played in Paris,[54] and, together with Bruneau, hoped that Debussy's opera would "push the official Wagner imitators into the tomb."

---

[46]Goncourt, *Journal* 4, p. 837.
[47]*Correspondance de Debussy et Louÿs*, ed. Borgeaud, p. 108.
[48]Lugné-Poë, *La Parade; Le Sot du tremplin; Souvenirs et impressions de théâtre* (Paris, 1930), p. 18.
[49]See A. B. Jackson, *La Revue blanche, 1889–1903* (Paris, 1960).

[50]*Claude Debussy: Lettres 1864–1981*, ed. François Lesure (Paris, 1980), p. 114.
[51]Scholars now know, of course, though few of Debussy's contemporaries would admit it, that the opera borrows many things from Wagner, and not just the music of the interludes. See Robin Holloway, *Debussy and Wagner* (London, 1979); and Carolyn Abbate, "Tristan in the Composition of Pelléas," *19th-Cen Mus* 5 (1981), 117-41.
[52]Busser, p. 108.
[53]References in this paragraph to Lalo's memoirs come from his *De Rameau à Ravel*, pp. 73, 365, and 371.
[54]Koechlin, p. 58.

The boldness of Debussy's innovations likewise provoked a more general, but also latently political discussion between those who advocated following rules and those who valued freedom and individuality—in extreme terms, between conservatives and anarchists. Critics of the first persuasion included not only the traditionalists but also the Wagnerians, for whom Wagner had by now become *the* formula for music drama. D'Harcourt, Fourcaud, Bellaigue, and Pougin were convinced that Debussy followed no logic or reason and ignored the laws of the "holy trinity" (the musical elements). While harmony, by definition, involves both "order" and "hierarchy," Bellaigue found it in Debussy's music to be synonymous with "anarchy," "disorder," and "confusion": "chance seems to direct all movement"; "the notes merely repel and detest each other." Odero referred to the opera as "musical anarchy" and Pougin deemed Debussy the "head of the anarchists in music." To such accusations, Vuillermoz had a direct response:

So it is anarchy, is it? Maybe, but how beneficial, since [the music] attains a beauty right off the bat that the thick web of rules had never allowed it to achieve.

In calling Debussy's music anarchy, these critics were not far from wrong, given the broad definition of the term during this period. The anarchist movement preached not only political but also artistic freedom for the individual, it questioned accepted institutions of all kinds, and it criticized bourgeois hypocrisy. Its followers hoped that, through a series of cataclysmic changes, life would evolve to a more perfect state, and believed that art should show the possibility for change and create new ideals. Debussy was certainly receptive to these ideas. In the late 1890s, he even formalized such thoughts in a collaborative project with René Peter; their play, *Les Frères en art*, concerned a group of artists who sought to educate the public about the necessity of overthrowing bourgeois standards. In aesthetic terms, this meant rejecting rules and insisting on the sole authority of the creative mind—ideas remarkably close to those of the anarchists.

In imputing an association of Debussy with the anarchists, the critics were correct, but only

before the turn of the century when he frequented certain literary circles, not later when, as Michel Faure points out, Debussy's political orientation turned markedly to the right.[55] In the 1890s, many of Debussy's friends and supporters were active in the anarchist movement, mostly the same group who defended Dreyfus, and whom we have already named above in this connection. Regnier collaborated on the anarchist literary magazine, *L'Endehors*, and was considered one of its editors. He also edited *Entretiens politiques et littéraires*, a symbolist review that was open to anarchist ideas. Mauclair, although he was more concerned with the unhampered freedom of the artistic elite than the welfare of the masses, chose to end his novel about Mallarmé's circle, *Le Soleil des morts*, with an anarchist revolution that included the participation of the poets. Mirbeau's involvement with the anarchists is the topic of an entire book by Reg Carr.[56] Three of the journals most supportive of *Pelléas*—the *Revue blanche*, *Mercure de France*, and *L'Ermitage*—also sympathized with the anarchists and often reviewed articles from the anarchist and socialist press.[57] Bauër's defense of *Pelléas* for the sake of freedom of expression, and Brussel's point that Debussy represented no school and was the perfect example of a "personal composer," certainly must have attracted anarchist support to the opera.

Audience response to criticism of the opera also took on a political air. Debussy's supporters up in the top gallery called themselves a "sacred battalion."[58] Some of these included the composers Maurice Ravel, Paul Ladmirault, and Charles Koechlin; the future conductor D. E. Inghelbrecht; the poet Léon-Paul Fargue; the pianist Ricardo Viñes; the music critics Louis Laloy, Emile Vuillermoz, and M. D. Calvocoressi; and the Abbé Léonce Petit. According to Vuillermoz, their principal organizer, these

[55]Michel Faure, *Musique et société du second empire au années vingt* (Paris, 1985), pp. 75–82.
[56]*Anarchism in France: The Case of Octave Mirbeau* (Montreal, 1977).
[57]Eugenia W. Herbert, *The Artist and Social Reform: France and Belgium 1895–1898* (New York, 1961), pp. 96–100, 128.
[58]The development of this audience is the subject of another paper, "A Sociology of the Apaches, 'Sacred Battalion' for *Pelléas*," first presented to the American Musicological Society in Philadelphia, 27 October 1984.

"mobilized troops" were needed "to assure the presence of police in the hall." But long after their demonstrations were said to have "frozen the opposition,"[59] this group continued to attend the opera for every one of the first thirty performances almost as a political act, as each of them attests in his memoirs. A young musician and friend of Vuillermoz, Édmond Maurat, went only three times, and was snubbed thereafter.[60] Political vocabulary permeates the supporters' descriptions of the resistance given to this *œuvre de combat*.[61]

The massive attention from the press that we have traced in this essay eventually succeeded in elevating Debussy to the status of a new god of music, a "French" music. But the continued controversy also turned *Debussysme* into music's Dreyfus Affair, as Vuillermoz attests in a later article that somewhat fatuously points to the similar initials of their names (**A**chille **De**bussy, **A**lfred **D**reyfus).[62] Different factions developed even among the Debussystes (Laloy, Mauclair, Vuillermoz). As one of them admitted, "the struggle became so bitter that the object was forgotten."[63]

In turn-of-the-century Paris, a scandal inevitably awaited any new masterpiece that demanded extensive public attention. "Toute vibration inconnue scandalise," as O'Divy wrote in his review of *Pelléas*. The complexity of values at the time made confrontation certain, and the number of critics on hand to represent each possible combination of social class, political preference, musical and aesthetic taste resulted in fierce competition. Because the critics for the most part either attacked *Pelléas* or embraced it depending on what they and their subscribers valued, Debussy's opera was seen to fulfill mutually exclusive purposes. It attracted both the snobs who came to be seen and the artists who

came to escape the world; it was held up as an example of the lowest morality, leading to humanity's dissolution, and the highest, teaching humanity grace; it was praised by both nationalists, who aimed to preserve tradition, and anarchists, who sought renewal. Likewise, the opera was panned for the same contradictory set of reasons, argued by members of the same groups. Even reviews addressed to similar readers, such as those by Bellaigue and Hallays, sometimes reached diametrically opposed conclusions.

What made the critics and their public sway one way or the other was often a complex issue. As discussed earlier and shown in table 2, the political orientation of the paper or journal, the social status of their readers, the perspective guiding the reader's interest in opera, and the critics' own principal profession, all played important roles in predisposing both the critic and the public toward either categorical opposition to the work or an openness toward it. Monarchists, aristocrats, *haute bourgeoisie*, anti-Dreyfusards, socialites, and the conservative musical public tended to feel threatened or antagonistic towards the opera, whereas republicans, businessmen, socialists, Dreyfusards, professional writers, art-lovers, and the progressive musical public tended to give the work a chance.

Any paper, reader, or critic, however, could belong to both one group resistant to the opera as well as a second group more receptive to it. This explains why a republican journal such as the *Revue des deux mondes*—otherwise sympathetic to new ideas—could publish a bitter attack of the opera, since its critic Bellaigue came from a high social class and had very conservative musical taste. Fervent devotion to another composer also kept some avant-garde enthusiasts, who otherwise should have needed no convincing, from fully embracing Debussy's opera. Whether they were Wagnerians or ferocious anti-Wagnerians—and the discussions invariably involved Wagner—a critic's attitude toward Wagner did not automatically imply either support or rejection of Debussy. Even though he was among the inner circle who helped introduce Wagner to the French public, Jullien had to admit that *Pelléas* pleased him. Others, such as Mendès and Willy, allowed their love for Wagner to color what they otherwise admired in Debussy's opera. Of the anti-

[59]Paul Locard, "La Quinzaine," *Courrier musical*, 1 June 1902, p. 167.
[60]Édmond Maurat, *Souvenirs musicaux et littéraires*, ed. Louis Roux (Saint-Étienne, 1977), p. 21.
[61]Critics and writers who used this expression include Paul Flat, Florencio Odero, René Peter, D. E. Inghelbrecht (in his *Mouvement contraire* [Paris, 1947], p. 275), Jacques Rivière, and Louis Laloy.
[62]Émile Vuillermoz, "Une Tasse de thé," *Mercure musical*, 15 November 1905, p. 505.
[63]Ibid., p. 509.

Wagnerians, only Lalo embraced *Pelléas* as a work which might lead French musicians out of Wagner's grasp, while Pougin, Imbert and their public placed Debussy and Wagner in the same camp—neither satisfied their passion for traditional form and virtuoso singing.

One should not exaggerate the role that social and political issues played, for some critics were clearly charmed or put off by the work for inherently musical reasons. But the number of extra-musical issues capable of affecting how a critic formulated his message was enormous; and that formulation, then as now, might well determine whether a work failed or succeeded. It is no wonder that Debussy's supporters felt they had to organize.

Le Soleil des morts:
A Turn-of-the-Century Portrait Gallery

SUSAN YOUENS

In an appendix to the first volume of *Debussy: His Life and Mind*, Edward Lockspeiser called attention to a *fin-de-siècle roman à clef* containing a series of fictionalized portraits of the major avant-garde artists, writers, critics, and composers of the 1890s. "It is still a most valuable historical document," he remarked, "deserving an up-to-date edition enlightened by a critical commentary."[1] The novel, Camille Mauclair's *Le Soleil des morts*, first published in 1898, has recently been reissued by Slatkine Reprints with a brief historical introduction,[2] but the commentary for which Lockspeiser called is still lacking. This fashionably pessi-mistic novel is a portrait gallery of artists in the Belle Époque and an indictment of the age. The overly refined, spiritually exhausted devotees of Pure Art in this *photo jaunie* of decadence persist, for a time, in contemplation of "le Beau, l'Œuvre, l'Idéal" amidst the insurrectionist unrest of the 1890s, in which the *milieux anarchistes* undermine the Third Republic en route to World War I. Their vitalities eventually dissipate in esotericism, and the hermetic *Élite* flee one by one into fashionable society, commercial success, or anarchy. There are few contemporaneous chronicles that recount so acutely the strains besetting the ivory tower of modern art, music, and poetry.

---

[1] Edward Lockspeiser, *Debussy: His Life and Mind*, vol. I 1862–1902 (Cambridge, 1978; 1st edn., London, 1962), appendix F, pp. 223–28.
[2] Camille Mauclair, *Le Soleil des morts*, introd. Raymond Trousson, "Collection Resources 41" (Geneva, 1979 rpt. of the Ollendorf edn., Paris, 1898). All further references to the novel will be given in the text of this article.

The novel first appeared in six installments in *La Nouvelle revue*,[3] despite its name, one of the oldest and most prestigious literary journals in France. Its author was Camille Laurent Célestin Faust (1872–1945), who in his early twenties discarded the family name Faust (a literary windfall, or an albatross, depending on one's point of view) and adopted the pseudonym Mauclair. He wrote copiously about art (essays and books on Fragonard, Rodin, Greuze, Chardin, Tiepolo, Leonardo da Vinci, and virtually all of the Impressionists), literature (the first serious study of Jules Laforgue in 1896, Maeterlinck, Poe, Mallarmé), music (*La Religion de la musique* in 1909, a study of Schumann, an *Histoire de la musique européenne 1845–1910*, and much music criticism), and travel.[4] His initial ambitions were poetic and theatrical (he was Aurélien-François Lugné-Poë's collaborator in founding the Théâtre de l'Œuvre),[5] and he seemed to know everyone, including Debussy, who appears in one of the principal episodes of *Le Soleil des morts* at the premiere of his *Prélude à "L'Après-midi d'un faune."* Mauclair, who later wrote on "La Fin du wagnérisme" and "Wagner vu d'ici," points out in the novel the contemporaneous association of "modern music"—Debussy's—with "unpatriotic" tendencies originating in pernicious foreign influence—Wagner's.[6]

One of the central experiences in Mauclair's life was his introduction to Mallarmé in 1891 at one of the Concerts Lamoureux and his subsequent friendship with the poet, which lasted until Mallarmé's death in 1898. The impressionable Mauclair gravitated from one powerful figure and movement to another, his attachments sincere in each instance. The critic Rémy de Gourmont wrote somewhat unkindly that "he lies down at the feet of idols whom he renounces the next day" (p. i), the *comparse toujours* of more important writers and artists, but the devotion to Mallarmé was longer-lived than most. Mauclair's pen-and-ink self-portrait from 1923 (plate 1) is clearly modeled upon the two lithographs of Mallarmé by Edvard Munch in 1897, lithographs based in turn upon a photograph of the poet by Nadar in 1885;[7] the impulse toward *Doppelgängertum* is still manifest twenty-five years after the poet's death. In his *Eleusis: Causeries sur la cité intérieure* of 1893,[8] Mauclair, described by Mallarmé's biographer Henri Mondor as "thin, quivering,

---

[3]The novel appeared in *La Nouvelle revue* for 15 February, ch. 1–2, pp. 603–28; 1 March, ch. 3–5, pp. 40–69; 15 March, the end of ch. 5, pp. 254–85; 1 April, ch. 8–9, pp. 422–50; 15 April, ch. 10–11, pp. 638–66; and 1 May, ch. 12, pp. 100–13. Book IV, ch. 13–15, only appeared with the complete novel as published by Ollendorf at the end of 1898.

[4]Most of Mauclair's huge output is nonfiction. His fictional works include the novels: *L'Amour tragique* (Paris, 1908); *Les Mères sociales, roman contemporain* (Paris, 1902); *La Ville lumière, roman contemporain* (Paris, 1904); *Étreindre*, vol. 28 of *Les Œuvres libres* (Paris, 1923), pp. 99–177; and the collection of *contes*, *Les Danaïdes*, with illustrations by Emile Besnard and Eugène Carrière (Paris, 1903). His collections of poetry include *Le Sang parle* (Paris, 1904), and the works on music include *Schumann* (Paris, 1906); *La Religion de la musique* (Paris, 1919); and *Histoire de la musique européenne 1850–1914* (Paris, 1914). Essays on both Paul Adam and Mallarmé, among others, are contained in *L'Art en silence* (Paris, 1901) and *Princes de l'esprit* (Paris, 1920). He also wrote a volume of reminiscences of Mallarmé, a roughly equal mixture of fact and fiction, entitled *Mallarmé chez lui* (Paris, 1935). One of the most informative assessments, not only of Mauclair but of the entire Symbolist and Decadent movements in the Belle Époque, is found in Jean Pierrot, *The Decadent Imagination 1880–1900*, trans. Derek Coltman (Chicago, 1981).

[5]See Jacques Robichez, *Le Symbolisme au théâtre: Lugné-Poë et les débuts de l'Œuvre* (Paris, 1957). Mauclair's important role in the production of *Pelléas et Mélisande* is recounted on pp. 163–67. Because of Mauclair's evident theatrical interests and expertise, Mallarmé interceded on his young friend's behalf with Prince André Poniatowski to write dramatic criticism for the *Revue franco-americaine*. See *Stéphane Mallarmé: correspondance*, ed. Henri Mondor and Lloyd James Austin (Paris, 1982), VII, 89–90.

[6]Mauclair, *La Religion de la musique*, pp. 237–60. See also Claude Digeon, *La Crise allemande de la pensée française (1870–1914)* (Paris, 1959); Léon Guichard, *La Musique et les lettres en France au temps du wagnérisme* (Paris, 1963); and Martine Kahane and Nicole Wild, *Wagner et la France* (Paris, 1983).

[7]Mauclair's self-portrait is the frontispiece to G. Jean Aubry, *Camille Mauclair* (Paris, 1905). In the *Documents Stéphane Mallarmé* (1968), I, "Correspondance avec Edvard Munch, 1896–97": Munch was in Paris in 1896–97 to show works at the Salon des Indépendants and printed a series of lithographs *chez* Clot. On 23 May 1897, Vève wrote to her father (p. 120): "M Munch, le dessinateur norvégien du commencement de l'hiver, envoie le portrait qu'il a fait de toi. . . . C'est assez joli, mais ressemble à ces têtes de Christ dont l'empreinte est sur le mouchoir d'une sainte et sous lesquels il est écrit: 'Regardez longtemps, vous verrez les yeux se ferme'."

[8]Mauclair, *Eleusis: causeries sur la cité intérieure* (Paris, 1894). Mauclair in the early 1890s endeavored to explain the Mallarméan aesthetic to the reading public, as in "Notes sur l'Idée pure," *Mercure de France*, September 1892, pp. 42–46.

Plate 1

lemma between the life of art and participation in history. Mauclair dedicates the novel "to those unsatisfied in this epoch . . . to those who dream without hope, exalting their ecstatic souls toward diverse suns, liberty, passion, asceticism or glory." The most important of the real-life figures in the *roman à clef* are Mallarmé and his daughter Françoise-Geneviève-Stéphanie (1864–1919), called "Vève." The episodic novel begins with an account by the narrator (Mauclair himself, under the name André de Neuze) of one of the poet Calixte Armel's *jeudis*, the fictional counterpart to the real Mallarmé's famous *mardis* at 81, rue de Rome. (In the preface to the new edition, Raymond Trousson, on p. i, incorrectly identifies Mauclair as the character Manuel Héricourt.) Like many of Mauclair's names, Armel bears an easily decipherable relationship to that of the actual person: it is a condensation of Mallarmé. The setting is recognizably Mallarmé's dining room, including the Rodin statuette that Mallarmé owned, along with a Gauguin woodcut, a pastel of flowers by Odilon Redon, a seascape by Berthe Morisot, and a nymph by Whistler.[10] There, de Neuze, under the auspices of Pierre Louÿs, meets Debussy, Whistler, and a curious synthesis of Renoir and Monet; he subsequently meets or refers to Catulle Mendès, Loïe Fuller, Georgette Leblanc, Ernest Chausson, Léon Bloy, Paul Verlaine, Paul Adam, Toulouse-Lautrec, Maurice Barrès, Gustave Charpentier, Willy, Jules Lemaître, the Rothschilds, Barbey d'Aurévilly, and Octave Mirbeau.

The depiction of Armel/Mallarmé is unmistakable, even though Mauclair invents a family history and life story that differ significantly from the facts. At the time of the novel, Calixte Armel is fifty-five years old, Mallarmé's age in 1897, and the physical description is precise and

puny, with a sharp and imaginative glance,"[9] paraphrases Mallarmé's aesthetics. By 1897, he was no longer the epitome of an uncritical disciple. In *Le Soleil des morts*, Mallarmé is depicted not only for his genius and the magnetism of his influence, but for the psychologically complex, solipsistic aspect of his nature,—the dark underside of adoration. Mallarmé becomes the focal point for Mauclair's gradual disengagement from the cult of the dream in Symbolist and decadent art.

Le Soleil des morts is one of a series of works on the theme of the artist caught in a tragic di-

---

[9]Henri Mondor, *Vie de Mallarmé*, 20th edn. (Paris, 1941), p. 646. See also A. N. Marchbank, *Mauclair: Life and Work, 1890–1909* (Ph.D. diss., Edinburgh University, 1975); and W. C. Clark, *Mauclair and the Religion of Art* (Ph.D. diss., University of California, Berkeley, 1976).

[10]Mondor, p. 643, describes the Mallarmé dining room. "Les murs s'enrichissent lentement de quelques toiles ou gravures: aux deux Manet s'ajoutent maintenant, une marine de Berthe Morisot, une nymphe de Whistler, un pastel de fleurs de Redon, un plâtre de Rodin groupant un Faune plus agressif, moins joueur de flûte que celui du poète et une nymphe sans étonnement; enfin ce bois orangé de Gauguin ou le profil d'un Maori permet à Mallarmé de taquiner Mauclair sur une ressemblance approximative." In the description of the *mardis* that follows, it appears that Debussy did not often attend.

accurate.[11] The "feline" head, appropriate for a cat lover like Mallarmé, with its triangular shape, aquiline nose, moustache, and pointed beard whose shape mimicked the faunlike contour of the poet's ears; the red clay pipe; the cloud of tobacco smoke he liked to put between himself and his listeners; the enigmatic expression—all are familiar from the numerous portraits and photographs of the poet (pp. 11–12). If the external appearance is true to fact and the aesthetic ideas largely a replica of Mallarmé's, the remainder of the characterization lies in an indeterminate region between fact and fiction, always an attraction of *romans à clef*.

According to Mauclair's biographer Jean-Aubry, Mauclair submitted *Le Soleil des morts* chapter by chapter to Mallarmé.[12] In the extant responses, Mallarmé says almost nothing about the incestuous relationship between Armel and his daughter in Mauclair's novel, unless the oblique reference to the Armel's "two or three fixations [*obstinations*], in a sense" is meant to be understood as inclusive of the perverse father-daughter kinship. Rather, Mallarmé declares his complete trust in Mauclair—"to whom more surely could I confide myself?"[13]—

and asks only that Mauclair not send Armel into industry or into the arms of a woman. After reading the entire book, Mallarmé expressed some serious reservations: "The years—the few that remain to me—would not excuse me, literarily, if I contented myself, for my Destiny, to have appeared to you as this man here."[14] Perhaps Mallarmé had some intimation of his death, three months later at age fifty-six. One wonders how Mauclair must have felt at the unforeseen event. Whatever his protestations to Mallarmé and Mallarmé's lukewarm reassurances, the depiction of Armel *is* in large part a portrait, easily recognizable. If Love and Work are the linchpins of life, then Armel fails conspicuously, although not entirely, in both.

CLEFS: THE COMPANY OF *L'ÉLITE*

Calixte Armel / Stéphane Mallarmé (1842–98). Like most of the characters in the novel, Mallarmé is given fictional membership in the aristocracy (a metaphor for intellectual elitism and spiritual aristocracy), although in fact both his paternal and maternal families belonged to the bourgeoisie.[15] Armel's father was the tormented, introspective marquis Armel d'Héricy de Novres, who renounced his ancestral estate to marry the English actress Maud Davensey (shades of Berlioz and Harriet Smithson, except that the *tragédienne* of Mauclair's novel is described as brilliantly gifted). Calixte is orphaned at age twenty when his mother is killed in the burning ruins of her theater, and his father dies of a stroke on hearing the news. Mallarmé's mother, Félicie Desmolins-Mallarmé, died on returning from a voyage in Italy when the poet was five, and the two children, Stéphane and his sister Maria, were raised by their maternal grandmother. The romanticized fictional background is the figment of a youthful imagination,

---

[11]There is a rich iconography of the poet. Whistler executed a magnificent lithograph of Mallarmé, now in the collection of the University of Glasgow and the National Gallery, Washington, D.C. The famous portrait by Manet in 1876, with its references to Zola and *japonisme*, is probably the best known of the contemporaneous images—the portrait hung in Mallarmé's dining room, but there are also portraits by Renoir and by Gauguin. The latter is an etching, which Gauguin made in 1891 during the five months he spent in Paris before his departure for Tahiti; there is also a pencil and pen sketch as preparation for the etching. Some dozen proofs were pulled and then presented to close friends; one is now in the Boston Museum of Fine Arts, Gauguin portraying a more gaunt, haunted looking artist than we are accustomed to seeing. Reproductions of the etching and drawing are included in Ronald Pickvance, *The Drawings of Gauguin* (New York, London, Sydney, Toronto, 1970), pls. 50 and 51. See also "Les Portraits de Mallarmé" and "Mallarmé et les peintres" in "Nos Rencontres," *Mercure de France*, 1931, pp. 182*ff*. and pp. 209*ff*.
[12]Jean Aubry, p. 9. Mallarmé, *Correspondance*, vol. VII (July 1894–December 1895), pp. 87–88.
[13]*Correspondance*, vol. IX (Paris, 1983), pp. 281–82. It is quoted in Mondor, p. 794. "J'aime cet effort même désesperé, je parle pour moi; parce qu'au fond et en dehors du monsieur très fixe et sur lequel les regards ont pu s'arrêter, j'en suis encore là, éperdument. Avec deux ou trois obstinations dans un sens. Ce moi, qu'il fait paraître et que vous, un des mieux, voulutes affectionner vous appartient, certes, littérairement; et, s'il doit rester, que ce soit selon votre vision, Mauclair; a qui plus sûrment me confier? Vous

dites qu'il s'achève, dans votre livre, autrement; n'allez pas, cependent, le faire choir dans l'industrie ni enlever par une dame."
[14]The letter is quoted in Trousson, p. xi. "Toujours est-il que si l'aspect que dégage un homme à plusieurs ne lui demeure extérieure totalement, vous êtes quelqu'un, Mauclair, qui m'aurez estraordinairement regardé. Les ans, pour peu qu'il m'en reste, ne m'excuseraient pas, littérairement, que je me contenterais, pour destin, de vous être apparu cet-homme là."
[15]Mondor, pp. 11–13. Mallarmé was raised by his grandmother, became a *bachelier-ès-lettres* in 1860 at the lycée of Sens, and went to London in 1863 with Marie Gerhard, whom he married in London. He became a teacher of English in the lycée of Tournon that same year—the beginning of eight years in the provinces (he moved to Besançon in October 1866 and again to Avignon in 1867, leaving for Paris in 1871).

seeking the explanation for genius in a family history of great artistic passion. After the deaths of his parents, Calixte flees France and vanishes from sight for twelve years, finally surfacing in Paris. Before his reappearance, his aristocratic relatives formally spurn him for his revolutionary activities on behalf of the Czech opposition in Bohemia. The real Mallarmé, although he expressed political opinions on occasion, was notoriously apolitical—"a common man can be democratic; the artist is divided in two and must remain an aristocrat."[16] But Mauclair had a purpose in endowing Armel with such bravura credentials: the earlier experiences of active involvement in history stand in contrast to his later retreat into hermetic Art. The Armel who teaches English in the fictional country of Christiana for a brief time is borrowed from the actual poet, who taught English at provincial schools in Tournon, Besançon, Avignon, and in Paris until his retirement in 1893, although Mallarmé's lifelong, uncongenial school-mastering is not Armel's lot.

During the Franco-Prussian War, Armel is taken prisoner in Germany. (Mallarmé had nothing to do with the military conflict.) He returns to Paris shortly after the Commune and publishes a volume of poems entitled *Faunes*, which makes him famous in a fortnight, and a controversial essay on Wagner. Mallarmé was in Avignon during the Commune, but *L'Après-midi d'un faune*, begun in Tournon in 1865, before the War and recast probably in 1867, was published, with illustrations by Manet, after the war. It appeared from Derenne near the end of March 1876, after being refused by the *Parnasse contemporain*. His "Richard Wagner, rêverie d'un poète français," "part article, part prose poem," was written for the first volume of *La Revue wagnérienne* (1885), well after the date Mauclair assigns it.[17] In 1874, Armel meets a Madame d'Aurécy, recently widowed after only two years of marriage, and marries her. Two years later, in 1876, she dies giving birth to Sylvaine. A poet comfortably married for many years, as was Mallarmé, might detract from, or at least complicate, Mauclair's portrayal of isolation and withdrawal from Life into Art. Before his wife's death, though, Armel writes another book of verse with the improbably portentous title *Révélations*.

Armel then moves to the country with Sylvaine, an appropriate name for the daughter of a faun-poet (sixteen of Mallarmé's many occasional verses are "Offrandes . . . du faune").[18] For three years, he lives in Germany and Austria and there meets Wagner, already ill and near death; the real Mallarmé never met the composer, whom he dubs the "Monstre-qui-ne-peut-Être" in his "Rêverie." Then once again, with his customary facility, he disappears. When his friend, the painter Niels Elstiern (James McNeill Whistler) next hears of him, Armel at age forty-four has fallen in love with a celebrated singer, Edith Wollman, vaguely reminiscent of Augusta Holmès (1847–1903). The singer-composer, whose songs have been recently republished,[19] was possibly the daughter of Alfred de Vigny, studied composition with Franck, was for a time the lover of Catulle Mendès, and idolized Wagner. Edith Wollman's Wagnerian credentials are impressive: she was discovered by none other than Wagner himself, and, to add a last Wagnerian touch, she and Armel live together in Venice. She falls out of love with Armel and eventually flees with a young artist. Old before his time, his health ruined, Armel returns to Paris. Edith Wollman never actually appears in the novel, but the brief account of her part in Armel's past is crucial. One leitmotif that runs throughout *Le Soleil des morts* is the depiction of strong-willed, creative women whose vitality is in stark contrast with their passive, reclusive aesthete-lovers. Notably, the depictions lack the fashionable misogyny of much *fin-de-siècle* art.

Luc Deraines / Pierre Louÿs (1870–1925). Mauclair's counterpart, André de Neuze, is given a few aristocratic airs as well: born into a noble family in the Touraine and is, like Armel, orphaned and forced to sell the family chateau of Aulnayes. He is brought to the Armel *jeudi* by Luc Deraines or Pierre Louÿs (an arty spelling of his real name "Louis"), who was Debussy's closest and most important friend for ten years, from 1893 to 1903. The composer and the author of the *Chansons de Bilitis* first met ca. 1890 at one of Mallarmé's *mardis*, but Louÿs's close ties to Gide and Valéry and his work on the revue *La Conque* did not leave him time to pursue the friendship until August 1893. Mauclair would have known

[16]Stéphane Mallarmé, *Œuvres complètes*, ed. Henri Mondor and G. Jean-Aubry (Paris, 1945), from "Hérésies Artistiques—L'Art pour tous," p. 259. "L'homme peut être démocrate, l'artiste se dédouble et doit rester aristocrate."
[17]Wagner by 1885 had become famous as "the insulter of France," with even Catulle Mendès, among the most ardent *wagnéristes*, declaring that he could no longer be Wagner's friend. Mallarmé's circle had come to be a dominant force on *La Revue wagnérienne*. Mallarmé's prose poem/article seemed unintelligible to many readers; had they understood it, they would have realized how sharply the poet separated himself from his recently deceased Teutonic contemporary. See Gerald D. Turbow, "Wagnerism in France" in *Wagnerism in European Culture and Politics*, ed. David C. Large and William Weber (Ithaca, N.Y., 1984), pp. 134–66.

[18]Mallarmé, *Œuvres complètes*, from "Offrandes à divers du faune," pp. 111–14, including one (p. 114) to Debussy on the occasion of the *Prélude à "L'Après-midi d'un faune"*: "Sylvain d'haleine première / Si ta flûte a réussi / Ouis toute la lumière / Qu'y soufflera Debussy."
[19]The new edn. was published by Da Capo Press in September 1984, ed. Marjory Irvin, and contains twelve songs, to texts *à la* Wagner by the composer herself. See also Paula Barillon-Bauche, *Augusta Holmès et la femme compositeur* (Paris, 1912); René Picard du Page, *Une Musicienne Versaillaise: Augusta Holmès* (Paris, 1921); Rollo Myers, "Augusta Holmès: A Meteoric Career," *Musical Quarterly* 53 (July, 1967), 365ff.

Louÿs both from *La Conque* and from the *mardis*, although Louÿs at first found Mallarmé's magus airs insufferable. Even before the close association between Debussy and Louÿs, Louÿs in 1890 wrote in his diary of a wish for the regeneration of lyric drama, with libretti of great poetic worth, an ideal they later shared.[20] For a time in 1893, Louÿs was even looking for living quarters to share with composer.

Deraines is described in *Le Soleil des morts* as "blond, elegant, exhausted by lung disease, complicated, sentimental, an avowed Hellenist whose novel *The Nymph*, with its feverish and refined eroticism, had made one forget his shiveringly sweet poetry" (p. 13). From the extant photographs of Louÿs, who had consumptive tendencies, the description is accurate. Other details are also drawn from life: at one point, Deraines leaves for Morocco, a journey that Louÿs made, first to Biskra, in July and August of 1894 and again, with Gide, in 1898. The novel *La Nymphe* is surely a reference to Louÿs's *Aphrodite, les mœurs d'antiquité* of 1896, a novel of a courtesan's life in ancient Alexandria written in a gracefully stylized mixture of licentiousness and erudition, while the "shiveringly sweet" poems could be either the *Astarté* of 1891 or the *Chansons de Bilitis* of 1898. Louÿs, the *helléniste passionné*, translated Meleager, whose Orientalizing style influenced his own, and presented the Bilitis poems as translations from a non-existent contemporary of Sappho, a hoax that convinced several academic classicists;[21] he was later to translate Lucian of Samosata's *Dialogues of the Courtesans*. By the end of the novel, Deraines, like so many of the other characters, betrays his earlier high ideals: he creates a sensation with his newest *néo-grec* novel, then marries a wealthy woman and becomes the darling of the most snobbish salons. The real Louÿs married in 1898 and retired into his large house at Passy, to work there on translations and write poems that were to remain unpublished until his death in 1925.

Rodolphe Méreuse / Ernest Chausson (1855–99). *Le Soleil des morts* is dedicated to Chausson, who ap-

pears briefly in the novel as "Rodolphe Méreuse, the composer whose symphonies, with those of César Franck, were the only original works to appear since Wagner" (p. 38), an exaggerated encomium to the friend who set three of Mauclair's poems (*Les Heures, Ballade,* and *Les Couronnes*) as his op. 27. Chausson is again fictionalized in Mauclair's later novel, *La Ville lumière,* where Eugène Ysaÿe and Chausson are described performing Franck's A-Major Violin Sonata in Rodin's studio.[22] Chausson was in fact a student of Franck, whose influence is discernible in the tone poem *Viviane* of 1882. Chausson only wrote one full-length symphony, the Symphony in B♭, completed in 1890, and his struggles to finish it were symptomatic of his divided loyalties, split between Franck and Wagner ("this blood-red ghost of Wagner who will not release me," "the terrible Wagnerian ghost—my refrain!"), and his compositional doubts. Until 1894, he and Debussy were close friends,[23] and the cause of their estrangement is not entirely clear. Chausson was shocked by the ending of Debussy's engagement to Thérèse Roger in 1894, and his daughter, Mme Étiennette Lerolle-Chausson, implied that they quarreled as well over money. Debussy did, however, attend his former friend's funeral, after a fatal bicycle accident, in 1899. Mauclair never depicts Méreuse and Harmor/Debussy in conversation or in close contact with one another, although Méreuse is present at the premiere of Harmor's two orchestral preludes in the third chapter. Since Mauclair was a close friend of Chausson, it is possible that the slightly unsympathetic portrayal of Debussy was influenced by his knowledge of the contretemps between the two composers. Unlike most of the other characters in the novel, Méreuse does not renounce or betray his art.

Urbain Decize / Auguste Rodin (1840–1917). Except for Debussy, Mallarmé, and the novelist Paul Adam, most of the artistic *élite* appear only in brief vignettes. Rodin is given a larger place than most and is introduced as "the sensuous poet of little groups in bronze whose amorous fury astonished Paris" (pp. 109–10). Decize is described as a native of Picardy (Rodin's father was Norman and his mother from Lorraine) with a red beard and gray eyes, who sings in patois while working on his sculpture from seven o'clock in the morning until late at night. His favorite subjects, according to Mauclair, were "faunesses" and groups of lovers sculpted in bronze, often with strange patinas concocted by unknown means, and marble, recalling Rodin's *Kneeling Fauness* (ca.

[20]See Gordon Millan, *Pierre Louÿs: ou, le culte de l'amitié* (Aix-en-Provence, 1979), p. 207. The author is seriously annoyed with G. Jean-Aubry for what he feels is a misrepresentation of the Louÿs-Debussy friendship, as something playful and amusing rather than truly intimate—in the introduction to the *Correspondance Claude Debussy-Pierre Louÿs 1893–1904,* ed. Henri Borgéaud (Paris, 1945). See also *Le Tombeau de Pierre Louÿs,* containing chapters on Debussy and Louÿs by Paul Valéry and Jacques-Emile Blanche (Paris, 1925). Valéry, when Mallarmé died, felt that Louÿs and Debussy should be the first to be informed. "I'm completely overcome, Mallarmé died yesterday morning," he wrote to Louÿs. "Tell Debussy."

[21]The German classical scholar Ulrich von Wilamowitz-Moellendorff took the "translations" of the *Chansons* seriously enough to write a scathing review, which Louÿs, tongue-in-cheek, included in the bibliography appended to the edn. of 1898.

[22]*La Ville lumière,* ch. 2.

[23]See J. P. Barricelli and Leo Weinstein, *Ernest Chausson* (Norman, Oklahoma, 1955) and "Correspondance inédite de Claude Debussy et Ernest Chausson," *La Revue musicale* (December 1925). See also Ch. Oulmont, *Musique de l'amour: Ernest Chausson et la "Bande à Franck"* (Paris and Brussels, 1935). The quotations regarding Wagner come from Oulmont, pp. 122 and 132 respectively.

1884), *The Centauress* (by 1887), *Zoubaleff Fauness* (1885), and *The Kiss*.

Mauclair began writing *Le Soleil des morts* in the spring or summer of 1897 and completed it in 1898; as events occurred in the interim, he incorporated them into the novel in all their immediacy. Between Decize's first appearance in chapter 1 and his later appearance in chapter 9, the Société des Gens de Lettres stripped Rodin of his government commission, awarded in 1891, to sculpt a monument to Honoré de Balzac. A plaster model was exhibited at the *salon* of the Société Nationale in early 1898 and created a public outcry. Zola and Mallarmé, among others, took up literary cudgels in Rodin's defense. Mauclair's description of a sculpture that is probably the Balzac monument is sympathetic, but reveals what so disconcerted officials and Rodin's detractors:[24] "It was a figure hardly human, disproportionate, convulsive, a boulder more than a human being . . . a sort of Druidic altar" (p. 143). When de Neuze visits Decize at his atelier in Neuilly, very much like photographs of Rodin's studio at Meudon, he finds him hurling wet clay on a giant statue of a nude woman, delirious in the throes of love. Those responsible for the "statuemania" of the Third Republic had been shocked from the beginning of Rodin's career by the redistribution of anatomical elements in his caryatids and the eroticism of his sculpted lovers.

The Prince Lannoy-Talavère / Henri de Toulouse-Lautrec (1864–1901). Toulouse-Lautrec, his fictional name similarly a double patronymic with the initials reversed, is invoked only briefly in the seventh chapter, where de Neuze enumerates the various neurasthenic artists who surround him (pp. 118–19). Mauclair describes him as a "hideous, cynical, spiritual gnome" who could forgive neither his family nor life for having created him a cripple, as a caricaturist who was once placed on trial for pornography and who painted with genius the prostitutes and other denizens of Montmartre. The historical Henri Marie Raymond de Toulouse-Lautrec Monfa was born of an aristocratic family in Albi; his residence in a Montmartre brothel, his propensity for the Cirque Fernando, and his dissolute life are all ingredients for Mauclair's thumbnail sketch of Lannoy-Talavère.

Toulouse-Lautrec was never tried for pornography, a Baudelairean or Flaubertian touch to his fictional biography, but his lithographs of prostitutes from the rue des Moulins in Montmartre, a series entitled *Elles*, might have suggested to Mauclair the possibility of such a trial. The artist was known in the 1880s as an illustrator, caricaturist, and chronicler for several Parisian magazines, *Mirliton*, *Paris illustré*, and *Le Courrier français*.[25]

Niels Elstiern / James McNeill Whistler (1834–1903). Whistler is an inevitable presence in any novel about the Mallarmé circle, both because he is a quintessential Symbolist artist, a creator of evanescent images on the verge of illegibility, and because he was a close friend of Mallarmé. Mallarmé's genius for friendship is nowhere more evident than here, since the litigious Whistler could and did "go for the hand that fed him like an amphetamine-crazed Doberman."[26] Although Whistler lived in Paris on and off since 1855 (he exhibited at the first 1863 Salon des Refusés with the Impressionists), he did not become a close friend of the Mallarmé family until 1888. Claude Monet arranged a meeting at the Café de la Paix between Whistler and Mallarmé, who that year translated Whistler's artistic Credo, *The Ten O'Clock* (1885) into French.[27] One can imagine Mallarmé's sympathy with Whistler's insistence that art is amoral and non-narrative, that the artist is selfishly concerned with seeking the beautiful. "As music is the poetry of sound, so is painting the poetry of sight, and the subject-matter has nothing to do with harmony of sound or colour."[28] For a London periodical, *The Whirlwind*, Mallarmé contributed a sonnet, *Billet à Whistler*, published in November 1890,[29] and when the

---

[24]See Albert Elsen, *Rodin* (The Museum of Modern Art, 1963), pp. 89–105 for more on the Balzac controversy. The statue, which was never cast in bronze during Rodin's lifetime, is in one sense a double portrait, as Rodin identified with Balzac's struggle and liked, as did Balzac, to wear flowing bathrobes or pseudo-monk's robes while working. The press was so outraged by the plaster model that the scandal could not be diminished or overshadowed even by the Dreyfus Affair. The catalogue of an exposition for 23 June–18 October 1976 at the Musée Rodin, *Rodin et les écrivains de son temps*, includes several of Rodin's drawings to illustrate *Les Fleurs du mal* and Louÿs's Lesbian poems from *Les Chansons de Bilitis*. Rodin apparently never illustrated any of Mallarmé's poems, although he does so in the novel.

[25]See Ph. Huisman and M. G. Dortu, *Lautrec by Lautrec*, trans. Corinne Bellow (New York, 1964), p. 74 and *Henri de Toulouse-Lautrec: Images of the 1890s*, ed. Riva Castleman and Wolfgang Wittrock (The Museum of Modern Art, 1985), pp. 77–81, for more on the artist's magazine and newspaper illustrations. The poster announcing "Elles / Lithographies / éditées par / G. Pelet / 9, Quai Voltaire à Paris / Exposées à la PLUME / 31, rue Bonaparte, à partir du / 22 Avril 1896" is reproduced in Huisman and Dortu, p. 119. The lithographs were published the following year.

[26]Robert Hughes, "Pleasures of the Iron Butterfly," *Time*, 18 June 1984, p. 80. Whistler often signed his later works with the image of a butterfly, especially after the publication of *The Gentle Art of Making Enemies* in 1890, in which many of its pages were adorned with butterflies.

[27]Whistler's lecture was translated by Mallarmé in 1888 and appeared in *La Revue indépendante*. See Mallarmé, *Œuvres complètes*, pp. 569–83.

[28]From lectures originally delivered at Cambridge and Oxford in 1885, *The Ten O'Clock* was published in London in 1888.

[29]Mallarmé, *Œuvres complètes*, p. 65. Whistler was delighted with the sonnet and referred to it in two letters: (London, 29 October 1890), "Oh! le sonnet! Si vous saviez comme je ne fais d'avance une joie de le lire. Ah! ah! ah!" and (London, 19 November 1890), "Vous devez bien savoir, mon cher ami, que j'ai été ravi en lisant le joli sonnet!"

artist moved for a time to the Faubourg St. Germain in 1892, one of his first works was a lithograph of Mallarmé, published as the frontispiece to the poet's *Vers et prose* of 1893.[30] Mallarmé acted as the middleman in the negotiations between Roger Marx, the Inspector of Fine Arts, Léon Bourgeois, Minister of Public Instruction, and the artist, in order that the French government might purchase Whistler's *Arrangement in Gray and Black No. 1: Portrait of the Artist's Mother* for eventual inclusion in the Louvre ("Bravo! O! Ministre Mallarmé!" the artist crowed at the conclusion of the negotiations). Mallarmé understood the dedicated artist beneath the frequently shrill exterior, and the warm friendship is preserved in the painter's emphatic, exclamation-filled letters and the poet's thoughtful responses.[31]

Whistler was born in Lowell, Massachusetts, although he later repudiated his birthplace ("I do not choose to be born in Lowell"). He is similarly an expatriate in *Le Soleil des morts*, a "great Norwegian painter of portraits and seascapes" who astonished the Salons for ten years with his portraits, "worthy of Reynolds," and shocked society with his outrageous behavior. ("If you were not a genius," Degas, a quick hand with a *bon mot* himself, once told Whistler, "you would be the most ridiculous man in Paris.")[32] Whistler's early notoriety in the 1860s and early 1870s was based largely on his portraits, and he exhibited *Lady Meux: Arrangement in Black No. 5* at the *salon* of 1882. Mauclair describes Elstiern accurately as sardonic of visage, a diminutive figure— Whistler was five feet, four inches tall—with a red rosette in the lapel of his elegant black coat. He and his art seem magical; no one ever sees Elstiern work, and he is notorious for his acerbic wit, evinced in words that are "rare but as sure as a knife in the hands of a juggler" (pp. 18–19). Proust's Elstir, the artist in *À la Recherche du temps perdu*, may well owe his name to the earlier fictional personification, even though Elstir's paintings are attributable to Monet, Renoir, Turner, Chardin, and Manet as well as Whis-

tler.[33] The *Harmonies en plusieurs couleurs* mentioned in Mauclair's novel are clearly derived from the *Nocturnes* and *Symphonies*, Whistler's transpositions of the Japanese aesthetic he loved into the texture of late nineteenth-century experience.

Germain Bussère / Auguste Renoir (1841–1919) and Claude Monet (1840–1926)[?]

André Lebois sees a conflation of Monet and Manet in the person of Germain Bussère,[34] but it is difficult to find any trace of the urbane Manet. Bussère is present at the *jeudi* salon in the opening pages and is described as "the creator of the famous *Bather* whose orange and blue tones caused a riot at the last *salon*, . . . brown-haired, imperious, with the velvety eyes of a wild animal, a violent mouth in the curve of a black, curly bear" (p. 10). Renoir had already begun his famous series of *Bathers* in the 1890s. Monet seldom painted human figures at all and never painted bathers, and it was Renoir who was associated with the official salons; his break with the Impressionist showings, the *Indépendantes*, was prompted in part by a desire for recognition from the Académie des Beaux Arts and the buying public. Renoir was a frequent guest at Mallarmé *mardis* and had, in 1888, provided Mallarmé with three pencil-and-India-ink drawings of Venus, a foreshadowing of the late Classicizing nudes, for the prose poem *Le Phénomène futur*. A photograph by Edgar Degas from ca. 1892 at Berthe Morisot's apartment shows Renoir and Mallarmé together, leaning on a mantelpiece.[35] That same year, Mallarmé helped persuade the government to purchase their first Renoir painting, the *Girls at the Piano*, as he had done the year earlier for Whistler.[36]

---

[30]The lithograph is reproduced, among other sources, in Pierre Cabanne, *Whistler*, trans. Nicholas Max Jennings (New York, 1985), p. 85. Mallarmé was apparently delighted with the lithograph, and, in his "Divagations: Quelques Médaillons et portraits en pied" of 1897, he praised Whistler as "the conjurer of a work of mystery enclosed in its perfection" (*Œuvres complètes*, p. 532).

[31]See *Correspondance Mallarmé–Whistler: histoire de la grande amitié et leurs dernières années*, ed. Carl Barbier (Paris, 1964). The letter from Whistler to Mallarmé on 13 November 1891, at the conclusion of negotiations for the purchase of Whistler's *Mother*, appears on pp. 114–15. Geneviève Mallarmé's telegram ("OH! CHER MONSIEUR WHISTLER PÈRE EST MORT CE MATIN") and Whistler's reply ("Je pleure avec vous deux—inconsolable! 'mon Mallarmé!—vous savez bien—je l'aimais tant!") are found on pp. 288–89.

[32]Donald Holden, *Whistler Landscapes and Seascapes* (New York, 1969), p. 11.

[33]Proust was so taken with Whistler that he purloined one of his gloves at a reception. In *Remembrance of Things Past*, trans. C. K. Scott Moncrieff and Terence Kilmartin, vol. I (New York, 1982), pp. 892–911, Elstir's artistic ideals are presented, and the narrator notes, "His efforts had gone toward dissolving that collocation of judgements which we call vision."

[34]André Lebois, *Admirable XIXᵉ Siècle* (Paris, 1958), "À propos de Mallarmé—un clairvoyant biographe" and "Le Faune protestaire," pp. 165–95.

[35]Renoir's drawings and etching were illustrations for the lines, "À la place du vêtement vain, elle a un corps; et les yeux, semblables aux pierres rares, ne valent pas ce regard qui sort de sa chair heureuse: des seins levés comme s'ils étaient pleins d'un lait éternel, la pointe vers le ciel, aux jambes lisses qui gardent le sel de la mer première." See Barbara Ehrlich White, *Renoir: His Life, Art, and Letters* (New York, 1984). Renoir's *Three Drawings for Venus* ("Le Phénomène futur") and the etching *Venus* are reproduced on p. 185. A photograph of Renoir, Thadée and Misia Natanson, Cyprien Godebski, Ida Godebski, and Pierre Bonnard at the Natanson home after Mallarmé's funeral is found on p. 213, and the 1892 portrait appears in a black-and-white reproduction on p. 193. Mallarmé's prose poem appears in the *Œuvres complètes*, pp. 269–70.

[36]White, p. 195. Mallarmé's correspondence in the matter is contained in the poet's *Correspondance*, V, 61–62 and

Bussère disappears from sight after the opening Armel *jeudi* and does not reappear until later that autumn, after de Neuze begins an affair with the *femme fatale* Lucienne Lestrange. In his rambles around the Isle de la Grande-Jatte, Asnières, and the park at Neuilly, de Neuze several times encounters Bussère painting by a river bank and at last strikes up a conversation with him. This is where Renoir turns into Monet. Behind the "sensual, almost brutal" aspect is a "naive pantheism," expressed in ill-formed phrases. The subjects that Mauclair lists are Monet's: expanses of water, poplars in the wind, great caravans of clouds, but there is no record that Monet ever stated the aesthetic theories that Mauclair devises for him in *Le Soleil des morts*. According to Bussère, the public and critics want "an agreeable, calm, finished art," as in the Renaissance, but the "patient resignation" of those historical works no longer accords with contemporary impatience and the revolutionary trends in art. He paints motion, he declares, and wants the viewer to see the leaves tremble, to sense a migraine coming on when confronted with the "atmosphères blanches" of his canvases, to fetch a coat when he paints rain. If this does not meet with critical or public approval, he cannot help it and will not change; after all, he paints for himself because "I have 'the malady'." *La maladie* is the true subject of Mauclair's novel (pp. 108–09).

Midway through the novel, Bussère disappears from the scene after abandoning his art to become an artisan of porcelain figurines (p. 142). Nothing of the kind ever happened to Renoir, Monet, or Manet.

Manuel Héricourt / Paul Adam (1862–1920). Mauclair selected the fictional name from one of his friend's own books: Manuel Héricourt is the protagonist of the novel *En Décor: Jeunesse et amours de Manuel Héricourt* of 1891. Paul Adam[37] made his debut on the literary scene with a naturalistic novel about a prostitute, *Chair molle* of 1885, which had a *succès de scandale*, and then crossed over to join the Symbolists with such works as *Thé chez Miranda* of 1886, a novel of incestuous love between a mother and son, and *Être* of 1888, later reissued as *Feux du sabbat*. In 1890, he left behind the occultist obscurities of his Symbolist novels—he was one of the founders of the Rosicrucian Order in Paris—and began writing realistic, moralistic novels of the Belle Époque, in particular, a series of sixteen "modern frescos" called collectively *Le Temps et la vie* and including such popular novels as *La Force*, *Le Trust*, and *Le Mystère des foules*. These heavily written works of social history, after the model of Balzac or Zola but without their genius, are so closely connected with their time that they have not survived it. Mauclair depicts Héricourt with blond hair, blue eyes, a moustache, flaring nostrils, and a customary languid posture, legs crossed while a finely shod foot taps impatiently, the dandyism more reminiscent of Adam's friend Maurice Barrès (1862–1923) than of Adam himself (p. 10). After both men had converted from the *culte de moi* and Pure Art to political concerns, they each ran for office in the General Parliament in 1889, Barrès successfully from Nancy, Adam unsuccessfully.

In *Le Soleil des morts*, Héricourt gives up literature for political activity and becomes a follower of Claude Pallat, a brooding, intense revolutionary. In 1888–89, Paul Adam allied himself with the Boulangists, the followers of General Georges Ernest Jean-Marie Boulanger, who had been a military hero in his youth and became War Minister in the Freycinet ministry in 1886. Thereafter, the malleable minister was espoused both by the radical left and by royalists opportunistically interested in fomenting anti-government rebelliousness. Barrès, a convert to *boulangisme*, nevertheless recognized the general's chameleonlike appeal, saying "the Royalists saw in Boulanger their king; Republicans saw their Republic; Imperialists their Caesar; patriots, the return of Metz and Strasbourg; peaceful folk saw order; and those who were restless saw an adventure which would solve all their problems." The phenomenon of so many people investing blind faith in a person so devoid of qualities of good leadership says much about political frustrations in the Third Republic.[38] Adam remained an enthusiastic supporter of Boulanger, even after the whole episode ended with the General's flight to England in 1890 and his suicide the following year.[39]

Claude Pallat is no General Boulanger, however. Mauclair's fictional revolutionary is an underground anarchist who seldom emerges in the open, whereas Boulanger courted publicity. Boulanger was a handsome figure, tall and commanding, with an aquiline nose, blue eyes, and regular features, while Pallat is described as having an ugly, craggy face, wrinkled and jaundiced, with two deep folds extending downward on either side of his nostrils (pp. 126–27). Since Mauclair intended to exalt involvement with life and

---

77–78. Mallarmé, amused and impressed, points out to Roger-Marx that Renoir has taken advantage of the situation to paint the same subject alongside the first canvas and "you will have trouble choosing."

[37]Mauclair wrote a biography of his friend, published the year after Adam's death: *Paul Adam, 1862–1920* (Paris, 1921). See also *L'Époque symboliste et le monde proustien à travers la correspondance de Paul Adam, 1884–1920*, ed. J. Ann Ducan (Paris, 1982).

[38]See Adrien Dansette, *Le Boulangisme* (Paris, 1946); Fresnette Pisani-Ferry, *Le Général Boulanger* (Paris, 1969); and James Harding, *The Astonishing Adventure of General Boulanger* (New York, 1971). Harding, p. 162, cites Barrès's assessment of the General's appeal. Barrès's violently anti-Dreyfusard stance led Gide to characterize him as a precursor of Hitler.

[39]See Francis Laur, *L'Époque boulangiste: essai d'histoire 1886–1887*, 2nd edn. (Paris, 1914).

history, the inglorious War Minister would inevitably require either drastic revision or replacement by a more committed character of a different nature, perhaps Paul Delesalle (1870–1948), who knew Verlaine and whose youthful portraits resemble Pallat,[40] or Émile Henry, Sadi Carnot's assassin.

Lucienne Lestrange / A Synthesis of Georgette Leblanc-Maeterlinck (1875–1941) and Loïe Fuller (1862–1928).

De Neuze has an affair in the course of the novel with a singer turned dancer named Lucienne Lestrange, a combination of the singer Georgette Leblanc and the American-born modern dancer Loïe Fuller. The green-eyed, blond beauty, whose looks are reminiscent both of Debussy's mistress Gabrielle Dupont and Georgette Leblanc, first appears as a singer who performs in the premiere of Debussy/Harmor's new preludes. Mallarmé knew her: in his review in March 1898 of a song recital she gave in Paris, he praises her, not for her "ordinary" voice (a more tactful version of Debussy's judgement), but for the power of her "musical mime" and her gestures.[41] In her memoirs, Georgette Leblanc wrote of her visits to the rue de Rome and Mallarmé's singular air of indulgence.[42]

The bearing and golden-haired, green-eyed looks of Georgette Leblanc are duplicated in Lucienne Lestrange, but near the end of the novel, she turns into Loïe Fuller, born Mary Louise Fuller in Chicago in 1862 (?; she offered one biographer a choice of eight birthdates). At age thirteen, she became a temperance lecturer and at eighteen toured America with a group of Shakespearean actors. In 1893, having moved to Paris, she began a new career as a modern dancer, a living embodiment of *art nouveau* and the *femmes fleurs* in art, with their expressive merger of botany and human anatomy. For her dances—"Gounod's *Ave Maria*," Salome's "Dance of Fear" to

music by Florent Schmitt, the "Dance of the Lily"[43]—she wore voluminous dresses made of thin India silk with immense trains; by manipulating the folds of cloth, she created effects of butterflies, lilies, and flames, the new technology of electric arc lights playing on the moving folds and pleats. In *Le Soleil des morts*, her debut at the Folies-Bergères is displaced forward in time to correspond with Verlaine's funeral in 1896 at the close of the novel, after she has angrily dismissed de Neuze from her life.

The Symbolists discovered "La Loïe" after her debut in 1893. Dance was an important element of Mallarmé's aesthetic theories: he saw the dancer in action as "a Sign," "the visual incorporation of the Idea." His article "Considérations sur l'art du ballet et de Loïe Fuller," published in the *National Observer* for 13 March 1893,[44] is one of the best literary evocations of the dance ever written, and Mauclair, in his description of Lucienne/La Loïe's debut, closely echoes the earlier work by his master. Rodin met La Loïe in 1896 and was thereafter a good friend, an association in which the dancer took great pride.[45] He seems never to have sketched or sculpted her, however; without a dozen yards of swirling silk, she was a stocky, rather plain Midwesterner. Toulouse-Lautrec was so taken with her dances that in 1893–94 he created a series of lithographs of her, works influenced by Whistler's *japonaiserie*. When the lithograph itself had been printed, he painted in watercolor on each of the fifty copies, heightened the color with pads of tint-soaked cotton wool and then sprinkled gold powder irregularly over the surface. The dancer is almost lost from sight in the billowing draperies, higher, wider, and larger than the human being at the center, the lithographs an abstraction of pure motion.[46]

Tristan Saumaize / Paul-Marie Verlaine (1844–1896).

Verlaine's counterpart never appears as a speaking character, but the novel ends with his funeral and de Neuze/Mauclair's meditations on its aftermath. The description of Verlaine is unmistak-

[40]Jean Maîtron, *Paul Delesalle: un anarchiste de la belle époque* (Paris, 1985).

[41]Stéphane Mallarmé, *Œuvres complètes*, p. 861. It first appeared in Alfred Athys, "La Quinzaine dramatique," *La Revue blanche*, 1 March 1898, 380–81, with the introduction, "Voici, touchant Mme Georgette Leblanc, que je n'ai pu entendre, l'opinion de M Stéphane Mallarmé."

[42]Georgette Leblanc, *Souvenirs (1895–1918)* (Paris, 1931), pp. 120–21. "Souvent j'allais lui rendre visite rue de Rome. Je voulait bien me recevoir dans l'intimité. Je le trouvais dans sa chambre, écrivant, son immortel plaid à carreaux sur ses épaules. Pourquoi étais-je si à mon aise en sa présence? Je sentais son indulgence. . . . Sa présence dégageait une qualité de bonté rare,—celle qui a tout traversé et dépassé. On goutait près de lui la paix absolue. Il semblait vivre au bout du monde, à la limite de toutes les beautés qui l'absorbaient, et pourtant il était proche, amène, simple comme un saint. J'imagine que les paupières de Saint François s'abaissaient comme les siennes sur les fleurs de la prairie. Il avait de hautes et lourdes paupières. Éloquentes, elles descendaient sur ses paroles et les impregnaient de gravité. Son expression était parfois tellement intense qu'il eut fallu du courage pour la soutenir si l'on avait été secouru par la grace de son sourire."

[43]Loïe Fuller, *Fifteen Years of a Dancer's Life* (Boston, 1913), includes photographs of herself in "The Dance of the Butterfly," pp. 143 and 181; "Gounod's *Ave Maria*," p. 159; "Dance of the Lily," p. 93; "Dance of the Flame," p. 59; "The Dance of Fear—Salome," p. 283.

[44]"Considérations sur l'art du ballet et la Loïe Fuller" first appeared in the *National Observer* for 13 March 1892 and subsequently in the first number (June–August 1895) of *La Revue franco-americaine* with the title "Étude de danse." It appears in the *Œuvres complètes*, pp. 307–09. Mauclair modeled the scene in which Lucienne makes her debut on Mallarmé's "Considerations" (p. 308): Au bain terrible des étoffes se pâme, radieuse, froide la figurante qui illustre maint thème giratoire où tend une trame loin épanouie, pétale et papillon géants, déferlement, tout d'ordre net et élémentaire, p. 720.

[45]Loïe Fuller, "A Visit at Rodin's," pp. 122–27.

[46]See Castleman and Wittrock, pp. 114–18, for reproductions of the lithographs of Loïe Fuller, also Huisman and Dortu, p. 117.

able: "the genial beggar, drunkard, infirm and sublime, one who shared with Armel the admiration of
the youth . . . before . . . these forty years of exquisite
songs and ardent prayers, agonizing on a bed in a
charity hospital, a tardy impulse for justice shook
Paris" (pp. 230–31). Mauclair would have known
Mallarmé's energetic efforts to fund a monument to
Verlaine.[47] In his account of Saumaize's *cortège* from
St. Étienne-du-Mont to the Batignolles quarter and
the cemetery of Père-Lachaise, Mauclair emphasizes
the lack of any official recognition and the *sympathies individuelles* that swell the processional. The
occasion serves one principal purpose near the novel's end: Mauclair juxtaposes the artistic *funérailles*
with an insurrectionary gathering at the *mur des fé-
dérés*, dramatizing the opposition of poetry-death
and politics-turbulent, violent life. The outbreak of
rioting among the revolutionaries, whose shouts of
"Vive l'anarchie!" drown out the funeral speeches—
nothing of the kind happened at Verlaine's funeral—
is the culmination of Mauclair's thesis that historical change usurps energies formerly given over to art
(pp. 237–46). In the final two brief episodes after the
confrontation at the cemetery, the President of the
Republic is assassinated (doubtless an allusion to the
assassination of Sadi Carnot in June 1894), mob fury
breaks out in the city, and a final meeting takes place
between Armel and de Neuze as the *soleil des morts*
rises over the defeat of both men. De Neuze realizes
belatedly that Armel alone, of all the elite, has understood the vanity and atrocity of action, while Armel
declares, "I disseminated death; I will not write any
longer. . . . I have been wrong, like all of you" (pp.
255–56).

Finally, there is an entire gallery of bit players who
make only brief appearances and then vanish from
sight. The "realist composer Gustave Doussy" (p. 46)
who attends the premiere of Harmor/Debussy's preludes is probably Gustave Charpentier, whom Debussy pilloried in a letter to Prince André Poniatowski in February 1893:

> A rising star on the musical horizon is one Gus-
> tave Charpentier, who seems destined to be re-
> nowned for both his fertility and his unbeautiful
> music. He is a follower of Berlioz, a tremendous
> humbug, I believe, who manages to believe in his
> own hoaxes. Charpentier lacks Berlioz's rather
> aristocratic nature. He is downright vulgar to the
> point of writing an opera to be called 'Marie'
> [eventually *Louise*] to take place in Mont-

martre. . . . What you can't imagine is its utter
lack of taste, the triumph of beer-hall music in the
opera house. . . . Our poor music! How it has been
dragged into the mud![48]

Among the intimates of Armel's *jeudis* is "Pierre
Peyronny, the Impressionist, the great harmonist of
vivid [daylight] colors, as Elstiern was the master of
nocturnal light" (p. 38), with no physical description
that might aid in identifying him. Théophile de
Broiseilles is Théodore Faullain de Banville (1823–
91), described as "the enchanting poet, of astonishing
wit, lovable for his goodness," who openly and
frankly supports Armel's art (p. 38). Banville was a
close friend of the Mallarmé family, and Mallarmé
praised him to the utmost in his "Symphonie Littéraire: Théophile Gautier—Charles Baudelaire—
Théodore de Banville," saying that when he reads the
poet "smiling, I drink nectar in the Olympus of lyri-
cism."[49] In *Le Soleil des morts*, Broiseilles dies suddenly, "the last ray of lyric grace" (p. 120), the same
spring that Harmor marries and renounces opera,
that Héricourt becomes a politician, and Deraines
becomes a creature of the snobbish salons. His death
and the defections from the élite spell the beginning
of the end. A personage who is perhaps a conflation of
Jules-Amédée Barbey d'Aurévilly (1808–89) and Octave Mirbeau (1848–1917) appears as Ludovic Marens
at the Concert Lamoureux in the third chapter. The
outrageous dress and behavior recall Barbey
d'Aurévilly, whose exhibitionistic dandyism and
corsets, of medieval severity, were notorious. Deraines hangs, draws, and quarters him verbally as a
"gossiper, despoiler of women, a courtesan of men
and women alike . . . neither writer nor journalist,
neither worldly nor debauched, not fish and not red
meat, but a little of everything. . . . But he is present-
able today, curled, painted anew, well-corseted" (p.
43). Later in the novel, Marens becomes the lover of
the baroness Esther Soldmann, a diamond-encrusted
morphine addict who lives in rooms decorated entirely in white and writes pastiches of Hans Christian Andersen-like tales (p. 121).

The acerbic critic Neuflize, who also attends Harmor's premiere and is described as "an elegant skep-
tic, a man of reticences" whom Deraines compares to
Flaubert's Spendius in *Salammbo* (pp. 48–49), could
be either Jules Lemaître (1853–1914) or, more likely,
Willy/Henri Gauthier-Villars, Colette's manager-
husband. The reference to a review of an *opéra bouffe*
could apply to either man, likewise the caricature of
a critic with a knife in one hand and a bouquet of

---

[47]See *Correspondance*, vol. VIII (1983), pp. 334–45, for the
committee organization and the responses to Mallarmé's
letters requesting help with the memorial. Mallarmé was
president both of the Comité d'Action and the Comité de
Patronage, with Rodin as the vice-president and a long list of
artistic luminaries as subscribers: Anatole France, Odilon
Redon, Regnier, Reynaldo Hahn, Emile Verhaeren, Zola,
d'Indy, Fauré, Huysmans, and many others.

[48]Debussy's letter about Charpentier is quoted in
Lockspeiser, p. 171. In the same letter, Debussy speaks of
washing the bad taste of Charpentier out of his mouth by
attending the performance of a Palestrina mass at the
church of St. Gervais.

[49]Mallarmé, *Œuvres complètes*, p. 264. See also Eileen
Souffrin-Le Breton, "Debussy lecteur de Banville" *Revue de
musicologie* 46 (December 1960), 200–22.

flowers in the other. The vituperative author of autobiographical novels, Léon Bloy (1846–1917), becomes the figure of Léonce Magne in *Le Soleil des morts*, a great pamphleteer with a brutal but magnificent style, someone who savagely insults the entire era and finally dies of hunger in a slum (p. 118).[50] Properce Defresne is the novelistic impersonation of Catulle Mendès (1842–1909), the Parnassian poet, novelist, playwright, and man of letters; Defresne, we are told, is a cover for the Jewish writer's true name Isaac Goltz. Roger Leumann, the art critic who enters the first chapter in Whistler's company, is described as around thirty-five years of age, sanguine and robust, a Saxon type and the "pontiff of *l'art indépendant*" (p. 21), possibly the critic Henri Bauer, while the blond, blue-eyed music critic and musicologist Stéphane Cernay is perhaps Debussy's friend Maurice Emmanuel (p. 44). The "nonentity Huffin who placed bad sonnets at the base of his confectionary watercolors but who gorged the press with lunches and teas at his home" could possibly be Puvis de Chavannes (1842–98). Toulouse-Lautrec kept in his Montmartre studio a parody of Chavannes's *Bois sacré*, hailed as a masterpiece at the 1884 *salon*.

Claude-Eric Harmor / Claude Debussy in *Le Soleil des morts*.

After Mallarmé and his daughter, Debussy is among the most prominent figures in the novel. Mauclair retains the composer's first name for a character described as

disdainful, vague, his moustache drooping onto a sensual and abnormally large chin, bright eyes, a noble forehead, [who] held himself with the dry elegance of an aristocrat. The grandson of a minister during the Restoration, he was a cousin of the dukes of Hautfeuil who had quarreled with his impoverished family. A tiny ducal coronet embroidered on his cravat was the sole ornament to his sober garb, apart from a shining monocle which his finely-shaped fingers made fly about at the end of its thread (p. 11).

The monocle and coronet-embroidered cravat

are more characteristic of the composer's friend Henri de Régnier, the principal poetic influence on Debussy's *Proses lyriques*, than of Debussy himself. Mauclair has, one suspects, transferred the real Debussy's prominent forehead and cranial bulges downward to the chin. The fictional Claude-Eric Harmor has become known to *L'Élite* for his orchestral *Motifs de songe* and his preludes, which caused a riot at the Concerts Lamoureux. His designation as a "malleable and bizarre symphonist" (p. 11) reflects both Debussy's preoccupations during the 1890s with orchestral composition and Mallarmé's theory, the subject of his disquisition at the *jeudi* in the first chapter, that the orchestral concert has become the new sacred communal ritual for humanity, with the elements of mystery necessary for sacred things.[51]

The third chapter is an account of the premiere of Harmor's two new preludes at the Concert Lamoureux. The first, a programmatic composition, is clearly modeled on the *Prélude à "L'Après-midi d'un faune,"* completed in September 1894 and first performed at the Salle d'Harcourt under the direction of the Swiss conductor Gustave Doret on 22 December 1894. In Mauclair's novel, the two preludes follow a performance of Mendelssohn's "Reformation" Symphony, and neither composition has any connection with Armel's poetry. The actual *Prélude* was performed at the end of a long and varied program (Glazounov's *La Forêt*, Bordier's *Suite serbe*, Duparc's *La Vague et la cloche*, Bougault-Ducoudray's *L'Enterrement d'Ophélie*, Saint-Saëns's Third Violin Concerto, Guy Ropartz's *Prière*, and Franck's *Rédemption*). The flute and the satyr of Harmor's program-

[50]Léon Bloy, the entry for 1 February 1896, *Mon Journal I: 1896–1899* (Paris, n.d.), 7–8. Bloy writes of the dead Verlaine thus: "Pauvre Verlaine au tombeau! Dire pourtant que c'est lui nous a valu cette cacade! Pauvre grand poète évadé enfin de sa guenille de tribulation et de péché, c'est lui que le repugnant auteur des *Rougon-Macquart*, enragé de se sentir conchie des jeunes, a voulu choisir pour se l'opposer démonstrativement a lui-même, afin qu'éclatassent les superiorités infinies du sale négoce de la vacherie littéraire sur la Poésie des Seraphins." Willy, in his *Souvenirs littéraires . . . et autres* (Paris, n.d.), p. 28, writes cattily of a Mallarmé poetry reading: "Des hurlements d'admiration s'élevèrent. Tous . . . tous acclamaient le maître aux gestes lents de sacerdote."

[51]Armel/Mallarmé's discourse on public concerts as communal ritual appears in *Le Soleil des morts*, pp. 13–17. Mauclair, in *La Religion de la musique*, pp. 5–6, writes "L'orchestre est le miroir de l'univers. Où aller pour trouver l'esprit qui vivifie? Où, sinon là? Heureusement il est convenu que la musique est un plaisir, et, pour certains, une névrose: sans quoi, si tous comprenaient qu'elle est *la dernière prière*, on devrait craindre que la vie ordinaire s'en vengeât. Mais, protegée par le snobisme, l'incompréhension et l'espoir de spasmes plus raffinés que ceux de l'amour physique, elle peut encore impunément nous donner, en plein modernisme athée, le spectacle mystique du moyen âge, avec ses moines, ses extasies, ses rituals et ses grands saints aussi, depuis saint Augustin, qui s'appelle en cette religion Beethoven, jusqu'à saint François d'Assise que nous appelons César Franck."

matic prelude recall Mallarmé's poem, but other details were invented from whole cloth, including the cock that crows at the beginning of an autumn day—a different season entirely—and the end of the composition:

The orchestra built up a slow, plaintive melody. . . . The plaint was amplified, then suddenly broken off and taken up once again, as in an autumn dawn, when the dry leaves chase about in the cold wind. Then, from the violins, evoking the rustling in the high trees, came the cry of a satyr, savage and obstinate. One heard the raucous breathing in the flute, stifled by a gust of wind. Panting, the satyr took up once again his harsh, poignant song, like sobbing as he leapt madly from rock to rock and launched shrill notes, swelling the breeze, which mingled . . . with the arpeggiated raindrops, overwhelming the continued melody. The voice of the satyr became more distant, fleeing like summer, humidity, and joy, before the rainy season. The rustic poem thus broke up, stanza by stanza, under the invasion of a musical storm sweeping in waves across the great plain. The song died away in their turn. . . . A silence: and suddenly the shrill clamoring of the cock, parodying the vanished voice of the satyr, burst forth upon the dawn of a livid, stormy day (p. 50).

The scenario has little in common, except for the figure of a satyr, with Mallarmé's *éclogue*. Louÿs also resorted to similar analogies from nature in his note to Debussy after the premiere of *Prélude à "L'Après-midi d'un faune"*: "Throughout, one hears the wind in the leaves, so varied, so changeable."[52]

The second prelude is a melange of different Debussyan traits and works in its quasi-Orientalizing melodies for the flutes, the sound of gongs, arpeggiated figuration, and the like. The addition of a wordless human voice to an orchestral composition immediately recalls *Sirènes*, but the nature of the solo (not a female choir) is carefully distinct from the last of the *Nocturnes*:

The voice, powerful and strange, breathing as if overcome in the midst of tears . . . rose higher and higher, almost hysterically. It was the voice of a priestess intoxicated by poison fumes, the voice of an enchantress arisen naked in the desert night, the supplicating voice of a hallucinating creature caught in the god's kiss. Suddenly the music fell silent: alone, her cry soared upwards and suddenly culminated in a burst of terrible laughter, which awakened the entire orchestra in a tumult of themes pounding together and then falling into the abyss (p. 52).

The description is riveting, but does not correspond to any work by Debussy.

The performance of the two preludes unleashes a riot, a literary foreshadowing of the riot fifteen years after the novel at the premiere of Stravinsky's *Le Sacre du printemps* and quite unlike the largely successful reception of Debussy's work.

Applause mingled with booing. Anger convulsed the arcades full of people. . . . 'Enough! . . . *Vive Harmor!* No! Enough! . . . It's shameful! Bravo! Let's go hear Paulus![53] Lunatics! Philistines! *À bas! à bas!* The Russian anthem!' A storm of cries and laughter came from the tiers: the black monster of the crowd, for a time annulled by the music, revealed three thousand cynical faces, illuminated by the pale light from the electric candelabras. . . . 'This is drunkards' music! Prelude to what? to a padded cell! . . . Composer! Singer! Yes, yes, pass her the smelling salts! Poor woman! to be forced to sing *that!* . . . This is more insane than Wagner! Go play this stuff abroad!' (pp. 51–53).

The cry a few lines later that this is *musique de sans-patrie* reflects the association of anything avant-garde in music with Wagnerism, on a political as well as artistic level. Héricourt/Adam shortly thereafter invokes the memory of that cry when he discusses the current (false) notion of patriotism (pp. 59–72). Deraines/Louÿs appropriately is the principal spokesman for the composer and his music in the third chapter, as he was in real life in the late 1890s. After the concert, de Neuze finds Harmor sitting alone in a café, and the two converse briefly about their respective arts. "Art," Harmor declares, "is a sad sickness . . . one has art as one has consumption," and the public does not understand the slavery of the body and of dreams that an artist must endure (p. 58): creativity is a malady, very like Thomas Mann's later coupling of genius and disease. Debussy did not, to my knowledge, ever say precisely those words, but he did

---

[52]Gordon Millan, p. 229, also *Revue de musicologie* 48 (1962), 62.

[53]Paulus was among the most famous of the Belle Époque café-concert singers. His Bastille Day premiere of the song, *En revenant de la revue*, with the refrain "Not' brav' general Boulanger," helped make the general famous overnight.

express in a letter to Chausson from 20 April 1893, a similarly aristocratic conception of the artist: "The Artist in modern times will always be someone whose worth is not recognized until after his death, and then only to take in him an often idiotic pride, or speculation that is always shameful."[54] One wonders what he would say to his current presence on French twenty-franc notes. Harmor is better able to sustain the disappointment of the concert because, he tells de Neuze, he is completing "a lyric drama, more important than those two poor preludes that Lamoureux asked me to write" (p. 58). The lyric drama is unnamed in the novel, but Mauclair would have known Debussy during the years of work on *Pelléas et Mélisande*; in fact, he was a go-between for Debussy and Maeterlinck. The opera's fictional counterpart suffers a disappointing fate later in *Le Soleil des morts*: it is rejected by the Opéra (*Pelléas* was accepted by the Opéra-Comique), and Lucienne Lestrange, for a time Harmor's mistress, attempts to present fragments of the opera in her recitals, to jeering reviews by the press.

Mauclair's ambivalence toward *L'Élite* is evident in the fate he assigns several of his characters, chiefly Harmor. After his disappointments with the preludes and his opera, Harmor marries one of the banker Soldmann's daughters (a fictional Rothschild clan?—"Jewish bankers, colossally rich . . . the foremost snobs of the elite," p. 121), gives up all dreams of more operatic composition, and becomes the composer of pleasant, refined, and tremendously popular salon songs. In fact, Debussy never relinquished the hope of still more theatrical projects until the war and illness intervened and wrote very little definable as a "salon song" after 1884.[55] From the 1890s on, his production of *mélodies* declined markedly, with the exception of a few banner years, 1904, 1910, and 1913. Harmor's involvement with the strong, passionate self-willed Lucienne Lestrange and his subsequent marriage to a wealthy woman recall in an imprecise way Debussy's stormy involvements with Gaby Dupont, Thérèse Roger, and Lilly

Texier in the last decade of the nineteenth century and the first years of the twentieth. The ending of Harmor's fictional biography stems, however, not from life, but from Mauclair's thesis that few *fin-de-siècle* artists could maintain their radical artistic ideals and instead pursued the easier paths of wealth and popular success.

The episodes of which the novel is composed—the Armel salon, the Lamoureux concert, the visit to Decize's studio, Verlaine's funeral, the encounter with Pallat by night in Montmartre—inspire on Mauclair's part meditations on the spirit of the times. His criticisms of the elite, many of them repeated in his *Servitude et grandeur littéraires* (Ollendorff, 1922), are cutting. They are assembled less to sustain a system of ideas than to present an ensemble of sensibilities. They live, he says, like the Byzantines, occupied with petty controversies in an illusory empire, surrounded on all sides by barbarians. Those ideas they *do* retain have endured too much use, and their caretakers already sense that they guard a tomb. They no longer have the requisite vitality necessary either for life or art; what remains to them are refined sensations, the cultivation of artificiality and abnormality, fatalism, and a combination of obstinacy and hauteur. All have turned their backs on life and are barely tolerated by the crowd, with whom, however, they share the same putrescent odor of decadence, even if exquisitely distilled from the prevailing rottenness. The light they shed is no more than a will-o'-the-wisp, a feeble phosphorescence born of the "putrefying fermentation of democracy, the last light of the Occidental twilight" (p. 117). The apocalyptic tone is quite strong at times.

If the novel strays from its center—Calixte Armel—to a periphery loosely composed of many other artists, Armel resumes center stage strongly near the end. By the third book (chapters 9–12), entitled "Sylvaine," Mauclair has disposed of virtually everyone except Armel, Sylvaine, and de Neuze, the trio at the core of the book, and it is the tragic sundering of their former alliances that constitutes the conclusion.[56] One wonders what Freud might have

---

[54]Oulmont, p. 60.
[55]The closest thing to an exception is perhaps *Dans le jardin*, a setting in May 1903 (published by J. Hamelle in 1905) of a sentimental poem from Paul Gravollet's *Les Frissons*.

---

[56]This is not the place for a close analysis of the final scenes, but they are among the best in the novel. Mauclair carefully

said, had he known of this novel: *Le Soleil des morts* is one of the most striking expositions of the Elektra/Oedipus complex to be found anywhere. Sylvaine is a literary representation of a crucial Freudian mechanism in the development of the personality, someone abnormally fixated at that stage, such that every aspect of her being functions only to support her intense psychosexual infatuation with her father, an infatuation Armel has fostered. Freud's insistence that there is no escape from our primary identification as *gens sexus* could be illustrated by the fictional Armel's inability entirely to deny, by means of intellectualization and sublimation in poetic creativity, his sexual self and its effects on those closest to him. *Le Soleil des morts* is almost exactly contemporaneous with Freud's discovery of the Oedipus complex, since Freud apparently first formulated the concept of a universal developmental crisis, whose prototype he found in Greek drama, within the course of his self-analysis in the summer of 1897.[57] By the end of Mauclair's novel, Sylvaine realizes that she is hopelessly infected with her father's dis-

dain for life—she is his Morella[58]—and is unable to go back, while Armel for the first time understands his responsibility for her existential crisis and renounces his art: "I was the poet of a bygone age, a listener to otherworldly sounds. . . . Pan is dead. The Elite is no more" (p. 213).

The tragedy of Calixte and Sylvaine did not, of course, happen in real life—Mallarmé never renounced his art, but there is some evidence that Mauclair was not merely exercising an overactive and vengeful imagination. Geneviève lived on after her father's death to marry one Edmond Bonniot, with whom she edited several of Mallarmé's works;[59] unlike Sylvaine, she *did* marry someone willing to dedicate himself, at least in part, to Mallarmé's cause. Mauclair's portrait-in-words of Sylvaine's grave beauty and reserved, enigmatic air is apparently accurate, from the evidence of photographs and two extant paintings: Mary Cassat's *Dans le loge de l'Opéra* of 1882 and Whistler's *Rose et gris: Mlle Geneviève Mallarmé* of October 1897.[60] Lockspeiser points out that some of

---

establishes earlier in the work Armel's too fond love for his daughter, especially when they listen to music together ("Armel regardait halêter le démon de beauté dans le corps tiède et souple de Sylvaine"), and the principal characters' massive scruples; they are too hermetically sealed off from life and from each other to speak home truths until the Vesuvian pressure of repressed feeling explodes. In the first of three confrontations, one between de Neuze and Armel, the younger writer realizes his rebellion against Armel's sublime indifference to life. In the second confrontation, Sylvaine rejects de Neuze's proposal of marriage because she is her father's daughter and can only live "in his soul as in my native country." In the final scene between Armel and Sylvaine, the daughter realizes that "amour de fille" and "passion de femme" have formed an unholy alliance, and both are destroyed by the realization.

[57] Sigmund Freud, *The Origins of Psycho-analysis: Letters to Wilhelm Fliess, Drafts and Notes: 1887–1902*, ed. Marie Bonaparte, Anna Freud, and Ernst Kris, trans. Eric Mosbacher and James Strachey (New York, 1954), the letters to Wilhelm Fliess from 3 October and 15 October 1897, pp. 219–24. In particular, the letter of 15 October, pp. 223–24, contains the statement that "everyone was once a budding Oedipus." Freud seems to have first used the actual term "Oedipus complex" in the first of his "Contributions to the Psychology of Love," 1910. In *Die Traumdeutung*, in *The Standard Edition of the Complete Psychological Works of Sigmund Freud*, trans. James Strachey in collaboration with Anna Freud, assisted by Alix Strachey and Alan Tyson (London, 1953–74), IV, pp. 262–64, including the line "It is the fate of all of us to direct our first sexual impulse towards our mother." Freud, as so often, speaks of men.

[58] Poe first published the autobiographical story "Morella" in 1835 in the *Southern Literary Messenger*. In the tale, the narrator is under the spell of his immensely learned wife Morella, whom he nevertheless loathes and dreads. She pines away and eventually dies giving birth to a daughter, with whom the narrator falls in love, an unnatural, obsessive love; the daughter exercises the same spell as the dead wife and seems possessed by her mother's spirit. Poe hints that the narrator murders them both by supernatural means. The tale foreshadows Poe's own fate: his wife Virginia burst a blood vessel while singing and was ill for five years, until her death in 1847.

[59] Edmond Bonniot and Geneviève together edited the collection *Stéphane Mallarmé: Poésies*. Edition complète contenant plusieurs poèmes inédits et un portrait. (*Éditions de la nouvelle revue française*, 1913.) Edmond Bonniot also edited the *Contes indiens* of Mallarmé with "decorations en couleurs" by Maurice Ray in 1927.

[60] Mary Cassat in 1882 painted a work entitled *Dans le loge de l'opéra*, depicting Geneviève Mallarmé and a friend, Mary Ellison. Geneviève was eighteen years old at the time and is shown seated, three-quarters length; she is blond, very reserved looking, with a full, sensitive mouth, a black velvet ribbon around her throat. She holds a small bouquet of pink flowers wrapped in tissue paper and wears a white and pale pink gown—a model of decorum. Whistler's *Rose et gris* was painted at Valvins on 20 October 1897. Whistler took the painting to Paris with him, had it framed, and sent it to Geneviève with a note: "Il est déjà dans son cadre le petit tableau de la princesse en son boudoir rose et gris." It is reproduced in *The Paintings of James McNeill Whistler* by Andrew McLaren Young, Margaret MacDonald, and Robin Spencer, vol. II (New Haven, 1980), p. 210.

Mallarmé's friends might well have been attracted to Geneviève;[61] in the novel, both Harmor and de Neuze are in love with her but, recognizing her devotion to her father, either do not declare their love (Harmor) or do so only belatedly (de Neuze). There is no hint in Debussy's extant letters or accounts by his friends that he was ever attracted to Geneviève as Harmor was to Sylvaine in the novel. If Mauclair's analysis of the relationship between father and daughter is drawn from life, however exaggerated in the service of his thesis about *la maladie*, the reality could possibly have been more complex than the novel. There is no Anatole, dead at age eight, no Madame Mallarmé, in the novel. Whatever the accuracy, exaggeration, or fictionalization of Mauclair's account, it is astonishing that neither reviewers nor friends from the *mardiste* circle discuss the depictions of the Mallarmé-Geneviève/Armel-Sylvaine relationship in print. That the portraits were unrecognizable is beyond credibility; moreover, no reviewer denies Armel's identity as Mallarmé. One wonders if the reticence regarding Geneviève might not be further evidence of Mallarmé's extraordinary influence, his attentive literary and artistic nurture reaping a harvest of silent support.[62]

The pleasure of identifying the famous names and faces of an earlier generation in Manet's *La Musique aux Tuileries* is experienced to an even greater degree when one reads *Le Soleil des morts*—the artists of the age themselves become art and play their parts in a tale part fact, part fiction. Beyond the attractions of a *roman à clef*, however, Mauclair chronicles the deep ideological split between those who remained true to the splendid isolation and chimerical universes of *fin-de-siècle* art and those who began increasingly to repudiate the tenets of Symbolism and decadence. Beginning in 1897 and culminating in 1900, Mauclair allied himself with the latter. Maxime Hersant, the protagonist of his novel *L'Ennemi des rêves* (1900), turns his back on poetry, on the uses of imagination as a form of hashish, "creating the paradise of those who had lost heart," and moves to Marseilles to begin a new life. Mauclair did likewise that same year and thereafter wrote mostly nonfiction, essays, criticism, and memorials to an age and a movement he had renounced.

---

[61]Lockspeiser, p. 227.

[62]Mondor, p. 793, is characteristic when he writes of the central plot only: "Peut-être a-t-il fait glisser, entre les pages, une Geneviève arbitrairement compliquée."

Wagner and Our Century

LEON BOTSTEIN

The extent to which the music, writings, theories, character, and politics of Richard Wagner continue to generate controversy more than a century after his death, as if he were still a dimension of the modern in our own times, is a circumstance perhaps unique for an historical figure and his work. There is little doubt that the American critic Arthur Elson was correct when he noted in 1904:

In the latter part of the nineteenth century the musical world was overshadowed by one of the few great geniuses that the art has produced. . . . It seemed as if he [Wagner] summed up in his works the whole range

of musical possibilities . . . beyond which no further progress was possible. He towered above his fellows like a veritable giant . . . as an unapproachable exponent of the school which he himself had founded and forced upon the public.[1]

Composers in the generations immediately following Wagner, whether in reaction, imitation, or avoidance, were unable to circumvent some confrontation with him. For Strauss, Debussy, Schoenberg, and Berg, there was no "alternative" to placing Wagner at the heart of the modern career of music, as Hans Mayer observed.[2] Writing in 1975, Pierre Boulez con-

---

A review article of Thomas Mann, *Pro and Contra Wagner*, translated by Allan Blunden, with an introduction by Erich Heller (Chicago: University of Chicago Press, 1985), and Jacob Katz, *The Darker Side of Genius: Richard Wagner's Anti-Semitism* (Hanover and London: University Press of New England, 1986; Tauber Institute for the Study of European Jewry Series, No. 5).

[1]Arthur Elson, *Modern Composers of Europe* (Boston, 1904), p. 1.

[2]Hans Mayer, Heinz-Klaus Metzger, and Rainer Riehn, "Diskussion über Recht, Unrecht und Alternativen," in *Richard Wagner: Wie antisemitisch darf ein Künstler sein?* (Munich, 1978), pp. 55–57.

cluded that Wagner's music "still is an essential fermenting element . . . of universal significance; the language of music as we know it today is quite simply unthinkable without that work."[3] The historical correctives emerging from the relatively recent revival and long overdue reconsideration of Liszt as an innovator and visionary have not diminished the enormity of Wagner's significance or aesthetic influence.

From the mid-nineteenth century on, for audiences and the cultural public in general, Wagner became an emblem of the radical and the modern. This association was problematic not only in the aesthetic sense. From the very start of his career, Wagner conjured up enthusiasms and fears well beyond the musical. During his lifetime, Wagner cultivated a significant following and achieved fame and popularity explicitly as a radical and a modernist. In contrast to the careers of his greatest musical antecedents (for example, in the case of Beethoven the late music was thought by Franz Grillparzer, a skilled amateur, to be merely the work of an overheated and somewhat imbalanced genius),[4] the anxieties provoked by Wagner drifted rapidly even beyond politics into the regions of morals and medicine. Henry T. Finck, the tireless American Wagner enthusiast who enrolled at Harvard in 1872, later recalled that when John Knowles Paine

found I was playing the Wagner scores on the official Harvard piano in University Hall, he was greatly distressed and warned me solemnly that I would corrupt my musical taste. As there were no police regulations on the subject, he could not put a stop to my nefarious conduct.[5]

Writing in 1909, Thomas Mann described the reaction of his contemporaries, the generation born after 1870, to Wagner as "much instinctive, albeit unvoiced mistrust" (p. 41). They re-

coiled at the effort to render Wagner a "classic, an authority." Thirty-five years after Wagner's death, Mann could write that: "Wagner is still a burningly topical issue, a problem, the problem of modernism itself—and everything that has followed, including *Elektra*, seems uninteresting by comparison" (p. 41).

Indeed, following the path of the young Nietzsche, Mann, in his youth, became almost obsessed with Wagner. He experienced both the intense allure and the revulsion Wagner seemed to engender simultaneously. In 1933 Mann described his response to Wagner as a love for "one of the most splendidly questionable, ambivalent, and fascinating phenomena in all artistic creation," and for "an enchanted *œuvre* that has been part of my life," which, in turn, revealed an entire century's "deep pessimism, its musical attachment to night and death, which will probably come to be seen as the dominant characteristics of the age" (p. 92). Particularly for Germans, here was the aesthetic itself writ large—an art that was consuming, "extremely modern and by no means innocent. . . . It is clever and ingenious, full of yearning and cunning; in its resources and characteristics it knows how to combine the narcotic with the intellectually stimulating in a way that is intrinsically exhausting for the spectator" (p. 52). In 1911 Mann wrote Ernst Bertram that after hearing *Götterdämmerung* "words of outrage" came to him: "In my bitterness I said to myself that only a barbaric and spiritually purblind nation could raise temples to a work like this" (p. 49). Wagner was a triumphant but "dubious" modernity.

In 1914, well after the corrupt and hagiographical propaganda (including the influential writings of Houston Stewart Chamberlain) issuing from the clique around Cosima in Bayreuth had made its initial round of Europe, Paul Stefan wrote a psychological and historical study, *Die Feindschaft gegen Wagner*, which attempted to expose and refute a new generation of Wagner detractors, among whom Stefan counted Mann. For Stefan, Gustav Mahler's great admirer and biographer and champion of *fin-de-siècle* modernism in Vienna, the new generation of Wagner critics followed Nietzsche's critique of Wagner too blindly. The

[3]Pierre Boulez, "Richard Wagner: The Man and the Works," in *Orientations: Collected Writings*, ed. Jean-Jacques Nattiez, trans. Martin Cooper (Cambridge, Mass., 1986), p. 225.
[4]Franz Grillparzer, Fragment, dated 1834, in "Zur Musik," in *Sämtliche Werke*, ed. Moritz Necker (Leipzig, n.d.), XV, pp. 199–200.
[5]Henry T. Finck, *My Adventures in the Golden Age of Music* (New York, 1926), p. 78.

young, Stefan believed, were mistakenly in search of the purely aesthetic, of an art divorced from the "social," the "human." Stefan believed that Wagner's work, stripped of its historically correct but artificially limiting theatrical appearances, such as Makart-like costumes and primitive symbols of the Teutonic, demanded rehabilitation as the proper inspiration of the modern for a new generation.[6] Yet it was Wagner, as Mann recognized, who inspired a Huysmans-like drift to pure aestheticism; to the world of Dorian Gray, to the decadent, the pessimistic. Wagner helped to propel Mann consistently (and Mann thought the influence was evident on others as well) in his own fiction back toward the linkage between art and death; between beauty, the enervatingly ecstatic, and morbid illness, rather than toward a conception of art as a means to engender a modern utopian social and political world—as an affirmative expression of palpable human possibility. Wagner drifted into the realms of "magic and ceremonial," Mann wrote in 1928. Like Ibsen, Wagner was the "true and awesome" finale of a century, an artist whose work was marked by all the signs of "lateness: recapitulation, retrospective, self-quotation, and dissolution" (p. 85).

The volume under consideration represents a not entirely felicitous translation (with some additions) of a 1963 German collection of Mann's writings about Wagner written between 1902 and 1951, including letters, fragments, excerpts from notebooks, published comments, and complete essays. We are reminded of how curiously Wagner and his work serve as a prism through which the career of twentieth-century modernism can be understood. The culminations of Mann's obsession with Wagner were the 1933 essay, "The Sorrows and Grandeur of Richard Wagner," the 1937 essay on the *Ring*, a 1940 letter to *Common Sense*, and last but not least, in an oblique sense, *Doktor Faustus* (obviously not included in the collection), written during the war.

---

[6]Paul Stefan, *Die Feindschaft gegen Wagner* (Regensburg, 1918), pp. 7–8, 60–81.

II

The 1933 essay, a version of a commemorative address on the fiftieth anniversary of Wagner's death, sparked a hostile reaction from Nazi enthusiasts, who saw it as an attack on "the deepest German sensibilities, now that the uprising of Germany as a nation has assumed a stable form." These self-styled guardians of Wagner's honor believed that a defense of "that great German Master," in the context of the rebirth of a true German spirit in the wake of the Nazi seizure of power, could no longer be regarded as "an unwarranted diversion." An "official" protest was published, signed by, among others, Richard Strauss, Hans Knappertsbusch, Siegmund von Hausegger, and Hans Pfitzner (pp. 149–51). The controversy over Mann's essay grew. Mann replied to the protest several times, among others, in a letter addressed to Pfitzner (p. 79), whose *Palestrina* Mann had praised in 1914.

Mann's 1933 essay was hardly critical. It described Wagner's work as "the most sensational self-portrayal and self-critique of the German character that could be possibly imagined; as such it is calculated to make German culture interesting even to the most doltish foreigner" (p. 145). It was a penetrating but balanced assessment that took Wagner to task for the "dehistoricization" of his subject matter (p. 127), for a tendency to "degeneracy" (p. 135), and for "elements of backward-lookingness and obscurantist worship of the past" (p. 147). Mann focused on the many contradictions in Wagner's work, as well as dwelling on its erotic and pessimistic dimensions. Despite Mann's conclusion that Wagner's work ought to be honored "as a powerful and complex phenomenon of German and Western European life . . . as a profound stimulus to art and knowledge" (p. 148), his explicit claim that Wagner's nationalism was apolitical and that, if anything, Wagner "would assuredly be branded a *Kultur*-Bolshevist today" rankled, as did his warning, "let no spirit of pious or brutal regression claim him for its own" (p. 148).

Of course, this is exactly what happened. For Hitler, who had written in *Mein Kampf*, "I saw the first opera of my life, *Lohengrin*. I was captivated at once. My youthful enthusiasm for the master of Bayreuth knew no bounds." Wagner stood "side by side" with Luther and Frederick the Great as one of the great "reformers" of Germany.[7] It is ironic that Mann's love of Wagner also stemmed from a charmed boyhood memory of *Lohengrin*—as did Ludwig II's. To the end of his life, the prelude was perhaps Mann's favorite musical fragment of Wagner.[8] In the end, the controversy surrounding the 1933 Wagner essay played a crucial role in Mann's decision to emigrate.

The appropriation of Wagner by the Nazis was indeed extensive, and was embraced enthusiastically at Bayreuth. It was no accident, therefore, that post-war musical modernism in Europe aggressively took the direction marked by Schoenberg and serialism; that in the aftermath of the war, the young embraced an aesthetic of modernism once condemned by the Nazis as "*Kultur*-Bolshevist." The modern in the twentieth century, as T. W. Adorno never tired of stressing, demanded that art serve in the struggle for liberation and against fascism. Fascism, in its aesthetic sympathies and alliances, exploited the deceitful denial of politics through art and encouraged a replacement of political hope by the phantasmagoric. Art, even in its pre-modern, late Romantic incarnation, could readily participate in a seductive utilization of the nostalgic, of the idea of the hero and the mythic, which all had key roots and extensive expression in Wagner's art and ideology.

The other post-war musical alternative was perhaps the truly radical nostalgic retreat embodied in Hermann Hesse's *Das Glasperlenspiel* (1943)—a withdrawal into a rigid antique classicism, as opposed to the creation (in Schoenberg's sense) of a radically new, modern classicism. Hesse was partly prescient in that the revival of interest in antique music, from the early Baroque, Renaissance, and Middle Ages, gained dramatic momentum in the postwar era. It gained this at the expense of an attachment to the inherited culture of the late nineteenth century, in terms of both repertoire and performance practice.[9]

The memory of the embrace of Wagner by the Nazis has faded significantly in America, but not in Germany or in Israel. The renascence of interest since the early 1970s in the musical language of Richard Strauss's later works and the contemporary symbiosis of minimalist and late nineteenth-century Romantic musical idioms are indications that we have forgotten the cultural and political significance of the anti-Wagnerian radical musical modernism of the 1950s. In view of the fascist embrace of what T. W. Adorno's generation regarded as regressive romanticism, the astringent and angular modernism adopted by younger composers after the war constituted a necessary declaration of independence from the fascist appropriation of Wagner and his imitators and successors. Beyond the fading of a collective memory about the war and its immediate consequences, the explicit role of progressive politics in shaping American art and culture continues to weaken in the 1980s, as it has since the late 1960s (and particularly during the mid-1970s). Within the context of a culture dominated by claims of cultural autonomy from politics or by a cultural politics of restoration and nostalgia (in the form of neo-conservatism) Wagner has experienced both a direct and an indirect revival. Obliquely, we see the resurgence of efforts at extended large-scale musical and dramatic work in Philip Glass's operas and Robert Wilson's staging, with their implicit Wagnerian ambition to span the grandiose and engage a larger public. There is a renewed interest in performance art using mixed media and, among composers, a return to a late nineteenth-century musical vocabulary and a reminiscently expressive language.

Directly, there is a shift away from Appia-like staging in favor of traditionalist revivals of Wagner—as, most recently in the 1986 production of *Die Walküre* at the Metropolitan Opera—which restore Wagner's literal scenic and dramatic meanings. Even in non-literal revivals, there is a reversal of Wieland Wagner's attempt in the 1950s to render Wagner through light, symbolic gesture, and staging. One fairly recent example was the widely televised Boulez-Chereau Bayreuth *Ring*, which sought to transform Wagner's narrative meanings—and in that very act, paradoxically, vindicated the grand literary and ideological ambition of

[7]Adolf Hitler, *Mein Kampf* (New York, 1941), pp. 23, 287.
[8]See Mann's letter from 1949 to Emil Preetorius, p. 210.
[9]An issue discussed by Mann in "Die Entstehung des Doktor Faustus," in *Doktor Faustus* (Frankfurt, 1967), pp. 728–30.

Wagnerian music drama. Last (and in this context, certainly least) we seem to possess, in a culture that has spawned *Star Wars*, the infantile fantasies of Steven Spielberg, and MTV, a fertile ground for the experiential flight into myth and forgetfulness that, as Mann argued, Wagner uniquely can afford us.

These books by Mann and Katz have appeared, then, at a time when audiences once again are beginning to respond to the facile pessimisms of late Wagner. There is a new sympathy for his decadent implicit rejection of practical collective social schemes and political aspirations, seen as ultimately futile and naive, in favor of mystical redemption through love, sacrifice, and faith. Perhaps we even share Wagner's residual cult of heroism. Has our sense of politics disintegrated into an implicit faith in new possibilities emerging from an heroic leadership in which we might place all hope? We find ourselves favoring the sensual, the private, the pursuit of temporary ecstasy, rapid gratification, and even flirtations with new religious enthusiasms as though in imitation of Wagner's biographical odyssey from politics to myth and finally to idiosyncratic notions of Christian redemption in death. In short, the 1980s have generated a cultural climate that is once again profoundly hospitable to Wagner, a world filled with superficial affinities for his aesthetic, particularly as Mann understood it.

Although this climate prevails in the United States, elsewhere—in Germany and Israel at least (among many intellectuals and in particular educated Jews)—Wagner, Wagnerism, and the contemporary reinterpretations of Wagner have not shed their inflammatory aspects. Apart from the echoes of classic pre-war critiques of Wagner, such as those written by Adorno (in his 1938 *Versuch über Wagner*)[10] and Mann, which drew their strength from an analysis of Wagner's work and its then contemporary political implications, there remain unresolved two famous biographical and historical issues that continue to render Wagner and Wagnerism controversial. One is the nature of Wagner's German nationalism, and therefore his influence on modern German nationalist thinking. The other is Wagner's anti-Semitism and, consequently, his influence on and the level of his "responsibility" for the creation of the world of the mid-twentieth century in which the extermination of six million European Jews occurred.

Mann tried to address the first issue directly. In 1949 he wrote Emil Preetorius that "there is in Wagner's bragging, his endless holding-forth, his passion for monologue, his insistence on having a say in everything, an unspeakable arrogance that prefigures Hitler—oh yes, there's a good deal of 'Hitler' in Wagner" (p. 210). Responding to Peter Viereck's scathing essay on Wagner in 1940, Mann observed, "I find an element of Nazism not only in Wagner's questionable literature; I find it also in his 'music,' in his work . . . directed 'against civilization,' against the entire culture and society dominant since the Renaissance" (pp. 201–02).

Mann wished to believe that there were two Germanys, one of Goethe and one which ended up in Hitler. Wagner, correctly understood, would clearly belong to the former. Whatever Wagner's shortcomings, he was for Mann a great artist and master of "the purely human dimension" (p. 177). At moments Mann was convinced Wagner would himself have been an enemy of Hitlerism. But at the same time, there was little denying that not only the explicit content and the ecstatic seductiveness of the work, its form and its heroes, but also its peculiar popularity—its ease of memory, its accessibility—all rendered Wagner somehow markedly dangerous.

At the heart of Mann's critique of Wagner was the lament that Wagner, that remarkable "dilettante" of the nineteenth century, had found both a style and a form of artistic expression that broke the sanctity of art as possession of the few and the educated. Theodore Thomas, the conductor who probably did more than any other single individual to popularize Wagner in America (and who once remarked *en passant* that Wagner "did not care for humanity, but in his later life he became sentimental"), noted that "the Wagner technique has something very fascinating about it, and one learns the music readily by heart. There is something spontaneous and melodious about its figures—symmet-

[10]First published after World War II (1952). Published in English as *In Search of Wagner*, trans. Rodney Livingstone (London, 1981).

rical, I might say."[11] In a similar vein, in 1896 Henry Edward Krehbiel recognized in Wagner a unique plasticity of expressiveness (accessible by the untutored audience) within a clearly defined and grasped range of thematic elements; within what Schoenberg later characterized as the specific legacy of Wagner for his own music: "the way it is possible to manipulate themes for expressive purposes and the art of formulating them in the way that will serve this end."[12]

Mann recognized that Wagner's innovative command of the art of expressive repetition made him accessible to a mass audience in ways unthinkable for the highest regions of "absolute" music, such as chamber music. Through his art Wagner created a cultural bridge, a vehicle, on behalf of the democratization not only of his own music but of the heritage of eighteenth- and nineteenth-century music.

For Mann, Wagner transformed the idea of music and its distinctiveness. The "insatiable chromaticism" of *Tristan* and much of the *Ring* was a "literary idea" (pp. 46 and 108). What Wagner wrote was, in some sense, no longer music, but an amalgam of acoustic and narrative inspirations, which "can persuade even the unmusical to listen to music"—which they did—and force new musical sounds "of unspeakable splendor" in service of the portrayal of "mythic concepts."[13]

A new public, and for Mann a dangerous one—the rapidly expanding urban middle classes of the late nineteenth century, was embraced, therefore, by Wagner (whose melodic texture Mann deemed "vulgar" when compared to Mozart or Beethoven) (p. 41). Wagner was the artist as "demagogue" rather than "aristocrat." Wagner flattered "the people" and craved popularity among the "vulgar bourgeoisie" whose spirit had come to dominate Bayreuth even in his lifetime. This "rabble" was different from

the "genuine middle class." The fact that Wagner was the master of the narrative, a novelist in music who "treated music in a literary manner," accounted for his mass popularity. That, in turn, made possible the corrupt political appropriation of Wagner into a racist German political nationalism, which finally culminated in National Socialism. In Europe outside of Germany, Wagner and Wagnerism helped to enlarge and define the concert and opera public well beyond the social (rather than demographic) limits evident in the public for music at mid-century in European and American cities.

Rather than confront Wagner's art and its impact on audiences since the 1870s, recent Wagner revisionists (in political matters) have cited Wagner's eventual rejection of Bismark and Prussian nationalism, the significance of his pre-1848 democratic radicalism, and above all the fact that the oft-quoted closing nationalistic lines of Hans Sachs in *Die Meistersinger* refer explicitly only to "holy German art." In a recent book, a contemporary apologist for Pfitzner claims that there was less difference in 1933 between Pfitzner and Mann than we might like to think.[14] Pages are devoted to sanitizing Pfitzner's anti-Semitism, his enthusiastic endorsement of the Nazis (which actually dated from the 1920s), and his lofty rejection, after the war, of any sense of collective guilt.[15]

The Mann collection exposes the murky and troublesome arena of art and politics, particularly in the era of Nazism. The issues that troubled Mann and his generation were perhaps most sharply evident in the case of Wagner. Yet they have been essentially sidestepped by most modern professional scholars of music history. In *The New Grove* we read the lie that Pfitzner "detested" Nazi rule.[16] Despite the respect ap-

---

[11]Theodore Thomas, *A Musical Autobiography*, ed. George P. Upton (New York, 1964), pp. 343–44, 347.

[12]Arnold Schoenberg, "National Music (2)," in his *Style and Idea*, ed. Leonard Stein (London, 1975), p. 174.

[13]See pp. 38 and 108. In 1937 Mann referred to "a structure of musical remembrance," to a nineteenth-century "naturalism . . . hallowed by myth," which, among other things, helped Wagner to become an artist with a potential for a mass audience. See pp. 188–91.

[14]Bernhard Adamy, *Hans Pfitzner: Literatur, Philosophie und Zeitgeschehen in seinem Weltbild und Werk* (Tutzing, 1980).

[15]Consider this sample of Adamy's logic. After all, Pfitzner tried to help an individual Jew. Hans Frank had to be more than just another high-ranking Nazi; he was a personal friend, and that made things hard for Pfitzner. *Adamy*, pp. 252, 272–321, 335–43.

[16]Helmut Wirth, "Pfitzner, Hans," *The New Grove Dictionary of Music and Musicians*, ed. Stanley Sadie (London, 1980), vol. 14, p. 612.

propriate to Pfitzner as a composer, his relatively minor stature makes such a glossing over comparatively invisible. But the "problematical personality" of Wagner, as Boulez observed, has not and may never "vanish" behind Wagner's "supreme artistic achievement."[17] On the thorny issue of Wagner and anti-Semitism, *The New Grove* had the audacity to print Curt von Westernhagen's bizarre and naive quotation of Hermann Levi's defense of Wagner in a letter to his father (a rabbi), and the assertion that Wagner once painted "an affectionate picture of Samuel Lehrs" as proof that, despite his many anti-Semitic writings, Wagner "was otherwise not hostile to Jews."[18] In the midst of today's renewed interest in Wagner, there is, in fact, a rehabilitation at work, an apolitical revisionism against the post-war analysis which attempted to underscore Wagner's importance in the history of modern German nationalism and European political anti-Semitism.

What makes the Wagner case difficult is the enormity of his artistic and historical genius and importance. The moral issues with respect to Richard Strauss and Hans Pfitzner can be reduced to precise questions of collaboration and responsibility. They were contemporaries of political horror, and their actions demand assessment. In the case of Anton Bruckner, whose work was also enthusiastically embraced by the Nazis, the issues are far easier than in either the Wagner case or those of Strauss and Pfitzner. By the late 1880s Bruckner had already become a political symbol, an oft-cited exemplar of simple Austrian and Christian values, a vital contrast to cosmopolitan and corrupt art and artists. By 1900 Bruckner had been enshrined, like Schubert, as an emblem of native Austrian virtues. These sentiments transformed Bruckner into a darling of Christian-Socialists and Austrian anti-Semites at the *fin de siècle*, especially in the anti-Semitic press in Vienna, which never tired of making invidious contrasts between Bruckner and Mahler.[19] But, even though Max Auer, in his edition of the massive Göllerich Bruckner biography from the late 1930s (dedicated to the "new Vienna"), could exult that Adolf Hitler himself had agreed to place a bust of Bruckner in "the Honorary Hall of United Germanness, the Valhalla near Regensburg,"[20] it remains clear that Bruckner and his music were innocent. Bruckner was a naive and simple God-fearing Catholic, in the political sense an entirely harmless, and ineffective fellow. His music can hardly be found to have nefarious political or aesthetic content. Its critics have been content to declare it merely dull and boring; the hint of moral culpability in the catastrophes of our century can never be raised legitimately, no matter how enthusiastic Nazis and Austrian anti-Semites have been about Bruckner.

Such issues and their lingering presence in the case of Wagner, therefore, are more than the consequence of Nazi appropriation. Since direct moral responsibility is historically a matter not at issue, the key questions that seem to recur are: what did Wagner think and believe; what was his political and cultural influence, and is he to be held responsible by modern audiences for that influence; what might he have thought of the Nazis? Even more to the point: are his works somehow still intrinsically dangerous for contemporary audiences (in the manner Mann alluded to) in the world. Does Wagner's art still influence the way audiences understand art and art's role in society in a way that would never have dawned on Bruckner?

[17]Boulez, p. 230.
[18]Curt von Westernhagen, "Wagner, Richard," *The New Grove Dictionary of Music and Musicians*, ed. Stanley Sadie (London, 1980), vol. 20, p. 111. This and other difficulties in *The New Grove* text when it was first published led to the replacement of Westernhagen's biographical account with a much more acerbic one by John Deathridge. This new text, which can be found in *The New Grove Wagner* (New York, 1984), appears to have been a discreet maneuver by the editors to compensate for the error of having printed the Westernhagen account. Unfortunately, the public, for whom *The New Grove* was in part intended and for whom it sets a standard as a reference source, will encounter in the bound volumes of this wonderful tool Westernhagen's and not Deathridge's narrative. See the review by Joseph Kerman of the Wagner literature in *The New York Review of Books*, 22 December 1983.

[19]See the discussion of this issue in Johannes Leopold Mayer, *Die politischen und sozialen Hintergünde von Musik und Musikpflege in Wien in den Jahren 1840 bis 1880* (Ph.D. diss., Vienna, 1978).
[20]August Göllerich and Max Auer, *Anton Bruckner: Ein Lebens-und Schaffensbild* (Regensburg, 1937; rpt. 1974), XVII, 129.

Central to Wagner's lifelong social and political philosophizing—and some would argue to his musical ambitions and career—was the so-called Jewish Question. It is perhaps on this crucial issue that the analytical dilemma with respect to Richard Wagner, in both the historical and moral dimensions, rests. For Wagner, and many of his contemporaries, particularly in German-speaking lands, the issue of what constituted a nation, a cohesive people and political entity, was ultimately inseparable in nineteenth-century society from the issues of religion and the place of Jews, Europe's most significant and visible international minority. Wagnerism gave the long history of anti-Semitism in Germany new impetus in a manner similar to the impact the Dreyfus trial would later have on the career of French anti-Semitism, which already had been influenced by French Wagnerism. Vincent d'Indy's anti-Semitism, for example, took much of its inspiration from Wagner.

It is significant that in his many musings about Wagner, the issue of the Jews never figured prominently or explicitly for Mann. From the start, Mann was convinced that "we can learn more about Wagner from Nietzsche's critique" than from all other sources. For Mann, Wagner meant *Tristan*, the world of eros, and the focus on seductive sexuality and its psychological centrality. Mann responded to the influence of Schopenhauer in Wagner and to the hypnotic power of late Romantic musical language. In his construction of *Buddenbrooks*, Mann adapted from Wagner the sweeping, ambitious, near-mythic narrative of decline. The psychological contradictions inherent in the personality of Wagner when he wrote *Parsifal* (if not the aesthetic atmosphere of the work) helped to focus the sort of ruminations about art, inspiration, and death that are present in *Death in Venice*. *The Magic Mountain*, the short stories, and *Faustus* document Mann's struggle with Wagner, with the artist as purveyor of spiritual and sensual experience at the expense of life and being-in-the-world. Wagner, for Mann, constituted the crucial heritage of aesthetic influence, as well as the object of modernist rebellion; he was the symbol of the dominant centrality of musical art in the life of the cultured German classes. It was only later, during the waning years of the Weimar Republic,

that an emphasis on the explicitly political in Wagner was forced on Mann, with some ambivalence and reluctance (despite Nietzsche's critique).

Even in his first extended piece on Wagner dating from 1908, however, Mann questioned Wagner in oblique political terms. He challenged Wagner's debt to theatrical tricks—to the theater in the "conventional" sense (bereft of Wagner's grandiose claims to have generated a new form)—and Wagner's affinity to the clearly dated historicist and vacuous aesthetics of Hans Makart. Mann's later concern for the political implications of Wagner and Wagnerism emerged from the sorts of insights he expressed in 1908: "We Germans are born with a reverence for the theater such as no other nation knows." The consequence was that Wagner created, through the "most unscrupulous use of non-artistic effects . . . an opiate to the fashionable bourgeoisie . . . a *trompe-l'œil* . . ." that has an "immediate impact" on an assembly but demands "so much forgetfulness." The "theater . . . has no yesterday." This forgetfulness, Mann concluded, accounted for the "highly artistic and diseased elements of a cosmopolitan European spirit" whose finest symbol was Bayreuth. This was all possible because Wagner was "terrifyingly expressive," his work filled with "gripping moments" (pp. 32–36).

With ambivalence, Mann noted in 1908 that while Walt Whitman probably had "more influence on the younger generation," Wagner was an embodiment—the essence—of the nineteenth century, in the sense that Tolstoy, Dostoevsky, Balzac, Zola, and Dickens were as well. In Mann's view, modern Germany had produced no great novel; Wagner provided the monumental German equivalent to one. By 1933 Mann had concluded that Wagner had captivated and subjugated bourgeois Europe through the manipulation of "the delicious, the sensual-pernicious, sensual-consuming, heavily intoxicating, hypnotically caressing, the thickly and richly padded—in a word, that supremely luxurious element in his music" (p. 137). In all Mann's ruminations, there are, at best, passing references to Wagner's bad character, his anti-Semitism, or other dubious moral qualities, those which prompted Nietzsche to call Wagner a "sickness," not a human. Anti-Semitism was little more than a persistent sign of Wagner's flawed character, but not a central aspect of that which "drew the bourgeois masses" into the "arms" of his works.

III

Jacob Katz, in contrast, has focused explicitly on Wagner's anti-Semitism in order to understand both Wagner himself and his role in modern political anti-Semitism. Katz is a distinguished historian working in Israel, perhaps the leading authority on the history of German Jewry and modern anti-Semitism. He may have been motivated, in part, to write his little book by the publication in 1978 of a series of papers in the *Text + Kritik* series entitled *Richard Wagner: Wie anti-semitisch darf ein Künstler sein?* (ed. Heinz Klaus Metzger and Rainer Riehn [Munich, 1978]).[21] Katz was struck by the contrasts in, and vitality of, the contemporary debate on the issue of Wagner's anti-Semitism in Germany. He cites a "glossing-over" in Georg Martin Dellin's biography of Wagner and the sharp anti-Wagner attack (contained in the 1978 volume) by Hartmut Zelinsky, which takes Wagner to task anew as a key historical force in the emergence of Nazism. Katz asserts an old-fashioned, indeed nostalgic, methodological credo: he claims that he writes history "remaining independent of the tendencies of the present . . . disregarding the consequences that still lay in the future," in order to understand "the past in light of what was then known . . . in the context of that time." Katz is harsh on those who seek to "backdate." He sticks to a "chronological order," convinced that "the known facts" dating from Wagner's lifetime prove incriminating enough, without "burdening him in addition with the horrible deeds of Hitler" (pp. ix, 3–4).

The theoretical possibility of achieving a genuine and adequate standard of historical objectivity through so seemingly simple a method has been the subject of compelling critical scrutiny since the days of Heinrich Rickert and Max Weber. From the standpoint of any overt pursuit of objectivity, however, more troubling is the fact that Katz refuses, in contrast to Mann and Adorno, to pursue Wagner's artworks or even Wagnerism after 1883. Oddly enough, he has written a sort of oblique vindication of Wagner in "obedience to [the] professional ethic, to research matters accurately and to describe them in accordance with the facts . . . [paying] attention to the factor of time" (pp. 129–31). For selfish reasons—among them fear of alienating Jews who were among the most enthusiastic members of the Wagnerian audience, not to speak of offending Angelo Neumann, the Jewish impresario who popularized Wagner throughout the continent—Wagner is plausibly depicted as having been unwilling to embrace the practical consequences of the organized political anti-Semitism that emerged in Germany in the late 1870s and 1880s. Although he remained a "central symbol" for anti-Semites all the way through the Holocaust, Wagner's anti-Semitism is termed by Katz as comparatively "naive" and even "restrained."[22]

Katz rejects the notion that Wagner's 1850 essay, "Judaism in Music," (published under a pseudonym) was a harbinger of modern racist thought. He finds no concrete evidence of anti-Semitism before 1850 in Wagner and rejects the Nietzsche hypothesis of Wagner's fear of his own Jewish origins, an idea that has survived owing to the currency of the claim that Wagner's stepfather, Geyer, had been Jewish. (But the fact that Geyer was, in the event, not Jewish does not refute the historical plausibility of a psychological fear on the part of Wagner that he, Wagner, might have been considered, however falsely, Jewish and illegitimate to boot.) Katz's contention that Wagner was not anti-Semitic before 1850 rests on no more than the absence of any recorded explicit anti-Jewish remarks. Such a psychological portrayal is finally too simplistic, perhaps the result of Katz's over-zealous wish to avoid the excesses of speculative pseudo-historians eager to vent moral outrage on Wagner.

Katz argues that Wagner became anti-Semitic because of his sense of rivalry with Mendelssohn and Meyerbeer; that his 1850 essay de-

---

[21]This collection also contains reprints of Peter Viereck's 1939 article on Wagner and Hitler and Mann's 1940 reply (also contained in the Blunden volume).

[22]See also pp. 115–20.

rives much of its logic from a "Zeitgeist" of which Bruno Bauer and Karl Marx were a part; and that his critique of Mendelssohn was not based on a biological or racist argument. In short, the 1850 essay was of little consequence, and its arguments were not prefigurings of late nineteenth-century racist anti-Semitism, which became an essential part of Nazism by way of Houston Stewart Chamberlain. Even the 1869 reprint, published under Wagner's own name, was undertaken on account of personal factors and was less politically significant than later historians might have wished or feared.

Katz, predictably, is best in depicting the history of anti-Semitism and political relations between Jews and Christians in the mid-nineteenth century, particularly in Germany. He summarizes effectively the nature and consequences of the changing expectations of emancipation on the part of Jews and Christians over the century; the persistence of evident Jewish differences in language and religion; the collapse of the hope of mass conversion; and the character of Jewish-Gentile interactions and the general progress of legal emancipation until the 1870s. In Katz's view, Wagner needed consistently to assert an enemy and a believable conspiracy that could explain and discredit any artistic, commercial, or critical failures he might encounter. The Jew was a convenient and universal explanatory device, a constant other. Nevertheless, the Jew ultimately was probably capable of some form of non-violent process of disappearance. According to Katz, Wagner did not consider the negative qualities of the Jew "ineradicable." Amalgamation, assimilation, "overcoming" were always possible for Wagner (perhaps, as in the case of Hermann Levi, through baptism and cultural self-cleansing). Katz sticks to the idea that the "complete negation" of the Jews' potential transformation into a healthy part of the German or European peoples was never expressed by Wagner.[23]

What Katz fails to take into account are the many contradictions and confusions in Wagner's theoretical writings—works that Mann, interestingly, never took seriously, despite their enormous influence in Wagner's lifetime

and afterwards, particularly on Gustav Mahler and his contemporaries. Katz goes so far as to suggest that "spontaneous remarks," such as those in Cosima's diaries, "Wagner cannot have meant to be taken seriously" (p. 91). The most notorious of these remarks, because it was reported in Glasenapp's massive biography, long before Cosima's diaries were made public, is Wagner's response to the tragic fire at the Ringtheater in 1881 in Vienna; all the Jews, he quipped, should be burned up during a performance of Lessing's *Nathan the Wise*. (Wagner knew and resented the fact that as early as 1881 a disproportionate segment of the audience for music and theater in Vienna was Jewish.) Katz seems unwilling to take such a remark seriously as evidence of a genuinely "modern" anti-Semitism!

At least Katz does not adduce Wagner's relative close relations with Tausig, Levi, and Joseph Rubinstein ("Malvolio," as Cosima liked to call him) as evidence against his antipathy toward the Jews. Katz correctly draws attention to the difficult pathology of self-hate engendered by European anti-Semitism among selected Jewish intellectuals. Yet, somehow he is determined to characterize Wagner as an almost benign pre-modern anti-Semite, despite Wagner's unquestioned ideological (not only personal) influence on the logic of German anti-Semitism.

Katz's final arguments about Wagner's anti-Semitism at the end of his career focus on the composer's psychology, ambitions, and circumstances. Katz cites the equivocations and the virulent anti-Semitic remarks that characterized Wagner's final years, when Hans von Wolzogen had already embarked on an editorial policy that helped turn the *Bayreuther Blätter* into an anti-Semitic organ. Although Wagner refused to sign the 1880 petition (von Bülow did sign it) calling for repeal of emancipation rights for Jews, he still occasionally took credit for the revival of anti-Semitism in its new, post-1873 political form and even ruminated about the appropriateness of "expulsion" for the Jews. Katz concedes that at the very end, race thinking did enter Wagner's anti-Semitism. Yet, Wagner's belief "in the corruptness of the Jews . . . led to the concept of race," not the other way around, Katz would like us to believe (p. 117).

For Katz, "anti-Semitism must have its his-

---

[23]See pp. 89–90; also pp. 117–19 and pp. 123–27.

torical causes and its psychological and sociological preconditions in order to summon the conceptual means for its justification" (p. 117). Katz concludes that although modern anti-Semitism is different from Wagner's and that although Wagner's own writings had less influence and were less innovative than a "fixed" and presumably a historical "conception" of anti-Semitism might suggest, Wagner's "mentality and way of thinking are indeed an anticipation of future horrors." Wagner can gain no "historical acquittal," even when the sins of the future cannot be legitimately ascribed to him.

IV

What is striking about Katz's book is its methodological stridency. It is as if restricting themselves to "direct statements" and other "testimony," avoiding "evidence from Wagner's artworks," and eschewing so-called subjective, imaginative interpretations of the artworks, is all that historians must or can legitimately do. It is as if in the writing of history "facts," as Katz calls them, are discrete, unambiguous objects handed down from the past. In contrast, Mann, although he does not confront anti-Semitism directly, engages the works and therefore the central issue of Wagner's impact on real audiences in real time.[24]

Rereading *Judaism in Music* and Wagner's other statements on Jews, one can easily come to a conclusion quite at odds with Katz: that Wagner's anti-Semitism was lifelong and had developed well before 1850. What he did in 1850, in my opinion, was to formulate a conceptual logic integral to both anti-Semitism and his political visions. Wagner's view of art and its proper connection to a spiritually "right" audience, as well as his view of Mendelssohn as flawed in a particularly Jewish way, both have their echoes in more "modern" political anti-Semitic campaigns. The one before 1907 in Vienna against Mahler is a notable example. Wagner's formulation of anti-Semitism in 1850 and after was consistent with his Romantic ruminations and his ensuing characterizations of groups in society, of masculinity, nations, and

heroism. It fits in with the characters and the social and mythic ideology present in *Siegfrieds Tod, Meistersinger*, and later *Parsifal*.

Wagner's sense of his own public after the 1869 republication of the essay on Judaism, as present in writings Katz did not choose to examine—his concept of *Volk*, his critique of the business of art and theater, and his vision for Bayreuth and music education—all demonstrate, despite their confusions, innovative dimensions in the way culture, nationhood, and the role of the individual in a nation were to be understood. These, in turn, bear directly on Wagner's view of Jews as entirely foreign as a group, incapable of true assimilation even on an individual basis; as the source of cultural and national decline, and as fundamentally diseased and decadent. The fact that Wagner's specific vocabulary was not the same as modern racist anti-Semites is not a sufficient argument. Katz's historical conception of race thinking may finally be too narrow, even though his understanding of changes in anti-Semitism during the nineteenth century constitutes a valuable historical corrective to simplistic static narratives.[25]

Katz's seemingly modest refusal to engage in analysis of Wagner's art leads one to suspect he has underestimated the influence and significance of Wagner between 1850 and 1883, especially as regards the logic and character of anti-Semitism. Wagner's ideas were, in fact, enthusiastically acknowledged by his contemporaries

---

[24]See p. 123. See also, for example, the awkward and narrow analysis of the 1850 essay, pp. 41–44.

[25]Katz's argument is really quite limited, particularly in its discussion of Wagner's writings and, therefore, his attitudes. No matter the early similarities with Marx, Wagner's recurrent focus on the Jews demands the kind of psycho-historical probing that Nietzsche began. Any analysis of Wagner also requires a discussion of Wagner's ambivalence on the subject of artistic success; Wagner's view of the Jews as quintessential examples of the corrupt public whose adulation he nevertheless craved. The Jew was the symbol of the journalist, the capitalist—in short, every evil type that surrounded the "true" artist and (ironically) dominated in every arena of potential support. Finally, just as Katz criticizes those with too static a view of anti-Semitism, he counters with a far too static view of language use, the concepts of biological and sociological thinking, and the idea of race. See for example Richard Wagner, "Publikum und Popularität" (1878) and "Das Publikum in Zeit und Raum" (1878) in Richard Wagner, *Gesammelte Schriften und Dichtungen* (Leipzig, 1888), X, pp. 61–102.

in Germany and Austria. The virulent anti-Semitism of the Bayreuth circle around Cosima after 1883 and the appropriation of Wagner by later political anti-Semites, including the Nazis, have deep historical roots in Wagner's work itself. Indeed, Katz refuses to confront the fascinating and crucial issue of Wagner and Wagnerism with which Mann and Adorno struggled: the ultimate political consequences of the vision of the world promulgated by Wagner through the heroes and villains of the *Ring*, the theology of *Parsifal*, and his views on sin and sexuality. Any discussion of the political significance of Wagner, inclusive of anti-Semitism, must address the ultimate political consequences of Wagner's interweaving of myth, fantasy, love, and death.

Therefore, one cannot dismiss lightly the observations made by Ludwig Marcuse in 1938 that Wagner's cult of the genius, his artistic elevation of tribal and racial conflict, the banishment of the historical from the stage, and the notion of an artistic "totality" are all items to contend with in discussing Wagner's historical and political influence. In the late nineteenth and early twentieth centuries, Wagner represented to a new public enmeshed in the daily world of industrial and commercial work, railroads, factories—a "prosaic" world—a desperate but unbridgeable gap between reality and the world of swans, knights, and the rescue of maidens. Wagner highlighted the monstrosity of the modern everyday which seemed escapable only through aestheticism, not real politics. Perhaps Wagner's cult of the single hero and, more to the point, the obsession with the corrupt outsider—the Alberichs and Beckmessers of this world (themselves evocative as caricatures of anti-Semitic stereotypes of Jews)—offered a simple, radical alternative to a bleak existence which otherwise resisted conventional liberal political efforts to make it more tolerable.[26]

By dangling the myth of simplistic radical transformation, by sentimentalizing death, love, and redemption, Wagner's operas made a magic and easy flight from an unforgiving world

into an unreal world seem somehow plausible to loyal audiences in the years between 1883 and 1933. At best, ordinary politics could no longer suffice. Such notions are foreign to Katz. He simply will not confront the massive ideological and cultural influence of Wagner and his art, even though those who do confront the "darker side" of Wagner usually freely concede the obvious: that nothing will, can or even should, discredit the greatness of Wagner as artist and composer.

In that realization lies the central dilemma. Taken together, these two books clarify and frame the continuing historical and cultural reconsideration of the tensions (and perhaps links) between moral, political, and aesthetic evaluations of art, past and present. In Mann we find an eloquent and honest coming to terms with a powerful art of many faces. Mann recognized the beauty and scope of the musical achievement, returning again and again to the opening measures of *Rheingold*, the consummate originality and magic of *Parsifal*, the dramatic power of the *Ring*, and to the extent to which Wagner succeeds in extending our sense of the poetic and the psychological through music and the drama. Mann wished to preserve Wagner for the tradition of Goethe, the critique of Nietzsche notwithstanding (but taking account of Nietzsche's lifelong interior recognition of his own debt to Wagner). Despite the consequences of Wagner, Mann sought to find a way to incorporate Wagner into a European and German heritage of humanism.

But Mann himself was scarcely able to resist the draw of the Wagnerian assertion of a conflict between the bourgeois (of which Wagner was himself, ironically a consummate ideal type) and the practical (including the conventionally moral, and the political) on the one hand, and the spiritual and the artistic on the other. Mann revealed his own conception, of the link between love and death, of the price paid for the aesthetic, the creative, the beautiful, and the sublime. From *Buddenbrooks* to *Doktor Faustus*, the price was, finally, personal health, a sense of historical optimism and continuity, moral stasis, and any hope of sustaining an ethical order.

Above all, for Mann and his generation, Wagner, in this sense, set the terms for the radical and modern. As Mann's albeit faulty use of

---

[26]Quoted in Klaus-Ulwe Fischer, "Von Wagner zu Hitler: Annahme oder Ablehnung einer These von Ludwig Marcuse," in *Richard Wagner: Wie antisemitisch darf ein Künstler sein?* (see n. 2), pp. 38–39.

Schoenberg as a model in *Faustus* revealed, Wagner defined the inheritance of the nineteenth century that needed to be transcended. (Alban Berg was reputed to have rebuked an anti-Wagnerian with the remark that without Wagner, *Wozzeck* would have been unthinkable.)

If this were not enough to grapple with, add to it the need to face the consequences of Wagner's musical and dramatic work, its success in terms of how the work was made to cohere with modern racially based nationalism, to coalesce with German nationalism and finally with Nazism. Also consider that few artists of such historical stature have been as outspoken and reprehensible as individuals as Wagner. Here we have no charming Mozart or distraught Beethoven with whom we can commiserate; no unhappy Tchaikovsky, no noble Verdi, or matter-of-fact Haydn. What must one make of this psychological case, this instance of megalomania, moral corruption, and self-deceit we call Wagner? Is Wagner's character any more relevant to an appreciation of his art than the consequences of Wagnerism in Germany? And what does one make, historically, of Wagner's influence elsewhere in Europe and in America, even on cultured Jews, before 1933?

The relation of morality and art—the interconnections between politics and art—can be framed, as Katz suggests (but far less narrowly than he attempts), in historical terms. Beyond that, what is also historically fascinating is why and how Wagner and his work accelerated the expansion of the cultural audience at the end of the nineteenth century. The history of musical reception has no better subject than Wagner. As Krehbiel implied in 1896, the new audience took to Wagner and, through him, to hearing music. They were nurtured in part on cultural journalism—a favorite Wagnerian *bête noir* and, not surprisingly, perhaps one of his best weapons of self aggrandizement. The collapse of a late eighteenth-century elite tradition of musical hearing, including the connoisseurship of instrumental music learned by cognoscenti who were often active amateurs was followed by the rise of a spectator culture of music, larger but in musical terms comparatively illiterate. Encouraged by their Wagnerian sensibilities, *fin-de-siècle* audiences listened to Beethoven as

to a dramatic literary narrative. Listening as they did in the larger and larger halls built in the two decades before 1900 (that even Theodore Thomas complained were singularly unsuited to playing and hearing Beethoven and Mozart),[27] they embraced the young Strauss, Tchaikovsky, and Mahler. Through habits of listening influenced by hearing Wagner, music, in all its forms, was rendered subservient to the literary, the visual, and the dramatic.

Against this new emotional and melodramatic bond between audience and composer, against a world of music filled with seemingly expressive plots, pictures, echoes, evident memories, moods, and sentiments, two radical voices were raised even before 1920. One was Schoenberg with his effort to restore the classical autonomy of musical language, and the other was Schenker with his critique of Wagner and "surface" hearing—a critique closely bound to the polemic against Wagner and the conventions of post-Wagner, polite, middle-class musical culture. Following the first generations of Wagnerians came the world of the Society for Private Musical Performances and the conceits of clean, historically true editions of Beethoven and of "structural hearing." It is not surprising that the self-conscious effort to peel off layers of nineteenth-century Romantic performance practices in the standard repertory by men as different as Weingartner, Toscanini, and Schnabel coincided with a revulsion against decadent Wagnerism. That reaction sometimes contained a concomitant affinity to post-World War I modernism. Here again was a struggle against the enormous shadow cast by Wagner and his writings on the way musical history and performance traditions were understood between the years 1870–1914.

V

What makes both these volumes worthwhile despite frequent repetitions in the Mann and recurrent awkwardness in the translations of both is that they contribute to both a needed historical and a contemporary reassessment of Wagner. Much work still needs to be done on music and culture in the Third Reich and on the

---

[27]Theodore Thomas, pp. 348–49.

influence of Wagner in European life (as the recent volume edited by David Large and William Weber, *Wagnerism in European Culture and Politics* [Ithaca, 1984] illustrates).

The historical role of Wagner and the manner in which he is to be assimilated—that is, interpreted in modern productions—remain central aspects of German political and cultural self-definition, particularly with respect to the Third Reich and German nationalism. It is more than an antiquarian matter. In Israel there is the need to confront the raw and finally counterproductive simplification of the relation of historical European political anti-Semitism to art maintained through bans on public performances of Wagner. This simplification ends up mystifying and falsifying musical history. Perhaps Katz's book is intended to 'prove' through historical research the wrongheaded nature of the continuing ban on Wagner performances in Israel. Restoration of Wagner (and even Strauss) in public performance need not constitute tacit forgiveness, nor the tacit assent to the proposition that art and politics—or art and morality—

are somehow magically separate. They are not. Only through recreation, reinterpretation, and performance in one's own day can the interrelationship between the aesthetic in music and the political be examined and confronted.

Finally, for American readers engaged in today's romance with that amorphous journalistic phenomenon called "post-modernism," and for scholars of the nineteenth century, both volumes offer an occasion to reflect on Wagner, his character, influence, and unusual greatness. At a minimum, readers will put these books down humbled by Wagner's staggering historical impact, his artistic vision, his musical and dramatic imagination, his sheer persistence, and his perverse but profound belief that in matters of art lie essential aspects of human life. As the case of Wagner amply illustrates, art, culture, and the life of the artist cannot be relegated to the periphery of contemporary life. And Wagner's case cannot be relegated to the margins of historical or normative inquiry and debate regarding the nineteenth and twentieth centuries.

Nineteenth-Century Ideas Developed in Bartók's Piano Notation, 1907–14

LÁSZLÓ SOMFAI

An appreciation of the full and authentic message of the notation written down by Béla Bartók's generation less than a century ago demands no less prudent investigation than the most important issues surrounding the "historical performance" of music of the eighteenth or early nineteenth centuries. With Bartók, as with the earlier repertory, we are confronted with the possibility that the signs, symbols, and performing instructions in the score have a slightly (or considerably) different meaning today. Moreover, the notational conventions—the implicit information—have to be understood as an integral part of the score. Obvious as this may seem, many editors of *Neue Ausgabe*-type *Urtext* editions of eighteenth-century music still do not make it their business to discover and explain the ever-changing conventions (or supposed conventions) of notation beyond mere orthography. Intelligent performers often prefer

a self-edited xerox of one source to the printed *Urtext* supposedly based on the analysis of all the available sources.

Neither the systematic teaching of the proper notation of musical ideas nor the furnishing of performing instructions was part of a composer's curriculum in Bartók's youth. The student taught himself hundreds of scores by reading the common-practice and contemporary repertory; and he learned from his piano teacher in the studio, from a great artist in recital, from hearing an orchestra, and from a comparison of different editions of the same work. Either because of the lack of relevant information, or sometimes because of the abundance and confusion of secondary data, there is little hope that we can discover in most cases—even at the distance of a few decades—which notational conventions were self-evident for a creative musician and, consequently, how he intended his own music to be played. Bartók can be considered a fortunate exception. First, the available relevant documentation is unusually rich.[1] Second, there is a special "triangle" of partly related sources, the comparative study of which could lead to important and objective observations. The three points of the triangle are as follows:

A
versions of Bartók's compositions made before and after publication[2]

B
Bartók's recorded performances of music by himself and other composers, made between 1910 and 1945, comprising altogether about ten hours[3]

C
performing editions of eighteenth- and nineteenth-century piano works, prepared by Bartók between 1907 and 1926, comprising altogether about 2,000 pages of printed music[4]

These three source groups are not equally well known. The 1981 Centennial Edition made group **B** available to the public; the only significant addition will be the issue of a recently discovered phonograph cylinder of Bartók playing his Sketch No. 3, a wedding present for Emma and Zoltán Kodály made in August 1910, and, in fact, the earliest recorded Bartók performance. Items from group **C**, Bartók's performing editions, are partly available (in unreliable new editions) in Hungary and neighboring countries only, but until recently have not been given serious consideration as a major source for investigating Bartók's musicianship and notation.[5] Group **A**, compositions by Bartók himself, includes not only different versions made during the compositional process, but also those prepared *after* the first authorized edition; the latter may represent either a true corrected form—a *Fassung letzter Hand*—or an alternative/variant form.[6] Many musicians are at present confused by the different editions, but until a complete critical edition makes the sources available only sporadic sources and cases can be studied.[7]

The three groups of the source-triangle are not equally important for Bartók studies in general. The extent of direct interconnections varies, as the graphic picture in figure 1 suggests. The overlapping between **A** and **B** is considerable, but is of value mainly to a handful of Bartók scholars.[8] Interconnections between **B** and **C** are very rare, although more straightforward.[9]

---

[1]Bartók was a very thorough man who kept, and indeed "recycled," practically everything. (For instance, the empty versos of letters which he received were usually used for drafting a new essay, or as a paper on which to stick smaller pages with folk music transcriptions, etc., practices which help to assign approximate dates to some of his miscellaneous works.) The majority of the printed scores he used during his school years are now either in the Budapest Bartók Archives or in the private collection of Béla Bartók, Jr., in Budapest. For a chronological list of Bartók's piano studies see D. Dille, *Thematisches Verzeichnis der Jugendwerke Béla Bartóks 1890–1904* (Kassel, 1974), pp. 217–45.

[2]On Bartók's compositional process, see my "Manuscript versus *Urtext*: The Primary Sources of Bartók's Works," *Studia Musicologica* 23 (1981), 17–66.

[3]*Centenary Edition of Bartók's Records (Complete)* (Hungaroton LPX 12326–33 and 12334–38) (Budapest, 1981); see my study in vol. I, "The Centenary Edition of Bartók's Records," pp. 19–32.

[4]On behalf of the Budapest Bartók Archives, András Wilheim and I are preparing all of Bartók's performing editions for publication by Editio Musica Budapest (EMB) in the series *Bartók Reprint Edition*, a scholarly reprint with commentaries in three languages. It will consist of eleven volumes:
1. Bach, *Wohltemperirtes Klavier* I–IV (1st edn.)
2. Bach, *Wohltemperirtes Klavier* I–II (revised 2nd edn.)
3. Keyboard Music by Bach, Scarlatti, and Couperin
4. Haydn, Sonatas
5. Mozart, Sonatas
6–7. Beethoven, Sonatas I–II
8. Beethoven, Piano Pieces
9. Piano Music by Schubert, Mendelssohn, Schumann, and Chopin
10–11. Piano studies I–II (Heller, Köhler, Duvernoy) (Vols. 1–2 and 4–7 are already prepared for publication.)

[5]An exhibition dedicated to the subject was opened recently in the Museum of Music History of the Hungarian Academy of Sciences, Budapest. See my catalogue, *As Béla Bartók Played Classics* (Budapest, 1986).

[6]See the catalogue of the permanent exhibition of the Budapest Bartók Archives, László Somfai, *Bartók's Workshop. Sketches, Manuscripts, Versions: The Compositional Process* (Budapest, 1987).

[7]In 1981 I outlined the disadvantageous situation for a complete Bartók critical edition ("The Budapest Bartók Archives," *Fontes artis musicae* 29 [1982], 59–65). In 1982 the widow of the composer, Mrs. Ditta Bartók-Pásztory, died; preliminary negotiations for such an edition are now in progress with the American heir, Péter Bartók.

[8]There are three major collections which contain nearly all of the primary sources: (1) the former New York "Estate" and "Archives," which since 1986 have been in the possession of Péter Bartók (Homosassa, Florida); (2) the Budapest Bartók Archives, the only collection open to the public as an institute, staffed by specialists; and (3) the private Budapest collection of Béla Bartók, Jr.

[9]For example, Bartók's test recording in a studio in December 1929 of two Scarlatti sonatas he had edited in 1926; or

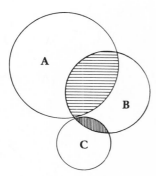

Figure 1

The indirect connections between groups **A** and **C**, however, have the utmost significance for the general study of notation and performing practice. It is a unique situation that one of the greatest composers of our century was also an extraordinary concert pianist who was intimately familiar with the Vienna-Budapest tradition of interpreting common-practice music around the turn of the century and who furnished detailed performing instructions for the whole *Well-Tempered Clavier* by Bach, nineteen sonatas by Haydn, twenty sonatas by Mozart, twenty-seven sonatas and five other piano works by Beethoven, as well as pieces by Couperin, Scarlatti, Schubert, Schumann, and Chopin. This study will suggest that Bartók's editorial work on the *Instruktive Ausgabe*-type publications, most of which can be accurately dated,[10] can be profitably compared with his compositions of the same years and months. His own works can also be illuminated by a careful study of the legends in several of his performing editions describing the meaning of musical signs.

I

A collation of two versions of Bagatelle No. 1 may serve as a basic point of departure. The Bagatelles, written in the spring of 1908, during the

most decisive period for the formation of Bartók's mature style, were seen by the composer himself to "inaugurate a new trend of piano writing," in which "a new piano style appears as a reaction to the exuberance of the Romantic piano music of the nineteenth century; a style stripped of all unessential decorative elements, deliberately using only the most restricted technical means."[11] The much-discussed Bagatelle No. 1[12] was presumably written on 14 April 1908, as the date on the first existing draft (plate 1) suggests.[13] Although the dual key signature, with four sharps in the upper staff and four flats in the lower one, prompted bitonal analyses in the 1920s,[14] Bartók himself interpreted the work as "simply a Phrygian colored C major."[15] In August 1908, the Fourteen Bagatelles were sent to the Leipzig engraver Röder, and were soon issued by Rozsnyai. As the facsimile of the original edition (plate 2) shows, the basic musical text of no. 1 was not significantly changed (Bartók corrected slightly the right hand in mm. 6–7, and he compressed the rhythm of the last two measures into one). But Bartók's notation of the performing indications underwent considerable revision. In addition to modifying tempo markings and metronome numbers, he increased the independence of dynamics in the right and left hands. These aspects were already fixed in a second draft from ca. May 1908

---

[11]*Béla Bartók Essays*, ed. Benjamin Suchoff (New York, 1976), p. 432.
[12]Two recent analyses include Hermann Danuser, *Die Musik des 20. Jahrhunderts* (Laaber, 1984), pp. 54–55; and Elliot Antokoletz, *The Music of Béla Bartók: A Study of Tonality and Progression in Twentieth-Century Music* (Berkeley and Los Angeles, 1984), pp. 52–54.
[13]Since this draft came to the Budapest Bartók Archives from the collection of Mrs. Emma Kodály, there is a slight chance that it may be a copy made (and dated) for Emma by Bartók. The manuscript, however, resembles Bartók's typical "first draft" for a piano piece in those years.
[14]The first significant classification of Bagatelle No. 1 as a typical example of "polytonality" achieved "through empirical means in counterpoint" appeared in the "Harmony" entry in Eaglefield-Hull's *A Dictionary of Modern Music and Musicians* (London, 1924); see ex. 27 on p. 220. The entry is signed by eight names, Bartók and seven English musicians (including Donald Tovey, Edward Dent, and Ralph Vaughan Williams). The text and selection of musical examples originated in a London conference at which Bartók was the only continental composer present.
[15]*Béla Bartók Essays*, p. 433. It was not just retrospectively that Bartók disliked his works being labeled "bitonal," or "polytonal." The original program of the Budapest premiere of the piece from Bagatelles (19 March 1910) lists No. 1 as "1. Molto sostenuto (C-dur)."

---

his performance in a radio studio in 1939, of the theme and first variation from Beethoven's op. 34, which he had edited in 1910.
[10]The majority of the original contracts in the archives of EMB (legal successor to the former private Hungarian music publishers) retain the date of delivery of Bartók's engraver's copy. Additional data can be found in letters, notes, drafts of prefaces, etc. in the Budapest Bartók Archives.

Plate 1: Bartók, Bagatelle No. 1, autograph draft (Budapest Bartók Archives).

Plate 2: Bartók, Bagatelle No. 1, Rozsnyai 1st edn.

plate 3).[16] Bartók also differentiated the touch of the two hands by turning the uniformly *portato* notation into slurred tenuto in the right hand and slurred "half-tenuto" (⨪) in the left. He arrived at this decision only at the last minute: on the printer's copy prepared by a professional copyist, he erased the staccato dots in the right hand and substituted tenuto signs, and he added the tenuto to the dot in the left (plate 4).

The fine differentiation in touch (timbre and gesture) between the ascending *mezzo forte* and the descending *piano* motives is indeed of great help to the pianist in expressing the tonal-modal conflict that is the very essence of Bagatelle No. 1. Consequently, a few fundamental questions come to mind. Did Bartók significantly change the intended style with these refine-

ments, or did the first notation of an idea and the edited version represent essentially the same piece for him—the first in a less detailed concert-style notation,[17] the latter in a quasi-performing-edition style? Before we consider this question, we must also ask: do we know how Bartók differentiated slurred staccato, slurred tenuto, and slurred half-tenuto (or half-staccato, ⨪) in actual performance? And when a slur appears in Bartók's piano notation in combination with additional signs (such as staccato and tenuto), is it intended primarily to suggest articulation or phrasing?

Fortunately, at this point we can refer to Bartók's edition of the *Well-Tempered Clavier*, on which he worked amidst feverish compositional activity in the first half of 1908.

---

[16]The facsimile of the whole page is reproduced in *The Piano Music of Béla Bartók: The Archive Edition*, Series I, ed. Benjamin Suchoff (New York, 1981), p. xvii.

[17]"Concert-style" is an expression I use for the notation specifically adopted by Bartók in piano works written originally for performance by himself, such as, the Suite, op. 14, the Sonata (1926), or the Piano Concertos Nos. 1 and 2.

Plate 3: Bartók, Bagatelle No. 1, intermediary draft (reprinted from *The Piano Music of Béla Bartók, The Archive Edition*, Series I, Dover Publications, Inc.).

Plate 4: Bartók, Bagatelle No. 1, copyist's handwriting with Bartók's corrections and additions (Budapest Bartók Archives).

II

In January 1907, without notable teaching experience, the twenty-six-year old Bartók was appointed professor of piano at the Budapest Academy of Music. He inherited the class and the chair from his former teacher, the Liszt pupil István Thomán, who had to retire suddenly at the age of 45. At that time there were only three principal piano professors on the faculty: the other two were the chairman, the vain Árpád Szendy (age 44), also a Liszt pupil and a composer of mediocre works in the well-worn national idiom; and Kálmán Chován (age 55), an expert in piano methodology trained at the Vienna Conservatory.

At about the same time an energetic music publisher in Budapest, Rozsnyai, decided to offer for sale domestically printed editions of piano and chamber music; these were intended to displace the imported German editions (issued primarily by Cotta'sche Buchhandlung in Stuttgart). Preparation of these new editions was entrusted exclusively to professors of the Budapest Academy. For the first volumes Rozsnyai urgently needed J. S. Bach's Two- and Three-Part Inventions; Szendy took these in hand. The "48" were assigned to the younger, more energetic Bartók.

Elsewhere I go into details of the Tausig edition of the "22" which had official status in Budapest prior to the new Hungarian *WTC*; of

Bartók's *progressiv geordnet* (according to technical and musical criteria) sequence of the complete "48," printed in four volumes (twelve in each); of his dependence on the text in *J. S. Bach Werke*; of his ideal, right or wrong, of the proper instrument, ornamentation, and performance style.[18] Here we must be content with a few aspects of the notation, considered chronologically. Table 1 presents a rough sketch of the sequence of events outlined by the date of the contracts. (Rozsnyai [R. K.] and the rival Budapest publisher Rózsavölgyi [Rv.] usually fulfilled the contract formula on the day Bartók delivered the engraver's copy of the work.)

We recall that the Bagatelles were actually written between 14 February and May 1908, and the Easy Pieces within the late spring months (by June).[19] It is not generally known that vols. I and II of Bartók's *WTC* edition were later (ca. 1913) carefully revised;[20] recent prints by Editio Musica Budapest (EMB) tacitly present only the

---

[18]"Critical Introduction" to Vols. I and II of the *Bartók Reprint Series* (in preparation).

[19]About the chronology and the known dates of pieces written February–June 1908, see my notes accompanying the record *Béla Bartók, Complete Edition, Piano Music 2* (Budapest, 1967) (Hungaroton LPX 1299), pp. 6–8.

[20]The "revised second edition" has no date; neither has Bartók's new preface, or the text for the appendix. Circa 1913 is suggested as the date of publication on the basis of an analysis of the earliest existing copies (price, address of the publisher, etc.); see my study mentioned in n. 18.

Table 1

Plate Number	Title	Honorarium	Date of Contract
R.K. 246	Bach *WTC* Vol. I	400.–K	[no date; ca. 1907]
R.K. 247	Bach *WTC* Vol. II	400.–K	15 March 1908
R.K. 248	Bach *WTC* Vol. III	400.–K	13 June 1908
Rv. 3199	Bartók Rhapsody op. 1	[no sum]	19 June 1908
R.K. 249	Bach *WTC* Vol. IV	400.–K	25 June 1908
R.K. 293	Bartók Ten Easy Piano Pieces[a]	350.–K	25 June 1908
R.K. 338	Bartók Fourteen Bagatelles	500.–K	15 August 1908

[a]Called "Eleven Pieces" in the contract; the series consists of 1 + 10 pieces, "Dedication" being the unnumbered first one.

text of the revised form. In the present study, based on original copies from Bartók's library, both the first and the revised second edition will be considered, designated as volume I[1] and I[2] or II[1] and II[2], respectively.

A comparison of the catalogue of performing signs and instructions in the four *WTC* volumes, as well as in the re-edited first two, reveals that while working out the precise notational ideal for Bach's keyboard music, Bartók enriched and chiseled his piano notation immensely.[21] The revisions of vols. I and II were made necessary not, I think, by a few wrong notes, but rather by Bartók being faced dramatically with the practical consequences of musical notation through the actual performance of the compulsory Bach preludes and fugues by his new pupils, by those of his colleagues, and by private students coming to Budapest from the provinces to pass the Academy's examination. The result was that as editor Bartók put more instructions into the performing editions of earlier piano music—in fact, an overdose of signs; as a composer, primarily in the pedagogical works, he then borrowed notational ideas from the performing editions.

Let us examine the micro-chronology of the application of a few selected signs (table 2): *marcato* and *marcatissimo*, both familiar from Bartók's works prior to 1907; the half-tenuto (÷), which Bartók had not used in his piano works before 1908; and the indication for the right

pedal (which appeared in earlier Bartók works in the traditional nineteenth-century 🎵 ❋ form). (Signs in parentheses in table 2 indicate rare occurrences.)

A few remarks are relevant (numbers refer to those in the left-most column of table 2):

1. Bartók used *marcato* in the *WTC* edition from the very beginning.
2. *Marcatissimo* was introduced in II[1]; later, in both I[2] and II[2], many ˃signs were changed to ʌ.
3. After sporadic use of staccato-plus-tenuto in vol. IV,[22] Bartók made abundant use of this touch, in the revised vols. I[2]–II[2], e.g. as in ex. 1.[23]
4. In the first edition of 1907–08 there are only a few linear pedal signs;[24] in the revised vols. I[2]–II[2] they occur frequently.
5. The linear pedal sign with a diagonal ending, suggesting the gradual release of the pedal, appears only in the revised volumes.[25]
6. In vols. III–IV Bartók occasionally uses a rare asymmetrical form, marking the precise place of pressing down the pedal.[26] This device was probably inspired by Busoni.[27]

---

[21]Piano music written by Bartók during the editorial work on *WTC*, i.e. from 1907 to June 1908, includes Three Hungarian Folksongs from the Csík District, No. 1 of Two Elegies, No. 1, Fourteen Bagatelles, and Ten Easy Piano Pieces.

[22]In Bartók's Vol. IV, Fugue No. 38 (F Minor, Book I) and Prelude No. 44 (E♭ minor, Book I) have half-tenuto signs.

[23]Vol. I, Fugue No. 6 (F Major, Book I). In the Budapest Bartók Archives there is a copy of the first edn. in which Bartók made preliminary penciled notes to the revision, including the half-tenuto signs here.

[24]Vol. II[1]: Fugue No. 16 (G♯ Minor, Book I), Prelude no. 22 (C Major, Book I); Vol. IV: Preludes nos. 37 (C♯ Major, Book II) and 42 (A♭ Major, Book II).

[25]Vol. I[2]: Preludes Nos. 2 (D Minor, Book I), 7 (C Minor, Book I), and 13 (F Major, Book II).

[26]Prelude No. 27 (C Major, Book II), Fugues Nos. 41 (B♭ Minor, Book I) and 43 (C♯ Minor, Book I).

[27]A similar sign can be found in Part I, C-Major Prelude, m. 1, of the Busoni edition: a dotted vertical line leads from the asterisk to the exact place where the pedal has to be released.

Table 2

Date	1907	1908			ca. 1913	
		15 March	13 June	25 June		
Volume of *WTC*	I1	II1	III	IV	I2	II2
1	>	>	>	>	>	>
2		^	^	^	^	^
3				(-̣)	-̣	-̣
4		(└──┘)		(└──┘)	└──┘	└──┘
5					└──╱	
6			└┘	└┘		
7a		(*senza* Ped. *con* Ped.)				(*senza* Ped. *con* Ped.)
b			(Ped. . . . :)			
c				(Ped. *)		

7. In the first edition, there are a few traditional pedal instructions as well; some perhaps occur through oversight,[28] some as a general direction (*senza Ped., con Ped.* in Prelude No. 22 in C Major, [from *WTC* Book I]).

My examples are selected more or less arbitrarily from the immense complex of musical notation. Nevertheless, subsequent volumes and versions of *WTC* confirm that two signs (lines 3 and 4 of table 2) were introduced into Bartók's piano notation only in 1908. We cannot be certain of the origin of these signs,[29] but can at least determine the date they were first used by Bartók. Returning to Bagatelle No. 1, we note that the half-tenuto sign indeed represented a completely new shade of touch in Bartók's notation when he revised the printer's copy.[30] Since the pedal sign in line 4 of table 2 (not used in this Bagatelle) was unfamiliar to the reader, Bartók explained its meaning in his short introductory instructions to the Ten Easy Piano Pieces and Fourteen Bagatelles.[31]

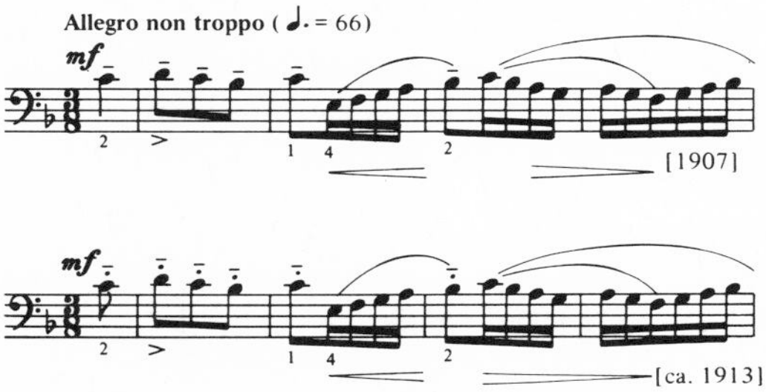

Example 1

Curiously enough, in the same two sets Bartók made no comment on the two types of crescendo–decrescendo hairpins, one engraved with heavy lines (see, for example, m. 13 in plate 2), the other in thin lines, although they were prepared with special instructions to the German engraver. These unusual signs are the manifest expression that in the notation of his new piano compositions of 1908 Bartók adopted in an experimental way ideas used in his recent performing editions. As a composer Bartók used this typographical aid to differentiate between specific nuances (dynamics usually in one hand or one part), and more general dynamic effects. In a similar fashion Bartók as editor differentiated between heavy and thin hairpins in his *WTC* edition.[32]

[28]Case (b), Fugue no. 27 (C Major, Book II); case (c), Fugue No. 45 (A Minor, Book I).

[29]In the second half of June, Bartók met Busoni in Vienna and played the Bagatelles in the latter's piano class. See D. Dille, "Dokumente über Bartóks Beziehungen zu Busoni," *Documenta Bartókiana* 2 (1965), 62–76. It is conceivable that the meeting with Busoni, in which notational problems may well have been discussed, encouraged Bartók to adopt half-tenuto signs.

[30]From 30 June to ca. 7 September, Bartók was in Switzerland and France (on the day of the Bagatelles contract, 15 August, in Val d'Isère at Lac des Tignes). Thus the final revision of the printer's copy had to be made abroad.

[31]An English translation of these "Instructions" can be found in Series I of *The Archives Edition* (see n. 16 above), pp. 68 and 105.

[32]"The < > sign with thin lines denotes a slight crescendo and decrescendo restricted to one voice, thicker <, a larger and more general crescendo affecting all voices alike" (from Bartók, "Appendix" to Vol. I2).

In the case of J. S. Bach's keyboard music, where the original text had no dynamics, it was possible (and clever) to differentiate editorially between the size and function of dynamic shadings by means of signs in different type sizes. The same technique could not, however, be used in editing Viennese Classical music, a task which Bartók had soon to face. Similarly, the relatively small number of authentic articulation signs in the *WTC* (an occasional slur or staccato) could easily be accommodated in footnotes, thus leaving Bartók free to use a two-level system of slurring, one for indicating legato performance (or, in combination with staccato and tenuto signs, other kinds of touch), and another for suggesting musical phrasing. It is not always immediately clear what is what: whether a long slur indicates legato and the short ones under it phrasing, or vice versa. In many cases, as in the developed piano notation of nineteenth-century composers, touch and phrasing are welded together in a refined network of slurs.

Consider, for example, the minute variations between Bartók's first and revised editions of Prelude No. 13 in F Major (*WTC* Book II; plates 5–6). His basic concept of an organ-like, uninterrupted, *sempre legatissimo* performance,[33] which is out of favor today but represents a typical pianistic rendering around the turn of the century, did not change at all between 1908 and ca. 1913. The revision (plate 6) simply represents a corrected, more precise notation—the spelling out of what was thought *musikalisch natürlich*, such as a cresc.–dim. for the first notes in the right hand; additional phrasing for the inner parts; heavier accent on long notes and accentuation of syncopated notes; different touch for a simple tonic chord and an altered one immediately after it (m. 3). Such elegant details throw light upon Bartók's musicianship and taste, and on characteristics of expression and articulation which he felt unnecessary to fix even in the notation of his own piano works.

Some details will remain ambiguous to the musician of the 1980s. For example, what is the exact meaning of a tenuto sign on isolated notes, alone or in combination with other signs, as on the first note in the left hand in m. 1, or on the second and third chords in the right hand of m. 3? Does it affect duration (indicating that the key is to be held down till the very end of the note value), accentuation (as the lightest accent sign), or touch (a special touch, a *Tenuto-Anschlag*)? In order to clarify this kind of problem, we shall now present a survey of the legends, listing and explaining the performing signs employed by Bartók.

III

There are four texts written by Bartók that explain performing signs.[34] Two of them are on the whole genuine legends (B and D), and two written in form of running notes (A and C):

A. The preface and the appendix to Bach, *Wohltemperirtes Klavier*, Bd. I (R.K. 246), 1907.
B. The *Zeichenerklärung* to each sonata in Beethoven, *Sonaten für Pianoforte* (Rv. 3281, etc.), 1909.
C. The new appendix to the "revised second edition" of Bach, *Wohltemperirtes Klavier*, Bd. I (R.K. 246), ca. 1913.
D. The Preface to the twelve pieces selected from Bach, *Notenbüchlein für Anna Magdalena Bach* (Rv. 3681), 1916.

Each was written by Bartók in Hungarian; the German in the bilingual original edition was either his own translation or authorized by him. There are of course many important short remarks by Bartók about the meaning and interpretation of certain signs in a given context, especially in the individual notes to the *WTC* and the Beethoven sonatas. Nevertheless, the texts of B, C, and D are also indispensable to the interpreter of Bartók's own music.

Plates 7–8 reproduce the original German version of D and B.[35] The former represents to my mind the most important of these texts. Since the Bach pieces are beginner's studies,

---

[33] Bartók's note: "This prelude is strikingly organ-like. In performance it should sound as if the unbroken sequence of counterpoint founded on eighth notes were leading through broad, sustained chords. This effect may be achieved through *legatissimo* and the cautious use of the pedal restricted to the appropriate places."

[34] The 1913 *Zongora Iskola* (Piano School), "written by Béla Bartók and Sándor Reschofsky" (Rózsavölgyi 3635), is in this respect no source at all; Bartók furnished the volume with short compositions, but the text and explanations are Reschofsky's alone.

[35] In earlier copies of plate 8 the last two lines of text were missing.

Plate 5: Bartók's 1st edn. (1908) of the F-Major Prelude (Rozsnyai edn., copy in the Budapest Bartók Archives).

Plate 6: Bartók's "revised 2nd edn." (ca. 1913) of the F-Major Prelude (old Rozsnyai print in the Budapest Bartók Archives).

Bartók provides elementary explanations. But the gradations of both length of notes (from *staccatissimo* to *legato*) and the accents are of value to more advanced players of Bartók as well. Note, for instance, that in *portato* (which Bartók erroneously but consistently called *portamento*)[36] the shortened notes "are joined with a special coloring." In text C, in a slightly different formulation, we read that

the sign ⁻⁻⁻ (tenuto sign and dot) means a sort of semishortness combined with *tenuto*-touch. The interpretation of the ⌢···· (*portamento* sign) is closely related to it. The only difference between the two is that the *portamento* [recte: *portato*] requires a greater degree of ease [*Leichtigkeit*].

It is significant that Bartók gave a second meaning to the tenuto sign placed above notes of a legato passage: it represents the slightest grade of accent, a gentle emphasis produced by a different touch.[37]

Basic to the Anna Magdalena preface is the explanation of two signs of separation, the comma and the vertical line, instructions

---

[36]Bartók was probably misled by the last sentence of Ehlert's preface to the *WTC* edition (twenty-two pieces) of Tausig: "Die horizontale Striche (- - -) bedeuten ein etwas accentuirtes Portamento."

---

[37]Speaking with musicians who had played with Bartók, I repeatedly discovered that in their memory there was some confusion whether a tenuto sign meant a slight accent, or only a change in tone quality.

The legends to the Beethoven sonata edition consist of only three accent signs (the tenuto is missing), but also include the sign of non-accentuation (⌣). Bartók himself very rarely used it in his editions and had not borrowed it from Schoenberg's similar *unbetont* symbol (as found in op. 23 and other works). But he also declares that the wider the angle of a crescendo sign is, the greater the crescendo effect should be. The proof-sheets of Bartók's own works are full of corrections of cresc.–dim. signs, either their proper placement or their angle.

Die erste Hälfte der in diesem Heft herausgegebenen kleinen Klavierstücke ist als Unterrichtsmaterial für das 2. Studienjahr, die zweite Hälfte für das 3. Jahr gedacht.

Die Stücke sind Bach's „Notenbüchlein für Anna Magdalena Bach" entnommen. Abgesehen von einigen Änderungen, die zumeist im Weglassen von Verzierungen bestehen und auf die wir gelegentlich immer hinweisen, haben wir den Original-Notentext übernommen.

Bezüglich der angewendeten Vortrags-Zeichen sei bemerkt:

Das Ende des zur Bezeichnung einer Phrase gebrauchten Bogens bedeutet nicht, daß der am Ende des Bogens stehende Ton staccato zu spielen, oder daß die Klangdauer desselben auch nur im geringsten zu verkürzen wäre. Dies hat nur dann zu geschehen, wenn über dem letzten Ton der Phrase das Staccato-Zeichen (Punkt) oder nach demselben das Trennungszeichen (|) steht.

Außer dem Trennungszeichen (|), das eine Unterbrechung bedeutet, benützen wir auch noch das stärkere Trennungszeichen ɔ (Komma), das nicht nur eine Unterbrechung, sondern auch ein kaum merkbares Innehalten bedeutet. Bei dem Trennungszeichen (|) ist also die Zeitdauer der Unterbrechung von dem Werte des vor dem Zeichen stehenden Tones zu nehmen, bei dem ɔ (Komma) erscheint diese Unterbrechung als Innehalten zwischen dem Werte des vorhergehenden und nachfolgenden Tones, mitunter verlängert durch die Klangpause, die durch die Verkürzung des vor dem Zeichen stehenden Tones ensteht.

Zwischen Staccato-Tönen bedeutet das Trennungszeichen (|) das Ende der Phrase.

Auf die zahllosen Abstufungen zwischen dem staccatissimo und legato können wir nur durch Anwendung folgender Zeichen hinweisen:

ꞏꞏꞏ : scharfes staccato (staccatissimo) womit eine gewisse Betonung und schärfere Tonfarbe verbunden ist.

ꞏꞏꞏꞏ : das gewöhnliche staccato wobei das Klingenlassen des Tones zwischen einem Moment und beinahe der Hälfte des Notenwertes schwankt.

ꞏꞏꞏ : portamento, bei welchem die Töne beinahe bis zur Hälfte des Notenwertes klingen zu lassen sind, verbunden mit einer gewissen besonderen Färbung.

ᵥᵥᵥ : das Zeichen der Halbkürze (das Klingenlassen der Töne soll nicht kürzer sein, als die Hälfte des Notenwertes).

—— : das Tenuto-Zeichen über einzelnen Tönen bedeutet, daß dieselben während ihres ganzen Notenwertes zu halten sind, über jeden einzelnen Tone einer Tongruppe, daß wir die Töne, ohne sie aneinander zu binden, womöglich durch ihren ganzen Notenwert klingen zu lassen haben.

⌒ : das bekannte Zeichen des legato, das wir bei Legatogängen in Ermangelung eines anderen Zeichens auch zur Bezeichnung der Phrase benützen.

Zur Bezeichnung der verschiedenen Betonungen (sf) benützen wir folgende Abstufungen:

sf : stärkste Betonung

ʌ : noch genug starke Betonung

⁻ : schwache Betonung

— : das Zeichen des tenuto über den einzelnen Tönen der Legatogänge bedeutet die zarte, durch eine andere Tonfärbung erzielte Hervorhebung des Tones.

R. & Co 3681

Plate 7: Bartók's preface to twelve pieces from Bach, *Notenbüchlein für Anna Magdalena* (Rozsnyai 1st edn., 1916).

which are often misunderstood today by even great performers. In a letter of 7 December 1939 to Boosey & Hawkes, Bartók described the distinction in English; " ɔ (comma) means not only an interruption, but also an additional rest (*Luftpause*); | means only an interruption (division of sound) without any extra rest."[38]

I find the fourth paragraph ("Das Ende . . .")

most illuminating. Indirectly it proves that an eighteenth-century practice was still valid in the first decade of this century: Bartók wanted to prevent the pianist from playing the last note under a slur automatically short. In text C, dealing with the same phenomenon, he put his finger on the source of the problem: both phrasing and legato were conventionally expressed with a slur.[39]

It was with this situation in mind that Bartók made the last-minute changes in the notation of

---

[38]Quoted by John Vinton, "Hints to the Printers from Bartók," *Music & Letters* 49 (1968), 228. The length of the interruption is, of course, the crucial factor! The Szigeti-Bartók performance of the second movement of the Violin Sonata No. 2, in the 1940 Library of Congress concert (*Centenary Edition*, LPX 12332−A), should be carefully studied as a model case.

[39]Bartók's German formulation: "Als Phrasierungs- und Legatobezeichnung dient ein und dasselbe Zeichen: der Bogen."

Zeichenerklärung.

⌐_____⌐ = ein auf das Pedalisieren bezügliches
Zeichen. Das Pedal wird genau bei jenem Tone nieder-
gedrückt, auf welchen der vordere Arm des Zeichens zeigt,
und bei jenem freigelassen, auf welchen der ausgehende
Arm hinweist.

sf = stärkste Betonung. ∧ = schwächer, > = noch schwächer.

⌣ ist das Zeichen für Nichtbetonung (in einzelnen Ausnahme-
fällen).

Kleine *fermata* (⌢); soll eine nur ganz geringe Verlängerung
bezeichnen.

Bei ◁◁◁◁◁ ◁◁◁ etc.: Je grösser der Winkel, um so stärkeres
crescendo zeigt das Zeichen an.

Sostenuto = plötzliches Zurückhalten, *ritard.* und *riten.* = all-
mähliches Zurückhalten.

Pochettino oder *pochissimo* wird in der Bedeutung von „ganz klein
wenig" angewendet.

Legatissimo bedeutet übermässiges *legato* (wenn jeder Ton beim
Beginne des folgenden etwas länger angehalten wird).

Plate 8: Bartók's explanation of signs as printed in his Beethoven sonata editions by Rózsavölgyi (1909–).

Bagatelle No. 1 to fix the length and character of the notes in both hands. Slurs indicate phrasing, whereas the intended length and touch of the notes is fixed by the tenuto and half-tenuto signs. The touch and character of the two hands are certainly not identical, nor are they merely optical variants of a *portato*, as written down in the autograph. With the revision did Bartók really intend to change (differentiate) his original concept of the performing style of the Bagatelle? Or had the original *portato* notation itself implied a certain (nineteenth-century) kind of freedom on the part of the professional musician, who would interpret such sensitive notes according to their melodic-harmonic context and their *Affekt?*

Clearly Bartók was still learning the nuances of notation in 1908, and the vast amount of earlier piano music for which he was to prepare performing editions in the following years became the central medium of his self-education.

IV

Table 3 offers a chronology of the performing editions Bartók prepared for three Hungarian publishers: Rozsnyai (1907–26), Rózsavölgyi & Co. (1909–19), and Bárd (1920). In addition, I list Bartók's piano transcriptions (1928–30), quite a different genre, which will not be dealt with in this study, as well as his (mostly unpublished)

contributions as an editor for the old Liszt edition (1911–18).[40]

The three chronological segments outlined in table 3 represent decreasing editorial activity. The years 1910–12 were by far the busiest. They were also productive years for Bartók's own composition: 1910: the completion of Two Rumanian Dances, Seven Sketches, Four Dirges for Piano, No. 2 of Burlesques for Piano, and Two Pictures for Orchestra; 1911: *Allegro barbaro*, No. 3 of Burlesques, the one-act opera *Bluebeard's Castle*, the orchestration of the Rumanian Dances, and Two Portraits II; 1912: the draft of Four Pieces for Orchestra.

The second period, which begins with the Anna Magdalena pieces in 1916, consists of a less significant series of piano study editions motivated simply by Bartók's desperate need for extra income during the last years of the war and those immediately following (1917–20). At the same time, in the slender volumes of Couperin and Scarlatti, Bartók's performing editions reach their highest level, for the selection as well as the editorial method were entirely his own.

It is fascinating to play the complete series of Bartók's Beethoven, Mozart, or Haydn in their editorial sequence. Since he quickly became more experienced in each repertory, one can speak of a genuine evolution. Bartók chose first those sonatas or pieces which he knew and liked best, such as Mozart's C-Minor Fantasy, K. 475, prepared for Rozsnyai (and marked *Bearbeitung von* instead of *Herausgegeben von*, as in subsequent editions; see plate 9).

Rozsnyai copied the house style of Cotta's *Instruktive Ausgabe* in many ways. The editor had to furnish the score with letters indicating first theme, transition, second theme, etc.— a practice which Bartók detested. Nor did he feel comfortable having to supply metronome markings: he often borrowed these in whole or in part from Lebert's edition for Cotta,[41] a fact

---

[40]A short report on this still unknown activity by Bartók is in my "Liszt's Influence on Bartók Reconsidered," *New Hungarian Quarterly* 102 (1986), 210–19.

[41]Or in some cases Bartók simply gave no metronome marks. Among his Haydn sonata editions, the first (in 1910 or 1911) and the last eight (1913 and 1920) were printed without them. Of the ten sonatas edited in 1911–12 with metronome marks, only in three or four cases did Bartók alter Lebert's suggestion substantially.

Table 3

DATE	ROZSNYAI	RÓZSAVÖLGYI	OTHER PUBLISHERS
1907–08	Bach, *Well-Tempered Clavier*, complete, 4 vols.		
1909		Beethoven, 5 sonatas[a]	
1910	Beethoven, piano pieces: ops. 33, 34, 35, 89, 119 Mozart, 4 sonatas,[c] Fantasia, K. 396	Beethoven, 11 sonatas[b]	
1911	Schumann, *Jugendalbum* Schubert, 2 scherzi Mozart, 15 sonatas[d] Haydn, 4 sonatas[e]		(1911–18: editing Liszt's Hungarian works for the Breitkopf & Härtel complete edn.)
1912	Mozart, 1 sonata[f] Haydn, 7 sonatas[h]	Beethoven, 9 sonatas[g]	
1913	Haydn, 6 sonatas[i] Bach, *WTC*, vols. I–II (rev. 2nd edn.)		
1916		Bach, "Anna Magdalena" selection (12 pieces) (rev. 1924: 13 pieces)	
1917–19		studies for piano: Köhler, op. 242 Heller, ops. 45–47, 119, 125, Sonatina-Album Duvernoy	
1920	Haydn, 2 sonatas[j] Scarlatti, vol. I (vol. II: 1926)		for Bárd: Chopin, 14 Waltzes Beethoven, Ecossaises
1924	Couperin, vols. I–II		
1928			for Carl Fischer, New York: transcriptions of Marcello, Rossi, Della Ciaia, Frescobaldi, Zipoli
1929			posth. edn.: Purcell, 2 preludes, transcription
1930		Bach, Organ Sonata in G major, BWV 530, transcription	

[a]According to the contracts, Bartók's correspondence with the publisher, and the research of András Wilheim (editor of two forthcoming Beethoven sonata volumes), these comprised op. 2, no. 1, in F Minor, op. 10, no. 1 in C Minor, op. 13 in C Minor, op. 27, no. 2 in C♯ Minor, and op. 49, no. 1 in G Minor. These sonatas were reedited (reengraved) ca. 1911.

[b]Op. 2, no. 3, in C Major, op. 10, no. 2, in F Major, op. 14, no. 1–2, in E Major and G major, op. 49, no. 2, in G Major (through 8 June) and op. 26 in A♭ Major, op. 57 in F Minor, op. 78 in F♯ Major, op. 79 in G Major, op. 90 in E Minor, op. 53 in C Major (through 6 October).

[c]K. 475/457 in C Minor, K. 331 in A Major, K. 310 in A Minor, K. 396 Fantasia in C Minor, K. 283 in G Major.

[d]K. 332 in F Major (27 January); K. 330 in C Major (9 May); K. 333 in B♭ Major, K. 576 in D Major (28 September); K. 279 in C Major, K. 280 in F Major, K. 309 in C Major (6 October); K. 281 in B♭ Major, K. 311 in D Major, K. 284 in D Major (13 October); K. 570 in B♭ Major, K. 282 in E♭ Major (27 October); K. 545 in C Major, K. Anh. 135 in F Major, K. 533/494 in F Major (13 November).

[e]Using the Wiener Urtext (ChL) numbers, WU 53 in E Minor (1910 or 1911?); WU 42 in G Major (20 November 1911); WU 48 in C Major, 50 in D Major (9 December).

[f]K. Anh. 136 in B♭ Major.

[g]Op. 2, no. 2, in A Major, op. 7 in E♭ Major, op. 10, no. 3, in D Major, op. 22 in B♭ Major, op 27, no. 1, in E♭ Major, op. 28 in D Major, op. 31, nos. 1–3, in G Major, D Minor, and E♭ Major.

[h]WU 49 in C♯ Minor, 56 in D Major, 55 in B♭ Major, 62 in E♭ Major, 30 in D Major, 54 in G Major (15 April); WU 52 in G Major (2 June?).

[i]WU 58 in C Major, 38 in F Major, 31 in A♭ Major, 59 in E♭ Major, 46 in E Major (21 January).

[j]WU 32 in G Minor, 12 in A Major (8 July 1920?).

Plate 9: Bartók's edn. of Mozart, C-Minor Fantasy, K. 475 (Rozsnyai, 1910).

which might surprise those aware of Bartók's fastidiousness about metronome marks and timings in his own works.[42] Fingering interested him to some extent, but he was especially conscientious in interpreting dynamics, phrasing, touch and character, and pedaling.

Fortunately, it is easy to separate Bartók's additions from those he believed to be in the *Urtext*.[43] Small-size dynamics, dots, and tenuti

(and ⌄); and thin crescendo–decrescendo hairpins and slurs were all editorial additions. Bartók occasionally overruled the composer's instruction, which he then placed in parentheses and explained in a footnote (see, for example, the *forte* in mm. 1, 3, and 5 of the C-Minor Fantasy). Bartók was, of course, familiar with the editorial procedure of distinguishing between normal and small type. As his library proves, as a youth he studied most of the standard repertory from the Cotta edition, including Schubert and Weber in the edition by Franz Liszt, who in his preface made precisely such distinctions.

Even his contemporaries might have found Bartók's performing editions unnecessarily laden with instructions. They allow us, however, to reconstruct his style and taste in a most vivid way. Note in the Mozart Fantasy, for instance, how deeply Bartók felt the Riemann upbeat-downbeat pattern of mm. 1–2, 3–4; how he played *legatissimo* in a slow Alberti bass (m. 6ff.); how he used the pedal (m. 8ff.)—achieving, incidentally, less of a blurring effect than on the piano of today.[44]

Yet how can we be sure of really playing Mozart's Fantasy according to Bartók's performing instructions? Can we know exactly what, for example, he meant by *sonore, p ma sonore,* or by marking the thumb *marcato* but *dolce?* One way of getting close to the editor's intention would be a careful compilation and analysis of all the verbal instructions. In his Mozart editions, Bartók used a rich Italian vocabulary. Leaving aside the modifications *poco, molto, subito,* we find:

sonore	*grazioso*	*marcato*
espressivo	*leggiero*	*pesante*
cantabile	*scherzando*	*energico*
dolce	*vigoroso*	*agitato*
sostenuto		*risoluto*
semplice		*martellato*
quieto		
tranquillo		
calando		

---

[42]About the ostensibly confusing contradictions between the metronome speed and the *durata* given by Bartók, see László Somfai, "Die 'Allegro barbaro'-Aufnahme von Bartók textkritisch bewertet," *Documenta Bartókiana* 6 (1981), 259–75.

[43]In the case of Mozart, Bartók acquired from his publisher individual sonata prints either from the old *Gesamtausgabe* volume (1878) or of the Ernst Rudorff "Urtextausgabe" (*Sonaten und Phantasien für Clavier von W. A. Mozart,* I–II, 1895), both printed by Breitkopf & Härtel. This was the "Urtext" which he then edited.

[44]In regard to the pianos used in those days in Hungary, it might be worth quoting a note by Bartók to Beethoven's op. 2, no. 2, II, m. 28 (where he used a ⌐⌐⌐ half-pedal sign). After the explanation of the rendition of a half-pedal, Bartók adds: "Bei Bechstein und andern, bei uns weniger bekannten Klavieren ist das Halb-Pedal vom ganzen in fühlbarer Weise abgesondert. . . ."

a.

b.

Example 2

Another method would be to make use of the above-mentioned "triangle" of sources: to compare Bartók's phonograph recording with his concert copy, preferably his own performing edition, if one exists. We can briefly compare Bartók's 1910 edition of the Variations, op. 34, by Beethoven (ex. 2a), with the phonoamateur recording of a studio concert broadcast by Radio Budapest on 13 January 1939 (Hungaroton LPX 12335–A).

The comparison is not straightforward, since there is no evidence that Bartók used his own 1910 edition in that concert. Indeed, it is likely he used a Breitkopf & Härtel *Urtext*.[45] Moreover, at the time he had prepared the performing edition, nearly three decades before his studio

concert, this work of Beethoven was not yet in his repertoire, although we may assume that his understanding of the basic *Affekt* and style of the variation theme had not changed radically. Yet, to take examples only from the first four measures: Bartók chose a different articulation for the last sixteenths in m. 3; the crescendo pattern leading from m. 1 to m. 2 became a nervous two-step action in Bartók's performance, and he made a beautiful rubato for the upbeat figure at the end of m. 4. (See ex. 2b; the boldface corrections and additions were transcribed by me from Bartók's recording.[46])

To return to our survey of the editions (table 3): the house style of Rózsavölgyi was less rigid than that of Rozsnyai. Thus in editing the Beethoven sonatas Bartók had a freer hand. He was not forced to introduce an abbreviated formal analysis, and he could write more extensive

[45]As a permanent member of the "Commission Internationale de la Cooperation Intellectuelle" of the League of Nations, Bartók submitted a draft resolution in 1932 concerning the promotion and support of *Urtext* editions (and of facsimile editions of significant manuscripts). Otto Erich Deutsch drew Bartók's attention to the matter, but at that time he already took sides with the *Urtext* editions.

[46]A closer, more direct connection between notation (edited ca. 1920 but printed only in 1926) and performance (23 December 1929; Hungaroton LPX 12326–B) is found in the case of the B♭-Major Sonata by Scarlatti (L. 50, K. 70).

notes, often including rather personal remarks
such as

Those who observed with what a tremendous emphasis [Richard] Strauss conducted the last two of the
following chords in the first movement of the *Eroica*,

and who experienced the shattering effect of the unexpected force almost surpassing the *fortissimo*, will
try to produce a similar effect—although to a lesser
degree—in these two measures [op. 2, no. 3, in C Major, I, mm. 67–68].

The twenty-seven Beethoven sonatas edited
by Bartók might prove the greatest contribution
to the study of Bartók's musicianship around
1909–12.[47] This is because, first, he knew Beethoven much better and played his works more
often than those of the other masters, and second, because his sources here were considerably
more reliable than those consulted for Mozart
and Haydn.[48]

V

My endeavor to interpret Bartók's performing editions as a highly informative source of
his musical personality might be received skeptically by those who believe they may merely
reflect the *Zeitgeist*, the musical taste around
the turn of the century in the major centers of
Europe: Vienna, Budapest, Prague, and Berlin.
Yet a comparative study will clearly show that
even within the framework of the general style

of those years in the German-Austrian-Hungarian musical traditions, Bartók indeed had individual concepts and put them on paper with
growing precision. Two examples may suffice,
the beginnings of both the Prelude and the
Fugue in D Minor from *WTC* I, (no. 2 in Bartók's
edition).

Example 3 shows the beginning of the prelude as edited by Tausig, d'Albert, Busoni, and
Bartók, in his two versions. Bartók almost certainly knew the earlier editions (the Tausig was
the official one in his school years). The articulation of the left hand in the Bartók is obviously
individual. The phrasing of the right hand (but
not the articulation!) seems to accord with Busoni in the first edition (I) and with Tausig in the
revised (II). Yet consider d'Albert's phrasing, or
play both hands of the five editions one after the
other—and one has a vivid image of the young
Bartók's musical inspiration and temperament.

The subject of the D-Minor Fugue has always
been an enigma. A slur and staccato[49] in Bach's
hand in m. 2, duly reprinted in the Bach *Werke*
(see ex. 4a), has led later editors to different
pseudo-solutions. Bartók, especially in the revised version (ex. 4f), seems to feel the intended
accent more strongly than his predecessors. In
these examples we also see how quickly the traditions of trill execution evolved, from the old
way, beginning on the upper auxiliary (ex. 4b),
to the more modern main-note beginning (ex.
4c–e), and back to the early method (ex. 4f).

VI

The nineteenth century was the first period
in which leading composers felt that outstanding works of the past needed not only to be rediscovered, but also rendered in a modern, more
precise notation.[50] (One thinks, for example, of

---

[47]The reprint edition of Beethoven in preparation will consist not only of twenty-five sonatas (the seven other, mostly
late, sonatas—ops. 54, 81a, 101, 106, 109, 110, and 111—
were not part of the official piano curriculum at the Budapest Academy of Music), but also the facsimiles of op. 101
and op. 111. These two works were carefully edited by Bartók but never printed; the intended engraver's copies came
to light only recently.

[48]András Wilheim has pointed out that Bartók first chose
d'Albert's edition as his main source for Beethoven (Leipzig,
1902–04), and later used the *Urtext* printed by Breitkopf &
Härtel (*Urtext classischer Musikwerke*). His library also
contains the sonata facsimile editions of the time.

Bartók's main source for Haydn was a nineteenth-century Breitkopf & Härtel version (Pl. No. 8252*ff.*), fascicles
from *Sonaten für das Pianoforte von Joseph Haydn [. . .]
Neue Ausgabe*. This is in many ways a corrupt Haydn text;
but Pasler's *Urtext* edition was not yet available.

[49]The staccato is a dot in the autograph; see the facsimile
edition of *WTC* Book I (*Faksimile-Reihe Bachscher Werke
und Schriftstücke* 5 [Leipzig, n.d.]).

Bartók's note: "The slur above the sixteenth notes of the
subject, as well as the staccato dash coming after it, are also
present in the original manuscript. As in Bach's time, both
the dot and the dash merely mean that the note so marked is
to be played relatively shorter. The staccato indicated by a
similar dash will therefore be used in the sense of a dotted
staccato throughout."

[50]An important precedent is Mozart's re-scoring of major
Handel works at van Swieten's request, even though these
comprise arrangements rather than the modernization of an
obsolete notation.

Tausig (1869)

d'Albert (1906)

Busoni (1894)

Bartók (1907)

Bartók (rev. ca. 1913)

Example 3

a. Bach *Werke* (Kroll) 1864

b. Tausig 1869

c. Busoni 1894

d. d'Albert 1906

e. Bartók 1907

f. Bartók (rev.) ca. 1913

Example 4

Mendelssohn's score of the *St. Matthew Passion*, Liszt's edition of Schubert and Weber for Cotta, Brahms's edition of Handel for Chrysander, etc.) Moreover, these composers sought to fit the notation of their own original works into a generally valid network of performing instructions, even if special additional signs were needed. By the end of the century, this sense of historical responsibility was widespread among central European composers. Indeed, it would be valuable to study how important a role the German performing editions of the standard piano repertory played during the formative years of composers born in the decades between 1860 and 1890. The impact on Béla Bartók was obviously great, first when as a teenaged piano student he learned the actual meaning of performing signs, and later, roughly during 1907–14, when as an editor he had to express his mature interpretation of earlier works in the form of performing editions with detailed notation.

As regards the notation of his own piano works—whether those in the new style inaugurated by the Bagatelles of 1908 or those belonging to a more Lisztian tradition (in which he continued to write until the 1920s)—there are two basic styles which have to be recognized:

1. Piano works in an "edited version," very much similar to, and clearly influenced by the spirit and technique of, "performing editions" of the late nineteenth century.
2. Piano works in a "concert-style" notation, first used by Bartók in pieces intended primarily for his own performance (e.g., the Suite, op. 14; Violin Sonatas Nos. 1 and 2, Sonata (1926), *Out of Doors*, Piano Concertos Nos. 1 and 2). Here pedaling and fingering instructions appear only when they are a part of the intended effect in harmony or touch.[51]

The performing-edition style of detailed notation was, to be sure, appropriate for works and series that had a clear educational purpose, such as *For Children* (1908–09), Ten Easy Piano Pieces (1908), Rumanian Folkdances (1915), and Rumanian Christmas Carols I–II (1915). There are also times, however, when Bartók's notation contains a great deal of detail, although the piece itself, from our point of view, seems not to belong in the educational sphere. Sometimes

---

[51]For example, the ⌐————⌐ pedal signs and the 1 + 2 fingering in the second movement of the *Suite*, op. 14.

we can guess his motivation in doing so. The Bagatelles, for instance, were in fact recommended as "free" pieces in the same Rozsnyai catalogue of piano music which listed the Bartók editions of the compulsory common-practice repertory. But why was Improvisations (1920), probably his most original arrangement of peasant music and a favorite item on his recitals, edited by Bartók so carefully that there is hardly a note for which the precise touch is not indicated? We can only assume that Bartók was especially careful in fixing the notation of works based on folk material because the intended style was alien to most of the customers of Universal Edition.

In the years following his most ambitious experimentation with different notations, Bartók's interest began to lapse. He soon became tired of fighting the house style of his new publisher (Universal from 1917). For instance, in a few piano scores Universal accepted the ⌐___⌐ pedal sign, but then switched back to the traditional, and less precise, ℛ𝒆𝒹. ✳.

In the 1930s the performing-edition style of notation gradually vanished from Bartók's new piano music. In *Mikrokosmos*—now in the house style of yet another publishing firm, Boosey & Hawkes—a third notation is manifest, fairly precise but clearly "simpler." Bartók appears to have recognized that the precise meaning of performing signs was differently understood and taught in different conservatories, countries, and cultures. Yet he did not give up his fight. He knew that musical notation was by nature inadequately precise,[52] and with the growing interest of major record companies, he made disks of many of his works, thus fixing the authentic performances (or one possible model).[53] Furthermore, in the 1930s he developed a microscopic (micro-acoustic) notation in transcribing thousands of vocal and instrumental folksongs and dances from phonograph cylinders and discs. He also thoroughly revised his older transcriptions. The role of these activities

in Bartók's creative self-expression is still not adequately recognized in the literature.[54]

The interpretation of works written in this third, simpler style of notation must be combined with the systematic study of recordings made or supervised by Bartók. Consider the Violin Concerto of 1937–38, commissioned in 1936 by Zoltán Székely, Bartók's chamber-music partner at the time. Bartók finished the work in the form of a *particella*, which he played and discussed with Székely. He gave a copy to the violinist for careful reconsideration of the solo part. In Bartók's original notation, the solo entry of the theme in the second movement (ex. 5a) has a fine, delicate articulation, surely intended as an upbow-downbow pattern, with a slight *portato* separating the first note from the rest.[55] Székely divides the two strokes of each measure into four (ex. 5b).

Did Székely change the character of the theme to suggest a fleshier, more vibrant performance, with more action and stress from the bow? And if so, why did Bartók not reject this notation, rather than seeing it into print? It would be a great (but common) mistake to compare the two notations in a post-Heifetz (or post-Oistrakh, post-Stern) reading and playing! Fortunately, the first performance, played by Székely with the Concertgebouw Orchestra under Mengelberg (23 March 1939), was recorded at the Hilversum studios and was later issued to the public (in 1971, on Hungaroton LPX 11573). We can thus hear Székely's reading of the published articulation of the slow theme. This is in fact the authorized "oral form," since Bartók worked with Székely and let the violinist play the concerto before fixing the performing signs and instructions. The notation was then "cor-

---

[52]Bartók, "Mechanical Music," in *Essays*, pp. 289–98.
[53]When a new print was prepared from the *Suite*, op. 14, in 1937, Bartók let Universal print the following text in the music: "Authentische Grammophon-Aufnahme (Vortrag des Komponisten): His Master's Voice AN 468, 72–671/2." This text is, however, missing from recent editions.

[54]For a better understanding of Bartók's transcriptions of recorded folk music, see and hear *Hungarian Folk Music Gramophone Records with Béla Bartók's Transcriptions*, ed. László Somfai (Budapest, 1981) (Hungaroton LPX 18058–60).
[55]From the mid-1930s on, in scores edited by Boosey & Hawkes, Bartók made a differentiation between two similar articulation patterns: a dot inside the slur (i.e., with the staccato between the note head and the slur) and a dot outside the slur. As he wrote to Boosey & Hawkes, 7 December, 1939, "In string (bow-) instruments (a) ⌣⌣ and (b) ⌣⌣ or (a) ⌣⌣ and (b) ⌣⌣ have a different meaning. (a) means an interruption before the last quaver, (b) means a shorter sound of the last note, without any interruption." (Bartók followed this principle to some extent in his late piano notation as well.)

a. Bartók's particella

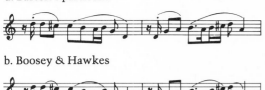

b. Boosey & Hawkes

Example 5

rected" to some extent, since Székely thought it should be put on paper properly so that violinists of his generation could play it according to Bartók's intentions. Those who have heard the record will realize that the delicate, elegant performance by Székely is totally alien to the reading(s) by most of our present-day violin superstars. Perhaps they would get nearer to the intended character if the printed score had retained the manuscript version. Shall we neglect the Székely articulation of the authorized score and restore the ms. version? In the future the conventions of understanding basic signs of notation may turn in still other directions.

An understanding of the full and detailed message of a Bartók score obviously cannot end with the act of reading and memorizing the printed music as the basis for reinterpretation. Or if this is going to be the routine henceforth, performers of music by Bartók may sooner or later have to cope with a rival approach: an "historical performance" trend, in which we cultivate a more individual, more interesting, and more boldly personal Bartók style.

Index